Lotteries in Public Life

Lotteries
in Public Life

A Reader

Edited and Introduced by

Peter Stone

imprint-academic.com

Published in the UK by Imprint Academic
PO Box 200, Exeter EX5 5YX, UK

Published in the USA by Imprint Academic
Philosophy Documentation Center
PO Box 7147, Charlottesville, VA 22906-7147, USA

ISBN 9 781845 402082

A CIP catalogue record for this book is available from the
British Library and US Library of Congress

Contents

Peter Stone

Introduction

In 1959, the Swedish sociologist Vilhelm Aubert published a paper entitled "Chance in Social Affairs." At the time, it enjoyed very little company. Scholars had almost completely neglected the topic of decision-making by chance, random selection, or selection using a *lottery*. Such attention as the topic had received almost always happened in passing, during a discussion of something else (say, the randomly-selected jury employed in Britain and the United States). Only one book had appeared in English on the general subject of random selection. That book, *Of the Nature and Use of Lots*, was published by Puritan theologian Thomas Gataker. But that book appeared in 1619, and was long out of print in Aubert's day.[1] And little new theoretical ground had been broken in the centuries between Gataker and Aubert.

Aubert's paper was thus critically important, but one must not overstate his achievement. Aubert hardly invented the idea of employing lotteries in decision-making.[2] Indeed, as Aubert documents, the practice has been around since the earliest days of civilization. Some examples of lottery use are widely known today. The Anglo-American jury and the military draft are perhaps the most famous of these. Some are more obscure; as Aubert notes, the Republic of San Marino selected its dual chief executives in this manner for many years (p. 38; all references in this introduction will be to the anthology unless otherwise indicated).[3] But Aubert did inaugurate the

---

1   A new edition of Gataker's seminal work has recently appeared. See Thomas Gataker, *The Nature and Use of Lotteries* (Exeter: Imprint Academic, 2008).

2   I shall treat as synonymous such expressions as "selection by lot," "selection via lottery," and "random selection."

3   Aubert's paper may well be the only English-language source on this subject. (The politics of San Marino is not a hot topic in comparative politics.) Subsequent works on lotteries have mentioned San Marino, and invariably they have cited Aubert. Apparently, however, San Marino had ceased use of the lot by the time Aubert's paper appeared.

modern study of random selection. Fifty years later, this study continues apace.[4]

The papers collected in this anthology all concern random selection as a means of public decision-making. Included here is virtually every significant theoretical paper on lotteries published in English between 1959 and 1998. By "theoretical," I mean papers that examine lotteries not at the level of application in specific contexts, but at a more abstract level. This means, for example, including papers on the general problem of allocating goods by lot — which goods to allocate by lot (if any), and why — and excluding papers on the specific problem of allocating a particular good (e.g., organ transplants) by lot. There is no shortage of case studies that apply lotteries to particular problems in public life.[5] The papers in this volume, however, take a step back, and ask more generally when and why anyone would ever consider doing this.

Even a theoretical study of lotteries and random selection, however, leaves many questions to be answered. Just what is a lottery? When have lotteries been used to make decisions? When *should* lotteries be so used? And why? Obviously, these questions are closely interrelated. If one claims that a particular decision ought to be made by lot, then one must naturally define what a lottery is, as well as justify one's claim that a lottery is appropriate for that decision. And surely one would expect there to be some relationship, however imperfect, between decisions *actually* made by lot and decisions that might *justifiably* be made by lot.[6] And yet to some extent at least these questions can be treated separately. Aubert tried to tackle all of them at once in his paper — understandably, given his lack of predecessors upon whom he could draw. The answers Aubert provides, equally understandably, were often unsatisfying. Subsequent authors have been able to take advantage of the growing literature on lotteries. But they have also tended to focus on one or a few pieces of the large lottery puzzle.

Such is the case with the papers in this anthology (except Aubert, of course). Three of them (Sher, Kornhauser and Sager, Wasserman) tackle

---

4   For a review of the recent literature, see Antoine Vergne, "A Brief Survey of the Literature of Sortition: Is the Age of Sortition upon Us?" in *Sortition: Theory and Practice*, eds. Gil Delannoi and Oliver Dowlen (Exeter: Imprint Academic, 2010).

5   For example, the bioethics literature has considered the idea of allocating organ transplants by lot for over four decades, usually in a sympathetic manner. For a sample of this literature, see Nicholas Rescher, "The Allocation of Exotic Lifesaving Medical Therapy," *Ethics* 79 (1969); James Childress, "Who Shall Live When Not All Can Live?" *Soundings* 43 (1970); Al Katz, "Process Design for Selection of Hemodialysis and Organ Transplant Recipients," *Buffalo Law Review* 22 (1973); and John F. Kilner, "A Moral Allocation of Scarce Lifesaving Medical Resources," *Journal of Religious Ethics* 9 (1981).

6   In his study of lotteries, Jon Elster treats the divergence between "does" and "ought" to be of fundamental importance. Any theory of lotteries, he argues, should explain, first, why do people use lotteries when they should not, and second, why do people fail to use lotteries when they should. He finds the latter phenomenon far more prevalent than the former. See Elster, *Solomonic Judgments* (New York: Cambridge University Press, 1989).

the problem of defining a lottery. Four of them (Mueller et al., Mulgan, Engelstad, Knag) focus upon the assignment of political office by lot. The rest (Wolfle, Greely, Goodwin, Eckhoff, Hofstee, Broome) consider the problem of allocating goods randomly.

Together, the overall effect is to map out much of the theoretical terrain generated by the problem of random selection. But while it may be possible to group these papers together according to the questions they answer, I have chosen to present them here in chronological order. Any grouping is bound to be imperfect and could be highly misleading. For example, all three papers concerned with defining a lottery also speak to the question of how lotteries might justly be used. In addition, there is a clear development of ideas taking place between the earlier and the later papers. This makes perfect sense, as the latter often reference, correct, clarify, and/or elaborate upon the former. And so while the papers may be read in isolation from each other, a reader will gain from reading them in the order they appeared.

Anyone reading this anthology will learn a great deal about the proper use of lotteries in public life. She will also learn much about possible ways of using lotteries — past and present, real and fictional, actual and hypothetical. And she will see how our understanding of lotteries has improved and deepened since Aubert's paper first appeared over five decades ago. Nevertheless, she will also learn that there remain both points of disagreement among lottery experts and unresolved questions regarding the theory of random selection. In the remainder of this introduction, I shall discuss, in a highly partisan way, a few of the topics considered in these papers with an eye to how we should understand them today. This will illustrate both what has been accomplished thus far and what remains to be done in terms of understanding lotteries.

If one wishes to consider the virtues and limitations of random selection, one must of course be able to distinguish random selection from alternative forms of decision-making. This task has proven far more difficult than it might appear at first blush. Several authors in this study, for example, note the use of lotteries as divinatory aids. Since the earliest times, societies throughout the world have employed "chance devices" (to use Aubert's expression) in order to seek instruction from gods, demons, spirits, etc. The Bible contains numerous examples of this practice. It is used, for example, to identify Jonah as the passenger aboard a ship whose conduct is responsible for the divinely-inspired storm threatening the ship (Jonah 1:7).

How should this practice fit into the theory of random selection? Torstein Eckhoff claims that

> The reasons for leaving decisions to a lottery can, to some extent, be the same for a distributor who believes in a supernatural interpretation of the outcome as they are for one who regards it as a pure chance device.

Both can conceive of a lottery as a way of simplifying decision-making
and of avoiding responsibility for the outcome (p. 162).[7]

Eckhoff is correct to point out how "simplified" appeal to a lottery makes
decision-making, regardless of whether that appeal has supernatural significance to its users. But he is quick to add that "there may be other
motives for choosing this device," and throughout the rest of his argument
he presupposes that the lottery is not being used for divinatory purposes.
And this is how it should be. If one believes that a higher power — presumably one whose opinion is of interest — directs the results of a chance
device, then one will employ the lottery in order to ascertain that power's
views. In effect, the use of the lottery under such circumstances is no different than a phone call placed to a trusted authority. A lottery can do no
such thing for those who see no supernatural force guiding the roll of the
dice or the drawing of lots.[8]

Ordinary language can generate much confusion on this subject. Consider the idea of "luck" or "chance" or "fortune." On the one hand, they
intuitively sound very different from the usual forces we like to believe
shape most of our decisions. But on the other hand, it is all too easy to
assimilate them to those very same forces. When Barbara Goodwin writes
that "Chance and causality are often misleadingly contrasted," and that
chance can in fact serve as a "primary cause" (p. 98), she is correct insofar
as people can indeed decide what to do via chance processes. But it would
be a mistake to infer from this that chance is a force that predictably determines behavior, the way that psychological drives can. Certain factors
might lead a person to select *an* option via lottery, but no factor can ever
lead a person to select a *particular* option via lottery. For by their very
nature, lotteries do not predictably select anything.[9]

Similarly, one can agree with Lewis Kornhauser and Lawrence Sager
that "a lottery assigns the goods on the basis of luck" (p. 159). But this does
not mean that people possess some property called "luck" to varying
degrees, with lotteries favoring those who possess more of it. Rather, a lottery favors no one, and we simply call "lucky" the people who happen to
wind up winning them. Assignment on the basis of luck, therefore, is not
equivalent to assignment on the basis of need, or merit, or desert, but a

---

7   Mulgan (p. 119) makes a similar point.

8   I have argued elsewhere that it is misleading even to use the term "lottery" for divinatory
    practices of this nature. See Peter Stone, "Three Arguments for Lotteries," *Social Science
    Information* 49 (2010): 159.

9   Aubert encounters the same issue in discussing "chance theories," a category that includes
    "everything from the calculus of probability to everyday attempts to explain events by
    reference to luck, accident, fortune, or the like, with the emphasis on the latter 'folk theories'"
    (p. 26). But the latter theories suggest that there is some factor that explains why some event or
    other happens — the presence of absence of a force called "luck." The former theories, by
    contrast, do not assume the existence of such a factor — indeed, they assume that no such factor
    exists.

radically different alternative to any of these assignment procedures. (Of course, such procedures can be combined with lotteries, as we will see.)

All of this presupposes, of course, that there are certain properties that all and only random selection procedures possess, properties that distinguish them from other procedures. But one need not presuppose this. When Aubert writes about "chance," he uses the term to describe a variety of meanings, each of which bears at best a "family resemblance" (to use Wittgenstein's phase) to each other.[10] He distinguishes between "manifest randomness," in which the people using a selection process know that it is random, and "latent randomness," in which they do not. Both can benefit the people that employ them. The Naskapi Indians of Labrador, for example, decided where to hunt caribou by heating animal bones and then interpreting the cracks that formed in them. They presumably regarded this process as divinatory, a means of making contact with informed sources in the spiritual world. But the process may have had the effect of randomizing the hunt, preventing the caribou from figuring out where the next hunt was going to take place (p. 24). While both manifest and latent random processes might reasonably be described as "chance processes," they obviously work in different ways. By definition, one cannot deliberately adopt a latent random process.[11] And so if there is a property that makes manifest random processes worth adopting, it must be considered on its own terms.

It is important, then, to determine just what property lotteries have that makes it possible for them to do what they do. The identification of such a property might make it necessary to exclude certain practices from the category "lottery" that ordinary language would include (divination, for example). Once such a property is discovered, one can ask just what decision-making processes with that property can do. And it might be found that other processes lacking that property — i.e., processes that are not lotteries — can do many of the same things. The literature on lotteries takes for granted this possibility. Sigmund Knag, for example, praises the tendency of political lotteries to place decision-making in the hands of amateurs, not professional politicians. But he also admits that this kind of amateurism does not require random selection; it can be seen, for example, in "unpaid honorary officials, such as justices of the peace of Britain and the United States, honorary consuls, and holders of various local offices of a legal nature" that persist up to the present (p. 255). He also believes that term

---

10   This is why he feels justified in including a wide variety of phenomena in the category "chance theory." See n. 9.

11   Aubert never addresses the question of why societies use latent random processes. Like many sociologists, he is content to speak of the *functions* that such randomness might serve, even though those functions cannot serve as *reasons* for making use of the randomness (because the randomness itself is unobserved). But this type of functionalist explanation is radically incomplete. For a critique of functionalism as traditionally practiced in sociology, see Jon Elster, *Explaining Technical Change* (New York: Cambridge University Press, 1983), ch. 2.

limits can encourage amateurism in politics (p. 255). And so even after the virtues of random selection are established, there remains the critical question of whether alternative processes can accomplish the same aims more effectively or with fewer drawbacks.

All of this raises an obvious question. If selection by lot ought to be distinguished from other decision-making processes by virtue of some property it possesses, just what is that property? The intuitive answer is that a lottery selects each of its outcomes with equal probability.[12] But probability remains a highly contentious term in philosophy, as do related concepts such as "randomness." And some arguments for random selection are valid on certain definitions of probability but not others.[13] Most commentators agree that a purely *subjective* account of probability—arguably the most popular account in philosophical circles today—is a nonstarter when it comes to defining a lottery. On this account, the probability of an event simply reflects some agent's psychological certainty that the event will occur. That agent cannot be wrong about this so long as she is consistent—as long, for example, as she properly updates her beliefs using Bayes' rule whenever she receives new information. But on a purely subjective understanding of probability, a lottery might be equiprobable to one person and not equiprobable to another, without either of them being wrong. While this may not pose a problem for a lone individual using a lottery for her private purposes, it raises insurmountable obstacles to any use of lotteries in public life. How can one select a proper lottery to use when people cannot, even in principle, agree on whether or not its outcomes are equiprobable?

Other contending definitions of probability are more plausible parts of a theory of lottery use, but there is no consensus upon which one to use. Kornhauser and Sager, mindful of the limitations of the subjective account, insists that a fair lottery must be *objectively* equiprobable. But as they quickly acknowledge, there are multiple conceptions of probability that might be described this way. Kornhauser and Sager mention both "frequentist views resting on observed physical properties of the world" and "logical notions that rest on a formal theory of rational inference" (p. 140, n. 12). The former view understands probability to be a property of a collection of events. On this view, a statement about the probability of a coin toss coming up heads is a statement about the set of all possible tosses of that coin, and the percentage of the members of that set possessing the

---

12   An equiprobable lottery is what ordinary language would describe as a *fair* lottery, although the latter term is ambiguous. I leave aside the topic, which several authors in this study consider, of *weighted lotteries*, lotteries which select some outcomes with higher probability than others. Needless to say, all of the considerations taken up here apply to weighted lotteries just as much as to fair lotteries.

13   For a fuller treatment of this problem, see Peter Stone, "Lotteries and Probability Theory," in *Sortition: Theory and Practice*, eds. Gil Delannoi and Oliver Dowlen (Exeter: Imprint Academic, 2010).

property "coming up heads." The latter view understands probability as a relationship between evidence and degree of belief. On this view, a statement about the probability of a coin toss coming up heads is a statement about how sure one should be in predicting a result of heads, given a certain body of evidence (like previous coin tosses).[14] Kornhauser and Sager seem to believe that all objective conceptions of probability are interchangeable. But as David Wasserman points out, this is far from obvious, and it is in fact difficult to construct an argument for lottery use that goes through equally well on either frequentist or logical accounts of probability (p. 242). Either lotteries contribute to decision-making only when they are equiprobable on one specific understanding of probability, or else lotteries that are equiprobable on different understandings contribute different things. Wasserman compares two distinct cases for lottery use based upon different understandings of probability, and finds one wanting, whereas Sher endeavors to construct a single unified understanding adequate for making sense of lottery use.[15]

Even those who associate fair lotteries with a particular conception of probability, however, usually suggest that equiprobability might not be an absolute requirement. In other words, if you're going to use an equiprobable lottery, then make it equiprobable according to one specific definition of probability. But you might not need an equiprobable lottery at all to enjoy the benefits of lottery use. Sher ultimately offers a definition of a fair lottery that avoids any reference to probability at all, although he apparently assumes that most ordinary examples of equiprobable lotteries (tossing a coin, drawing straws, etc.) will meet his definition. Kornhauser and Sager suggest that an "impersonal" procedure, one which expresses "a refusal to prefer or disprefer members of the lottery pool because of their attributes or circumstances," may do much of what an equiprobable lottery can do (p. 136). Similarly, John Broome suggests that a "fixed rule" might work just as well as a fair lottery under a variety of circumstances (p. 220). And Wasserman suggests that the best argument for lottery use requires only that a procedure "must prevent bias and partiality" (p. 233).

Each of these arguments tacitly rely, not only upon an account of how lotteries work, but also upon an understanding of how alternatives to lottery use work. When pressed, some of these understandings present problems. Take, for example, Kornhauser and Sager's understanding of "impersonality" as an alternative to equiprobability. What does it mean to "refuse to select one option over another because of their attributes or circumstances?" Does it mean refusing to make conscious use of a reason? If so, it is not at all obvious why that would be enough. After all, people are

---

14 For the frequentist understanding, see Richard Von Mises, *Probability, Statistics and Truth*, 2nd revised English ed. (New York: Dover, 1981). For the logical understanding, see John Maynard Keynes, *A Treatise on Probability* (New York: Dover, 2004).

15 I critique Sher's argument in "On Fair Lotteries," *Social Theory and Practice* 34 (2008).

far from transparent to themselves, and they act on the basis of reasons they cannot or will not acknowledge. No merely "impersonal" procedure could screen out unconscious motivations. And even if agents understand their own motivations, they are perfectly capable of lying about them. As Kornhauser and Sager acknowledge, it might be very difficult to distinguish between an "impersonal" procedure and a procedure based upon unacknowledged or hidden biases and desires (pp. 142–143).

If a procedure systematically favors one type of option over another, then that procedure is vulnerable to exploitation by an agent with a desire (which she may or may not admit to herself) to favor the first type of option. An equiprobable lottery, properly understood, would presumably prevent that. If the outcomes occur with equal probability, then the agent has no ability to predict which outcome will occur, and thus no ability to favor one type of option for any reason. Presumably, this plays a key role in the justification of lotteries. If alternatives to equiprobable lotteries are to perform the same job, they surely must demonstrate an ability to prevent the wrong types of motivation from entering the process.

The question of how to define a lottery tends to get raised in conjunction with one of the two leading uses to which lotteries are put—the allocation of scarce goods. The good might be admission to a desirable school, or a radio broadcasting license, or access to a dialysis machine. The good might even be exemption from a burden or punishment, such as military service.[16] The distribution of all of these goods is subject to the demands of allocative justice. And not coincidentally, all of these goods have been allocated by lot at some point in history.

How might lotteries contribute to the allocation of scarce goods? The intuition has been well-expressed by George Sher: "It is generally agreed that when two or more people have equal claims to a good that cannot be divided among them, the morally preferable way of allocating that good is through a tie-breaking device, or *lottery*, which is fair" (Sher's emphasis; p. 85). Lotteries, under the circumstances detailed by Sher, advance justice in the allocation of goods. This idea—which I elsewhere call the *just lottery rule*[17]—is widely, though not universally, accepted. The question, then, is why it should be that justice demands this.

Some arguments connecting lotteries to justice make use of other important concepts in political theory. But those concepts themselves generate problems if they are not used with care. One such argument holds that lotteries contribute to equality of opportunity. In Hank Greely's words, "Where equality of result is impossible…equality of opportunity is the next best goal because it parcels out equal chances to receive the good.

---

16 Sher (p. 95) explains well the equivalence between receiving a benefit and being exempted from a burden.

17 See my *The Luck of the Draw: On Lotteries and Decision-Making* (New York: Oxford University Press, 2011), ch. 3.

Random selection is the only allocative method which honestly can claim the objective equality of opportunity from which the satisfaction of equality of expectation springs" (p. 67). But it seems strange to suggest that equality of opportunity requires selection with equal probability. We don't ordinarily assume that when people apply for a job, equality of opportunity will be violated if some people are systematically selected for the job over others, so long as the basis for the systematic selection is relevant to the job.[18] Of course, equality of opportunity is more complicated than that; one might argue, for example, that equality of opportunity requires people to have equivalent background starting conditions, and that when the conditions have been set in this manner people will be selected with equal probability.[19] But selection by lot all by itself can do nothing to accomplish this, and so the connection with equality of opportunity seems forced.

Greely argues that lotteries ensure equality of opportunity, and that from equality of opportunity "the satisfaction of equality of expectation springs." Others bypass equality of opportunity entirely, and connect lotteries directly to equality of expectations. Kornhauser and Sager argue that

> what a social lottery offers is an equal division of a good that is otherwise indivisible. A lottery constitutes a probabilistic division of the good ex ante; instead of getting one unit of the good each member of the lottery pool gets a G/P chance at one unity of the good, where G is the number of units of the good available and P is number of persons in the entitlement pool. On this account a social lottery is just because it permits an equal allocation of the good consistent with the equal entitlements of the claimant pool (p. 146).

Eckhoff makes a similar point, contending that "Objective equalization can be obtained in two ways: either by giving the recipients equal shares of the allocated values or by holding an even-chance lottery" (p. 163). Broome carries this logic furthest. He writes that "By holding a lottery, each can be given an equal *chance* of getting the good," and this generates a sort of "surrogate satisfaction" that represents a "partial equality in satisfaction" of claims to a good (Broome's emphasis; p. 227). And if it makes sense to give equal amounts of this surrogate satisfaction when people have equal claims, then it also makes sense to give *unequal* (but nonzero) amounts of this good when people have *unequal* (but substantive) claims to the original good. Thus, according to Broome, when one party has a

---

18 Richard Mulgan argues effectively that selection by lot is a rival to the modern idea of "equality of opportunity or the career open to talents," not an instantiation of it (p. 130). And Greely himself admits that he is using the term "equality of opportunity" in an unconventional way (p. 60, n. 15).

19 Even then, the link is controversial, and there are accounts of equality of opportunity that have no relationship with equiprobability. See, e.g., Lesley A. Jacobs, *Pursuing Equal Opportunities: The Theory and Practice of Egalitarian Justice* (New York: Cambridge University Press, 2003).

slightly stronger claim to a good than another, the right allocative decision
is not to give the first party the good 100% of the time, but to employ a
weighted lottery that gives the first party the good most, but not all, of the
time. Anything less would not provide appropriate amounts of the surrogate satisfaction to all parties.[20]

On all of these accounts, one good cannot be distributed equally, and so
as a second-best substitute another good — expectation of receiving the
original good — is distributed equally instead. But this argument is difficult to sustain. As Wasserman's paper ably documents, the treatment of an
expected good as a good generates some counterintuitive implications.
Does the value of the expectation vary depending upon how long it is
held? If it does, then the allocator can provide all of the recipients with
more of the good by announcing the lottery well before it actually takes
place. That way, every recipient enjoys the expected receipt of the good for
a long time. If it does not, then the allocator could expand the amount of
the good provided by holding multiple lotteries, each one eliminating one
claimant but leaving the others in the pool. If p individuals held claims to
the original good, then p of those individuals can enjoy the expected
receipt of the good until the first lottery is held, then $p\text{-}1$ of those individuals can enjoy another good after the second lottery, and so on. Both of these
conclusions are hard to swallow (p. 246). If lotteries contribute to the just
allocation of goods, they most likely do not do so by placing an additional
good on the pile of things to be allocated.

A more promising route to explaining the relationship between lotteries
and allocative justice lies through the notion of *impartiality*. Most of the
authors who discuss lotteries in this context note this link. In particular,
they focus upon the *negative* demand that impartiality places upon the
allocation of goods. An impartial allocation of goods ignores certain information about the potential recipients of those goods. It does not, for example, discriminate for or against claimants based upon race. This can indeed
be a very valuable achievement, as most of the authors in this volume will
attest. An exception is Dael Wolfle, who of all the authors collected here is
the one most suspicious of lottery use. Wolfle asserts that "To use a lottery
to allocate risks or benefits is not only a denial of rationality, it is also a
denial of man's humanity; each man is reduced to a cipher, distinguished
from other ciphers only by the uniqueness of the combination of digits that
identify his records in a growing number of office files." And he concludes

---

20 Elsewhere, Broome argues forcefully that "we should not value equality in expected utilities,"
and that in particular "valuing equality in utilities gives us no reason to do so." It is difficult to
see how Broome reconciles this position with his endorsement of equality of "surrogate
satisfaction." Presumably, the answer lies in the distinction Broome draws between fairness
and overall welfare. See John Broome, "Uncertainty and Fairness," *Economic Journal* 94 (1984):
631.

with the rhetorical question, "Should Judgment wear a blindfold, or should she be required to see the persons judged" (p. 46)?

Contrary to what Wolfle implies, however, it is sometimes very desirable for justice *not* to see certain features of those being judged. In the courtroom, justice is supposed to be blind to any qualities the defendant might have apart from her guilt or innocence. Similarly, the agent charged with allocating scarce goods ought to be blind to any features of the recipients apart from their claims to the good. Justice should, in a very real sense, be blind. Anything else would be a violation of impartiality.[21] And as Wolfle recognizes, lotteries do indeed ignore this kind of information. This may be just what impartiality demands.

But to say that justice ought to be blind in some ways is not to say that justice ought to be blind in every way. To misunderstand this is to misunderstand impartiality. A judge is not being impartial if he acquits every defendant, regardless of guilt or innocence. He is also not being impartial if he simply tosses a coin to resolve every case, as did the judge in Rabelais' *Gargantua and Pantagruel*. Similarly, it might well make sense to toss a coin when deciding which of two equally worthy recipients ought to receive a good. But there would surely be something absurd about tossing a coin when deciding between two *unequally* worthy recipients.[22] Impartiality requires the exclusion of irrelevant reasons from allocative processes, but it also requires the *inclusion* of relevant reasons. And where there are relevant differences between claimants to a good, the use of a lottery would not impartial.

If this argument is correct, then the random allocation of goods must always be justified in terms of a specific conception of justice. This conception would spell out precisely what gives a person a claim to a good, and what makes one claim stronger or better than another. A lottery would then make sense whenever the conception does not provide a basis for distinguishing between the members of a group of claimants. In such a situation, the conception would prove *indeterminate*, in that it would not provide a sufficient basis for selecting a single unique distribution of the good. There would be no legitimate reasons for distinguishing between certain claimants. The lottery would then prevent any illegitimate reasons from doing so. The lottery would thus ensure impartiality, but only after the conception of justice had done all the work that it could.

Of course, in practice it might be very hard to say when a conception of justice has drawn all the distinctions between claimants it can. Suppose

---

21 I discuss this point further in "Why Lotteries Are Just," *Journal of Political Philosophy* 15 (2007); "Lotteries, Justice, and Probability," *Journal of Theoretical Politics* 21 (2009); and *The Luck of the Draw*, ch. 4.

22 Even those who advocate using weighted lotteries to allocate goods (such as Broome) recognize that stronger claimants ought to receive goods with higher probability than weaker claimants. The fact that one person has a stronger claim than another is a reason to favor the former, and impartiality does not require ignoring this reason.

that some good is to be distributed according to need. At first glance, it might appear that x is just as needy as y, but a closer scrutiny of their respective cases might reveal differences between their claims, however small. Hofstee presses hard on this point, arguing that indeterminacy is always "equioptimality within the limit of what it pays to find out" (p. 201).[23] He then tries to argue that a lottery is always less efficient than "sloppy choice." Even the most quick and dirty scrutiny of candidates, he argues, can detect *some* difference between them (p. 203). But perhaps Hofstee's point can be addressed by distinguishing between reasons for favoring one candidate over another and *justice-related* reasons for favoring one candidate. Hofstee gestures at such a distinction by suggesting that allocation by lot may be "irrational" and yet defensible in some sense.

On this understanding of justice—an understanding endorsed clearly by Broome, and possibly by Kornhauser and Sager as well as Hofstee—there may be many reasons for giving one person a good rather than another. But only some of those reasons give that person a *claim* or a *right* to the good. Justice demands that allocation respect claims. It may be the case that some other reason favoring one candidate over another exists, and that reason might justify overriding the power of claims. Suppose that x has a much weaker claim to a lifesaving organ transplant than y, but that x is a physician who is needed to find a cure for some terrible epidemic. In that case, it might make sense to say that it would be *unfair* to give the transplant to x and not y, but that it would be *better all things considered*.[24] This distinction plays a critical role in Broome's account of the demands of fairness and justice (see pp. 221–222).

If this is right, then there may well be many cases in which lotteries are highly appropriate. It may be implausible to suggest that two options yield the same total overall benefits, or that two options generate the exact same amount of social welfare. But it is much more plausible to suggest that two people may have the same *right* to a good.[25] Rights are like that. As Kornhauser and Sager put it,

> Robust moral entitlements—often called rights—typically derive their force not from a complex calculus of personal worth or a wide-ranging measure of moral consequence, but from rather stark and general features of the situations in which they arise. Hence the rights of Rose and Jasmine not to be killed by Violet can be equal, notwithstanding the fact that Rose has rather little to commend her to the world, while Jasmine has led a life of energetic virtue, has a handicapped husband who is heavily dependent on her, and is engaged in a research project of

23 Hofstee follows Jon Elster here. See Elster, *Solomonic Judgments*.
24 Of course, one might argue that the potential victims of the epidemic have claims to the cure. If so, justice with respect to one good (the cure) might demand injustice with respect to another good (the organ transplant for y).
25 Hofstee further suggests that "wisdom" might call for the use of weighted lotteries as a method for taking into account the full demands of justice (pp. 206–207). But he does not develop the point.

great social importance, along with colleagues who are emotionally and professionally invested in her continued work with them. Equal moral entitlements are thus less rare than the moral complexity of the world may suggest (p. 144).

But even if the just allocation of goods rarely required tiebreaking, the justice-based case for lotteries would remain the same. Lotteries ensure impartiality whenever two or more people have equally good claims to a good according to some conception of justice. Impartiality demands that the reasons provided by that conception, and not others, determine the allocation. Once the valid reasons have done all the work they can, lotteries can keep out the invalid reasons.[26]

The argument discussed here holds that lotteries have a role to play in the allocation of goods by helping to ensure the impartial employment of a conception of justice. "Selection by lot" is thus not a conception of justice in its own right, comparable to "selection according to need" or "selection according to merit." But some of the papers in this anthology connect random selection to impartiality in a different manner. They see random selection, if not as a conception of justice, then at least as an alternative to any particular conception of justice. The impartiality of lotteries arises out of this alternative role. It is therefore worth briefly exploring this alternative effort to connect lotteries with impartiality.

Consider first the contrast Aubert draws between two types of equality. He notes that before a good can be distributed equally among those with equal claims, one must first decide "with respect to what criteria are individuals to be grouped as equal or unequal." Distribution according to need will yield one distribution; distribution according to merit will yield another. But, Aubert notes,

> There exists another concept of equality, however, which makes it possible to avoid this dilemma by assuming that all men are equal, independent of special characteristics. It brings to the fore another method of establishing and observing equality and justice. "Independence" is the key word when absolute concepts of justice are involved. One way of achieving independence between "in-put" in a decision-making agency, and the "out-put," the decision, is to insert a randomizer, a chance device. What is then achieved is not that each contribution or merit receives its just reward, but that it can be established that rewards and penalties are at least unrelated to those criteria that are deemed as irrelevant biases (p. 42).

Knag makes a similar point, arguing that

> reason and analysis generate reliable answers only where the relevant facts, well defined and accepted, are at hand; where the objectives are

---

26 Lotteries have no such role to play in the criminal justice system. Judges are supposed to convict *all* the guilty, and acquit *all* the innocent. Indeterminacy thus never arises. But if for some reason it was necessary to punish only some of the guilty, or (less plausibly) acquit some but not all of the innocent, then a lottery might make sense. This practice has been employed in the past, as Eckhoff explains.

clear and agreed upon; and where the alternatives are few. But such conditions rarely exist. When reason has done what it can, something else must complete the job: intuition, faith, or chance. Of these, only chance is objective and has no bias (p. 256).

Aubert and Knag are suggesting that, instead of achieving the *positive* goal of ensuring allocation according to need, merit, utility, etc., lotteries can achieve the *negative* goal of preventing allocation according to "irrelevant biases." This might prove valuable if negative goals (e.g., preventing racial discrimination) are politically less controversial than positive goals (e.g., rewarding merit).[27] And it may well be true that people can agree much more readily upon negative rather than positive criteria for allocating goods. This negative goal is completely compatible with the understanding of impartiality sketched above. If everyone agrees that racial discrimination is bad, then everyone can agree that lotteries contribute to justice insofar as they keep racial discrimination out, even if they cannot agree upon anything else.

But one must not take the point too far. In relying upon a lottery as an allocative method, one has not somehow substituted a less controversial conception of justice for a more controversial one. One has, in effect, decided to "punt" on the question of achieving justice. One has decided that the default assumption is that all potential recipients of a good have equal claims, and that this presumption of equality can only be defeated when a social consensus exists upon a theory capable of differentiating between claimants. Absent such a consensus, the default assumption reigns, all parties are to be treated as equal claimants, and so a lottery is appropriate.

Politically, this strategy might make sense. Then again, it might not. It could be that, as Knag suggests, "Accepting the principle of random selection and knowing that chance has given rise to a public decision, one has little to complain about if one dislikes the outcome" (p. 256). But it could also be that people with strong but different opinions regarding justice will be dissatisfied with the default assumption of equal claims. If I believe in allocation according to need, I might prefer allocation by lottery to allocation according to merit. But then again I might find a lottery as bad if not worse than a meritocracy. (Perhaps merit correlates loosely with need, whereas lotteries correlate with nothing.) And if this were the case then lotteries would not work as a political compromise. In Greely's words,

> An honest lottery is objectively fair, but this fact may escape the applicant who believes that merit, wealth, or patience is the proper classification criterion. The literally homeless applicant who is denied admission to public housing or the applicant who has waited for years for that benefit likely will not be satisfied by the objective equality a

---

27   Hofstee stresses the role of lotteries as a form of political compromise, although he envisions weighted, not fair, lotteries in this role.

lottery offers if a relatively well-housed person who applied last month is rewarded by the luck of the draw. Abstract equality may be a poor substitute for the good which potential recipients desire (pp. 67-68).[28]

And regardless of the merits of this compromise, it is important to stress that it is a *political* compromise, not a philosophical one. There exist competing conceptions of justice. A lottery might make political sense as an alternative to any one of these conceptions. But it is a solution guaranteed, from the standpoint of all of these conceptions, to get things wrong. At best, it won't get things as wrong as the adoption of an opposing conception.[29]

Yet another approach treats allocation by lot, not as a supplement to a conception of justice, or as a political alternative to such a conception, but as an integral part of a unique and distinct conception. This is the approach taken by Barbara Goodwin in "Justice and the Lottery." Of all the papers in this collection, this one provides the most elaborate account of the demands of justice and why those demands involve lotteries. Goodwin believes those demands to be extensive. Taking Jorge Luis Borges' short story "The Lottery in Babylon" as her inspiration, Goodwin argues that most benefits and burdens in modern societies should be regularly allocated and reallocated randomly (although her argument requires "embroider[ing] and dissect[ing] Borges's fable out of all recognition;" see p. 107). In subsequent work, she dubs this idea the "Total Social Lottery," and the term is very appropriate for what she has in mind.[30]

Goodwin's defense of this radical proposal has a great number of moving parts, not all of which fit together seamlessly. The flavor of the complexity of her argument is well captured in the following passage:

In summary, then, the Babylonian lottery can be seen as a just distributive process firstly because of the elements of contractualism, due process and impartiality in its constitution. Some people might argue that these elements alone guaranteed its justice. Secondly, from the perspective of someone who believes that a key component of justice is equality, I would argue that the equaling effect which arises from the random, repeated casting of lots, also makes it a just system, given the

---

28   At the same time, Greely (p. 60) suggests that "the lottery is particularly neutral" as compared to its major alternatives (merit, willingness to pay, "first come, first served"). The lottery is "neutral" in the sense that it does not embrace any particular alternative principle of distribution. But this will not appear "neutral" to someone wedded to one such alternative principle. Just as a judge is not "impartial" if he acquits innocent and guilty alike, so a mediator is not "neutral" if she ignores all the merits of the cases put forward by the opposing sides.

29   There is a story about an absent-minded physician who delivers two sets of twins on the same day. The doctor mixes up the twins, forgetting which pair belongs to which mother. His solution is to switch one twin from one pair with another twin from the second pair. This guarantees that he will get things half-right, even if it also guarantees that he will get things half-wrong. A lottery works the same way as a political compromise. It guarantees that the wrong conceptions of justice will be ignored, even as it also guarantees that the right one will be ignored.

30   See Barbara Goodwin, *Justice by Lottery*, 2nd ed. (Exeter: Imprint Academic, 2005), ch. 1.

immutable nature of the Babylonian social structure. The lottery
serves to make an intolerable system more just, and therefore more
bearable by the circulation of inequalities. I would not, of course,
argue that *any* chance distribution is just (for this would imply that any
system whatever could be regarded as just): it is the complete impartiality of the Babylonian lottery and the repetition, which are in themselves fair, which bring about an egalitarian form of justice
(Goodwin's emphasis; p. 107).

Goodwin seems to make three distinct arguments for a political system
that allocated benefits and burdens at random. First, it is just because the
people living under it have consented to it. This argument presumably
does not distinguish a system of lotteries from any other allocative system.
Moreover, it runs into the usual problems regarding consent with which
the social contract tradition has grappled for centuries. Second, it is just
because it distributes goods "impartially." Third, it is just because the
repeated allocation of goods over time leads everyone to enjoy more or
less amounts of whatever valuable things the society has to offer — providing what Goodwin dubs "equal life chances" (p. 106).

The relevant point here is Goodwin's understanding of impartiality and
its relationship to lotteries. She stresses that the "two basic conditions for
justice" are "*impartiality*" and "*a reduction of inequality*" (Goodwin's
emphasis; p. 102). The repeated use of lotteries, she claims, accomplishes
both aims. Goodwin never defines what she means by "impartiality," but
she appears to have in mind the exclusion of irrelevant criteria for distribution. But it is therefore important to her argument that there be no *relevant* criteria for distribution. If there are legitimate justice-related grounds
for discriminating between people, then using a lottery to decide between
them would be wrong. It is therefore important to Goodwin's argument
that there be no such grounds. Goodwin is ambiguous on this point. On
the one hand, she is completely dismissive of the very idea of distinguishing people on the basis of merit or desert (p. 111–112). On the other hand,
she also claims that "indivisible and positional goods could be distributed
by lot or by rotation, *first taking account of basic and special needs*" (my
emphasis; p. 109). Apparently, there are some goods that should not be
distributed by lot according to Goodwin — the goods that are needed to
meet people's "basic and special needs." Goodwin here assumes some
radical form of egalitarianism that embraces need but not merit, desert, or
(implicitly) any other criteria for distinguishing between claims. But as a
result, her argument stands or falls with this egalitarian conception of justice, a conception she does not develop in the paper.

Equally important for Goodwin is the problem of reconciling her twin
lottery-related goals of "impartiality" and the "reduction of inequality."
Goodwin does not merely want everyone to enjoy an equal *probability* of
receiving goods; she also wants them to enjoy equal *amounts* of those

goods over the course of their lifetimes.[31] After all, if all that matters is the equal *chance* of enjoying each good — which is all that impartiality seems to demand — why bother with periodic reallocations of goods? Why not give each person a once-and-done random draw at birth, without regard for how unequal the resulting distribution is? But if the equal distribution of goods over lifetimes is a goal of justice, then surely it can be better ensured simply by dividing up society's goods equally, and dispensing with lotteries altogether. Lotteries leave things to chance, but if lifetime equality of goods is an important goal, why allow chance to enter into things at all? (A completely equal distribution would presumably, on Goodwin's account, also satisfy the demands of impartiality.) Goodwin must add a number of additional assumptions — in particular, the near-universal possession of zest for gambling and risk (which the people in Borges' story all share) — in order to maintain a place for lotteries (p. 104).

In the end, "Justice and the Lottery" demonstrates well a point that is implicit in most of the other papers in this collection dealing with justice. Any argument for allocation of goods by lottery will make sense only in light of a particular understanding of justice. That understanding might be reasonably abstract, or it might involve a fully-worked out conception of justice. But disagreement about the proper understanding will lead to disagreement about when and why lotteries should be used to allocate goods. Inquiry into allocation by lottery thus leads naturally into inquiry into the nature of justice more generally.

As noted before, the allocation of goods is one of the two most common uses to which lotteries have been put. The other is the assignment of public responsibilities — basically, political offices. (One can include in this category the Anglo-American jury, and perhaps even military conscription as well.) As with the allocation of goods, there is a wide measure of agreement in the papers collected here as to the role that lotteries might play when selecting people for political office. And as with the allocation of goods, there are also persisting theoretical problems, mostly at the level of the theoretical underpinnings of the practice. While the allocation of goods by lottery raises deep questions about the nature of justice, the assignment of public responsibilities by lottery raises deep questions about the nature of democracy.

No two of the authors here offer exactly the same case for selecting public officials by lot, but a number of arguments repeatedly arise. Aubert (p. 39) notes that the practice can preserve the "independence" and "objec-

---

31 Goodwin is a bit slippery here. She also writes at one point that "The premise of the lottery is that perfect equality of welfare, functions and resources is unattainable" (p. 107). She seems not to have noticed that any allocation that ensures equality of welfare will almost certainly fail to generate equality of resources, and vice versa. The latter seems compatible with equality of life chances, but the former clearly is not (even if one makes some kind of allowance for "basic and special needs"). Goodwin is clearly an egalitarian, but at times she seems unclear as to what she wants to be equal.

tivity" of officials. This is because no faction or special interest can stack the offices in question with partisans favorable to its cause. Nor can it bribe or threaten officials once selected, at least if the lottery draw is not conducted well in advance. This independence, note Aubert (p. 39), Mulgan (p. 122–123), and Engelstad (p. 184), can in turn prevent intrigues and power rivalries; factions will not be driven into conflict by the quest to control positions of power. Random selection can also ensure descriptive representation due to the law of large numbers; if $x\%$ of the population holds some view, or possesses some characteristic, then $x\%$ of a randomly-selected decision-making body (such as a jury) will on average do the same. (The size of the deviations from the average will vary depending upon the size of the random sample drawn.) Descriptive representation is noted as an advantage of random selection by Mulgan (p. 123–124), Engelstad (p. 182), and Knag (p. 254). And as Mueller et al. stress (pp. 49–50), random selection severs the connection between representation and geographically concentrated special interests, with all the negative effects (logrolling, pork barrel spending, etc.) that this connection can generate.[32]

Finally, political office might reasonably be regarded as a good in itself. If it is, and if all citizens are equally worthy of receiving it, then selection by lot serves the demands of allocative justice. Mulgan attributes this position to the Athenian democrats as follows:

> The conception of justice peculiar to democracy was that social goods should be divided equally among all free citizens. Equality of distribution was implicit in the original slogan of the [Athenian] democrats, *isonomia*, "the fairest word of all" according to Herodotus, which incorporated the notions of equality (*ison*) and law/rights (*nomos*). Among the goods to be distributed equally in a democracy was political office (p. 120).

This justice-based argument for the random assignment of political office is also made by Engelstad (pp. 181–182). If this argument is applicable, then it would be slightly misleading to suggest that the two primary uses of lotteries are the allocation of goods and the assignment of public responsibilities. It would be more accurate to say that the latter is simply a special case of the former. But modern liberal societies hold very different ideas regarding political office than ancient Athens did. And so these two uses are best regarded as distinct.

Most of these arguments take for granted that the lottery will select from the entire citizenry. This was the practice in Athens, and it certainly squares with modern assumptions about the equality of all citizens (as demonstrated by the practice of universal suffrage). But one can easily imagine foregoing this assumption. Knag, for one, sees merit in doing so.

---

32 Andrew Rehfeld develops a similar argument for randomly assigning voters to congressional districts. See Rehfeld, *The Concept of Constituency* (New York: Cambridge University Press, 2005).

He criticizes U.S. presidential elections for being "maximally politicized." "By politicized," he writes, "I mean simply that considerations of merit and utility as understood by the typical citizen take second place to the desires of political insiders and organized special interests" (p. 256). Knag assumes here that "merit and utility" constitute legitimate reasons for favoring some citizens with political office, whereas the preferences of special interests do not. If random selection nevertheless makes sense, it must be because the dangers of bad reasons influencing elections are so serious as to make it worthwhile to forego the possibility of good reasons influencing them. Random selection can keep out the bad and the good reasons that can sway electoral results. This argument parallels the political argument for the random allocation of goods — sometimes it is more important to disable bad reasons than to enable good reasons.

Of course, it may be worthwhile to risk some intrusion of bad reasons into the selection process in order to enable good reasons to do some work. One way to do this would be to select randomly, not from the entire population, but from those suitably pre-screened according to merit or talent. A number of the authors, including Knag and Engelstad (p. 186), make this point. This need not require a complete meritocracy, in which only the best get selected for office, with lotteries breaking the occasional tie. (In effect, this is what happens whenever a coin toss decides a disputed election.) One could believe that political officials must meet some standard of qualification — should be "good enough" — and that lots should be drawn from among all those meeting this standard. At the extreme, one could even believe that virtually everyone is "good enough" in this sense, so that selection with pre-screening for ability becomes indistinguishable from selection from the whole. This seems to have been the Athenian position, as Mulgan notes:

> But use of the lot, it should be noted, did not imply that superior ability and experience were not *discernible*, only that they were not *required* for the job in question. It is most unlikely that the Athenians were unaware of differences in capacity among those who filled the various positions appointed by lot…Participating in various public offices was an honor which should be shared as equally as possible among all the citizens, even at the price of a certain degree of inefficiency, and lot was vital as a means of selecting citizens at random, regardless of their personal qualities (Mulgan's emphasis; pp. 121–122).

This position would, of course make no sense if citizens did not possess equal claims to the good of political office. There is a loss incurred whenever a political system selects the "good enough" instead of the best to fill its offices. If this loss is worth incurring, it must be because there is some additional value advanced by ignoring considerations of merit or ability past a point. For the Athenians, this additional value was allocative justice, and it justified ignoring the very real differences between citizens.

The Athenians may or may not have had the right idea. But one thing is clear. Any form of prescreening may advance certain values, but only at the potential expense of other values. Prescreening may ensure that better qualified candidates take office, which could have very positive effects upon system performance. But such prescreening would, as the Athenians knew, compromise allocative justice, assuming political office to be a good to which all citizens have equal entitlement. It would also compromise descriptive representation; a random sample of prescreened candidates will resemble, not the people as a whole, but only the subset of the people who could survive the screening process. Which tradeoffs are worth making here is probably an impossible question to answer in the abstract; the answer will almost certainly vary from office to office and from political system to political system.

Finally, proponents of the assignment of political office by lot must make a variety of assumptions about political decision-making. Those assumptions may prove difficult to justify, however much their intuitive appeal. This is nowhere more evident than in the sophisticated analysis offered by Mueller et al. These authors note that direct democracy, while desirable, is not feasible in a large and complex industrial society. This is because of the problem of "rational ignorance." Each ordinary citizen can have only a negligible influence on the political process. As a result, no one has an incentive to gather much information about important issues of the day, or to devote much effort to analyzing the information she does acquire.[33] A randomly-selected decision-making body, however, can overcome this problem. The members of such a body would have much more incentive to become politically informed, given the much greater impact they would be able to have upon decision-making. Moreover, the random sampling process would ensure that the body resembled the entire population (descriptive representation), and so could ably "stand in" for the entire population. Thus, random selection offers the benefits of direct democracy without its major disadvantage.

Mueller et al.'s argument has a definite intuitive appeal. But it crucially depends upon the assumption that a random sample of the entire population can in some sense "speak for" the entire population, such that the normative force of its decisions is equivalent to the normative force that a direct consultation of the people would have. This normative force is supposed to be a product of descriptive representation. The random sample "looks like" the people, therefore it speaks with the "voice of the people." And this is the case even if the *actual* people (due to rational ignorance) disagree with the decisions made by the random sample. The idea has some plausibility, but it clearly doesn't always apply. If someone very much like

---

33   The classic source on the problem of rational ignorance remains Anthony Downs, *An Economic Theory of Democracy* (New York: Harper, 1957).

me signed my name to a contract, I would not thereby be bound by his decision. To make this argument work, one would have to answer a number of theoretical questions. In what sense does descriptive representation produce the "same" decision as the people as a whole? How does it do this? And when does this matter, given that different cases of descriptive representation have different normative force? These questions have proven remarkably difficult to answer in the years since Mueller et al.'s paper first appeared.

As this brief overview should make plain, the papers in this anthology cover a lot of ground. Decision-making by lottery, a deceptively simple-sounding idea, raises many questions. The papers collected here tackle many of them. The answers provided are far from perfect, and yet a great deal has been learned about the practice since Aubert's paper first appeared over five decades ago. The hope is that this collection of papers will promote the further development of the theory and practice of random selection, a process largely initiated by those very papers.

*   *   *

The papers collected here are reprinted without changes to the text. I have, however, standardized the formatting to the best of my ability. All references are presented in footnotes using the Chicago-style documentation system. Several authors listed sources as "forthcoming;" I have changed the citations to reflect the published versions of these works. And I have silently corrected a few citation errors. Hopefully, these changes will make it easier for readers to continue their investigation of lotteries past the papers in this volume should they so choose.

Work on this project began at Stanford University, where I enjoyed the able research assistance of Cristiana Giannini and Christina Nguyen. I am grateful for their help. I completed the project while a Faculty Fellow at Tulane University's Center for Ethics and Public Affairs. The Center provided me with an excellent home for a year, which made possible the completion of a number of projects. I would also like to thank Imprint Academic for its encouragement and support. Last but not least, I would like to thank the authors of the papers reprinted here, all of whom enthusiastically supported this project.

Vilhelm Aubert[1,2]

Chance in Social Affairs

The Norwegian Law of Courts § 51 states: "Well in advance of each session of the circuit court, hearing criminal cases, the chief judge, or another judge authorized by him, or the court's clerk shall, in the presence of a legal witness, *by drawing lots*, select fourteen jury-members and two alternates." This is one among a great many cases where society has institutionalized a recognized chance device as the proper mode of reaching a decision with social implications.

More than 150 years ago the English minister-philosopher Paley advanced the embryo of a general theory about the social functions of such chance decisions:

> In a great variety of cases, and of cases comprehending numerous subdivisions, it appears, for many reasons, to be better that events rise up by *chance*, or, more properly speaking, with the appearance of chance, than according to any observable rule whatever. This is not seldom the case even in human arrangements. Each person's place and precedency in a public meeting may be determined by lot. Work and labour may be *allotted*. Tasks and burdens may be *allotted*. Military service and station may be *allotted*. The distribution of provision may be made by *lot*, as it is in a sailor's mess; in some cases also the distribution of favours may be made by *lot*. In all these cases it seems to be acknowledged that there are advantages in permitting events to chance superior to those which would or could arise from regulation. In all these cases also, though events rise up in the way of chance, it is by appointment that they do so.[3]

And he goes on to say that "even the acquirability of civil advantages, ought perhaps in a considerable degree to lie at the mercy of chance. Some would have all the virtuous rich, or, at least, removed from the evils of poverty, without perceiving, I suppose, the consequence, that all the poor

1   Originally published on pp. 1-24 of *Inquiry* 2 (1959). Copyright © 1959 Taylor & Francis Ltd. Reproduced with kind permission from Taylor & Francis Ltd.

2   I am indebted to Tom Broch for collecting material to this paper, and also for having contributed with new insights.

3   William Paley, *The Works of William Paley*, vol. 5 (London: 1819).

must be wicked. And how such a society could be kept in subjection to governments, has not been shown…"[4]

Paley refers to chance devices that "by appointment" are used to make decisions. The chance element is, as in the selection of juries, a *manifest* characteristic of certain institutionalized types of decisions. If we leave our own rationalistic culture, or those areas where we are the most deliberate and utilitarian, we come across another vast class of decisions that *are* random, but without being recognised as such. The chanciness of these decisions is *latent*.

One interesting step towards extending the concept of the chance device in social decisions has been taken by O. K. Moore in his analysis of hunting-magic among the Naskapi Indians in Labrador. The magical practice consists of heating bones of animals over hot coals, usually the shoulder-blade of the caribou or a bone of the kind of animal which the Naskapi are about to hunt. When heated, the bone cracks. It is then fitted into a wooden handle, and while held in specified ways, the cracks of the bone are read so as to give directions for the hunt. "An impersonal device of the kind used by the Naskapi might be characterized as a crude 'chance-like' instrument. It seems that the use of such a device would make it more difficult to anticipate their behaviour than would otherwise be the case."[5]

The practice serves to increase the likelihood of successful hunting under conditions where game is scarce and where the animals tend to learn from previous experience with hunters. The Naskapi are, however, quite unaware of the randomness resulting from these decisions. They believe that they are seeking, and getting, guidance from the super-natural, i.e. that the decision is "systematic." This seems to be generally true for all similar practices among primitive people. The conscious *notion* of chance appears to be a late comer among the basic conceptual tools by which man gains mastery over his world of action and perception. Sigerist states categorically that primitive men always deny chance or randomness in the occurrence of disease.[6] Illness is always precipitated either by natural causes or by the sick or somebody else's actions. Similarly, death is usually not explained as due to chance.[7] On the whole, it seems to be the consensus of anthropological opinion that misfortunes and other events, are never explained by reference to a chance concept. On the contrary, primitive man's systems of belief usually give evidence of a very vigorous

---

4 Paley, *Works*.

5 Omar Khayam Moore, "Divination: A New Perspective," *American Anthropologist* 59 (1957): 72.

6 Henry E. Sigerist, *The History of Medicine*. Vol. I (New York: Oxford University Press, 1951), 127.

7 Leo W. Simmons, *The Role of the Aged in Primitive Society* (New Haven, CT: Yale University Press, 1945), 217ff.

denial of chance and uncertainty, and a similarly desperate affirmation of their capacity to master the world by secular skills or by magic.[8]

It has already been suggested that there is a need to distinguish between what we, as scientific observers, would characterize as chance elements in social life, and what any particular individual or social group happens to classify as a chance event. It may actually be useful to distinguish between three sociological types of chance phenomena: random responses precipitated by ignorance, chance devices, and chance theories.

Ignorance

Several years ago Moore and Tumin published a paper on the functions of *Ignorance* in social affairs. Some of their conclusions merit serious consideration in a context of chance decisions, although the writers themselves were unconcerned with this aspect of their problem: "The central theory of this paper holds that, quite apart from the role of ultimate values and the attitudes relative to them, perfect knowledge is itself impossible, and an inherently impossible basis of social action and social relations. Put conversely, ignorance is both inescapable and an intrinsic element in social organization generally, although there are marked differences in the specific forms, degrees, and functions of ignorance in known social organizations."[9] And they go on to describe some possible functions of ignorance in modern western societies: "The function of ignorance that is most obvious, particularly to the cynical, is its role in preserving social differentials."[10] "Ignorance operates to maintain smooth social relations by preventing jealousy and internal dissension where differential rewards to approximate status equals are not based upon uniformly known and accepted criteria."[11] "The success of military or law-enforcement undertaking, and the security of its participants, may depend upon the element of *surprise*."[12] "Another way in which ignorance serves to protect the traditional normative structure is through reinforcing the assumption that deviation from the rules is statistically insignificant."[13]

Whenever there is ignorance, secrecy, or deception about an event, the actor's response and decision relative to that event, must in one sense be random. He does not fully know what he is doing. The influence of ignorance and secrecy upon his *perception* of order or randomness depends upon the reason why he is kept ignorant. If his ignorance is related to the

8   Cf. Bronislaw Malinowski, *Magic, Science, and Religion* (New York: Anchor Books, 1955).
9   Wilbert E. Moore and Melvin M. Tumin, "Some Social Functions of Ignorance," *American Sociological Review* 14 (1949): 788.
10 Moore and Tumin, "Social Functions," 788.
11 Moore and Tumin, "Social Functions," 790.
12 Moore and Tumin, "Social Functions," 790.
13 Moore and Tumin, "Social Functions, 791.

unacceptably random nature of the events (like unequal rewards in an office organization) it may give him more sense of orderliness than is warranted. If his ignorance is due to a need to hide a system in certain events, he will perceive more randomness in the events than there "is." One might venture the hypothesis that ignorance of randomness is most likely to be kept up within co-operative social bonds; while ignorance of systematic responses is most likely to be kept up in antagonistic social relations and in conflict behavior.

Chance Theories

By "*Chance theories*" is meant everything from the calculus of probability to everyday attempts to explain events by reference to luck, accidents, fortune, or the like, with the emphasis upon the latter "folk theories." The functional significance of such theories has been discussed by Merton:

> In sociological terms, the doctrine of luck as expounded by the successful serves the dual function of explaining the frequent discrepancy between merit and reward while keeping immune from criticism a social structure which allows this discrepancy to become frequent. For if success is primarily a matter of luck, if it is just in the blind nature of things, if it bloweth where it listeth and thou canst not tell whence it cometh, or whither it goeth, then surely it is beyond control and will occur in the same measure *whatever the social structure.*
>
> For the unsuccessful and particularly for those among the unsuccessful who find little reward for their merit and their effort, the doctrine of luck serves the psychological function of enabling them to preserve their self-esteem in the face of failure. It may also entail the dysfunction of curbing motivation for sustained endeavour…
>
> This orientation toward chance and risk-taking accentuated by the strains of frustrated aspirations may help explain the marked interest in gambling—an institutionally proscribed, or at best, permissive rather than preferred or proscribed mode of activity—within certain social strata.[14]

The idea of Fortune as a category of events appeared in Aristotle's works. But, beginning with him, the concept of Fortune has always been very close to its opposite pole, Fate.[15] This ambivalence reappears in people's everyday philosophies relative to a large number of social situations; what seems to be determined by chance is at the same time decided in advance by fate. The ideology of romantic love gives an explanation of the decision on whom to love and/ or marry, which has a strong element of

---

14   Robert K. Merton, "Social Structure and Anomie," *Social Theory and Social Structure* (Glencoe, IL: Free Press, 1949), 139. Empirical studies have indicated more readiness to explain success by *luck* among lower class respondents than among respondents with higher rank. Cf. Richard Centers, "Attitude and Belief in Relation to Occupational Stratification," *Journal of Social Psychology* 27 (1938).

15   Vincenzo Cioffari, *Conception of Fortune and Fate in the Works of Dante* (Cambridge, MA: Harvard University Press, 1940); and Vincenzo Cioffari, *Fortune and Fate from Democritus to St. Thomas Aquinas* (New York: Columbia University Press, 1935).

chance, with overtones of fate. The English term "to fall in love" carries with it associations of randomness and chance. The more extreme cult of romantic love, is full of expressions like "love at first sight," "love in spite of reasons." A Norwegian proverb says that "love may fall upon a dirt as soon as upon a lily." One implication seems to be that love is unpredictable, irrational and divorced from other systems of social interaction.

The notion of "the happy accident" in science is another case in point, irrespective of whether this is a correct explanation or not, of how inventions and discoveries actually are made. A more special case is the institution of "free association" in psychoanalysis. The norm directed to the patient is that he should permit "random" thoughts to become conscious and verbalize them, while the explanation applied by the therapist is a systematic one. We may look upon the recent method of "brainstorm" as an extension of free association on the psychoanalyst's couch.

Chance Devices

The objective chance device is a physical test to the outcomes of which are assigned values in advance. Man has under a great variety of circumstances chosen to delegate decisions to such tests—ranging from matters of life and death to mere trivia.

Games of Chance are the prototype of chance mechanisms. The mathematical theory of chance and probability itself has developed out of experiences with lot-drawing, dice-throwing, card-playing and roulette. Games of chance are found as far back as we can go in the history of Western society, and among a large number of primitive societies. On the basis of a threefold division of games; games of chance, of skill, and of strategy, it has been found that the relative frequency of occurrence of these three kinds of games varies with geographical and political factors. In 51 cultures represented in the Cross-Cultural files of Yale University, which were judged to be adequately covered on the topic of games, 20 had games of chance.[16]

Games of chance belong in a specific sheltered area of existence, the sphere of "play" as against the serious business of living. It is an activity of Homo Ludens.[17] But games of chance interest us here, not because they represent a retreat from the serious business of living, but because the games effect settlements that impinge upon "serious" social reality, e.g. by redistributing money, goods, prestige, the benevolence of the gods, future

---

16   John M. Roberts, Robert R. Bush, and Malcolm J. Arth, *Dimensions of Mastery in Games* (Mimeo, Center for Advanced Study in the Behavioral Sciences, 1957).

17   Cf. Johann Huizinga, *Homo Ludens* (London: Routledge and Kegan Paul, 1943). Cf. also John Cohen and Mark Hansel, *Risk and Gambling* (London: Longmans, Green, and Co., 1956).

prospects in love and business, the joys of victory, and frustrations of defeat.[18]

Trial by ordeal is another institutionalized chance device. Vinogradoff divides the ordeals into three types: Struggle, appeals to chance, and appeals to miracles against a human presumption.[19] The distinction between the two last ones is probably one of degree, the odds being very heavily stacked against one of the parties in the latter case, leaving less scope to the operation of chance factors.

Concerning those ordeals which apparently appeal to chance, one recent writer has claimed that they were set up so as to give the innocent, and therefore psychologically relaxed, a strong advantage over the guilty and psychologically tense.[20] There is some slight plausibility for this view in the bread-eating ordeal and a few others. On the whole, this theory, which likens the old Germanic ordeals to modern legal-psychiatric observations, seems rather far-fetched. Most writers on the subject appear unconcerned with the degree of system and uncertainty in trials by ordeal, which makes it hard to determine whether the ordeal functioned as a chance device or not.

Trials by ordeal are best known from mediaeval Germanic law.[21] From early mediaeval times such trials were occasionally fought by the church;[22] but the last remnant of the English statute authorizing trial by battle was not repealed until 1819. Trials by ordeal are also well-known from old Indian laws.[23] Very few examples are known from the other great civilizations of antiquity, the Babylonian, the Judaic and the Greek. The Bible does, however, in a few places, refer to trial by lot-ordeal, the one ordeal most obviously based upon a chance device.[24] Finally, trial by ordeal is known from many primitive legal systems.[25]

An omen is not a decision on how to act, but a way of deciding on what to expect. The prediction may or may not have consequences for action. It may become a self-fulfilling prophecy, or a self-defeating one, or it may

18 In this respect our approach differs from that of Huizinga and also from that of Roger Caillois, "Unity of Play: Diversity of Games," *Diogenes* 19 (1957).

19 Paul Vinogradoff, "Ordeal," in *Encyclopaedia of Religion and Ethics*, Vol. 9, ed. James Hastings (Edinburgh: T. T. Clark, 1917), 519.

20 Hermann Nottarp, *Gottesurteile. Eine Phase im Rechtsleben der Völker* (Bamberg: Bamberger Verlagshaus, 1949), 12ff.

21 Cf. Nottarp, *Gottesurteile. Eine Phase im Rechtsleben der Völker*; Vinogradoff, "Ordeal;" and Herluf af Trolle, *Om ordalierna hos de germanska folken* (Stockholm: Aktiebolaget Nordiska Bokhandeln, 1915).

22 Charlotte Leitmaier, *Die Kirche und die Gottesurteile* (Wein: Herold, 1953), 41ff.

23 A. F. Stenler, "Die Indischen Gottesurteile," in *Bibl. Soc. Orien. Germ* (1907).

24 Joshua 7:13ff., Samuel 14:24ff., Proverbs 16:33 and 18:18; and Joshua 1:7.

25 Cf. E. Adamson Hoebel, *The Law of Primitive Man.* (Cambridge, MA: Harvard University Press, 1944), 251, 262. The use of oracles in witchcraft cases should be included here, cf. E. E. Evans Pritchard, *Witchcraft, Oracles and Magic among the Azande* (Oxford: Oxford University Press, 1937).

result in a conviction with more diffuse behavioral implications, e. g. greater or less self-assurance in general. Unlike the known ordeals, which fall in relatively few distinctive types, there exists an indefinite variety of methods of divination and tests from which omens are drawn. Frazer's "Golden Bough" contains a fabulous wealth of material on omens and divination.[26]

We find here two groups of tests, which differ in one apparently significant respect. The first group of tests is made up of games of skill, the outcome of which depends very largely upon physical prowess and the will of the actor. The outcome of the second group of tests lies at the mercy of chance. The importance of this distinction may nevertheless be doubted in this particular context since the relationships between the tests of skill and the predicted events, unlike relations between examina or I. Q. tests, and later occupational performances, seem to be random. In other words, the pre-established codes of interpretation, by which numerous outcomes of the tests are assigned meanings, are so constructed that they closely parallel modern lists of random numbers, transform systematic responses into a random distribution of values. Thus, any coincidence between test result and individual fate in real life would appear to imply super-natural interference, either in the test or in the life of the person. It should be noted, however, that in tests of skill, the person may express his motivation relative to the predicted event, and thus render the test into a rational symptom of the predicted state of affairs.

Functions

Communication with the supernatural

All known cultures, except possibly the emergent communist civilizations, assume the existence and significance of a supernatural world. To communicate with this vital sphere of existence presents grave problems, however. Man may speak to the supernatural, but will the supernatural answer? Or rather, how is it possible to obtain "answers" from the other world which do not obviously originate within everyday profane existence? Natural events can, of course, be viewed as symptomatic of states in the other world and of man's relationship to the other world. But there are two ways in which men may obtain answers that are inexplicable in terms of ordinary experience, and therefore achieve a special status relative to the supernatural: through dreams and chance devices.

Chance devices, as we know them from games, ordeals, omens, oracles, divination and other chance contraptions, have in common that the outcome, to varying degrees, is unpredictable on the basis of the natural or

26 Cf. also Reo Fortune, "Divination," *Encyclopaedia of the Social Sciences.* Vol. 5 (New York: MacMillan, 1931), pp. 174-6; and for a very detailed description of techniques of divination, S. G. Nadel, *Nupe Religion* (London: Routledge and Kegan Paul, 1954), 38-67.

moral qualities of the person with regard to whom a decision is being reached. It is, furthermore, unpredictable on the basis of the known characteristics, interests, motives, abilities, etc. of the social agent administering the test. The answer from the chance device is unpolluted by any carrier of the message, a priest, a prophet or a judge. Answers given by chance devices cannot meaningfully be ascribed to a human choice. Neither can they be ascribed to the laws of nature, since the test is set up precisely in such a way as to make the outcome uncertain on the basis of known laws of nature. It is not unnatural to conclude that what is not decided by men or by nature, must be decided by the gods.

The close relationship between games of chance, divination and man's communication with the supernatural world was pointed out by the outstanding nineteenth century anthropologist Tylor:

> The uncivilized man thinks that lots or dice are adjusted in their fall with reference to the meaning he may choose to attach to it, and especially he is apt to suppose spiritual beings standing over the diviner or the gambler, shuffling the lots or turning up the dice to make them give their answers. This view held its place firmly in the middle ages, and later in history we still find games of chance looked on as results of supernatural operation.[27]

Roberts and associates have furnished a more precise argument in favour of the view that games of chance are specifically connected with supernatural categories. They attempted a statistical test, upon nineteen cultures in the Cross-Cultural Survey files which contained adequate information on the presence of such games, of the following hypothesis: "If games of chance are associated with control of the supernatural, they ought to be associated with the belief that the gods are benevolent, with the belief that the gods can be coerced, and not with the belief that the gods are aggressive."[28] The data seemed to support the hypothesis.

That not only games of chance, but also chance-like omens, oracles and divinations have been used in large measure to test out the supernatural, appears likely from much material in Frazer's *Golden Bough*. He reports a large number of omens and divinations concerning marriage, death and other important events. What these omens had in common was that, to the people in question (as to us), no natural link of cause and effect existed between the device from which predictions were derived, and the likelihood of the predicted event occurring. Relative to the omens drawn, these tests were arbitrary. The relationship between the test and the predicted event was random on the basis of known empirical laws. Most likely it was precisely this, although not this alone, that gave them their social function, a function which concerns the contact with the supernatural. Either the

27   Edward B. Tylor, *Primitive Culture*, 2nd ed., Vol. 1. (London: Murray 1873), 79.
28   Roberts et al., *Dimensions of Mastery in Games*, 8.

test served to coerce the gods and obtain reassurance concerning an uncertain future, in accordance with Malinowski's theory of the psychological functions of primitive magic. Or the function was the more modest one of making predictions by drawing omens, and then seeing whether one had been successful in establishing rapport with the supernatural, irrespective of whether the omen was good or bad.

It is possible that we should also include, among the chance devices which serve to provide communications from the gods, phenomena such as runic inscriptions.[29] Old Norse runes served magical functions, and mastery of the runic art was very different from present-day literacy. Runic inscriptions often have many meanings, depending upon the scheme of interpretation applied. Two letters might be collapsed, one hidden in the other; or the message might be cryptic, in the sense that individual runes could be substituted for others according to pre-established systems of codes. From the point of view of communication between persons, these characteristics of runic inscriptions seem unnecessarily dysfunctional; but maybe not if we look upon the runes as means of contact with the supernatural. What is important here is not primarily that the receiver of the message would be in doubt and risk surprise by hidden meanings. But also the sender of the message, the inscriber, would be somewhat ignorant of what he was doing. His message might have meanings, according to one scheme of interpretation or another, which he had not foreseen. In other words, through the runes spoke not only men, but also an agent independent of human knowledge and volition, the supernatural. It is characteristic that a great many runes contain a term for protection, (*alu*), which may well refer to protection against unknown dangers inherent in the rune-writer's own text (*meinruner*), runes that might become magically turned against himself.

In societies, or segments of societies, which have lost faith in the blatantly supernatural, chance devices may still be used to consult with Fate on vital issues, often issues of life and death. Weiss concluded on the basis of interviews with 156 people who had attempted suicide:

> Many suicidal attempts have at least in part, the character of a gamble with death, a sort of Russian roulette, the outcome of which depends to some extent, on chance. The attempts are consciously or unconsciously arranged in such a manner that the lethal probability may vary from almost certain survival to almost certain death; and "fate," or at least some force external to the conscious choice of the person is compelled in some perhaps magical way to make the final decision.[30]

And, referring to the work of two other psychiatrists: "Stengel and Cook have noted that the outcome of the attempt is almost invariably accepted

29 I owe this idea to Tom Broch.
30 James M. A. Weiss, "The Gamble with Death in Attempted Suicide," *Psychiatry* 20 (1957): 21.

for the time being and further attempts are rarely made immediately even if there is no lack of opportunity. The outcome of the attempt is accepted like that of a trial by ordeal in mediaeval times."[31]

A case parallel to the one I have made above concerning man's attempts to get "answers" from the supernatural or from Fate, can be made for man's relationship to Law. Ordeals are, at least in part, chance devices, the outcomes of which are interpreted as the judgment of God. A decision which is unintelligible and unpredictable in terms of human volition and natural laws, but which is nevertheless definite, must, by some simple principle of elimination, express the judgment of higher authorities.

I should like to close this section with a few remarks on the game of solitaire. Solitaire may be used as a kind of divination, from which omens are drawn about marriage, acquisition of wealth and what not. But it seems especially pertinent in the present context that the playing of solitaire is a means by which even the isolate can communicate. Through manipulation of the cards, in accordance with the rules, the lonely player transmits messages and impinges upon his environment, such that unforeseen, unintended, uncontrolled and surprising "answers" are fed back from the cards. The meanings do not, except in cases of bad cheating, come from the player, but from something or somebody else. Thus, the playing of solitaire becomes a simple and ingenious way of relieving loneliness. It may be related to the same function of relieving loneliness when we find so many superstitious beliefs in magic and omens among lonely dairymaids, lumberjacks, sailors and fishermen.

Innovation and creativity

By innovation I refer to new relations between people. Such new relations often spring out of new relationships between man and nature after a change in climate or a technical invention. Because society is incapable of reproduction and survival on the basis of a set of social bonds established once and for all, creation of new ties are a functional prerequisite of any society, human or animal. And because man's environment is unstable, old social bonds must be capable of transformation, permitting adaptation to new conditions. If social innovations are a functional prerequisite of society, so are normative patterns bestowing legitimacy upon these innovations. Man cannot just act; he must be capable of giving reasons for his actions. And he must be capable of giving reasons *before* he acts.

In most societies of the world other than our modern industrial one empirical knowledge has been very limited, and man's capacity to shape the future according to his own volition was likewise limited. The arsenal of "rational" reasons for doing things is severely limited in primitive cultures, and chance happenings are not accepted. How then, if man cannot

31   Weiss, "Gamble with Death," 24.

act without knowing why, are such societies to achieve a sufficient degree of elasticity in social relations and to avoid a rigidity which exposes it too much to the variability of an environment which lacks respect for normative structures? Somehow, there must be available reasons, arguments, principles of decision for actions that so far lack a good empirical, utilitarian rationale.

Going back to the hunting magic among the Naskapi of Labrador, I would be inclined to interpret the practice as a means of breaking routine, of doing something new, not only in order to surprise the game, but as a way of achieving a wider experience, from which new systematic knowledge may accrue. The technique of divination is a primitive method of trial and error in cultures which do not accept trial and error. The method gives acceptable reasons, drawn from the folkloristic arsenal, for doing things which have the primary function of widening the sphere of experience. It is a primitive experiment, which, if successful, may be included in the commonly accepted stock of rational experience, knowledge of natural laws.

A random device is functional from the point of view of innovation because, in the absence of empirical knowledge, the best bet is the randomly distributed response. Such a mechanism may be operating in a fishing magic from Norway, the use of the "fish-tray." On the bottom of a tray is drawn a simple map of the coastline with the major fishing banks outlined. The tray is filled with water. Small bubbles of air will rise from the bottom to the surface. The location of these bubbles determines where the fish are most likely to be caught.[32] In this case the element of surprise is not likely to be important as it was in the Naskapi example. But the device is essentially similar and of a chance nature. I believe that the major function of the "fish-tray" may be to provide a decision-making device in the face of great empirical uncertainty, and one which permits some leeway from routine operation.[33] The sociologically significant aspect of these kinds of divinations is that they establish between family members or co-workers rights to carry out activities that also concern others, in a non-routine fashion.

If divination in the shape of objective contrived devices, like the fish-tray, may serve the function of breaking routine, so may pre-established codes of interpretation of natural events. A possible case in point is the codes for dream interpretation. In instances where dreams, without

---

32 Johan Theodor Storaker, *Tiden i den norske folketro* (Kristiania: Norsk folkeminnelag, 1921), 175-177.

33 Chance devices may be especially needed in situations of great uncertainty, since the alternative predisposition in risky situations is stereotyped, precedent-ridden behavior.

forethought, are confronted with pre-established codes,[34] "dream books" or the like, the codes may resemble the modern lists of random number. Theories of dreams may serve the innovative function in society by multiplying the number of reasons for doing things beyond that which is empirically warranted or morally permitted without dream justification.

There exist "lists of random numbers" for the interpretation of other natural events. Astromedicine is one example, based as it is upon the (empirically unfounded) assumption of definite relationships between celestial phenomena and the functioning of the human body. From astromedical laws were derived a number of principles for the intervention of a doctor in the state of health and sickness of his patients, medication, surgery and other kinds of treatment. These interventions were, in part, completely random, leading to similar prescriptions for entirely different diseases, and different treatments of the same disease, because of the (as we know) largely random relationship between human and celestial phenomena. But the innovative function may have been served by the astrological and other magical beliefs of early medicine. It does not seem unlikely that Paracelsus' achievements were, in part, due to the vast store of astrological and magical belief upon which he drew.[35] His unscientific beliefs gave him reasons for a ceaseless series of break-neck experiments. But out of these experiments grew empirical knowledge, modern medicine. A similar case may be made for the innovative function of the random hodge-podge of beliefs upon which the art of the goldmakers rested, and out of which chemistry developed. The sheer number of culturally accepted beliefs, formulas, statements, assumptions, appears essential in relation to creativity and innovation. If this view is sound, it opens up a new perspective upon the social function of non-rational thought in general. It may possibly give us a key to the understanding of such phenomena as water-witching, still widely practised in the U.S.A. and other industrialized societies. Vogt and Hyman interpret it as an anxiety-reducing ritual practice employed in the face of great empirical uncertainty about the location of underground water.[36] In terms of the present analysis it seems that water-witching serves as a legitimizer for random behaviour, where randomness is rational, but where "trial and error" is unacceptable as an explicit value basis for action partly because of the high costs of drilling new wells.

The innovating functions of divination, games of chance and magical belief of the random number type are in modern industrial societies often

---

34   Such a code is presented in Thomas A. Sebeok and Frances J. Ingemann, *Studies in Cheremis. Volume 2: The Supernatural* (New York: Wenner-Gren Foundation for Anthropological Research, 1956), 269ff.

35   Cf. Henry M. Pachter, *Magic into Science: The Story of Paracelsus* (New York: Henry Schulman, 1951).

36   Cf. Ray Hyman and Elizabeth G. Cohen, "Water-Witching in the United States," *American Sociological Review* 22 (1957).

served by other mechanisms. The *chance ideology* has taken the place of the cumbersome objective devices; the conscious notion that experiment, trial and error, originality are values in themselves within the institution of science.

The most famous and systematic modern ideologies of science tend to avoid the innovative aspect of scientific work. Logical positivism depicts the scientist as a producer of statements, verifiable, communicable and true. The niceties of this ideology have a purely retroactive function. They provide norms for evaluating scientific statements that have been made already. Our problem is to locate the norms and mechanisms by which it is possible to legitimize in advance the production of previously unverified or not accepted statements. It is commonly recognized that logic or "the logic of science" gives little or no clue as to how ideas are to be produced, but it is restricted to laying down rules about how they are to be handled once they have been produced. There is in the institution of science a fundamental ambivalence, a tension between truth and novelty. Ideas are, sociologically speaking, either true, that, is, communicated and accepted, or novel. They can be both only in a brief moment when a new discovery is being proven.

The value of originality or novelty is, in the nature of things, much less systematized than the value of truth; although truth is a value which science shares with many other institutions, while the emphasis upon originality is unique to science, a new value. As Whitehead put it, man made his greatest discovery when he invented the method of invention.[37] The institution of science was born when the value of novelty, invention, creativity, discovery and originality had become sufficiently embedded in a culture to motivate large numbers of well-equipped people to dedicate their lives to the production of new ideas. The scientist became then, not so much a man in search of truth, as a man who was permitted, forgiven, even encouraged and praised for making many false statements, as long as he did not abandon his basic attachment to the value of truth.

There is no stronger testimony to the institutionalization of the value of originality and novelty in science than the recurrent priority fights that have ravaged scientific communities for centuries. Merton has recently given a historical exposé of priority strifes from the sociologist's point of view, and emphasized their functional significance in enforcing the value of originality.[38] Another recent writer on the social system of science stresses the values by which "pure scientists" are ranked and rewarded:

> The core of the value system of pure science consists of two related beliefs: first, that new knowledge should be evaluated according to its

37   Bernard Barber, *Science and the Social Order* (Glencoe, IL: Free Press, 1952), 192.
38   Robert K. Merton, "Priorities in Scientific Discovery: A Chapter in the Sociology of Science." *American Sociological Review* 22 (1957).

significance for existing theory, and second, that scientists should be evaluated according to their contributions of new knowledge. Highest honours go to those whose work involves radical reformulations or extensions of theory or conceptualization. Next come those who do the pioneer experimental work required by a theoretical reformulation. Next come those who carry out the work logically required to round out the conceptual structure. Next come those who carry out redundant experimental work of a confirmatory nature, or concern themselves largely with relevant data accumulation. Last are the doers of sloppy and dull work.[39]

According to this scheme of ranking, it is the originality and not the degree of adherence to truth (which may be equal in the four first groups) that distinguishes scientists from each other in terms of merit.

Whether or not scientific progress has been characterized by chance innovation or not, it is a widespread belief within the scientific community that discoveries and inventions depend in large part upon luck. As a supplement to the common notion that science demands systematic and unusually hard work, the "happy accident" has also become an article of faith. Many great creative scientists and artists have put much emphasis upon the chance event as initiator of a discovery or an invention.[40]

Ernst Mach said in his paper "On the Part Played by Accident in Invention and Discovery:" "It is well to ask, are we justified in placing a low estimate on the achievement of an inventor because accident has assisted him in his work? Huygens, whose discoveries and inventions are justly sufficient to entitle him to an opinion in such matters, lays great emphasis on this factor. He asserts that a man capable of inventing the telescope without the concurrence of accident must have been gifted with superhuman genius."[41] "The disclosure of new provinces of facts before unknown can only be brought about by accidental circumstances, under which are *remarked* facts that commonly go unnoticed."[42] "I do not know whether Swift's academy of schemers in Lagado, in which great discoveries and inventions were made by a sort of verbal game of dice, was intended as a satire on Francis Bacon's method of making discoveries by means of huge synoptic tables constructed by scribes. It certainly would not have been ill-placed."[43]

A more contemporary writer on the same topic emphasizes, with some misgivings, how widespread the belief in the happy accident is, even outside the scientific community: "The radio, popular literature, the loose parley of the streets, all exalt such moments in the course of human prog-

39 Herbert A. Shepard, "Basic Research and the Social System of Pure Science." *Philosophy of Science* 23 (1956): 50.

40 Brewster Ghiselin, ed., *The Creative Process* (New York: Mentor Book, 1955).

41 *Monist* 6 (1896): 163.

42 Mach, "On the Part Played," 169.

43 Mach, "On the Part Played," 174-175.

ress as Goodyear's 'lucky' and chance discovery. Not so prevalent, however, is the emphasis on all the substantial progress, all the hours of dull,
minute and precise scientific prying that eventually crystallized in that
sparkling moment of the spilled mixture."[44] Nevertheless, the writer ends
up by giving new credence to the belief in the chance basis of significant
scientific discoveries.

What concerns us here is not whether the above statements are true or
not; but whether these beliefs in the happy accidents are representative
and express something significant in the ethos of the scientific community.
I shall assume that such is the case.[45] On the basis of our previous reflections it seems possible to guess what functions are served by this belief.
The scientist faces the problem, if he wants success, of investing a long
education and arduous work in the pursuit of novelty, of original ideas,
the truth and social acceptance of which he may only make uncertain
guesses about. The social situation of the gifted and ambitious scientist has
been that the stakes involved in the proper performance of his role are very
high, and the likelihood of reaping the fruits of the work is unpredictable.
In such a situation a doctrine of luck may serve much the same function as
in highly competitive social structures of other kinds.[46] It reduces the
probability of investing ability and hard work in pursuits, for the possibly
unsuccessful outcome of which one has to shoulder the responsibility. In
some measure the homage paid to the "happy accident" bestows freedom
of responsibility for failure upon the daring adherent of the novelty value
in science. It prevents failure from being interpreted as a reflection of
inability, and it may protect the successful from unbearable envy. In short,
the doctrine of chance in science seems to be a necessary ideological link
between the partly contrasting values of truth and novelty.

Representativity

If we look upon social bonds as patterned relations between Egos and
Alters exchanging performances, it will often happen that only a sample of
possible Egos can perform, or that the Egos can only respond relative to a
sample of all possible Alters. Thus, some select few will have to govern on
behalf of a larger group; and the police can only detect and punish a few of
all those who break the law. How are Egos and Alters selected in situations
presenting such a sampling problem?

Let us first look at the problem from the side of the actors, the Egos. It
presents itself, first of all, as the question of how to decide who shall make

44   Franklin McLean, "The Happy Accident," *Scientific Monthly* 53 (1941): 61.
45   For confirmatory evidence, see Barber, *Science and the Social Order*, 191ff; P. W. Bridgman,
     "Impertinent Reflections on History of Science," *Philosophy of Science* 17 (1950); Joseph
     Rossman, *The Psychology of the Inventor* (Washington, DC: W.F. Roberts, 1931), 117ff; and
     Arthur Koestler, *The Sleepwalkers* (London: Hutchinson, 1959).
46   See Merton, "Social Structure and Anomie," p. 139.

decisions *on behalf of* a group or category of persons. It is the problem of government and power.

The classical example of the selection of rulers through a chance device is the use of the lot in the Athenian democracy. The population of the city districts, the demes (there were about 100 of them) proposed lists of candidates from which Athenian jurymen and Athenian councillors were selected by lot. The demes elected candidates for membership of the Council (of which there were 500 in all) on a proportionate basis according to the number of inhabitants. The eligibility of the candidates was dependent upon passing a test of their qualifications. When the qualifications had been determined the final selection for a Council seat was made by lot.[47]

The system of selection to the Athenian council consisted in a blend of three principles: the choice by a population, determination of innate qualities and, finally, random selection. As for the functions of the last element, Barker makes this suggestion: "In fact, the qualification of election by the additional use of the lot was perhaps largely due to the desire to avoid election intrigues."[48] The use of the lot was criticized both by Socrates and Plato because it gave an equal chance to those unqualified to govern. Their opposition shows, by the way, that they did not trust the lot as an instrument of the deity.

A modern example of the use of chance devices to select political leaders is to be found in the small European state of San Marino, known for its famous Casino. San Marino is governed by two *capitani regenti*, traditionally elected by the 60 Man's Council of the republic, the *arengo*. The arengo designates twelve nominees that again designate their candidates. They vote for candidates by means of white and black balls, and the six who receive most white balls are further divided into three pairs of candidates. These three pairs are then led in a procession to the cathedral where the archbishop receives them. Then an innocent child of San Marino draws from an urn one of three scraps of paper furnished with two names — and the republic has been provided with two new governors.

In modern times, however, the judiciary is the branch of government where chance devices have been most frequently used as a mechanism of recruitment to positions of authority. As the jury system (and a system of lay judges) is practised in Norway, however, selection of jurors is based upon mixed principles. A general supply of prospective jurors is deliberately chosen by municipal authorities. In other words, the general recruitment to the roles of jurors is not a chance happening in any strict sense, although much "arbitrariness" may be involved. What is a matter of chance, although not without modifications, is the decision as to who, among a group of candidates, should pass judgment on the question of

47   Ernest Barker, *Greek Political Theory: Plato and His Predecessors* (London: Methuen, 1918), 34-35.
48   Barker, *Greek Political Theory*, 35.

guilt in any particular case. In other words, what has been left to the mercy of chance is the decision as to who, given a possible deviant, should be the sanctioning agent vis-à-vis *him*.

The custom of using chance devices to select incumbents of positions of public authority is not restricted to cultures which have been influenced by the democratic tradition originating in Athens. Frazer gives several accounts of how rulers are pointed out by divination, including, in the case of the election of the Dalai Lama of Tibet, the drawing of lots from a golden jar.[49] Another custom that provides for a random principle in the selection of rulers has to do with the institution of the Saturnalia. Frazer believed that the Latin kings were sons of unknown fathers, their mothers having become pregnant in the course of a Saturnalia, during which time they were promiscuous.

Through divination, the drawing of lots or even the Saturnalia, the gods were permitted to point out the rulers, thereby giving the government a sacral touch. That this may be functional from the point of view of establishing authority seems fairly clear.[50] Selection for office by chance may also reduce political strife and competition for power. Emulation and display of strength of gifts, or the rallying of supporters is unnecessary and actually useless. In the Athenian democracy, with its fear of hubris, this line of reasoning seems even to have been quite explicit. By making the terms of office brief and the incumbency dependent upon random mechanisms, a counter force is built up against political ambition. Scheming for power is rendered futile. If Ranulf is anywhere near right in his analysis of the climate of opinion under the democracy of Athens, with great emphasis upon equality, much envy and interpersonal aggression,[51] it would seem to give a good explanation of the election to political office by lots.

Election to a jury by lot may be viewed as a just way of distributing inevitable burdens. But it is also perceived as one means by which the independence and objectivity of the courts are secured. The juror, like the lay judge, is the representative of the people in an activity which is largely professional and therefore hard to control. Since he is untrained, he performs his role under some suspicion of emotionalism and partiality. The election by lot secures, however, a minimum of independence. Nobody can designate him with a view to his subjective disposition vis-à-vis one or the other of the contending parties. That decision is left to chance. Although this gives no guarantee that the juror will be an unbiased person,

49   James George Frazer, *The Golden Bough. Volume 1: The Magic Art and the Evolution of Kings* (New York: MacMillan, 1894), 411-412.

50   This may have been an important aspect of the Old Norse tradition of having pretenders to the throne, or their mothers, in cases of doubt, submit themselves to ordeals, especially the hot iron tests.

51   Svend Ranulf, *The Jealousy of the Gods and Criminal Law at Athens*, 2 vols. (London: Williams and Norgate, 1933).

it does prevent the occurrence of systematic biases in any particular case, both in fact and in appearance.

Let us now turn to the sampling problem in power and government as it presents itself from the other side. If social control is to be exerted, rules enforced within a collectivity, how are the specific targets of sanctions to be selected? There are two main reasons why direct social control of everybody standing under the force of a social norm is difficult or impossible in a great many situations. Reasons of "economy" often make it impossible for every case of deviance from a norm to be punished, even if they are known to the agencies of social control. Secondly, many deviant acts remain hidden to the sanctioning agents, thus preventing enforcement. The magnitude of these problems of social control, created by secrecy of deviance and need for economy with sanctions, is very forcefully brought to our attention by the now existing statistical data on so called "hidden criminality."[52] According to the best available information most criminal acts remain unknown to the agents of law enforcement. And if they were to become known and punished, it would imply an expansion of the watchdog institutions of society beyond the limits of what the social system could endure.

If, from a universe of deviant and partly hidden acts, a relatively small sample has to be selected for exposure to sanctions, one can give two theoretical arguments in favor of random social control. If we assume perfect ignorance of the distribution of deviance within a group of actors, which is only a marginal case, any systematic principle for the selection of the accused is exposed to the risk of going systematically wrong, hitting deviance less frequently than it hits conformity. The consequences would be that groups of deviants, if we assume less than perfect ignorance of sanction policy on their part, would learn that they had little to fear. Social control by random terror, like shooting every 10th person in a town, may rest upon considerations of this kind.

Ordeals are sometimes reported to have been used to detect the guilty person when ignorance was great and no specific person was suspected. The group of possible perpetrators were collected and exposed to the test. The ordeal has the advantage that the guilty person is at least exposed to a risk of sanction and the ordeal appears to demonstrate that what is hidden to man, is nevertheless revealed to God. It is paradoxical that the vehicle by which God's "limitless vision" should be expressed is a device of "blind chance."

Suppose that a thousand criminal acts are known, or easily knowable, to the law-enforcing agents. If there is only time and personnel available for handling a hundred cases, which ones are to be selected? The answer in terms of justice would be to rank the sets according to their seriousness,

52   Cf. Vilhelm Aubert, *Om straffens sosiale funksjon* (Oslo: Akademisk Forlag, 1954).

and sanction the hundred most serious offences. And, actually a higher number of murderers and robbers are sanctioned than of petty thieves and pilferers. But a rigid adherence to "justice" in this sense means that the police would have their hands full with the most serious offences, and the less serious offences would go systematically free of sanctions. This situation is intolerable, since large numbers of completely unsanctioned small offences may bring total disorder to vital institutions in an urban industrial society.

What actually develops is a compromise between the principle of justice and random distribution of threats. The spread of sanctions to cover the many petty offences as well is not, in modern society, achieved by chance devices in the objective sense. It is achieved by decentralization and specialization of control agencies, that is by ignorance and barriers of communication. The criminal police are so dedicated to the idea of worst things first, that if control of socially important, but undramatic offences, like price violations, etc., are left under their jurisdiction, these norms will be enforced with insufferable laxity. So, a vast number of independent or semi-independent organs of legal control have developed, each specializing on certain types of deviance. Justice has become specialized, because rigid justice is something which society cannot afford if it is to survive.

In primitive societies the problem of sanction economy is solved in a more elegant fashion. They draw upon the natural supply of suffering by ingeniously transforming them into morally meaningful sanctions. They achieve this by their theories of disaster, above all, their explanations of illness and death. Suffering, illness, or death may be viewed as the consequence of deviance on part of the sufferer, in which case fear of falling ill may be a deterrent against moral transgressions. Or, illness and death may be viewed as a consequence of black magic or sorcery on the part of somebody else. This theory is a two-edged sword. It makes people afraid of incurring enemies because enemies may give them diseases through sorcery, and also because they are afraid lest their enemies fall sick and accuse *them* of sorcery. This implies that the serious offender, the petty offender and the relatively blameless citizen stand an equal chance of being sanctioned. Such a system of sanctions can, by virtue of its randomness, not teach anybody the difference between right and wrong. But given that the cognitive discrimination between right and wrong is learned already, theories of illness, just like police terror, create a general feeling of uncertainty, fear of doing anything offensive, since no-one knows exactly what it takes to release these supernatural sanctions. And the randomness of the system has the consequence that it serves no purpose to hide offences — secrecy is no protection against sanctions.

But if sanctions hit individuals in a random fashion, will it not be empirically observed that there is no relationship between merit and reward, sin and punishment? In the first place such observations are hard to make. Furthermore, people are in general sinful in the sense that they are aware of something for which they might deserve punishment. Therefore, any case of sickness, or accusations of sorcery may be viewed as a confirmation of the theory by the sick person.

Equality and justice

There is one, and only one area of life into which all men are born equal, and also remain equal throughout their lives, independent of physical, pecuniary, intellectual, or moral achievements: the pure game of chance. Small wonder then that so many people representing so many different cultural backgrounds have sought refuge from the inequalities and injustices of real life in this model of an egalitarian society. Interpreted as divination, as we have seen a fairly universal pattern, it creates an egalitarian distribution of God's grace. The egalitarian distribution of "answers" from chance devices may, on the other hand, be one of the reasons why a religious interpretation of games of chance and other chance devices has become so widely accepted.

What are "equality" and "justice" in our present sociological context? One possible answer, a Platonic answer, is that equality means that equal contributions, merit or failure, are met with equal sanctions, rewards or penalties. To further this kind of equality or justice, chance devices are by definition unsuited. The establishment of this kind of justice suffers, however, from disequilibriating tendencies. It is a constant problem, as we see in all negotiations concerning wages, to reach and retain consensus on the criteria of performance on the basis of which the sanctions should be adjusted. In other words, with respect to what criteria are individuals to be grouped as equal or unequal?

There exists another concept of equality, however, which makes it possible to avoid this dilemma by assuming that all men are equal, independent of special characteristics. It brings to the fore another method of establishing and observing equality and justice. "Independence" is the key word when absolute concepts of justice are involved. One way of achieving independence between "in-put" in a decision-making agency, and the "out-put," the decision, is to insert a randomizer, a chance device. What is then achieved is not that each contribution or merit receives its just reward, but that it can be established that rewards and penalties are at least unrelated to those criteria that are deemed as irrelevant biases.

Under what conditions is each one of the two types of equality adapted to further harmony within a social system? In order to practice justice in the sense of "to each according to worth and merit," two conditions must be fulfilled. There must exist a reasonable consensus concerning the criteria of merit; and it must be possible in the individual case to observe whether the criteria agreed upon are fulfilled or not. In situations where these two conditions are not present, we might expect the occurrence of chance devices, or of chance theories.

The classical example is trial by ordeal. It took place in a context where there was general consensus about what sanction should be adjusted to what specific types of performance, the crime of the person with regard to whom a decision had to be reached. But there was ignorance concerning the presence or absence in the individual case of the relevant criterion, the guilt. We have come to solve such problems by increased fact-finding skill on the part of a professional agency, the police, and by the rule *in dubio pro reo*. Both of these factors are products of the sophistication of urbanization. If they are non-existent, by what method can the court establish a just relationship between deed and sanction? It seems that a chance device is the only available means, because it does secure, and give the appearance of, independence between sanction and irrelevant characteristics of the defendant and of the judges. On the manifest level the ordeal serves to discover the facts of guilt or innocence by divine intervention, thus permitting an application of the Platonic concept of justice as a basis for meting out punishments. On the latent level the ordeal demonstrates the independence between the decision and possible prejudices of the judge or particularistic relationships between defendant and judge. It may be claimed that as far as *apparent* independence goes, no chance device is needed, only an appeal to sources apparently outside the control of the judge. Both oaths, battle and falsified ordeals may serve this function. The divine chance device is only one among several mechanisms that may serve to uphold the court's claim to be a dispenser of justice, through the apparent independence between outcome and existing biases. It is however, superior to the others in the sense that in the long run it can be statistically observed that there is no correlation between these factors.

When we conclude that decision by chance mechanisms is functional when the problem of individual guilt or merit is uncertain, it must be recognized that it rests upon one further assumption, which may appear obvious. A chance device is only useful if we assume that the decision sought must effect *uneven* distribution of sanctions. And this carries us back to the control aspect of trials. Trials serve not only to achieve justice or equality, but also to threaten, by demonstrating the different consequences of different courses of action on the part of the citizens. We see this most clearly in the old cases where a limited number of people had been pointed out as suspects, and the choice of the guilty one was made by submitting them all to ordeals. It is close to axiomatic under such a condition that they cannot all be treated equally in the sense that they will all get the *same* treatment. To uphold the law, there must be an uneven distribution of sanctions.

This is, however, not a necessary constraint in all situations where an agency is faced with the problem of distributing sanctions under conditions of imperfect or non-existent knowledge of relative guilt or merit within a group. There are only two types of situations where mechanical equality of sanctions is ruled out as a way of coping with ignorance concerning contributions of the actors. There is the situation mentioned above, where differential deprivation or reward is functional as a means of social control or socialization. The other type arises out of scarcity and indivisibility of the advantages and disadvantages which are to be distributed. Exemption from military duty on the basis of lot-drawing is well known from several countries before the last war. The government took recourse to a chance device, not so much because there was ignorance with regard to the presence or absence of merit in individual cases, but rather because it appeared highly doubtful what criteria determine whether a young man "deserves" to be enrolled or not. Had it been possible, and practical, to divide the "disadvantage" indefinitely, no sampling would have been necessary, and a solution in terms of absolute mechanical equality would probably have been sought.

Nowhere is the close relationship between chance and justice brought more forcefully to our attention than in children's games and some of their ways of coping with the problem of distributing scarce values. From an early age, children learn that many, and to them important decisions, are best made by random devices, like saying "eenie, meanie, miney, mo," when selecting players for a specific role in a game, by drawing straws when dividing pieces of chocolate, etc. Parallel to the indoctrination of the achievement pattern as a basis for later adult conceptions of justice, we find a development towards an adult sense of justice through a learning to observe the rules of pure chance.

Dael Wolfle[1]

Chance, or Human Judgment?

For some kinds of decisions, chance may be better than human judgment. Adoption of the policy of selecting draftees by a random drawing of birth dates has been widely commended as the most democratic method available when the number of men who must be drafted is only a fraction of the number of men available.

If risk should be allocated by lot, perhaps benefit should be also. The Federal City College (the new land-grant college in Washington, D.C.) had many more applicants than could be admitted to its first class. Selection on the basis of grades or test scores was inappropriate, for the institution was intended to be an "open door" community college. A lottery solved the selection problem. In December, the arts and sciences college of the University of Illinois used a lottery to choose its quota of 3350 new students from among 4200 well-qualified applicants for admission in the autumn of 1970. In this case, the 850 losers were less impressed with the democratic fairness of a lottery than were the 3350 winners; public pressure, including pressure from parents of rejected applicants, persuaded the university to reconsider, and to accept all 4200 qualified applicants. The university has, however, announced that, if necessary, it will use random selection for 1971.

There are other selection decisions that could be made by chance. Traditionally, the best medical care has been available to the affluent, and in some places also to the indigent. If excellent medical care is not available to everyone, would not allocation on a random basis be more equitable?

A general principle can be stated: when the number of eligible people exceeds the number who must bear a particular burden or who can receive a particular benefit, the most democratic, equitable, and moral basis for allocation is by chance.

1   Originally published on p. 1201 of *Science* 167 (1970). Copyright © 1970 American Association for the Advancement of Science (AAAS). Reproduced with permission from AAAS.

The use of a lottery to decide who will receive a benefit that cannot be granted to all or who will bear a burden that need not fall on all is a denial of rationality. Under an earlier method of selecting draftees, local draft boards could take into account the particular circumstances of individual men and the particular needs of the country or the communities in which they lived. Errors and biased decisions no doubt occurred, but the system honored the rational judgment of a group of one's fellow citizens, not the luck of the draw.

To choose students by a random process is to deny the ability of the faculty to select those applicants who show greatest promise or who appear most likely to benefit from higher education.

In times of battle or catastrophe, a triage officer selects the ill and wounded who most need, and who are most likely to respond favorably to, prompt medical attention. A physician is surely more competent than a pair of dice to make such decisions and to determine which patients should be given access to limited medical resources.

To use a lottery to allocate risks or benefits is not only a denial of rationality, it is also a denial of man's humanity; each man is reduced to a cipher, distinguished from other ciphers only by the uniqueness of the combination of digits that identify his records in a growing number of office files.

Should Judgment wear a blindfold, or should she be required to see the persons judged?

Dennis C. Mueller, Robert D. Tollison
and Thomas D. Willett[1,2]

Representative Democracy via Random Selection

It has been generally accepted in political science literature that no matter the advantages of full participatory (town meeting) democracy, for a large polity, such as almost any country, this form of government is not feasible. Hence, on purely technical grounds the closest that a country like the United States could come to a pure democracy would be representative government of some form. In a recent article in this *Journal*,[3] James C. Miller, III, pointed out that given present rates of technological advance, it may not be long before this technical constraint will not be binding for rich countries such as the United States, at least in the sense of conducting national referenda.[4] Miller proposes to employ referenda along with "proxy politicians," whose function is to represent blocs of voters on issues and to be subject to instant recall by them, as an alternative to present forms of representation. The goal of such a reform is to give primary control over democratic process to the voters.

In a subsequent paper[5] Martin Shubik questioned the desirability of Miller's proposal on the grounds that there is a wide disparity in the infor-

1   Originally published on pp. 57-68 of *Public Choice* 12 (1972). Copyright © 1972 Center for Study of Public Choice. Reproduced with kind permission from Springer Science+Business Media B.V.

2   The authors are Associate Professor of Economics, Assistant Professor of Economics and Public Finance, and Associate Professor of Economics and Public Affairs, Cornell University. Useful comments were made on an earlier version of this paper by Professors James M. Buchanan, Edward Burton, C.M. Lindsay, J.C. Miller, III, Roger Sherman, and Gordon Tullock. Responsibility for any errors remains with the authors.

3   James C. Miller III, "A Program for Direct and Proxy Voting in the Legislative Process," *Public Choice* 7 (1969).

4   For the mention of a similar proposal, see Don K. Price, *The Scientific Estate* (New York: Oxford University Press, 1965), 84, and the reference cited there. Also, for a general discussion of public policy toward emerging communications technology, see Bruce M. Owen, "Public Policy and Emerging Technology in the Media," *Public Policy* 18 (1970).

5   Martin Shubik, "On Homo Politicus and the Instant Referendum," *Public Choice* 9 (1970).

mation possessed by various types of voters. Shubik's argument turns on a fear of getting "uninformed" choices in national referenda from a wide cross-section of voters and is closely related to the classic problems of obtaining adequate debate before voting or collecting opinions in a poll.[6] Shubik raised the correct issue because, if anything, the average complexity of public issues has increased over the same period that the technical capacity to conduct large referenda has been developed. The time costs of having the general public cast votes based on reasonable levels of information is still high, if not higher than in earlier periods. Thus, one could argue that the case for delegating authority to "experts" has increased. In this paper we extend the thrust of Shubik's argument to discuss how one can combine the advantages of collecting decentralized information through polling with the efficiency of representation and suggest a system of representation that we feel would yield a better mix of efficiency and information than either the present, geographic-based national legislature or Miller's referenda system.

I

Proposals for holding a national town meeting via computer technology to obtain actual choices under some voting rule or to obtain advisory opinions on certain issues are open to objection on several grounds. To the pure elitist some people may be wiser, more intelligent, more moral, and so on. Hence, these persons "should" lead. However, even to one who wants to follow a form of democratic procedure, there will remain certain specialized or technical knowledge required for representation, and some members of the society may be more experienced in the "ways of government" (e.g., parliamentary procedure), perhaps due to professional necessity as in the case of the lawyer. Finally, and importantly, it is tremendously costly for everyone to become generally informed and to listen to the argument of experts, and where there is a need for quick legislative action, this problem would be compounded. Advanced technology helps reduce these problems by lowering the money cost and increasing the speed and ease with which information could be received by the polity and their votes registered. But short of major advances in the efficiency with which individuals can absorb information, the value of the time the polity would have to expend in becoming reasonably well informed on political issues would remain staggering.[7] In essence, the principle of the division of labor

---

6   See, for example, the discussion in Howard R. Bowen, "The Interpretation of Voting in the Allocation of Economic Resources," *Quarterly Journal of Economics* 58 (1943).

7   Of course, in calculating the cost of becoming informed, one should exclude the time spent talking politics and the like, which individuals expend directly for its enjoyment value. On the money or economic value of time see Gary Becker, "A Theory of the Allocation of Time," *Economic Journal* 75 (1965), and Roger Sherman and Thomas D. Willett, "The Standardized

implies that some degree of representation will generally be efficient, and all the reasons for representation that we have discussed here are variants of this principle.[8]

The reason that this elementary view of representation is important in the case of national referenda is because of the information possessed by the various individual voters. Political representatives who specialize in political activity will probably have more and a different mix of information on public issues than their constituents. One might argue in this case that the representative ought to educate his constituents, or distribute the different information that he has to them. Nonetheless, a difference in the information possessed by the representative and by his constituents seems inevitable in a system of political specialization.[9] Thus, if the populace is sampled, choices based on a different quality of information than if representatives decide will be obtained. Which method is better? This depends, among other things, on the amount and mix of information that one feels it necessary for decisionmakers to have and how representatives are chosen, and such decisions would be among the more important ones made in a constitutional period. Clearly, however, the possibility for different political outcomes is possible as between some form of representation and the national town meeting due to differences in the information possessed by the decisionmakers in each case.

Much of the interest in a national referendum procedure stems from dissatisfaction with the present form of national representation. One of the major problems with the present form of national representation, which is compounded by the monopolistic seniority system in the Congress, is its geographic base.[10] Tying representation to location gives rise to the much discussed incentives to logroll for the home district, forcing the polity into negative-sum games. Purely national issues presumably have no representatives except the President and Vice-President who are the only nationally elected officials in the present system, and even in this case there is considerable implicit logrolling via campaign platforms that

Work Week and the Allocation of Time," *Kyklos* 25 (1972), and the references cited in these papers.

8   The sense in which we speak of efficiency here is that it is very costly for voters to become informed, and the gains over present forms of representation from having a political system where the responsibility for making informed decisions rests with the voters are probably nil. Also, the gains in terms of more accurate reflection of the underlying array of preferences of the polity are probably very slight.

9   Miller seeks to avoid this problem, as previously noted, by having so-called proxy politicians. This is an interesting proposal, but in addition to relying on the voters to become informed on issues as Shubik points out, Miller fails to clarify fully how his system would operate. What would happen to lobbyists? What would happen to party structure? What would be the role of bureaus? What would be the reaction of the media under such a system? It might well turn out in realistic circumstances that these proxy politicians are not such "proxies" after all.

10   For a more extensive proposal to deal with the following problems, see Dennis C. Mueller, Thomas D. Willett, and Robert D Tollison and Thomas D. Willett, "A Normative Theory of Representative Democracy," *Annals of the New York Academy of Sciences* 219 (1973)..

serves to vitiate the President's ability to take a purely national stance on many issues. A related problem is that possibly intense minorities, which are not geographically concentrated, may not be represented at all where representation is based on geography and legislators are constrained to cast one vote per issue. Nor is there any check that voters are reasonably informed in their voting choice, and there is considerable evidence that they frequently are not.[11] This results (at least in part) from the time costs of becoming informed through debate or otherwise in a specialized and complex world, and as stressed by Downs[12] and others, this may be quite rational. This defect in political procedure will persist so long as at some stage choices about representatives or policies are taken *directly* to the people. So a proposal, for example, to elect a national house of representatives from an at-large list of candidates would suffer from the same problem. Another problem with the present representative forms is that in a large number setting the individual voters may feel powerless to affect outcomes and may rationally decide to abstain on these grounds.[13] Finally, the present political process in the U. S. yields much power to the Executive and Administrative branches on expediency grounds.

II

If we accept that some form of national representation is efficient, the remaining task is to decide on the best practical form of such representation. We would like to propose for consideration the selecting of a national legislature *at random* from the voting populace. Dahl[14] recently suggested a similar procedure, although only to give advisory votes, and the idea has historical origins in Athenian democracy[15] and in the work

---

11   One of the more interesting examples of this—as an alternative to such perennial findings on that a sizable portion of citizens polled respond that the Bill of Rights may be considered subversive (when it is quoted to them without citation), or that "From each according to his ability, to each according to his needs" is a Biblical quotation—is the poll taken by one of the major television networks immediately preceding the 1968 New Hampshire Presidential primary which discovered that a majority of the voters polled did not know that Eugene McCarthy was a "dove" candidate. For a survey stressing that U. S. voters are typically not well informed on public issues, see Thomas R. Dye and L. Harmon Zeigler, *The Irony of Democracy* (Belmont, CA: Wadsworth, 1970). For a discussion of the degree of public information and ignorance about fiscal variables, see James M. Buchanan, *Public Finance in Democratic Process* (Chapel Hill: University of North Carolina Press, 1967), ch. 13, and the references cited there.

12   Anthony Downs, *An Economic Theory of Democracy* (New York: Harper and Row, 1957).

13   Perhaps pure forms of democracy may be defended on the grounds that voters learn over time. This may be the case, but where you have rational abstention, democratic outcomes are controlled by less than the whole collectivity. Who actually controls in these circumstances is a function of the costs of voting and the individual's perceived stake in the outcomes. One way to handle the problem of non-voting would be to have poll payments instead of poll taxes.

14   Robert Dahl, *After the Revolution* (New Haven: Yale University Press, 1970), 249-253.

15   C. Northcote Parkinson, *The Evolution of Political Thought* (New York: Viking Press, 1958), 172-173.

of Rousseau.[16] Such a procedure would be a significant improvement over the existing political system in several ways. The incentive for pork barrel activities in order to secure votes would no longer be present since random selection would be independent of geographic base, and for the same reason minorities would be represented in correct proportion to their numbers in the society. Representation by random selection would also return political power to individual voters and give better articulation of voter preferences in the legislative process without sacrificing the efficiencies of representation. The legislature would not be composed of median position representatives as under two-party, geographic representation. Voter abstention or uninformed voting would not be problems under this proposal, and perhaps voter alienation would be less in this case also.[17] If viewed as a replacement for the current forms of national representation, the random selection system removes direct sanctioning power through the ballot from the voter and replaces this control mechanism with a more subtle method of articulating voter preferences on national issues. We would argue that although the final outcome is not clearcut, such a change in representative procedure could be understood by voters as the formal embodiment of democratic equality in an ex ante rather than ex post sense.[18] One could also argue that the mass media aspect of political campaigning would be less of a problem under the random selection system,

16   Jean-Jacques Rousseau, *The Social Contract* (Amsterdam: M.M. Rey, 1762), bk. IV, ch. III. See also Peter Bohm, "An Approach to the Problem of Estimating the Demand for Public Goods," *Swedish Journal of Economics* 73 (1971), for a proposed use of random sampling to estimate the demand for public goods, Tollison and Willett, "A Normative Theory," for a discussion of the role of random selection in establishing and operating a system of proportional representation, and B. Ward, "Toward More Democratic Elections?" (unpublished manuscript, 1969), for a proposal to use sample electorates to vote in various elections (e.g., the Presidential election). The latter, unpublished proposal of Ward is different from ours in that he does not extend his random selection proposal to a form of representative government, but only to choose groups of voters. Thus, although his system would probably be an improvement over existing methods of selecting representatives, we would argue that it would be hampered by many of the same problems of the existing system, such as high information costs to the sample electorates, that can only be minimized by combining random selection with a form of representative government.

17   We should note that it is true that randomly chosen individuals who are not concerned with re-election to office will have no direct incentive themselves to become informed. Even though absenteeism from legislative functions could be controlled, daydreaming could not be. Thus, there would be a problem similar to that of the absence of direct incentives for judges to devote much effort to reaching informed decisions which has recently been analyzed by Gordon Tullock, "Public Decisions as Public Goods," *Journal of Political Economy* 79 (1971). (University professors with tenure provide a somewhat similar example.) We feel, however, that in case of important, highly publicized decisions, social pressures such as desires to be respected and the like will generally provide rather strong personal incentives for informed choice. Thus, we would expect that with our randomly selected legislature, this would not be a major problem. This consideration could be one argument for public rather than secret balloting, however, and also for making terms fairly limited in duration so that the legislator's reputation might have some influence on his later career (similarly the prospects for advancement to higher courts may be an important incentive for lower court judges to make knowledgeable decisions).

18   For the distinction between ex ante and ex post equity, see Mark W. Pauly and Thomas D. Willett, "Two Concepts of Equity," *Social Science Quarterly* 53 (1973).

although this is not certain since the outcome depends on how this system of representation is meshed with existing political institutions (e.g., the Presidency). Finally, and importantly, it should be stressed that random selection of representatives avoids all of the traditional problems in voting theory of intransitivities in voting outcomes and the like in establishing a system of proportional representation.[19] The application of voting theory is confined in this case to the operations of the random legislature once selected, and this feature of representation by lot is an important justification for establishing and operating proportional representation in this way.[20]

III

The operational details of how such a body would be selected and how it would function are important considerations. Who would be eligible for the legislature? We would argue that everyone in the voting populace would be eligible except those barred by constitutionally agreed upon restrictions. Including as many people as possible in the selection pool would effectively guarantee the representation of the whole cross-section of voter preferences. Thus, there would be few deferments from electoral eligibility for the randomized legislature. When one is born, he automatically goes into the electoral pool. Practically speaking, however, the polity may wish to bar some groups of individuals constitutionally. Examples might be children, the mentally ill, criminals, civil servants, and individuals who receive government subsidies. The latter two categories raise the prospect of policing the random legislature to insure against the threat of the selected representative passing laws or raising subsidy rates for his particular pressure group. One might argue that the random legislature would have higher costs of policing against bribe taking and the like, since legislators do not have to run for re-election. However, the present system of electing representatives has similar problems, especially when pressure groups are geographically concentrated. The pool of eligible individuals for the random legislature might have to be restricted to achieve genuine representative behavior, but such restrictions, which set up basically a system of weighted voting would have to be balanced against the loss of sampling accuracy.[21]

19 See Duncan Black, *The Theory of Committees and Elections* (New York: Cambridge University Press, 1958), ch. 11.
20 In a related vein William A. Niskanen, *Bureaucracy and Representative Government* (Chicago: Aldine-Atherton, 1971), ch. 20, recently suggested that review committees in the legislature be subject to random assignment and periodic reassignment. Under majority rule in the legislature this procedure would yield (with some sampling error) an approximation to the median committee member's demand for the output supplied by the bureau under review.
21 For example, take the case of individuals who receive a government subsidy. Pursued literally, this would not only exclude welfare recipients, but also homeowners, holders of stock in oil

How large would the legislature be and what sampling procedure would be followed? The size of the representative group would depend on how large a sample would be required to insure that on average over a series of electoral periods, a good depiction of the cross-section of voter preferences is obtained. In essence, more accurate measurement would have to be traded off against the additional costs of a larger legislature. Dahl argues that 500 or 600 at most is the number of people who could participate effectively in a random legislature.[22] This may or may not be the case depending on the amount of sampling error one is willing to tolerate vis-à-vis the costs of a larger legislature and depending on how one meshes the random body with the existing legislative process. Given that there is no prior knowledge about the population proportion being sampled for (50-50), a sample size of 500 would yield a chance of 95 percent that the value being estimated lies within a range equal to the reported percentages, plus or minus an error of 4.9 percent. Doubling the sample size to 1000 would yield a 95 percent chance with a 3.6 percent error. So it is probably true that very accurate samples of the voting populace would have to be large. However, this does not mean that a large random legislature is not feasible or cannot be effective. To judge the feasibility of this method of representation one would have to compare its costs with the costs of the present system of elections and operation and with costs of high information voting. In terms of the effectiveness of such a representative body, it could be meshed with the existing political process by making it a purely advisory body, or as will be discussed below, one house of a bicameral legislature could be designated primarily to respond (i.e., vote on) rather than initiate legislation. In these cases large size would not necessarily be a constraint on its effectiveness. Finally, for less important issues, smaller subsets of the large random body could be used for decision making, allowing many less important issues to be handled at the same time.

The proposed sampling procedure would be random sampling with replacement. The latter condition is not strictly required with a large pool of voters from which to sample; so operationally one might argue that legislators could serve only one term, although this would cause the problem of perpetual "rookie" legislators. Although we propose random selection from the required pool of voters, one might be concerned about insuring the selection of x percentage of a certain race or income level. In this case stratified sampling could be implemented and the legislature would be proportionally random by strata. Indeed, if such a variable as tastes and

and mineral companies, veterans, and so forth. Furthermore, it would be hard to argue that individuals should be excluded on the grounds of educational qualifications given current attitudes which do not allow literacy tests.

22   Dahl, *After the Revolution*, 152.

income are highly correlated, then stratified sampling would lower the required total sample size. However, there would be a new set of problems associated with determining how many strata there should be and in what terms the strata are defined, and we would not want to employ stratified geographic sampling for previously mentioned reasons. Also, the problem of policing the legislature against pressure group legislation would be more difficult under stratified sampling.

Probably the strongest argument for some form of stratified sampling is that under a continuous system of unrestricted random sampling, the probability will approach 100 percent over time that for some draw of the legislature a set of representatives which reflect only a small portion of the underlying population will dominate the legislature (the American Nazi party, for instance) with the possibility of extremely adverse consequences as a result. Strong constitutional provisions and the use of a second house of Congress (see Section IV) could also be used to limit the effects that an unrepresentative, intolerant legislature might have while in office, and we would argue that the frequency of occurrence of such situations under our proposals is likely to be considerably less than what we have historically observed under alternative forms of government.

A problem related to the selection of the randomized legislature is how to compensate the selected legislators. One might argue that the opportunity costs of selected individuals ought to be paid and therefore a system of discriminatory wages would be required. In such a system an individual would be no more or no less better off for being selected.[23] However, while attractive on efficiency grounds (and in one sense of equity), this procedure is probably not feasible because of all the problems of estimating and discounting the appropriate opportunity costs and also of maintaining a well-working legislature with differential rates of pay. An obvious second-best solution would be to take existing Congressional pay scales as approximate to the "proper" common wage for national legislators and pay this wage and any extraordinary costs to those selected. The problem in this case consists of whether or not you require people to be in the selection pool. On the grounds of obtaining the proper sampling characteristics, there would probably have to be a requirement to be in the pool. However, this creates problems of compensation when, for example, an individual with a $100,000 opportunity cost is selected.[24] This problem

23   In part this is a question of how much society should invest in government, and it is an implication of recent work on vote trading that a well-working government may embody great potential gains from trade for democratic citizens. Hence, investments in democratic process may have big payoffs. See Dennis C. Mueller, Geoffrey C. Philpotts, and Jaroslav Vanek, "The Social Gains from Exchanging Votes," *Public Choice* 13 (1972).

24   It might be possible to allow individuals with high opportunity costs to buy substitutes in this case. There would be a sacrifice of randomness here, but the rich may be "over-represented" in democracy in the first place.

is precisely analogous to the economics of conscription for military or jury duty where non-economic objectives such as racial balance may require violating strict opportunity cost dictates in recruiting or conscripting for such tasks.[25] In the case of the randomized legislature we would argue that an initial wage commensurate with existing Congressional pay scales would vitiate the major problems of requiring people to be in the selection pool. For those individuals with low opportunity costs who are selected, we would propose that they simply be allowed to earn the fortuitous rents caused by paying the uniform, high base wage. Also, if one were worried about random legislators voting themselves pay raises due to their lame duck status, Congressional pay scales could be set constitutionally and adjusted for productivity growth or increases in the cost of living. As another possibility, pay increases could be made for the subsequent session of legislators. So long as there were not a large proportion of staggered terms (see the discussion in the next paragraph), this procedure would help ensure against lame duck pay raises.

In terms of the functioning of the legislature, what would be the most desirable term of office? One cannot say for sure, but the fundamental reason for changing office under this system would be to detect changes in the distribution of voter preferences across the spectrum of national issues. In practice one would have to establish the trade-off between start-up costs (perpetual rookie legislators) and career dislocation costs (which would probably rise exponentially in relation to time in office) and the desire to collect accurate decentralized information while maintaining the appropriate incentives for representative behavior. Possibilities would range from short, non-staggered terms to career appointments upon selection with staggered terms.

How would this legislature mesh with the existing forms of national government? Several of the following alternatives for the new legislature might be explored:

a)   An additional national legislature to the present two,

b)   An additional national legislature replacing one of the present two,

c)   An exclusive national legislature replacing the present two,

d)   An exclusive national legislature with another nationally elected body,

---

25   To be fully analogous to the costs imposed by the military draft, any costs associated with the disruption of one's civilian career would also have to be estimated and discounted at the appropriate rate of time preference. See James C. Miller III and Robert D. Tollison, "The Implicit Tax on Reluctant Military Recruits," *Social Science Quarterly* 51 (1971), and Thomas D. Willett, "Another Cost of Conscription," *Western Economic Journal* 6 (1968).

e)   A mandatory national legislature to be used if requested by the present two legislatures or the President, and

f)   An advisory national legislature to be used if requested by the present two legislatures or the President or to be required to give advisory votes on selected issues.

Perhaps the more feasible alternative, at least on a short-run experimental basis, is the last. In this case, the central problem is whether the votes of the randomized legislature would be binding (and if so, in what form, i.e., what voting rule would be required to pass a law?). If the votes of such a body were binding in some form, then the political system could be characterized as government by randomized jurors. In this form the randomized legislature could be viewed as a more formal embodiment of its current functional equivalents — the Presidential commission, the White House conference, and the like. The Presidential commission, for example, is a method under present institutional arrangements to gather a range of informed public opinion on a given issue (of course, this is not the only function which commissions sometimes perform). Also, the advisory random body would officially sanction and improve (due to fuller information) public opinion polls. If the voters of the randomly selected body were to be only advisory, a smaller body could be maintained, and in a sense the polity would seek the counsel of a smaller number of randomly selected qualified persons on certain issues.[26]

Our basic point is that the use of randomly selected bodies is a powerful method for reconciling the specialization advantages of representation with a fuller representation of voter preferences and to show that one can get a better representation of voter preferences than exists under the present system without going to a pure referenda system. Also, one avoids traditional voting theory problems of aggregating voter preferences by selecting representatives (though not in the operations of the random legislature) in this method. While the operational details under any given embodiment of our proposal present problems and we have surely missed many important points that would have to be considered in meshing the random body with the rest of the process of government, these are no more insurmountable than those of organizing our present national legislatures,

---

26 Another interesting issue is whether the votes of the random body would be open or secret. The present national legislature has to have open voting so that constituents know how their representatives vote. This is not necessarily the case with the random body, particularly if one does not allow re-election of legislators. Thus, the issue of open or secret voting in the random body would revolve partially around the kind of voting response bias that the collectivity desired since both open and secret balloting would have inherent response bias. Of course, under either open or closed voting, care would have to be taken to insulate the legislators from lobbying pressures and to see that they cast informed votes. Closed voting might help in the former regard if it increased the uncertainty in vote buying, whereas open voting would help the latter cause since the impact of one's decision can affect his future career.

and we would urge experimentation along the lines of our proposal. Following Dahl,[27] we could argue that such experimentation is essential if democracy is to be given an opportunity to work and democratic power is to be returned to the people.

IV

A final point is that political entrepreneurship would probably suffer under an exclusive random system. In some respects, such as the problems of mass media and the technology of modern politics (dollar democracy), this would be desirable. However, to maintain the production of innovative policies and to produce what one might term "political X-efficiency," we might add to the random system a sort of executive committee or senate, to be elected nationally from an at-large list of candidates. For example, twenty seats for this group could be established, and political entrepreneurs could campaign for seats. This group in a sense would represent the formal continuation of the present Senate in much smaller size and would serve to lessen the problem of Executive discretion in the present system. This senate could be elected by the general public or by the larger random body. The advantage of having the senators elected by the general public would be to maintain a sense of voter participation in the system whereas the advantage of having them elected by the random body would be the attainment of virtually the same electoral outcomes for less costs of political entrepreneuring. There would be problems with defining which decisions this group would control and which decisions the President would control, but the principle on which such a division of issues would be undertaken would basically be how quickly a decision needed to be taken by the Executive Branch. Also, if one desired a very large random body for sampling accuracy reasons, then this smaller body could originate legislation. In this way the larger random group could function effectively, despite its size, with its primary function being to vote on proposals originated and debated by the smaller, elected senate.[28]

The persevering reader may be convinced by now that we are writing a piece of science fiction rather than analyzing a serious proposal to reform democratic decision making.[29] We argue, however, that the time is long

---

27   Dahl, *After the Revolution*.

28   Mill advocated an executive council or small group of experts to write and initiate legislation in his system of proportional representation. Presumably, this group in Mill's system would be the functional equivalent of the modern committee staff. This is related, but somewhat different, from our proposal where the initiating body is elected. For Mill's discussion, see John Stuart Mill, *Considerations on Representative Government* (London: Parker, Son and Bourn, 1861), ch. V.

29   He is somewhat justified in this regard as Robert Heinlein discusses a random selection proposal in Robert Heinlein, *The Moon is a Harsh Mistress* (New York: Putnam, 1966). However, as we indicated earlier, there are also precedents for this type of consideration in the practice of Athens, the work of Rousseau, and more recently, the work of Robert Dahl. Indeed, in popular

since past when this country should have a commissioned body to look analytically at its electoral procedures. In such a setting proposals like ours and Miller's and the work of others in this vein can be discussed seriously on their practical and theoretical merits.

commentary William F. Buckley's frequently repeated statement that "he would rather be governed by the first thousand names in the New York telephone directory than the faculty at Harvard" also comes to mind. We might also note that more than one work of science fiction has made worthwhile contributions to political science. See, for instance, the discussions in Dennis Livingstone, "Science Fiction Models of Future World Order Systems," *International Organization* 25 (1971), and Price, *Scientific Estate*, 5-7.

Hank Greely[1]

The Equality of Allocation by Lot

The government cannot distribute scarce[2] goods[3] equally to all potential recipients. This allocative problem challenges the equality on which our government is theoretically based,[4] because citizens, all of whom present justified claims to the good, must be treated differently. Traditional methods of allocation do not resolve this conflict between the necessity of unequal treatment and our notions of equality.

The major legitimate models[5] of government allocation include distribution by merit, market, and temporal priority. Allocation by merit requires individual examination of the merit or need of each potential recipient, ordinal ranking of the applicants, and distribution of the good to as many recipients as the supply permits. Civil service jobs are allocated this way.[6] Allocation by market gives benefits or exclusion from burdens to those most willing and able to pay for the good. The government uses

---

1   Originally published on pp. 113-141 of *Harvard Civil Rights-Civil Liberties Law Review* 12 (1977). Copyright © 1977 by The President and Fellows of Harvard College. Reproduced with permission from the journal and the author.

2   Scarcity of a benefit implies that the supply of the good is so limited that every applicant cannot receive it; a scarce burden is one which it is not necessary to impose on all citizens. See Armen Alchian and William R. Allen, *University Economics*, 3rd ed. (Belmont, CA: Wadsworth, 1972), 14. Scarce goods are effectively non-divisible, since division would relieve the scarcity. While anything can be divided either physically or temporally, some goods lose much of their value if so divided. For example, if twelve daily hours of treatment by a kidney machine is necessary to sustain the life of a patient with renal failure, giving two patients twelve hours of treatment is much more useful than giving twelve patients two hours of treatment. Cf. 1 Kings 3:16-28 (Solomon's wisdom: a child as a non-divisible good).

3   For convenience the term "good" will be used to denote any material possession, service, burden, or legal relationship to be allocated. See generally Alchian and Allen, *University Economics*, 20. Private organizations are also faced with the allocative decisions discussed in this Comment, and may find random selection a useful alternative.

4   See U.S. Declaration of Independence; U.S. Constitution Amendment XIV.

5   Some methods of allocation, such as patronage, are no longer considered legitimate. See *Elrod v. Burns*, 96 S.Ct. 2673 (1976) (invalidating the patronage distribution of police jobs in Chicago).

6   The competitive civil service operates on a point system. Points are given for test scores and relevant experience. Some applicants receive additional points as special preference, as for example in the case of veterans. 5 U.S.C. §§ 3311, 3313 (1970). The final choice must be made among the three applicants with the most points, 5 U.S.C. § 3318.

this method to allocate oil drilling leases on government land.[7] Thirdly, benefits can be distributed on a first-come/first-served basis,[8] rewarding those who have the best access to information or a greater ability to apply or wait for a benefit.[9] Often this allocation is coupled with merit standards to define the pool. Spots in public housing[10] and crowded park areas[11] are sometimes distributed in this manner.

Random selection[12] is the fourth alternative response to allocative situations. By using randomly selected priorities as its classification criterion, the lottery is particularly neutral.[13] Everyone within the lottery pool[14] has a mathematically equal chance of receiving the good.

The significance of the lottery is political. The method of governmental allocation of benefits and burdens unavoidably affects the citizen's perception of the fairness of the government's procedures and its evaluation and treatment of him; his perceptions in turn condition his emotions toward the government and his willingness to play a role in the system. With merit allocations, a citizen may feel honored or unjustly stigmatized, thanking or blaming the government or some official for the benefit or burden awarded. Because random selection does not give reasons and presents mathematical equality of opportunity[15] which could lead to equality

7   30 U.S.C. § 226b (1970).

8   It is difficult to conceive of burdens being allocated in this manner, because no one would volunteer to be served. Exemptions to burdens could be distributed on a first-come/first-served basis: similarly, the decision-maker could also impose burdens on the first V people he finds who meet minimum qualifications. Military conscription could proceed in this manner.

9   See generally Yoram Barzel, "A Theory of Rationing by Waiting," *Journal of Law and Economics* 17 (1974). The first-come/first-served system has the advantage of encouraging the acquisition of information by rewarding those who get information quickly.

10   See Barzel, "A Theory of Rationing," 126-130.

11   John Brannon Albright, "A Return to Chaos at Campsites?" *New York Times*, February 16, 1975, § 10. at 5. col. 5.

12   When used in this Comment, the phrases "the lottery," "random selection," and "by lot" will be used interchangeably to describe any method of allocation based on mathematically equal chances — luck.

13   The term here means only that no judgments are made on the basis of one's "desserts." Other morally neutral allocations include distribution alphabetically or by birthdate. While the ultimate choices made by the lottery are neutral, the decision to use random selection for allocation can be rational but not morally neutral, for it affirms, *inter alia*, the value of equality.

14   The "pool" is the group from whom final selection will be made by lot. The pool itself is selected from the general population by conventional classification schemes.

15   As used in this Comment, "equality of opportunity" is the mathematically equal chance of receiving a good that each member of a lottery pool enjoys. This objective term is not the same as the subjective notion of "equal opportunity" expressed in Title VII of the Civil Rights Act of 1964. 42 U.S.C. §§ 2000e to 2000e-17 (1970 & Supp. V 1975), nor does it reflect subjective estimates of likelihood. Equal opportunity traditionally means that "the expectations of those with the same abilities and aspirations should not be affected by their social class," (John Rawls, *A Theory of Justice* (Cambridge, MA: Belknap Press, 1971), 73). Distribution by merit could be considered the ideal of equal opportunity.

of expectation,[16] it is a useful neutral buffer between the government and its citizens. Though currently limited to representative uses such as choosing jury pools,[17] the lottery is too often ignored as a potential method of allocation where other systems are weak or choices are difficult.

This Comment will illuminate the way in which allocation by lot challenges the government's commitment to equality of opportunity and expectation, and forces it to articulate the goals of its allocation. It will formulate a theory of the lottery by examining the method's relative strengths and weaknesses, illustrate that theory, and outline the constitutional limits on the use of allocation by random selection. Because of the breadth and speculative nature of the topic, the Comment does not purport to be an exhaustive analysis of the subject matter, but is instead intended as a provocative treatment of the problems involved.

I. The Theory of Random Selection

In deciding which method of allocation to use in distributing benefits and burdens, the government must accommodate its desire to accomplish a substantive goal with considerations of efficiency and overarching objectives of equality and fairness. The choice is sometimes difficult but unavoidable, as in the case of the Vietnam War draft.[18] This section com-

16   "Equality of expectation" is the subjective feeling of a potential recipient who believes his chance of receiving the good is the same as that of anyone else.

17   Federal jury venire members are drawn by lot from a pool determined by district voting lists and legal eligibility. 28 U.S.C. §§ 1863-66 (1970 & Supp. V 1975). State jury pools may also be drawn in the same manner. See *Quadra v. Superior Court*, 411 F.Supp. 451, 452 (N.D. Cal. 1976) (voluntary adoption of random selection for a state grand jury).
         See also *Eisen v. Carlisle & Jacquelin*, 52 F.R.D. 253 (S.D.N.Y. 1971), rev'd, 479 F.2d 1005 (2d Cir. 1973), aff'd, 417 U.S. 156 (1974) (lottery used to determine class members to be notified in antitrust class action).

18   The draft furnishes an interesting example of changing approaches to allocation. See generally John O'Sullivan, *The Draft and Its Enemies: A Documentary History* (Urbana: University of Illinois Press, 1974). The first rational draft was instituted in the Civil War. See Jack F. Leach, *Conscription in the United States: Historical Background* (Rutland, VT: Charles E. Tuttle, 1952), 162. It allowed those selected to provide replacements for themselves, thus effectively selecting recruits by a market system (Leach, *Conscription*, 167, 169). The draft was used again in World War I, when a lottery was conducted. See Edward A. Fitzpatrick, *Conscription and America* (Milwaukee, WI: Richard, 1940), 31-78. This method was carried over to the peacetime draft of 1940; however, during World War II the Selective Service System, with its local boards, exemptions, and deferments, became the method of choosing draftees. See National Advisory Commission on Selective Service, *In Pursuit of Equity: Who Serves When Not All Serve?* (Washington, DC: U.S. Government Printing Office, 1967), 18-22.
         In the Vietnam era, the Marshall Commission recommended limiting deferments and exemptions and selecting among eligible men by lot (National Advisory Commission, *In Pursuit of Equity*, 37-46). However, the Congress refused to cut back on deferments and exemption, while simultaneously indicating that, without an expanded pool of eligible men, the lottery would be meaningless. See Military Selective Service Act of 1967, Pub. L. No. 90-40, § 5(a)(2), 81 Stat. 100; House Rep. No. 267, 90th Cong., 1st Sess. (1967).
         In 1969, in response to an initiative by President Nixon, Congress eliminated § 5(a)(2) to permit the President to institute a lottery system. Selective Service Amendment Act of 1969, Pub. L. No. 91-124, 83 Stat. 221. The lottery system that was instituted was limited by the

pares the uses of typical allocative methods, particularly merit allocations and random selection, in an effort to sketch the advantages and disadvantages of the lottery as a mechanism for allocation. It proceeds by outlining the competing and complementary goals to be met by the system.

Goal: Maximization or satisficing?

Governmental allocations which seek the "best" or "most needy" are based on a maximizing goal.[19] By ordinally ranking applicants, the government accepts the time and cost involved in the interest of supporting one goal as fully as possible. When only one goal exists, as in choosing the best Secretary of State or an Olympic basketball team, maximization is the preferable objective.[20]

When more than one goal exists, however, the government may prefer to trade off its various ends in an attempt to reach a certain minimum level of each. If the substantive end of the distribution is not crucial or too costly to achieve, satisficing[21] — finding enough satisfactory applicants — may well be more important than finding the best applicants. All in the lottery pool should meet the statutory minimum standards for receiving the good. Often a first-come/first-served system proceeds in this fashion,[22] and random selection by definition pursues a satisficing goal. Thus military conscription by lottery[23] did not seek the best soldiers, but merely a set

retention of the deferment and exemption provision and by the retention of state and local draft calls. The latter provision meant that men with identical lottery numbers would he treated differently depending on the requirements placed upon and men available to their local draft boards.

In 1971, both these limitations were eliminated and the Marshall Commission's recommendations were adopted in essence; Congress prospectively eliminated the college student deferment and permitted the President to institute national, rather than state and local, draft calls. Military Selective Service Act of 1971, Pub. L. No. 92-129, 85 Stat. 348. The Selective Service is still in existence, 50 U.S.C.A. app. §§ 451-73 (Supp. 1976), but the lowered manpower requirements of the post-Vietnam era have combined with higher pay for servicemen to eliminate the need to draft soldiers.

19 See generally Graham T. Allison, *The Essence of Decision* (Boston: Little, Brown, 1971), 20, and Herbert A. Simon, *Models of Man* (New York: Wiley, 1957), 204-205, 241-260.

20 Allocations based on a market mechanism maximize desire, though not necessarily the goal of the government. For example, auctions of oil drilling leases on government lands (see n. 7) maximize the amount of revenue flowing into federal coffers but do not necessarily promote the most speedy or efficient production of oil. Moreover, market allocations disadvantage less wealthy but possibly more meritorious applicants. For these reasons a government seldom adopts a market method of allocation.

21 See generally Allison, *Essence of Decision*, 72-74; Simon, *Models of Man*, 204-205, 261, 270-271; James G. March and Herbert A. Simon, *Organizations* (New York: Wiley, 1958), 48; and Gordon Short, "Period Price Determination in Theory and Practice," *American Economic Review* 38 (1948): 265, 269-271.

22 A first-come/first-served system does maximize whatever entitlement is gained by waiting time. An applicant for public housing may claim that his five year old application deserves acceptance before his neighbor's two week old application, assuming that both are in similar circumstances. See also n. 75.

23 See n. 18.

number of satisfactory soldiers. By hypothesis then, the lottery can be useful where satisficing is preferable to goal maximization.

Goal: The best allocative structure

It is basic that in an allocative situation the government should adopt the decision-making structure which advances the goal of the allocation at the lowest cost. The merit method of allocation focuses most clearly on maximizing the governmental end of relieving need, rewarding merit, or finding those most suited to imposition of a burden, but only at the cost of an often cumbersome, costly procedure.[24] Ranking applicants and offering hearings to those rejected[25] is a mammoth task suited only to the most important allocations.

In contrast, a market mechanism, first-come/first-served allocation, and random selection are all relatively objective. With fewer criteria, less information is needed concerning each applicant and allocation can be made more quickly and inexpensively, and thus more efficiently.

For an example from the private sphere, each year the admissions office of Yale Law School is forced to allocate its approximately 325 acceptances among over three thousand applicants.[26] Because the criterion is merit,[27] the administrative costs of the process are very high. Each seriously considered application is read and ranked by at least three faculty members. Though an attempt is made to pick the "best" applicants, and a decision at both extremes is relatively easy, the real problem for the decision-makers involves the differences between the applicant ranked 250 and the applicant ranked 350. The records of those applicants vary only slightly by objective standards,[28] and those differences are of questionable signifi-

---

24 For example, distributing welfare benefits is extremely costly. New York state spends approximately nine percent of the amount of welfare payments distributed on the administration of its program. See Hearings Before the Subcomm. on Fiscal Policy of the Joint Economic Comm., *Problems in Administration of Public Welfare Programs*, 92d Cong., 2d Sess. 331 (1972) (submission of state of New York). See *Mathews v. Eldridge*, 424 U.S. 319, 347-48 (1976); cf. *Goldberg v. Kelly*, 397 U.S. 254, 284 n.3 (1970) (Burger, C.J., dissenting) (prediction of increased administrative costs if hearings are required for termination of welfare benefits); and Jerry L. Mashaw and Richard A. Merrill, *Introduction to the American Public Law System* (St. Paul, MN: West, 1975), 373 (affirming the prediction of increased cost of welfare hearings).

    Of course, merit allocations need not adopt such subjective and cumbersome procedures. More objective criteria would be less costly to administer, and random selection would have a smaller comparative advantage.

25 Statutes may require hearings for those denied a government benefit. See, e.g., 42 U.S.C. § 1437d (c)(3)(i) (Supp. V 1975) (hearing upon denial of eligibility for federally assisted public housing). Though due process does not protect denial of a benefit, it guarantees a hearing prior to imposition of a burden depriving liberty or property. See pp. 71–74 and notes 61-76 infra.

26 Yale Law School, Admissions Information and Forms for the Class Entering September 1977 (1976), 2, 5 (On file at *Harvard Civil Rights-Civil Liberties Law Review*).

27 Preferential admission of minority group members has been another goal at Yale. See Macklin Fleming and Louis Pollak, "The Black Quota at Yale Law School," *Public Interest* 19 (1970), 44.

28 The application form calls for a college transcript, LSAT scores, SAT scores (verbal), a listing of college extracurricular activities, a 250 word essay, and two letters of recommendation. Yale

cance. While less careful subjective consideration and emphasis on the more objective criteria could speed up, and reduce the cost of, the review of marginal applicants, those actions mark a shift to satisficing. Once the pretense of maximization is dropped, the cheapest and fairest method of allocation is random selection.[29]

Goal: Reducing discretion

The discretion necessarily vested in the distributing official creates a potential for abuse or corruption that constitutes a cost of any merit system of allocation. Such discretion permits the possibly unintentional inclusion of irrelevant criteria such as the friendliness of the recipient or forbidden variables such as ability to pay a bribe. While more objective criteria can be employed to limit the objectionable aspects of discretion, no system of allocation can completely eliminate the potential for corruption. Yet the smaller number of criteria needed in random methodologies simplifies the policing of any attempt to submerge or fail to follow those criteria.[30]

Discretion still plagues the lottery in the decision-maker's role of setting up the initial pool from which the ultimate recipients are drawn. Yet even here the motivation for corruption is reduced because inclusion in the pool does not guarantee receipt of the benefit;[31] it only produces a chance to receive it. In addition to eliminating discretion at the ultimate choice level, the use of a lottery reduces the chance of successfully hiding systematic bias. The random nature of any distribution can be tested,[32] and the probability that any particular deviation from the expected outcome would occur randomly can be determined if the characteristics of the whole pop-

---

Law School, supra note 26, at 7-11. For the class of 1979, Yale Law School received 267 applications from people with LSAT scores of between 700 and 749, and grade averages of between 3.75 and 4.00. Eighty-eight of those applicants were accepted. Fleming and Pollak, "Black Quota," 5. The numerical differences between the members of that group accepted and those rejected could not have been great.

29 The lottery has occasionally been used to allocate tickets to rock concerts for efficiency reasons. In 1972 the Rolling Stones allocated 20,000 tickets for a Madison Square Garden appearance by lot from 560,000 mail order applications (*New York Times*, July 13, 1972, 28, col. 1). This may have been the result of ticket related riots at earlier concerts during that tour (*New York Times*, June 5, 1972, 5 (Vancouver); *New York Times*, June 15, 1972, 49, col. 3 (Tuscon)).

30 Those choosing from the lottery pool could simply destroy the names drawn or record different names. Supervision would limit this problem, but even supervisors can be corrupted. Even so, policing this system is easier than when the criteria are as subjective as comparisons of relative need.

31 Corruption is still possible in the random allocation of burdens because a bribe could remove one from the pool.

32 See Hubert M. Blalock, *Social Statistics* 2nd ed. (New York: McGraw-Hill, 1972), 168-169, and John E. Freund, *Modern Elementary Statistics* 3rd ed. (Englewood Cliffs, NJ: Prentice-Hall, 1972), 236-238. See generally Blalock, *Social Statistics*, 155-169, and Freund, *Modern Elementary Statistics*, 61-69, 172-178, 181-186, 243-248, 287-290.

ulation are known.[33] An unanticipated outcome of statistical significance affecting a group[34] can be detected and investigated.

Yet there are disadvantages in reducing the role of discretion in the allocation of goods. With less discretion, the ability of the decision-maker to maximize is reduced. Moreover, consideration of individual circumstances would be submerged in a lottery, reducing the feedback of information on the effectiveness of this allocative method; this lessens the chance that conditions disfavoring random selection will be recognized and the method of allocation altered. The costs and benefits of discretion must be weighed in choosing an allocative method, but random selection can effectively reduce discretion when that is a desired goal.

Goal: Avoiding undesirable self-perceptions from the allocation

Whether or not an allocative system maximizes its substantive goal, it imposes burdens upon or awards benefits to citizens. The fairness of the substantive result as perceived by the citizen affects his evaluation of the government's treatment of him and his willingness to participate in and support it.

Allocation of benefits by a merit criterion can operate to reward the recipient and encourage him to continue his meritorious efforts. In contrast, exclusion from benefits by merit can stigmatize those judged to be unworthy, as in the case of the person not allowed access to adequate hemodialysis treatment facilities.[35] Use of non-rational criteria for the allocation of goods eliminate both effects; no one can feel justifiably honored or unfairly condemned by the government when the allocation is determined by the luck of the draw.

Non-rational criteria also can provide potential recipients with the satisfaction arising from equality of opportunity. Since equal treatment is impossible, the notion that government allocates by a previously defined rule which rewards or stigmatizes no one reduces the impatience traceable

---

33 The benefits of statistical analysis have often been recognized by legal commentators. See, e.g., John M. Dawson, "Probabilities and Prejudice in Establishing Statistical Inferences," *Jurimetrics Journal* 13 (1973): 191 (use of chi square analysis in Title VII case); Michael O. Finklestein, "The Application of Statistical Decision Theory to Jury Discrimination Cases," *Harvard Law Review* 80 (1966): 338, 349-373; and "Beyond the Prima Facie Case in Employment Discrimination Law: Statistical Proof and Rebuttal," *Harvard Law Review* 89 (1975): 387 (use of analysis of variance and multiple regression techniques analysis in employment discrimination actions).

34 Statistical methods cannot detect discrimination against any one individual in any one distribution, because someone has to receive the worst lottery priority.

    The lottery could be given a presumption of validity which would be overcome by an outcome which has a low probability of occurring randomly. For example, if the probability were less than five percent, the operator of the lottery could be given the burden of showing that the lottery was honest. If the outcome were sufficiently improbable, it could be entirely disregarded, as long as uneven outcomes in the opposite direction were also disregarded. The result would be a truncated distribution with the same median.

35 See n. 59 infra.

to the allocation which is felt by those demanding goods.[36] The factors of citizen perception must be considered when the method of allocation is chosen.

Goal: Recognizing human dignity by equality of opportunity and fair treatment

The constitutional protections of the Bill of Rights and the fourteenth amendment affirm a commitment to the worth of individual citizens which is a basic value of Western society.[37] Besides passing constitutional muster,[38] allocative decisions must respect this ill-defined value by avoiding subtle coercion of potential recipients, striving for equality, and fostering a fair and accountable decision-making structure.

Satisficing criteria and allocations by merit which attempt to rank applicants can effectively coerce the conduct of potential recipients who seek to meet or avoid the classification. For example, a Selective Service System[39] report once boasted that the standards for exemption from the draft encouraged young men to attend college or enter the learned professions.[40] The influence wielded by an allocative system is most troubling

---

36   Radicals might attack allocation by lot by arguing that equal expectation diffuses the pressures for an increase of production to eliminate the scarcity that makes allocation necessary. The discrimination felt by those stigmatized by a merit distribution can be translated into a political demand for more of the good, and this impetus could be lost by the adoption of a lottery.

37   See, e.g., Charles Fried, "Privacy," *Yale Law Journal* 77 (1968): 475, 478-479; see also *Furman v. Georgia*, 408 U.S. 238, 270-74, 286-91 (1972) (Brennan, J., concurring) (death penalty is "cruel and unusual" because it is degrading to human dignity). Cases under many different constitutional provisions identify aspects of personal autonomy which reflect a concern with human dignity.
      In *Woodson v. North Carolina*, 96 S.Ct. 2978, 2991 (1976) (plurality opinion), the Court pointed to "the fundamental respect for human dignity underlying the Eighth Amendment" to require an individual determination before infliction of the death penalty. See also *Roe v. Wade*, 410 U.S. 113 (1973) (abortion cannot be prohibited by state in the first trimester of pregnancy); *Stanley v. Georgia*, 394 U.S. 557 (1969) (viewing of obscenity in one's home cannot be made criminal); *Katz v. United States*, 389 U.S. 347 (1967) (fourth amendment protects a reasonable expectation of privacy); *Griswold v. Connecticut*, 381 U.S. 479 (1965) (distribution of contraceptives to married persons cannot be prohibited by state); *Robinson v. California*, 370 U.S. 660 (1962) (status of narcotics addiction cannot be made criminal). Cf. Lawrence H. White, "On Private Questions and Public Questions," *Harvard Political Review* 1 (1976): 3 (certain issues should be removed from political arena).

38   See pp. 81-84 infra.

39   Military Selective Service Act of 1967, 50 U.S.C. app. §§ 451-73 (1970 & Supp. V 1975). See generally John Griffiths and J.W. Heckman, *The Draft Law*, rev. ed. (New York: Barnes & Noble, 1970).

40   "One of the major products of the Selective Service classification process is the channeling of manpower into many endeavors, occupations, and activities that are in the national interest...From the individual's viewpoint, he is standing in a room which has been made uncomfortably warm. Several doors are open, but they all lead to various forms of recognized, patriotic service to the Nation. Some accept the alternatives gladly — some with reluctance. The consequence is approximately the same." Selective Service System, "Channeling" (July 1, 1965). In Thomas Reeves and Karl Hess, Jr., *The End of the Draft* (New York: Random House, 1970), 193, 199.

because it is submerged in a scheme whose explicit goal is distribution of a benefit or burden.

Though no classification system with merit standards can eliminate this coercive effect, selection by lot for receipt of a benefit[41] reduces it. Applicants can no longer guarantee that they will receive the good by reordering their conduct; the most to be gained is a spot in the pool. Random selection has a comparative advantage in avoiding coercion.

The guarantees of the equal protection clause and the civil rights laws[42] exemplify the commitment of the United States to equality. The goal of equal treatment is derived from the idea that it is degrading to a citizen to deny him the benefit given to his similarly situated neighbor.[43] Where equality of result is impossible, however, as in an allocative situation, equality of opportunity is the next best goal because it parcels out equal chances to receive the good. Random selection is the only allocative method which honestly can claim the objective equality of opportunity from which the satisfaction of equality of expectation springs. It is the allocative method which maximizes the goal of equality.

Citizens may also demand a fair and accountable allocating structure. An honest lottery is objectively fair,[44] but this fact may escape the applicant who believes that merit, wealth, or patience is the proper classification criterion. The literally homeless applicant who is denied admission to public housing or the applicant who has waited for years for that benefit likely will not be satisfied by the objective equality a lottery offers if a relatively well-housed person who applied last month is rewarded by the luck

---

The Service also utilized deferments to "channel" protesters out of college, although it did not boast of that activity. General Lewis Hershey at one point issued a directive that the deferments of all known demonstrators be re-examined (*New York Times*, November 9, 1967, 2, col. 4-5, 3, col. 1; see *National Student Ass'n v. Hershey*, 412 F.2d 1103 (D.C. Cir. 1969) (a registrant's protest activities are not to be considered in determining his selective service classification).

41 Distribution of burdens by lot may still be coercive if potential recipients are able to exclude themselves from the pool.

42 See 42 U.S.C. §§ 1971, 1975a-1975d, 1981-1986, 2000a-2000h (1970).

43 William K. Frankena, "The Concept of Social Justice," in *Social Justice*, ed. Richard B. Brandt (Englewood Cliffs, NJ: Prentice-Hall, 1962); Gregory Vlastos, "Justice and Equality," in Brandt, ed., *Social Justice*.

44 Random selection is a system that peculiarly requires its performance to justify its fairness. Rawls suggests that "[p]ure procedural justice obtains where there is no independent criterion for the right result: instead there is a correct or fair procedure such that the outcome is likewise correct or fair, whatever it is, provided that the procedure has been properly followed...A distinctive feature of pure procedural justice is that the procedure for determining the just result must actually be carried out; for in these cases there is no independent criterion by reference to which a definite outcome can be known to be just. Clearly we cannot say that a particular state of affairs is just because it could have been reached by following a fair procedure. This would permit far too much and would lead to absurdly unjust consequences. It would allow one to say that almost any distribution of goods is just...A fair procedure translates its fairness to the outcome only when it is actually carried out." Rawls, *A Theory of Justice*, 86.

of the draw. Abstract equality may be a poor substitute for the good which potential recipients desire.

Random selection also denies the citizen's demand for participation in and accountability of the method of allocation.[45] In merit or need determinations, the potential recipient can argue with the allocating official about his satisfaction of the relevant criteria, and if the good is denied the citizen can blame the official. The lottery eliminates both options. It may thus have the cost of political withdrawal if citizens begin to feel they cannot affect the decision-making process. More damaging is the thought that random systems of allocation cut down on social interaction, producing the psychological alienation of being treated as an object.[46] The frustrations engendered by the unaccountable allocation of the lottery may be the greatest cost of random selection.

Goal: Choice avoidance

The above goals can be accommodated by rational choice among the available allocative systems. Yet random selection holds another advantage over traditional methods of allocation: when the policies to be furthered are in conflict or the good cannot be allocated rationally, the luck of the draw avoids the difficult ultimate choice between people. The premise is that people are better able to accept and reconcile themselves to certain kinds of decisions when made by fate, rather than through the application of principles they dislike or of limited human reason.

When policies conflict, the lottery provides a way to allocate without explicitly subordinating one policy to the other. For example, many collective bargaining agreements provide that seniority in industrial plants will determine the proper order of layoff and recall, with the last hired being the first fired.[47] Because of past discrimination, blacks and women have less seniority, making them particularly vulnerable to layoffs in times of recession.[48] Plants charged with racial discrimination under Title VII of the

---

45   Professor Tribe finds in the hearings mandated by due process a desire to provide the catharsis of participation to a citizen deprived of some benefit. Denying a person the right to speak when governmental acts affect him is treating him like an object. "[T]he very fact of conflict-resolution by judicially compelled resort to hearings…can avoid undermining the fraternal aims — the aims underlying a demand for explanation and participation rather than merely justification — which such hearings should be designed to further." Laurence H. Tribe, "Structural Due Process," *Harvard Civil Rights-Civil Liberties Law Review* 10 (1975): 269, 312 n. 128. See generally Tribe, "Structural Due Process," 303-314.

46   See Tribe, "Structural Due Process," 310-314.

47   Analysis of a 400-contract sample indicates that, in 1973, 42 per cent of collective bargaining agreements relied exclusively on seniority for layoff determinations. It was a factor in 85 per cent of all contracts. Bureau of National affairs, "Collective Bargaining Negotiations and Contracts," in Bureau of National Affairs, *Basic Patterns in Union Contracts*, 8th ed. (Washington: Bureau of National Affairs, 1975).

48   *New York Times*, November 10, 1974, §3, at 1, col. 5; *Wall Street Journal*, November 5, 1974, 1, col. 6.

Civil Rights Act of 1964[49] are barred from using facially neutral criteria, unrelated to job performance, which perpetuate the effects of past discrimination,[50] and plaintiffs have challenged last hired/first fired seniority under this principle.[51] One problem which may have deterred courts otherwise inclined towards granting relief to low seniority minority and women plaintiffs is that no obvious fair alternative to seniority exists should layoffs become necessary.[52]

The perceived problem with remedies in this area has been the impossibility of knowing which individuals benefited and which suffered from past discrimination. The black worker whose job is saved by a strict quota remedy[53] may never have applied for the job earlier even absent discrimination. The white worker laid off might have won his job even with honest competition from blacks. Ordering jobs to be given to a percentage of blacks equal to the population of the plant or the community at large is essentially arbitrary and clearly chooses affirmative action over the justifi-

---

49   42 U.S.C. § 2000e-2(a) (1970).

50   See *Griggs v. Duke Power Co.*, 401 U.S. 424 (1971).

51   See *Waters v. Wisconsin Steel Works*, 502 F.2d 1309 (7th Cir. 1974), cert. denied, 96 S. Ct. 2214 (1976); *Watkins v. United Steelworkers, Local 2369*, 369 F. Supp. 1221 (E.D. La. 1974), rev'd, 516 F.2d 41 (5th Cir. 1975); cf. *Franks v. Bowman Transp. Co.*, 96 S. Ct. 1251 (1976); *Jersey Cent. Power & Light Co. v. IBEW Local 327*, 508 F.2d 687 (3d Cir. 1975) (declaratory judgment sought by employer to reconcile its obligations under the Act and an EEOC conciliation agreement with those in its collective bargaining agreement), vacated sub nom. *EEOC v. Jersey Cent. Power & Light Co.*, 96 S.Ct. 2196 (1976). See also Clyde W. Summers and Margaret C. Love, "Work Sharing as an Alternative to Layoffs by Seniority: Title VII Remedies in Recession," *University of Pennsylvania Law Review* 124 (1976): 897, n. 18. See generally John H. Powell, Jr., "Reconciling Equal Employment Opportunity With Seniority: The Case for Sensitive Application of Equitable Principles," *Dickinson Law Review* 80 (1976); Donald R. Stacy, "Title VII Seniority Remedies in a Time of Economic Downturn," *Vanderbilt Law Review* 28 (1975); "Last Hired, First Fired Seniority Layoffs, and Title VII: Questions of Liability and Remedy," *Columbia Journal of Law and Social Problems* 11 (1975).

52   "It is fair to say that the real sticking point in all this controversy has not been the violation but the remedy." Caroline Poplin, "Fair Employment in a Depressed Economy: The Layoff Problem," *UCLA Law Review* 23 (1975): 194. This same logic also applies in other job-related situations. For instance, one commentator recommends the use of the lottery to reconcile the competing interests of equal opportunity and academic freedom. See Thomas M. Divine, "Women in the Academy: Sex Discrimination in University Faculty Hiring and Promotion," *Journal of Law and Education* 5 (1976): 443-450.

     Various remedies have been suggested. See generally Poplin, "Fair Employment," 194-234. One remedy is to give additional seniority to those minority workers who had applied previously and been denied employment. Cf. *Franks v. Bowman Transp. Co.*, 96 S.Ct. 1251 (1976) (additional seniority as part of a remedy for initial discriminatory refusal to hire). Another proposed remedy is to give additional seniority to those who, on the basis of age, residence, and employment history, might have been applicants but for the discriminatory policy. Yet another possibility is work sharing. See Summers and Love, "Work Sharing." Finally, a frequently discussed remedy is the imposition of racial quotas on layoffs and recalls. See *Watkins v. United Steelworkers Local 2369*, 369 F.Supp. 1221 (E.D.La. 1974) (remedial order), rev'd 516 F.2d 41 (5th Cir. 1975).

53   See *Watkins v. Steelworker's Local 2369*, 369 F.Supp. 1221 (E.D. La. 1974) (remedial order), rev'd 516 F.2d 41 (5th Cir. 1975).

able expectations engendered by the seniority system. The result is that any remedy appears to be a choice among presumptive innocents.[54]

Since a layoff is generally an allocative situation,[55] however, a court could order a lottery to be held among those holding jobs to be cut back or among all the workers in the plant.[56] From that pool priorities for layoff and recalls would be drawn. This use of random selection allocates the benefits and burdens of the remedy in accordance with a neutral criterion, and it attacks the real racial discrimination involved, that between groups, not between individuals. Rather than attempting the impossible task of determining which individuals benefited or suffered because of discrimi-nation, the lottery makes the remedy affect the groups. It promotes equal-ity at the expense of seniority, but the choice of policies is submerged by the luck of the draw. The difficulty of this choice-avoidance use of the lot-tery is that it also avoids the clarification of goals and policies that emerges when such hard choices must be made. An explicit decision between seniority and remedying discrimination may be valuable in itself.

Some burdens of vital importance cannot be allocated rationally, for doing so denies the human dignity of the recipient.[57] The classic example is what must occur when shipwrecked lifeboat occupants run out of food:

> There is…one condition of extremity for which all writers have pre-scribed the same rule. When the ship is in no danger of sinking, but all sustenance is exhausted, and a sacrifice of one person is necessary to appease the hunger of others, the selection is by lot. This mode is resorted to as the fairest mode, and, in some sort, as an appeal to God, for selection of the victim.[58]

Rational objective choices between individuals are impossible in hemodialysis programs[59] and in determining those couples who should have children.[60] In allocating such vital goods, the limits of judgment and

---

54   See *Franks v. Bowman Transp. Co.*, 96 S.Ct. 1251, 1272 (1976) (Burger, C.J., concurring in part and dissenting in part).

55   Small layoffs might be avoided by work-sharing. This would mean that the good is divisible, and therefore not scarce. See generally Summers and Love, "Work Sharing."

56   The exact scope of the pool could be difficult to determine. The problem involved in defining it solely in terms of the level of job involved in the layoff is that those with the lowest level jobs are probably those with the lowest seniority. Therefore, the pool has to include higher level jobs or it will become merely a roundabout seniority system. The class could be defined in terms of the group of workers who could replace each other. These difficulties would have to be faced in any layoff.

57   See n. 37.

58   *United States v. Holmes*, 26 F. Cas. 360, 367 (C.C.E.D. Pa. 1842) (No. 15.383) (Baldwin, J.) (dictum); cf. Jonah 7:17 (Jonah gets the short straw and is forced overboard).

59   A Seattle hospital originally regulated access to its artificial kidney equipment on the basis of social worth. A "Lay Advisory Committee" composed of various community members made the decisions. See David Sanders and Jesse Dukeminier, Jr., "Medical Advance and Legal Lag; Hemodialysis and Kidney Transplantation," *UCLA Law Review* 15 (1968): 371, 377-378.

60   See pp. 78–81.

reason are reached, and explicitly irrational random selection becomes the rational choice for avoiding decisions.

Governmental choice of an allocative method depends upon the balance struck among the goals outlined above. No method will always be satisfactory, but random selection offers advantages that often are unrecognized. Its comparative advantage will depend on the importance of maximizing the goal to be achieved, the objectivity or subjectivity of the pooling criteria, and the disparity in size between the pool and the recipients. Discussion of the lottery illuminates the nature and extent of the government's commitment to equality and forces a direct confrontation with its real goals.

II. The Lottery Applied to Three Allocative Situations

The examples presented in this section range from the illustrative to the provocative. The allocation of public housing usually is made on the basis of merit or first-come/first-served methods. Comparing the lottery with these more conventional methods of distributing places in public housing challenges efficiency criteria and excessive discretion of the present methods. The Federal Communications Commission licenses the broadcast media under a merit system that implicates first amendment values and the desire to protect the public from offensive programming. Random selection posits a less coercive resolution of the conflict among applicants for licenses. Should limits on procreation become necessary, speculation about the preferable method of allocation of birth rights will stretch our notions of the utility of, and limits on, existing allocative systems.

A. Public housing

Traditional methods of governmental allocation of public housing have proved slow and costly and have sheltered abuses of discretion, undue coercion, and stigmatization of the individual applicant. These evils are clearest in a system which allocates public housing according to the need of the applicants. These problems may be reduced or eliminated, however, by the use of simpler and more objective criteria to form a pool of eligible applicants from which recipients are drawn by lot or first-come/first-served. Although the result of such a system would only be satisficing, the nominal loss from the shift from maximization may be outweighed by the gains that flow from its use.

Although public housing in the United States is financed in part by federal funds,[61] the operation of the system, including decisions on the method for allocating the housing, is left to state and local authorities.[62]

---

61   42 U.S.C. §§ 1437, 1437b (loans), 1437c (annual contributions) (Supp. IV 1974).
62   See 42 U.S.C. § 1412 (1970). However, HUD regulations do govern procedures for determining eligibility, 24 C.F.R. § 860.204 (1976), and for denying admission to undesirable tenants, id. § 860.205.

The only federal requirement for admission to federally aided public housing is that a certain percentage of tenants meet specified income requirements,[63] and that certain procedures be followed in processing applications.[64] The result is that local authorities have actually used a wide variety of systems for allocating scarce public housing units.

In the 1960's the New York City Housing Authority selected its tenants on the basis of their need for public housing. This determination revolved around both their financial status and the condition of their current housing.[65] In contrast, the New Haven Housing Authority currently allocates its public housing through a slightly modified system of first-come/first-served among those who meet the federal income standards.[66]

The New York need system of selection can lead to abuses of discretion. In situations where the number of applicants exceeds available units,[67] housing can be used to punish or reward groups or individuals based on the decision-maker's conclusions as to their relative "merit." In the past it has been used against tenant organizers,[68] unwed mothers,[69] and unmarried couples living together.[70]

The Act formerly did recommend certain groups for special priorities. Those groups included persons displaced by public housing projects, veterans, the disabled, the elderly, and those in emergency need. 42 U.S.C. § 1410(g)(2) (1970) (repealed by the Housing and Community Development Act of 1974, Pub. L. 93-383, Title II, § 201(a), 88 Stat. 653).

63   See 24 C.F.R. §§ 860.406, 860.407 (1976). The term "low income families" is defined by statute to be those families "who cannot afford to pay enough to cause private enterprise in their locality or metropolitan area to build an adequate supply of decent, safe, and sanitary buildings for their use." 42 U.S.C. § 1437a(2)(Supp. IV 1974). "Very low income families" are defined by that statute to be those families with incomes less than 50 percent of the median income for their area.

64   42 U.S.C. § 1437d(c)(2) (Supp. IV 1974) requires that the local authority follows its "duly adopted regulations" in the admissions process. 42 U.S.C. § 1437d(c)(3)(ii) (Supp. IV 1974) requires an informal hearing for applicants ruled ineligible. 42 U.S.C. §1437d(c)(3)(ii) (Supp. IV 1974) requires that applicants found eligible be notified of their eligibility and be given an estimate of when they can expect to be housed. See also "Procedural Due Process in Government Subsidized Housing," Harvard Law Review 86 (1973).

65   New York City Hous. Auth. Resol. No. 62-7-473, reprinted in Brief's Joint Appendix at 39a-53a, Holmes v. New York City Hous. Auth., 398 F.2d 262 (2d Cir. 1968).

66   In contrast, New York City chose to allocate scare units distributed under its recent "urban homesteading" program by a lottery (New York Times, June 22, 1976, 39, col. 3, New York Times, January 11, 1976, § 1, 1, col. 4).
     The New Haven Housing Authority does have special priorities paralleling those formerly suggested in the Housing Act of 1937 (see n. 62). Those persons not in one of the special priorities are given housing in the order that they filed their applications. Interview with Susan Whetstone, New Haven Housing Authority, in New Haven (Nov. 4, 1976).

67   During the late 1960's the New York City Housing Authority annually received approximately 90.000 applications for approximately 10,000 places. Holmes v. New York City Hous. Auth., 398 F2d 262, 263 (2d Cir. 1968).

68   See Thorpe v. Housing Auth., 393 U.S. 268 (1969) (eviction from public housing allegedly because of organizational activities). Cf. Act of July 31, 1953, Chap. 302, title 1, 67 Stat. 307 (barred "subversives" from federally-aided housing as part of Appropriations Act).

69   See Thomas v. Housing Auth., 282 F.Supp. 575 (E.D. Ark. 1967).

70   Atkisson v. Kern County Hous. Auth., 59 Cal.App. 3d 89, 130 Cal. Rptr. 375 (1976). Individualized determinations however, can pursue worthwhile goals, as when the New York City Housing

New York City's attempt to determine the neediest applicants created mammoth administrative problems. The effort required to rank 90,000 applicants ordinally on the basis of their need for public housing was overwhelming; some applicants were forced to wait for over five years for action on their applications.[71] The kinds of determinations which the City attempted to make were not only susceptible to abuse,[72] but were time-consuming and costly, particularly in light of required hearings for rejected applicants.[73]

The use of the lottery instead of this need-oriented ordinal-ranking system would serve to simplify the procedure considerably. A pool would be established, consisting of all persons meeting income requirements who had applied for housing in the system.[74] At stated intervals all those within the pool would be subject to a drawing for priorities. These priorities would determine when and if applicants would receive public housing. They would be placed in available spaces in the order of their lottery numbers.

A first-come/first-served system is similar to the lottery in some respects. It could operate on a pool formed by the simple criterion of maximum income. Selection in this case would be by priority of application rather than random selection, which will likely result in lower administrative costs on the same order as the random number generator used for the lottery.[75] The first-come/first-served allocative system meets the considerations of fairness embodied in the applicant's assertion that his longer wait entitles him to the good more than someone who had waited a shorter time.[76]

Authority sought to maintain an integrated neighborhood by limiting minority representation in public housing projects. See *Otero v. New York City Hous. Auth.*, 484 F2d 1122 (2d Cir. 1973). See also *Hills v. Gantreaux*, 96 S.Ct. 1538, 1541-42 (1976).

71   *Holmes v. New York City Hous. Auth*, 398 F.2d 262, 264 (2d Cir. 1968).

72   The "objective scoring system" used by the Authority had five categories, each encompassing a number of specific criteria. Some of the criteria were objective: "illegal fire escape," "no facilities for hot water." Others were subjective: "general poor repair;" "sagging, sloping or worn floors;" "lack of privacy due to room arrangement." New York City Hous. Auth, Resol. No. 62-7,473 reprinted in Brief's Joint Appendix at 52a-53a, *Holmes v. New York City Hous. Auth.*, 398 F.2d 262 (2d Cir. 1968).

73   See n. 62, 64. See also *Holmes v. New York City Hous. Auth.*, 398 F.2d 262 (2d Cir. 1968).

74   There may need to be exceptions in any pooling criteria to accommodate emergency cases, as for example when an applicant's private housing has been destroyed by fire or other accident. Moreover, applicants disadvantaged by the luck of the draw for some period of time, say for five years, could be given immediate priority for entrance.

75   The first-come/first-served method can also be viewed as a variation on the need-fulfillment system in light of the likely depletion of the applicant's financial resources caused by the period required to receive the good. This depletion is almost certain to occur because the applicant's income is, by definition, insufficient to meet his housing costs. See 42 U.S.C. § 1437a(2) (Supp. IV 1974). That is, the longer the wait; the greater the applicant's need becomes.

76   The corollary wrong suffered by an applicant denied admission by a lottery system is not simply the denial of an expectation which could be relieved by sufficient advance notice of the institution of the lottery. Compare note 16 supra. Because waiting for public housing does not

Adoption of either a lottery or first-come/first-served system of allocation would result in a lowering of direct administrative costs, since the
housing authority would no longer be required to determine anything
beyond income, and its hearings would be reduced to consideration of that
issue. More importantly, the lottery would force other grounds for denial
to be either foregone or made explicit. Under the need system, the quality
of an applicant's present housing can be used as an excuse to avoid placing
the applicant, an excuse difficult to challenge in an administrative hearing.
Under a lottery, only the pooling characteristics, which were postulated
above as solely income, would be considered. Any other values would
have to be explicitly added to the pooling criteria.

The conclusion to be drawn is that in the context of public housing, the
policies that underlie allocations by any of the three above-discussed
methods are somewhat similar, although their effects and costs can vary
drastically. The first-come/first-served system allows the use of simplifying techniques but does not necessarily maximize the goal of providing
the needy with housing. It does, however, seem to meet certain
"entitlements" arising out of a sense of fairness. The use of the lottery in
this situation affirms a different notion of fairness: that of equality of
opportunity. The method chosen will ultimately depend on which of the
competing goals of maximization, entitlement, or equality the local
decisionmaker decides to embrace as paramount.

B. Broadcasting licensing

Random selection could be used to allocate broadcast licenses when more
than one technically and financially competent applicant exists. The present system of licensing attempts to promote the public interest through a
web of covert pressures on programming. The lottery would reduce those
pressures which threaten the artistic and political independence of the
broadcast industry from federal officials.

Spots on the broadcast spectrum are allocated by the Federal Communications Commission in accordance with the "public interest, convenience,
and necessity."[77] The FCC grants, subject to renewal every three years,[78]

---

exclude other activities, the opportunity cost of waiting for public housing is less than that
involved when one must actually wait in line for the goods. There is some notion that one's
diligence should earn some preference in the allocation process, although in fact the
differences as to priority may be due to informational imperfections rather than a lack of effort.
See generally Barzel, "A Theory of Rationing."

77   47 U.S.C. § 309(a) (1970).

78   47 U.S.C. § 307(d) (1970). While every contested renewal provokes a comparative hearing, the
practice of the Commission, with the exception of one short period, has been to renew the
present license almost automatically. See Henry Goldberg, "A Proposal to Deregulate
Broadcast Programming," *George Washington Law Review* 42 (1973); Albert H. Kramer, "An
Argument for Maintaining the Current FCC Controls," *George Washington Law Review* 42
(1973). WHDH, Inc., 16 F.C.C.2d 1, 15 RAD. REG.2d (P-H) 411 (1969), aff'd sub nom., *Greater
Boston Television Corp. v. FCC*, 444 F.2d 841 (D.C. Cir. 1970), cert. denied, 403 U.S. 923 (1971),

limited, non-transferable licenses to use certain frequencies.[79] When more than one party applies for a frequency, either initially[80] or on renewal,[81] the Commission must grant a hearing to determine which of the applicants meet the minimal legal, technical, and financial requirements of the Act.[82] All those meeting these standards are then involved in a comparative hearing to determine which applicant will best serve the public interest. The standards that enter into that decision are not clear-cut.[83]

The present system of licensing applies the public interest standard by inevitably, though obliquely, restraining the freedom of the broadcaster. Both ownership and programming are regulated. Recognizing that ownership affects program content,[84] the FCC scrutinizes station ownership, and thus has an indirect but highly coercive effect on programming. Radi-

---

was a departure from this norm. The Commission there refused to renew the television license owned by the *Boston Herald-Traveller* on the ground that the public interest would be better served by licensing one of the challenging applicants.

The Commission, after membership changes, has pulled back from the WHDH position. Although its official policy statement announcing the return to the status quo was ruled invalid, *Citizen's Communications Center v. FCC*, 447 F.2d 1201 (D.C. Cir. 1971), the Commission has merely returned to its previous lax scrutiny of renewal applications. See RKO General, Inc., 44 F.C.C.2d 123, 28 RAD. REG.2d (P-H) 1501 (1973), aff'd sub nom., *Fidelity Television, Inc. v. FCC*, 515 F.2d 684 (D.C.Cir.), cert. denied, 423 U.S. 926 (1975). See also Robert A. Anthony, "Towards Simplicity and Rationality in Comparative Broadcast Licensing Proceedings," *Stanford Law Review* 24 (1971): 106-110; Henry Geller, "The Comparative Renewal Process in Television: Problems and Suggested Solutions," *Virginia Law Review* 61 (1975); and "Comparing the Incomparable: Towards a Structural Model for FCC Comparative Broadcast License Renewal Hearings," *University of Chicago Law Review* 43 (1976).

79   47 U.S.C. § 3 10(b) (1970). While the statute requires Commission approval for the assignment of licenses, the FCC routinely approves assignments made after the first three year term. See Anthony, "Towards Simplicity and Rationality," 24-26; Louis L. Jaffe, "WHDH: The FCC and Broadcast License Renewal," *Harvard Law Review* 82 (1969).

80   47 U.S.C. § 309(e) (1970); *Ashbacker Radio Corp. v. FCC*, 326 U.S. 327 (1945).

81   *Citizens Communications Center v. FCC*, 447 F.2d 1201 (D.C.Cir. 1971).

82   These requirements have been developed by the Commission. The legal requirements include ownership by a citizen, absence of a previous license revocation for antitrust violations, absence of relevant convictions, and compliance with the Commission's rules on multiple ownership and chains. The technical requirements involve the details of broadcasting so as to minimize interference with other licensees while maximizing service to the area. The current financial requirement is that the licensee be able to construct and operate the station without income for one year. See Anthony, "Towards Simplicity and Rationality," 17-19.

83   The Commission in a 1965 Policy Statement claimed that maximum diffusion of control and best practical service to the public were the primary considerations in comparative broadcast licensing. The latter includes efficient use of frequency, integration of ownership and management, proposed programming, past record of broadcasting, and the character of the owner. Policy Statement on Comparative Broadcast Hearings, 1 F.C.C.2d 393, 394-400, 5 Rad. Reg.2d (P-H) 1901, 1908-14 (1965).

84   Rejecting the FCC's argument that color blindness was an appropriate posture to take in the licensing process, the Court of Appeals for the District of Columbia recently ordered the Commission to give positive weight to the factor of partial black ownership where diversity of content was likely to result. *TV 9, Inc. v. FCC*, 495 F.2d 929, 938(D.C. Cir. 1973). cert, denied, 419 U.S. 486 (1974). The court said that "[i]t is upon ownership that public policy places primary reliance with respect to diversification of content, and that historically has proven to be significantly influential with respect to editorial comment and the presentation of news."

cal links[85] and racial and religious bias[86] are obstacles to applicants seeking issuance or renewal orders from the FCC; it has even been charged that
licenses have been granted on the basis of political affiliation.[87] This policy
of considering the ownership of the station was criticized by Commissioner Loevinger, who argued that "[t]he FCC [is not] the moral proctor of
the public or the den mother of the audience. The Commission is not only
forbidden to disqualify an applicant on the basis of his religious and political statements, it is prohibited from inquiring into them as a basis for official action."[88]

Programming is also directly evaluated by the Commission. Applications for a license must contain a detailed breakdown of the expected percentage of programming by category.[89] Failure to propose a balanced
schedule has resulted in the denial of an unopposed application.[90] In
renewal proceedings past programming rarely is taken explicitly into consideration, but it always lurks in the background.[91]

The "regulation by raised eyebrow"[92] is the most pervasive and least
visible supervision by the Commission, and is therefore the most sinister.

---

85   See Ralph S. Brown, Jr., "Character and Candor Requirements for FCC Licensees," *Law and
      Contemporary Problems* 22 (1957): 652. In Dispatch, Inc., 22 F.C.C. 1369, 13 Rad.Reg. (P-H) 237
      (1957), a lawyer who owned a station was involved in a long renewal proceeding because of his
      alleged radical ties. In Pacifica Foundation, 36 F.C.C. 147, 1 Rad. Reg.2d (P-H) 747 (1964), final
      renewal of a station's license was delayed by charges of Communist affiliation and unsuitable
      programming.

86   See Brown, "Character and Candor," 650 (discussion of *New York Daily News* application for
      radio license and charges of anti-semitism); George E. Borst, 4 Rad.Reg.2d (P-H) 697 (1965)
      (case involving the extremely conservative, fundamentalist minister, Rev. McIntyre).

87   Bernard Schwartz, "Comparative Television and the Chancellor's Foot," *Georgetown Law
      Journal* 47 (1959): 689-694. Schwartz charged that Republican newspapers had a marked
      advantage in hearings for VHF television stations. Former President Nixon was also aware of
      the FCC's coercive power. "The main, main thing is *The [Washington] Post* is going to have
      damnable, damnable problems out of this one. They have a television station…and they're
      going to have to get it renewed." Richard M. Nixon to H. R. Haldeman and John Dean, Sept. 15.
      1972, quoted in Senate Select Committee on Presidential Campaign Activities, Final Report, S.
      Rep. No. 981, 93d Cong., 2d Sess., 149 (1974).

88   George E. Borst, 4 Rad. Reg.2d (P-H) 697, 707 (1965) (Loevinger, concurring in part and
      dissenting in part).

89   See Rad. Reg. (P-H) 98:303-07 for an application form.

90   Lee Roy McCourry. 2 Rad. Reg.2d (P-H) 895, 898-907 (1964) (Loevinger, C., dissenting).

91   For a discussion of the present system's indirect restraints on programming, see Goldberg, "A
      Proposal," 75-84; Glen O. Robinson, "The FCC and the First Amendment: Observations of 40
      Years of Radio and Television Regulation," *Minnesota Law Review* 52 (1967): 97-111. Cf. Oscar
      G. Chase, "Public Broadcasting and the Problem of Government Influence: Towards a
      Legislative Solution," *University of Michigan Journal of Law Reform* 9 (1975): 71, 89-98, 106-112
      (violation of first amendment interests by the content-based funding allocations made by the
      Corporation for Public Broadcasting (CPB), contrary to CPB's purpose of serving as a "buffer
      between the government and the broadcasters, producers, and artists").

92   Theodore Pierson, "The Need for Modification of Section 326," *Federal Communications Bar
      Journal* 18 (1963): 19-20 (report of a committee of the Federal Communications Bar Association).
      A federal district judge recently held that the television industry is under a duty to resist
      informal FCC coercion and that a failure to do so, by virtue of the industry's adoption of

A speech by a Commissioner, a letter forwarding a viewer's complaint, or the establishment of a new category for reporting programming,[93] all provide signals to the licensee and its counsel about what the Commission likes. The triennial renewal process puts the licensee under subtle but effective pressure to follow these signals. Moreover, the vague nature of the standards applied encourages litigation about every possible factor. Contested hearings involve massive records and take years to conclude.[94]

The lottery would be an improvement over the present system or allocating licenses.[95] About fifty contested allocations are made each year for new frequencies, involving primarily UHF television and FM radio licenses.[96] These comparative hearings could be replaced by a lottery. The technical, legal, and financial requirements which currently form the minimum standards required to reach the comparative hearing stage could define the lottery pool, thereby avoiding any consideration of ownership or programming. Within the pool, choosing by lot saves the time and cost of comparative hearings.

"family hour" broadcasting standards, violates the first amendment. *Writers Guild v. FCC*, F.Supp. (C. D.Cal., Nov. 4, 1976).

93   The Commission is not always subtle: "To underline our interest in children's programming aired on television…[w]e have added as Question 6…the following. 'Attach as Exhibit — a brief description of programs, program segments, or program series aired during the license period that were primarily directed to children twelve years old and under. Indicate the source, time and day of broadcast, duration, and program type.'" Formulation of Rules and Policies Relating to the Renewal of Broadcasting Licenses, 43 F.C.C.2d 1, 149, 27 Rad. Reg.2d 553, 613 (1973). In the midst of public concern about children's programming, the broadcaster would be likely to receive a message from this added question.

94   "Observers of the procedures employed by the [Federal Communications] Commission agree that the issues litigated are unreal and a mass of useless evidence, expensive to prepare, is required to be adduced." James M. Landis, Report on Regulatory Agencies to the President-Elect (1960), 22. See also Anthony, "Towards Simplicity and Rationality," 47-50. Anthony states that the cost per applicant in a major television contest has been estimated at about $500,000 (51, n. 274), although costs are lower for the UHF and FM comparative proceedings.

95   The lottery has been mentioned by several participants in and observers of the FCC process. Former Commissioner Nicholas Johnson wrote that "[e]ven a random drawing or first-come basis for awarding licenses between competing applicants would save a great deal of time and expense and promise results no less arbitrary than our present comparative process…" Farragut Television Corp., 8 F.C.C.2d 279, 291, 10 Rad. Reg.2d (P-H) 50, 63 (1967) (separate opinion).

      Judge Leventhal expressed similar feelings in dissent in *Star Television, Inc. v. FCC*, 416 F.2d 1086, 1092 (D.C. Cir.), cert. denied, 396 U.S. 888 (1969). "Maybe all it can do as to the other applicants is say: These applicants are all reasonably qualified; we have no meaningful way of choosing on principle between them; all we can really do is speculate who will do the best job in the public interest; and our best possible hunch is X…[S]uch a candid disclaimer would perhaps crystallize other and more acceptable solutions…Perhaps a lottery could be used, for luck is not an inadmissible means of deciding the undecidable, provided the ground rules are known in advance."

      Anthony, "Towards Simplicity and Rationality," 102, devotes two paragraphs to the lottery and considers it the first alternative to his proposal for more objective public interest standards.

96   See Jaffe, "WHDC."

The lottery could also be extended to the renewal process.[97] Because almost all the available VHF television licenses have been allocated and additional allocations to major markets are infrequent,[98] the renewal process is particularly significant. Any renewal process that gives discretion to the FCC inevitably puts pressure on the licensee to conform to the Commission's desires. By selecting by lot among all applicants for a license at the end of each term, this pressure would be limited to meeting the pooling criteria.[99] The Commission would have less discretion[100] with which to influence the conduct of the licensee.[101]

This comparative advantage of the lottery is also its major problem. It solves the problem of abuse of the public interest standard by eliminating the standard. Implementation of random selection would force a rethinking of just what the public interest does require in broadcasting. Though this desirable goal does not flow exclusively from a lottery, and the lottery's reduction of discretion and coercion does not seem great, a critic hostile to the discretion and the cost of comparative hearings could advance random selection as a means of forcing the government to avoid programming control or to use visible standards which act on programming directly, rather than covertly through licensing.

C. Allocation of procreation rights if births should be limited by the state

The federal government of India has embarked upon a national program for slowing population growth by using incentives to encourage sterilization.[102] Several Indian states, with federal approval, are considering com-

---

97   Anthony, "Towards Simplicity and Rationality," 61 (by implication).

98   Anthony, "Towards Simplicity and Rationality."

99   This use of the lottery could be criticised on the grounds that continuity of good broadcasting would be threatened if an applicant who was currently supplying good service was eliminated by the luck of the draw. The use of objective pooling criteria, however, should ensure that all members of the pool could provide adequate service.

100 Discretion is still present in the formation of the pool, although this problem is somewhat alleviated by the lottery's facilitation of the use of more objective criteria.

101 Other solutions have been suggested. One is that the standards for allocation on renewal be made more specific. See Anthony, "Towards Simplicity and Rationality;" "Comparing the Incomparable." This suggestion can be criticized on the ground that the public interest is and always will be a discretionary matter. As the criteria become objective and hence less subject to administrative discretion they also become less meaningful and more susceptible to parroting by applicants.
        Another solution would end the pressure stemming from the renewal process by ending that process. Making licenses permanent, or nearly so, eliminates programming pressure, but it also eliminates any public check as well as the possibility of change. See Goldberg, "A Proposal."
        Finally broadcast licenses could be auctioned off, see Ronald Coase, "The Federal Communications Commission," *Journal of Law and Economics* 2 (1959), though this method would not be desirable if diversity of ownership is a goal.

102 *New York Times*, April 17, 1976, 1, col. 6; *New York Times*, May 2, 1976, 17, col. 1.

pulsory sterilization.[103] The United States presently does not have a coherent population policy,[104] but before this century ends our government may have to set explicit population goals.[105] While voluntary methods of population control may be successful,[106] some commentators suggest that only compulsion ultimately will be effective[107] — a troubling prospect for a society which values children and family life so highly.[108]

In order to provoke thought about the potential of random selection in resolving a novel and complex distributive problem, we can hypothesize that Congress will find it necessary to mandate slower population growth by specifying that an uneven number of births—for example 1.7 per woman—will henceforth be permitted.[109] Contraception rights would

103 *New York Times*, August 13, 1976, 8, col. 1 (Maharashtra); *New York Times*, April 21, 1976, 11, col. 1 (Uttar Pradesh); *New York Times*, Feb. 26, 1976, 1, col. 3 (West Bengal).

104 Procreation is presently influenced by state and federal statutes on marriage, sex crimes, taxes, education, contraceptive distribution, and the availability of welfare benefits and abortions. See Guido Calabresi and Philip Bobbitt, *Tragic Choices* (New York: Norton, 1978).

105 See generally Lincoln H. Day & Alice Taylor Day, *Too Many Americans* (Boston: Houghton Mifflin, 1974), 11-74; Paul R. Ehrlich, *The Population Bomb*, 2nd ed. (New York: Ballantine Books, 1971); "Legal Analysis and Population Control: The Problem of Coercion," *Harvard Law Review* 84 (1971). Governmental allocation of the right to bear children is presented merely as an example, not as a prophecy; indeed, it is difficult for this Comment to forecast the value structure that would be used to judge the possible methods of allocation.

106 See Anthony M. Dileo, "Directions and Dimensions of Population Policy in the United States," *Tulane Law Review* 46 (1971); Frank W. Notestein, "Zero Population Growth: What Is It?" *Family Planning Perspectives* 2 (June 1970): 20-23.

107 See, e.g., Edgar R. Chasteen, *The Case for Compulsory Birth Control* (Englewood Cliffs, NJ: Prentice-Hall, 1971); Judith Blake, "Population Policy for Americans: Is the Government Being Misled?" *Science* 164 (1969).

108 The Supreme Court often has recognized the importance of families in human life. In *Meyer v. Nebraska*, 262 U.S. 390 (1923) (right to have children learn German) and *Pierce v. Society of Sisters*, 268 U.S. 510 (1925) (right to send one's children to private schools), the Court gave the family unit constitutional significance. In *Skinner v. Oklahoma ex rel. Williamson*, 316 U.S. 535, 541 (1942), the Court recognized the importance of conception by invoking the equal protection clause to strike down a statute compelling the sterilization of some criminals. But cf. *Buck v. Bell*, 274 U.S. 200 (1927) (upholding compulsory sterilization of the mentally deficient).

  Justice Goldberg once expressed reservations about the government's power to limit birth. "[S]urely the Government, absent a showing of a compelling subordinating state interest, could not decree that all husbands and wives must be sterilized after two children have been born to them." *Griswold v. Connecticut*, 381 U.S. 479, 496-97 (1965) (Goldberg, J., concurring) (invalidating Connecticut's restrictions on the use of contraceptives as an invasion of the right of privacy). But cf. *Dandridge v. Williams*, 397 U.S. 471 (1970) (rejecting claim that failure to increase assistance through Aid to Families with Dependent Children program upon the birth of more than four children infringed on the right to have children). This Comment will not discuss the constitutionality of the allocation of procreative privileges.

  See generally "Legal Analysis," 1875-1903; and "Population Control: The Legal Approach to a Biological Imperative," *California Law Review* 58 (1970).

109 Long run population stability for a given country requires the birth of between 2.1 and 2.5 children per woman. See Ansley J. Coale, "Man and His Environment," *Science* 130 (1970): 135; Tomas Frejka, "Reflections on the Demographic Conditions Needed to Establish a United States Stationary Population Growth," *Population Studies* 22 (1968): 379. With this birth rate and the current age composition of the population, the number of American citizens would continue to grow until about 2040. See Paul R. Ehrlich and Anne H. Ehrlich, *Population, Resources, Environment*, 2nd ed. (San Francisco, W.H. Freeman, 1972), 32 (figure 3-4), 34-35;

have to be allocated so that only seven out of ten women would be permitted to bear a second child.[110] In this context of governmental coercion, random selection is the least distasteful method of allocation.

Distribution by merit would deliver birth rights to those couples identified by the government as the most "meritorious" prospective parents. An effort could be made to identify the couples with the best genetic structure in terms of strength, intelligence,[111] or resistance to disease.[112] Alternatively, birth rights could be awarded to the parents who would appear to take the best care of the child or offer it the most stimulating environment.

Those possible criteria highlight the dangers of a discretionary merit system. Besides the inherent potential for corruption or bias in such subjective judgments, disagreement about the ultimate goals of the selection process will be profound if the society continues to embrace the values of equal opportunity and diversity. The magnitude of conflict would likely preclude a merit criterion for birth allocation.[113] Furthermore, it would be wrong for a society committed to pluralism to choose a "best" child. No one could know what characteristics would be needed for the future, so no one could allocate births in the present.

If allocation of birth rights becomes necessary, random selection is the most acceptable method. The use of the lottery in this situation affirms the value of equal opportunity by giving each woman a mathematically equal

Tomas Frejka, *The Future of Population Growth* (New York: Wiley, 1973), 165-166. The number of births required to keep the country at its present population is slightly more than one child per woman. See Frejka, *Future of Population Growth*, 165 (estimates 1.1-1.2 children per woman); and Coale, "Man and His Environment," 135. Cf. Ehrlich and Ehrlich, *Population, Resources, Environment*, 38-39 (problems of immediate cessation of growth). Thus the postulated number of births would end growth more quickly. We can assume some provision would be made to reallocate the birth rights of women who are unwilling or unable to bear children.

110 Presumably some method of enforcement would be necessary. Perhaps contraceptives would be added to everyone's water, with antidotes distributed by the government. See "Legal Analysis," 1875-1903; "Population Control: The Legal Approach to a Biological Imperative;" "Population Control in the Year 2000: The Constitutionality of Putting Anti-Fertility Agents in the Water Supply," *Ohio State Law Journal* 32 (1971). Of course, it is likely that government would avoid the allocative problem by allowing each couple two children (see Calabresi and Bobbitt, *Tragic Choices*) and controlling population growth by manipulating immigration. See "Population: The Problem, the Constitution, and a Proposal," *Journal of Family Law* 11 (1971-1972): 331.

111 These concepts could have racist implications. See Ralph Z. Hallow, "Blacks Cry Genocide," *Nation*, April 28, 1969; *New York Times*, May 2, 1971, § E. at 7, col. 1-4.

112 See "Eugenic Sterilization: A Scientific Analysis," *Denver Law Journal* 46 (1969): (survey of various hereditary and possibly hereditary diseases and conditions).

113 One can also advance a market mechanism as the preferable method of allocating children on the basis of desire. Granting birth rights to couples who are willing to pay the most for them in real terms helps to ensure the best treatment for the child. See Calabresi and Bobbitt, *Tragic Choices*; Edward H. Rabin, "Population Control through Financial Incentives," *Hastings Law Journal* 23 (1972). Yet this option also seems objectionable because it imparts a class bias to the allocation of children. Moreover, allocating children to those who desire them could make the population as a whole more "childloving," aggravating the population problem in the long run. See Garrett Hardin, "Population, Biology, and the Law," *Journal of Urban Law* 48 (1971): 567-568.

chance to bear a second child. Its use also removes governmental discretion from the decision-making process as much as possible. When such vital human choices are taken from citizens, the governmental intrusion is most limited by abandoning choice to the luck of the draw.

These examples have illustrated the comparative advantage of the lottery over methods of distribution based on such traditional criteria as merit and wealth. When allocative choices are particularly costly, in real or political terms; when traditional methods allow abuse of discretion or class or group bias; and when equality of opportunity and expectation is an importantly felt goal, then random selection is a proper policy tool.

III. Constitutional Limitations

Like all government policies, allocation by random selection must meet the requirements of the equal protection and due process clauses. This section will outline the constitutional objections which could be raised to the use of the lottery in any context. Leaving detailed considerations, as it must, to the factual context in which challenges might arise, the Comment will sketch the kinds of objections which could be raised by a citizen harmed by the use of random selection as an allocative system.

The equal protection clause requires that governmental classifications have a rational relationship to a legitimate legislative purpose,[114] either hypothetical[115] or articulated.[116] An equal protection challenge to random selection seems apt because the choices a lottery makes are purposefully non-rational. Any citizen deprived of a benefit or visited with a burden which does not fall equally on all in similar circumstances can complain that the difference is not-rationally related to a valid state purpose.

The government's response will be that the citizen has identified the wrong level of decision for equal protection scrutiny. The choice of this method of allocation is rational and serves the central purposes of the equal protection clause: to protect minorities from the tyranny of majority rule. As Justice Jackson noted in his concurring opinion in *Railway Express Agency v. New York,*[117] "there is no more effective practical guarantee against arbitrary and unreasonable government than to require that the principles of law which officials would impose upon a minority must be

114 See generally "Developments in the Law: Equal Protection," *Harvard Law Review* 82 (1969).
115 See, e.g., *Williamson v. Lee Optical Co.*, 348 U.S. 483 (1955); *Kotch v. Board of River Port Pilot Comm'rs*, 330 U.S. 552 (1947). See also "Developments in the Law," 1077-1087.
116 See *San Antonio Indep. School Dist. v. Rodriguez*, 411 U.S. 1(1973); *McGinnis v. Royster*, 410 U.S. 263 (1973); John Hart Ely, "The Wages of Crying Wolf: A Comment on Roe v. Wade," *Yale Law Journal* 82 (1973); Gerald Gunther, "Forward: In Search of Evolving Doctrine on a Changing Court. A Model for a Newer Equal Protection," *Harvard Law Review* 86 (1972): 46-48. But cf. *San Antonio Indep. School Dist. v. Rodriguez*, 411 U.S. 1, 98-110 (1973) (Marshall, J., dissenting) ("sliding scale" analysis).
117 336 U.S. 106, 112-13 (1949) (Jackson, 1. concurring).

imposed generally."[118] The allocative situations upon which the Comment is based, however, postulate that equality of result is impossible. A lottery adopts the best alternative policy: equality of opportunity due to the placing of all similarly situated citizens in the same pool. In traditional terms, random selection satisfies the equal protection clause because it is a rational choice of method, even though this method avoids the ultimate choices involved in relating each individual allocation to the desired end.

The due process clause applies to government action when it deprives citizens of liberty or property;[119] under current doctrine the clause would thus protect the allocation of burdens and the distribution of benefits to which there is an entitlement created by state or federal law.[120] The general substantive requirement of the due process clause,[121] demands non-arbitrary and non-capricious action: the government's choice must bear "a rational relation to a constitutionally permissable objective."[122] The citizen disadvantaged by an allocation by lot can complain correctly that the decision to include or exclude him was arbitrary. Once more the government's response must be that its choice of this method of allocation is rational and defensible, since any other plan of distribution would be more arbitrary.

---

118 The lottery makes the entire pool potentially subject to a governmental action. It is an important change from a conventional classification system because it puts more people in the pool, selecting from them by lot, rather than limiting the applicability of the action through classification. Therefore, it would seem to advance the interests with which Justice Jackson identified the equal protection clause. Cf. Rawls, *A Theory of Justice*, 118-192, especially 130-150. Rawls identifies as "principles of justice" those which would be selected by free and rational people with no knowledge of their natural capacities, their position in life, or the nature of the society whose rules they are to make — behind what Rawls calls a "veil of ignorance." One result of this "original position" would be that all the principles adopted are selected despite the fact that they may be applied to the disadvantage of those who create them.

119 U.S. Constitution, Amendments V & XIV.

120 See, e.g., *Bishop v. Wood*, 96 S. Ct. 2074 (1976) (no statutory entitlement to job as a policeman); *Arnett v. Kennedy*, 416 U.S. 134 (1974) (plurality opinion) (right to government job plus denial of procedures equals no right); *Perry v. Sinderman*, 408 U.S. 593 (1972) (officially fostered common understanding ensured due process protection for a professor's tenure despite lack of a contractual right); *Board of Regents v. Roth*, 408 U.S. 564 (1972) (no due process protection for a professor whose one year contract was not renewed). When there is no right to a government benefit, then, a plaintiff cannot raise a due process attack when it is denied (*Bishop v. Wood*), even though the good may be extremely important. Cf. *San Antonio Indep. School Dist. v. Rodriguez*, 411 U.S. I (1973) (a decent education is not a fundamental interest under equal protection clause); *Dandridge v. Williams*, 397 U.S. 471 (1970) (no constitutional right to welfare payments). It is unlikely that a government which faces allocation of a scarce good would create a statutory entitlement to it, since by definition the needs of all citizens cannot be satisfied.

121 Substantive due process attacks could be raised against any particular allocation; for example, see the discussion of procreation licensing at pp. 78–81 and n. 108. The discussion in text only treats the objections attaching to any allocation by lot.

122 See, e.g., *Ferguson v. Skrupa*, 372 U.S. 726, 733 (1963) (Harlan, J., concurring).

Procedural due process requires that citizens be given a hearing or statement of reasons for a deprivation of liberty or property.[123] The substantive content of the required hearing is the facts legislatively prescribed as relevant.[124] Accordingly, if the procedures used for determining the pool are fair and the lottery was honest, procedural due process should be satisfied. The factors to be considered in a hearing in the context of random selection are (1) inclusion or exclusion from the pool and (2) the statistical fairness of the lottery. Considering the actual selection of the recipients of goods is useless because by definition no reasons can be given. Allocation by random selection precludes notions of traditional procedural due process at the selection of recipients stage.

A fundamental due process objection remains, however, when the burdened or excluded citizen asks, "Why me?" Without advancing a traditional substantive or procedural argument, this citizen can object that despite the rationality of the overall process and the guarantee of procedures at stages other than actual selection, the lottery should not be applied to him. Professor Tribe labeled this third methodology "structural due process,"[125] which requires that governmental decisions about which there is deep moral and social disagreement must be made by an individualized determination.[126] The challenge is to the use of an otherwise rational policy as applied to a burdened individual. In essence, the citizen making this argument demands that a lottery cannot be used with respect to him, that merit or need criteria, or his greater purchasing power, or his greater ability to wait entitle him constitutionally to the good to be allocated. A satisfactory response to this developing doctrine, which has yet to receive explicit judicial recognition,[127] is difficult at this stage of theorizing.

Traditional constitutional objections to the use of a lottery can thus be successfully answered. Closer questions would be raised in the factual context of the specific use of a lottery and the developing doctrine of structural due process. These provisions may impose constitutional limits, and

---

123 See generally *Goss v. Lopez*, 419 U.S. 565 (1975); *Goldberg v. Kelley*, 397 U.S. 254 (1970); "Specifying the Procedures Required by Due Process: Toward Limits on the Use of Interest Balancing," *Harvard Law Review* 88 (1975).

124 See Paul M. Bator; Paul J. Mishkin; David L. Shapiro; and Herbert Wechsler, *Hart and Wechsler's The Federal Courts and the Federal System*, 2nd ed. (Mineola, NY: Foundation Press, 1973) 330-360 (Professor Hart's "Dialogue").

125 See generally Tribe, "Structural Due Process."

126 Tribe, "Structural Due Process," 307. This notion that burden can be imposed only after an individualized determination precludes the use of random selection in the criminal law. See *Woodson v. North Carolina*, 96 S.Ct. 2978 (1976) (death penalty can only be imposed after an individual determination). See also *San Francisco Chronicle*, Nov. 9. 1976. § 1. at 2. col. 1 (Louisiana Supreme Court disciplines a municipal judge who, inter alia, flipped coins to determine guilt or innocence).

127 But cf. *Woodson v. North Carolina*, 96 S.Ct. 2978 (1976) (death penalty can only be imposed after an individualized determination).

should certainly spark doctrinal developments when applied to the use of random selection for allocation of governmental goods.

Conclusion

When equal distribution of governmental benefits or burdens is impossible, impersonal and value-free decision-making to further equality of opportunity may be the fairest goal. In allocative situations, distributions by merit, money, or patience criteria stress goals conflicting with the norm of equality. Random selection is often the best, or least objectionable, alternative method of allocation, and its use as a distributive device should be considered more often.

The lottery abandons substantive goals that are difficult to reach or choose between, withdrawing active allocations from government decision-makers. Yet random selection is not an abdication to irrationality and amorality; it is neither irrational to recognize the limits of reason, discretion, and judgment, nor is it amoral for a democracy to reaffirm its commitment to human equality.[128]

---

128 The author wishes to thank Professors Bruce Ackerman and Owen Fiss for their assistance.

George Sher[1]

What Makes a Lottery Fair?

It is generally agreed that when two or more people have equal claims to a good that cannot be divided among them, the morally preferable way of allocating that good is through a tie-breaking device, or *lottery*, which is fair. Intuitively, we have little difficulty recognizing which lotteries are fair. Tossing ordinary coins, drawing straws, and picking numbers from one to ten are all clearly fair, whereas awarding goods on the basis of personal preference, of flips of "loaded" coins, or of racial or religious characteristics, are generally not. However, the principle behind these intuitions is not nearly as clear as the intuitions themselves. When one is asked about this principle, one is apt to reply that a lottery is fair provided that it affords each claimant an equal chance of obtaining the contested good; but this is helpful only to the extent that the relevant notion of equal chances can then be specified in its turn. Failing such specification, it will not be clear why lotteries based on personal preference or racial characteristics do not afford *their* entrants equal chances; and neither, conversely, will it be clear how coin tosses or straw drawings can offer genuine chances to any but their eventual winners. In this paper, I shall try to develop an adequate account of the principle that underlies our intuitions about fair lotteries. This will involve asking (a) exactly what conditions are necessary and sufficient for a lottery to be fair, and (b) why it should be morally preferable to allocate indivisible contested goods through lotteries which satisfy these conditions.

I

Suppose that n, o, and p are persons with equal claims to a good G, and that G cannot be divided among them. If any member of this group is to have G, then someone will have to institute a lottery L to determine who it will be. Assuming that m is entitled to institute the required lottery (and waiving the interesting question of how m acquires this entitlement) let us begin by

1   Originally published on pages 203-216 of *Noûs* 14 (1980). Copyright © 1980 *Noûs* Publications. Reproduced with permission of Blackwell Publishing Ltd.

asking what determines whether the lottery established by m is fair. We have seen that L's fairness depends on its affording all claimants an equal chance; but what exactly does it mean to say that L affords equal chances in this context?

A first possible way of interpreting "equal chances" here is to say that L affords such chances if and only if its outcome is not at all fixed in advance. Because the crucial procedure's outcome is not predetermined, the identity of the winning entry will be simply a matter of luck. This interpretation has the virtue of reflecting the common belief that in a fair lottery, the outcome rests on "the luck of the draw." Nevertheless, despite its familiarity, the proposed interpretation of "equal chances" could not possibly explicate our intuitive notion of fairness. If a lottery's fairness did depend on its outcome not being predetermined, then *all* lotteries would be unfair if determinism were true. In fact, however, the truth of determinism would simply not imply that coin-tosses, straw-drawings, and all similar devices are unfair.

In light of this difficulty, a different interpretation of "affording equal chances" is plainly called for. Because the notions of chance and probability are so closely connected, the obvious next move is to say that n, o, and p have equal chances of winning if and only if the probability of winning is equal for each. Moreover, because the events whose probability is at issue are single occurrences, the most natural way to interpret probability here is in terms of degrees of confirmation by available evidence.[2] If we do interpret probability in this way, then our proposal will become

P1:   A lottery L held at t is fair if and only if the hypotheses that the different claimants will win are all equally well confirmed by the totality of evidence available at t.

Because it construes a lottery's fairness as relative to what is known when the lottery is held, P1 implies that the fairness of a particular type of lottery may change as our state of knowledge increases. That this is so is confirmed by the intuition that an ordinary coin-flip would cease to be fair if the person calling it became able to predict its outcome from a set of causal laws and statements of antecedent conditions.[3]

---

2   For a comprehensive elaboration of this logical conception of probability, see Rudolf Carnap, *Logical Foundations of Probability* (Chicago: University of Chicago Press, 1950).

3   Although P1 has been couched in terms of the logical rather than the frequency approach to probability, nothing important rests on this choice. A frequentist who is willing to countenance single-case probabilities can formulate an analogous principle by saying that a lottery is fair if and only if each entrant would win equally frequently in an indefinitely long sequence of trials. Since Reichenbach has shown that single-case probability estimates lead to difficulty if they are not relativized to the narrowest known reference class, the relationship between a lottery's fairness and what is known when it is held would on this account be captured by the fact that the hypothetical sequence in question must incorporate all the features of L about which statistics are known at t. For discussion of Reichenbach's rule in particular, and the frequentist

P1 is clearly a step in the right direction. Nevertheless, a closer look reveals that it requires modification in at least two ways. An immediate difficulty with P1 is that it does not specify which persons must know at t that the entrants' probabilities of victory are equal. Because it is silent on this point, P1 implies that a lottery may be rendered unfair even by the foreknowledge of someone whose interest in the situation is merely academic, and who does not intend to communicate his predictions to anyone. However, this seems highly counterintuitive. We are not inclined to say that an otherwise fair lottery is rendered unfair by the mere existence of a hidden Laplacian calculator who does not plan to publish his predictions. To avoid such judgments of unfairness, we must modify P1 so that it applies only to certain relevant persons. These persons will include those responsible for deciding which lottery is to be held, and also those whose choices (of particular straws, heads or tails, etc.) will determine the chosen lottery's outcome. Since the feature common to all these persons is that each can at some moment affect the contested good's allocation, the natural way of restricting P1 is to make it apply only to those persons who exercise *control* over L's outcome at a given moment.[4]

A second difficulty with P1 is raised by a lottery whose controlling parties know *nothing* about the entrants' respective probabilities of victory. To illustrate this difficulty, let us imagine that n, o, and p are all about to undergo surgery, and that m, knowing nothing about their medical histories, decrees that G will be awarded to whichever claimant has some physical characteristic (say, the smallest liver) which will be discovered during the surgery. Although this lottery is somewhat bizarre, it does not intuitively seem unfair. However, it is unclear whether m's ignorance warrants any conclusion about the entrants' respective probabilities of victory, and so it is *a fortiori* unclear whether the lottery satisfies P1. m *will* be warranted in believing that the entrants are equally likely to win if he is permitted to invoke the principle of indifference; but since this principle is widely held to be suspect, we will do better to reformulate P1 in a way which makes an appeal to it unnecessary. To accomplish this, we must replace P1's positive evidential requirement with something a bit weaker. Instead of demanding that the controlling parties must *have* evidence that the entrants' probabilities of victory *are* equal, we must require only that the controlling parties *lack* evidence that the entrants' probabilities of victory are *not* equal.

When both of the suggested modifications are incorporated into P1, the result is

---

approach in general, see Hans Reichenbach, *The Theory of Probability* (Berkeley: University of California Press, 1949).

4   For a useful discussion of the various ways in which control can be exercised, see Nicholas Rescher, "The Concept of Control," in *Essays in Philosophical Analysis* (Pittsburgh: University of Pittsburgh Press, 1969).

P2:   A lottery L is fair if and only if, for every time t and every person q
      with control over L at t, there is nothing which q knows at t which
      confirms the hypothesis that one claimant will win any more highly
      than it confirms the hypothesis that any other claimant will win.

Since P2 has been arrived at through successive refinements of the
notion of equal chances, it expresses clearly the suggestion that fair lotteries are just those which offer all their entrants an equal chance of winning.
However, once this suggestion is clarified, it is readily seen to be false.
Although P1's conditions are indeed (roughly) necessary for fairness, they
fall far short of sufficiency; there are many lotteries which do afford equal
chances in the way specified by P2, but which nevertheless remain clearly
unfair. As one example of this, we may imagine a case in which n, o, and p
are persons of unknown racial and religious backgrounds, and in which m
decrees that G will be awarded to whichever one of them is discovered,
through a genealogical search, to have the fewest Jewish ancestors.
Although this lottery conforms to our amended P2 and is formally analogous to the smallest liver lottery just sketched, it raises intuitions of unfairness as the previous lottery did not. Moreover, similar intuitions are also
raised when we imagine m to decree that the contested good will be
awarded to whichever entrant turns out to belong to the highest (or lowest) social class, to be the most intelligent, or to be the most attractive. If
these intuitions are to be accommodated, then some further restriction on
P2 will obviously be required.

   What is most immediately striking about the unfair lotteries just
described is that their victory criteria all involve characteristics which significant segments of society hold to be either positive or negative in value.
Because this is so, the most obvious way of ruling them out is to augment
P2 with a clause prohibiting lotteries with victory criteria involving such
characteristics. In fact, however, we cannot simply rule out all such lotteries; for there would be nothing unfair about a lottery in which (a) each
entrant designated some proxy about whose racial background he was
ignorant, and (b) G was then awarded to the entrant whose proxy turned
out to have the fewest Jewish ancestors. To complete our account, we must
establish why this proxy Jewish ancestor lottery is fair while the original
Jewish ancestor lottery is not.

   The answer to this question is not difficult to discover. Although both
Jewish ancestor lotteries have victory criteria which involve characteristics which are value-laden, the mode of involvement is radically different
in the two cases. In the case of the original Jewish ancestor lottery, any person who satisfies the relevant victory criterion must himself possess the
associated value-laden characteristic; while in the case of the proxy Jewish
ancestor lottery, nothing like this is true. Taking our cue from this, let us
distinguish between those value-laden victory criteria whose satisfaction

does imply the possession of the associated value-laden characteristic (call these *primarily* value-laden victory criteria) and those others whose satisfaction does not imply this (call these *secondarily* value-laden victory criteria). Besides "being the claimant with the fewest Jewish ancestors," the class of primarily value-laden victory criteria will also include such specimens as "being the claimant whose mother and father have the fewest Jewish ancestors" and "being the claimant with the fewest ancestors who observed the Jewish laws." Of these further criteria, the first guarantees the possession of a value-laden characteristic via an analytic connection, while the second implies the possession of such a characteristic via a well-known empirical generalization. Given the distinction between primarily and secondarily value-laden victory criteria, the way we must modify P2 to rule out the original Jewish ancestor lottery is clear. What we must add is simply that no fair lottery can have a victory criterion which is primarily value-laden.[5]

When this final modification is incorporated into P2, what we get is

P3: A lottery L is fair if and only if

(a) For every time *t* and every person *q* with control over L at *t*, there is nothing which *q* knows at *t* which confirms the hypothesis that one claimant will win any more highly than it confirms the hypothesis that any other claimant will win; and

(b) *L*'s victory criterion is not primarily value-laden.

Unlike our earlier attempts, P3 does specify conditions which, at least for the most part, are satisfied by just those lotteries we intuitively consider fair. In this respect, P3 constitutes a major advance in our discussion. Nevertheless, P3 still remains deficient in at least two ways. First, its requirements for fairness are not related in any obvious manner. There is little apparent connection between P3a's strictures on knowledge and P3b's restrictions on admissible victory criteria, and so P3 leaves unexplained the unity which our notion of fairness appears to possess. Furthermore, and even more damaging, P3's requirements for fairness are not airtight. There are, as we shall see, a number of odd cases which violate P3 without any intuitive loss of fairness, and these must somehow be accommodated if our account is to stand. In the next section, both of these difficulties will be explored. They are, of course, not unrelated.

---

5 An interesting test case for this addition is the practice of awarding indivisible inheritances to the first-born. Thomas Hobbes, *Leviathan* (New York: Collier Books, 1962), 121, considers this practice to be an acceptable form of lottery; but I suspect many readers will disagree. Some of our intuitions of its unfairness may stem from the facts that few inheritances are genuinely indivisible, and that primogeniture was often restricted to males. However, a further source of unfairness may well be the value that has traditionally been attached to the property of being born first.

II

To see that P3 is not airtight, consider the following anomalous cases:

(1)   *m* knows in advance that lottery *L* will lead to *n*'s victory; but *m* has no special preference for this outcome. *m* does select *L*, but he does so on some basis which is totally independent of, and unaffected by, his foreknowledge of *n*'s victory.

(2)   *m* knows in advance that *L* will lead to *n*'s victory, and *m* does want *n* to win. However, *m* uprightly and successfully refuses to let his desires determine his decisions on such matters. Thus, *m* chooses *L* on some basis which is totally distinct from his preference for *n*.

(3)   *m* has no racial or religious preferences at all. However, for entirely independent reasons, he decrees that *G* will be awarded to whichever claimant turns out to have the fewest Jewish ancestors.

(4)   *m* is biased against Jews, and promulgates a lottery whose victory criterion does in fact imply non-Jewishness. However, *m* is unaware of this implication, and selects the lottery on other grounds entirely.

(5)   *m* is biased against Jews, and so decides to award *G* to whichever claimant has the fewest Jewish ancestors. Since claimants *n*, *o*, and *p* all share *m*'s bias, they all willingly acquiesce in his decision.

Of the lotteries just described, (1) and (2) violate P3's first clause, while, (3), (4), and (5) violate its second. However, none of them is intuitively unfair. By discovering why these violations of P3 are not unfair, we may hope to deepen our understanding of what it is for a lottery to be fair.

Let us begin by considering counterexamples (1) and (2). These lotteries both have outcomes foreseen by controlling parties; and yet neither lottery is unfair. Because this is so, it cannot be merely the controlling parties' foreknowledge which is responsible for the unfairness of most violations of P2a. Instead, the operative factor must be something which usually accompanies foreknowledge, but is strictly distinct from it. Given the fairness of (1) and (2), this further factor is not hard to find. The salient fact about (1) and (2) is that although their initiators do know the crucial procedures' outcomes, they do not use this knowledge to guide them in their choice of lotteries. Unlike most predictable lotteries, (1) and (2) are not instituted with the aim of awarding the contested good to any claimant whom a controlling party happens to favor. Since this is so, it must be not the controlling parties' foreknowledge, but rather their use of that foreknowledge to channel goods to favored claimants, which really renders most predictable lotteries unfair. Strictly speaking, foreknowledge is not a sufficient condition for unfairness at all, but rather is a necessary condition for, and a reliable sign of, a further condition — manipulation to favor a preferred claimant — which is genuinely sufficient for unfairness in its turn. In light of these considerations, P2's first clause must plainly be recast. Properly expressed, this clause must assert not that it is the controlling parties' foreknowledge, but rather that it is the meshing of this foreknowledge with the controlling parties' preferences to guide their actions, which really determines a lottery's unfairness.

This reorientation of P2's first clause naturally suggests a corresponding reorientation of its second as well. P3's second clause rules out primarily value-laden descriptions as victory criteria for fair lotteries. Since the pertinent values are those of the controlling party's society, and since someone who values a given characteristic will ceteris paribus prefer to award goods to the type of person who has it, P3's second clause in effect makes it unfair for controlling parties to award contested goods to any of the types of claimants they are most likely to favor. Because this is so, we can bring P3a into line with P3b by saying that just as most violations of P3a are unfair because they are intended to award goods to individuals favored by controlling parties, so too are most violations of P3b unfair because they are intended to award goods to types of individuals favored by controlling parties.[6] If this suggestion can be defended, then the underlying conception of fairness in lotteries will indeed be a unified one. In the last analysis, a lottery will be fair if and only if those who control it have not exercised their power in any of the ways they prefer.

The proposed revision of P3b is easily seen to be confirmed by counterexamples (3) and (4). Of these counterexamples, (3) is a racial lottery whose initiator lacks racial preference, while (4) is a racial lottery whose initiator is biased but unaware that his victory criterion is primarily racial. If value-laden victory criteria are themselves sufficient for unfairness, then the fairness of these lotteries will be hopelessly anomalous. However, their fairness will make good sense if what determines a lottery's unfairness is not simply the value usually attached to its victory criterion, but rather the intention with which the person initiating it has *adopted* that criterion. If the real determinant of unfairness is a controlling party's effective aim of awarding the contested good to a preferred type of claimant, then (3)'s fairness will be a straightforward consequence of the fact that m has no preference for claimants of the chosen race; while (4)'s

---

6 Of course, any lottery is intended to award its contested good to one type of claimant — namely, the type of claimant who wins. However, this intention cannot reflect the initiator's independent preference, since the "type" in question cannot be fully specified without mentioning the lottery itself. In what follows, such trivial "types" should be understood as excluded from consideration.

fairness will follow just as naturally from the fact that m's racial preference is not effective in determining his choice of what is in fact a racial lottery.

Given the ease with which the revised P3b explains these counterexamples, there is clearly a strong case for the view that a lottery is fair if and only if no one has exercised control over it in any of the ways he prefers. However, before we can accept this view, we must deal with a problem that is raised by our final counterexample, (5). This counterexample, we recall, is a racial lottery which is agreed to by a set of claimants whose racial preferences coincide. Like the other counterexamples, (5) is fair even though it violates P3. However, unlike the other counterexamples, (5) *is* chosen with the aim of aiding a favored type of claimant, and so violates our new conditions for fairness as well as the older conditions they replace. Because this is so, and because the new conditions are clearly superior on other grounds, the best way of accommodating (5) is through an appropriate restriction on the new conditions' scope. The exact strength of this restriction is not immediately obvious; for it is not entirely clear whether (5)'s fairness is due to (i) the fact that its victory criterion is *agreed to* by all claimants, or (ii) the fact that m *knows* that his preference accords with those of all the claimants, or (iii) the fact that m's preference *just does* accord with those of all the claimants. To decide among these alternatives, we must imagine two further variations of (5), the first of which satisfies only (ii) and (iii), and the second of which satisfies only (iii). Our intuitions about these further lotteries may be somewhat hazy; but I do not think we would consider either of them unfair. If this is so, however, then only the weakest of the three possible restrictions on our new principle would be called for. Properly amended, that principle will state that any lottery initiated to aid a preferred claimant or type of claimant is unfair *unless its initiator's preference is shared by all the claimants involved*.

This concludes our discussion of the counterexamples to P3. The outcome of that discussion is that our intuitions about these counterexamples all fall into place once we suppose that a lottery is fair if and only if no one has exercised his control over it in any way that he, but not all the claimants, prefers.[7] More precisely, our intuitions about the counterexamples fall into place once we reject P3 and accept in its stead

P4: A lottery L is fair if and only if there is no person q such that

---

[7] It has been suggested to me that there is one further counterexample which may resist such treatment. This is a case in which m does not know in advance who will win in L, but claimant n foresees that he will lose, and so declines to participate. If m initiates L over n's objections, then there may be some temptation to view the lottery as unfair to n even though m has not initiated it to further his own aims. However, if n is permitted to exercise a veto on the basis of his foresight, then the choice of any alternative lottery may seem unfair to those claimants who lack n's gift. In light of this, I am inclined to view the lottery in question as not unfair, but rather merely as a case in which one of the losers knows his fate a bit sooner than the others.

(a) q desires that L's contested good be awarded to a particular claimant or type of claimant, and

(b) q's desire is not shared by all the claimants to L's contested good, and

(c) q knows that his performing an action of type A will increase the probability of his desires being satisfied, and

(d) q performs an action of type A on the basis of this desire and the belief-component of this item of knowledge.

Setting aside certain well-known difficulties with "know" and "on the basis of" (which are standard problems of epistemology and action theory, and so need not be decided here), P4's conditions for fairness are not open to any further counterexamples that I can envision. Furthermore, P4's clauses bring together, in an extremely natural way, all the disparate elements of our previous discussion. Of these clauses, (a) brings out the underlying unity of P3's seemingly disjoint requirements by stressing the continuity between the different desires which they in effect proscribe. (b) incorporates the refinement, brought to light by counterexample (5), that such desires are pernicious only insofar as they are not shared by all the claimants to the contested good. (c) captures a basic insight of section I, that fairness in lotteries has an ineliminably epistemic component; and (d) connects knowledge and desire by specifying a relationship in which each plays an essential role. Taken together, (a)-(d) fuse all the earlier strands of our discussion into a single natural whole. These considerations strongly suggest that P4's conditions for fairness are the correct ones; and I shall hereafter accept them as such.

III

Having clarified the conditions under which a lottery is intuitively said to be fair, we may now turn to the moral grounding of the intuitions we have regimented. Granted that all and only those lotteries which satisfy P4 are fair, it may still be wondered why it is morally preferable to *use* such lotteries to allocate indivisible goods to which several persons have equal claims. Since fair procedures are ceteris paribus definitionally preferable to unfair ones, there may be a minimal sense in which P4 itself provides a reason for adopting the sorts of lotteries it describes. Nevertheless, the moral preferability of these lotteries would obviously be grounded more deeply if it could be deduced from other, more general moral considerations. To complete our discussion, we must now ask whether any such deeper derivation of P4 is possible.

To see why it is morally preferable to use lotteries conforming to P4 to allocate indivisible goods to which several persons have equal claims, let us begin by examining the assertion that someone has a (strongest) claim to a good. It is no part of our concept of strongest claims to goods that a person with such a claim is entitled to delegate the relevant good as he prefers. Many claims to goods, such as claims to jobs or admission to competitive institutions, are non-transferrable. It is part of our concept of strongest claims to goods, however, that when someone has such a claim, no one else is entitled to enjoy or dispose of the relevant good as he alone prefers. If n has the strongest claim to G, then any other person who either arrogates G to himself or delegates it to another on the basis of preference different from n's is *ipso facto* infringing on n's rightful claim to it. Given this conceptual truth, the rationale for ruling out the allocation of contested goods on the basis of personal preference should not be hard to see.

For suppose, again, that n, o, and p all do have equal (strongest) claims to an indivisible good G. In this case, all but one of their claims to G will have to be cancelled or overridden if any claim to G is legitimately to be satisfied. It is extremely difficult to specify the exact circumstances under which, or the mechanism through which, such claims are legitimately cancelled;[8] but what we can say with confidence is that the strength and equality of the initial claims impose severe limits on the permissible ways in which this can be done. More specifically, since it is part of the concept of claims to goods that no one without the strongest claim to G may delegate G as he pleases, the mere fact that n, o, and p share strongest claims to G must itself entail that no person different from them can legitimately take any step aimed at awarding G to a person or type of person whom he, but not all the claimants, favors. Any non-claimant who took such a step — including the step of advancing a lottery with this aim — would *ipso facto* violate at least some claimant's strongest equal claim to G. Furthermore, given the equality of their claims, it also follows that no member of n, o, and p may *himself* take any step towards directing G to a person or type of person whom he, but not all the others, favors. Any claimant who took such a step — including again the step of advancing a lottery with this aim — would necessarily violate the others' equal claims by attempting to impose his preferences on them. Taken together, these considerations entail that no person at all may legitimately advance any lottery with the

---

8   If it could be shown that claimants concerned to maximize their legitimate access to goods could only gain from the implementation of fair lotteries, it might be possible to explain how such lotteries eliminate claims by invoking the fact that all the claimants either have consented to them or would consent if they were rational. See Thomas Nagel, "Rawls on Justice," in *Reading Rawls*, ed. Norman Daniels (New York: Basic Books, 1974), 5-6. However, it is simply false that all claimants concerned to maximize their legitimate access to goods can only gain from the implementation of fair lotteries. We can easily imagine a situation in which n and o have equal strongest claims to G, but in which getting G is of less value to n than is o's failing to get G. In such a case, it would be irrational for n to consent to a fair lottery; and yet such a lottery, if held, would still eliminate all but one strongest claim to G. In light of these considerations, I suspect that a satisfactory explanation of the binding force of fair lotteries must await the construction of a full theory of the grounding of obligations.

purpose of awarding the contested good to a person or type of person whom he, but not all the claimants, favors. This conclusion, however, is identical to the principle whose grounding we have been trying to understand. Since this is so, our account leaves little mystery about the moral preferability of fair lotteries. Given the conditions for fairness we have sketched, the moral preferability of using fair lotteries to allocate indivisible contested goods is merely an analytical consequence of the lottery situation itself.

Although this derivation of the moral preferability of fair lotteries seems adequate for the range of cases we have considered, it may be wondered whether this range has been quite broad enough. Our discussion to this point has focused entirely on lotteries whose purpose is to allocate indivisible *goods*. There are, however, also cases in which lotteries are called for to allocate indivisible *burdens*. One example of a burden that may best be allocated in this way is the burden of military service. Since our account has derived the demand for fair lotteries from the concept of claims to goods, it may seem unable to account for the demand for fairness in lotteries which distribute burdens rather than goods. To suppose this, however, would be to overlook the internal connection between the concepts of burdens and goods. If B is a burden for n, then escaping from B is necessarily a good for him. Moreover, the mere fact that there is a moral problem about allocating a burden among a group of people implies that each of them has an equal claim not to bear that burden. Given these facts, there should be little difficulty in extending our account to explain the demand for fairness in lotteries distributing burdens. To do this, we need only view such lotteries as devices for distributing the goods of avoiding these burdens.[9]

9   I have benefitted from discussions of this topic with Steven Cahn, Patricia Kitcher, Michael Levin, William Mann, and Alan Wertheimer. I owe a special debt to Philip Kitcher, whose many helpful suggestions have greatly improved the final product.

Barbara Goodwin[1]

Justice and the Lottery

> But some things there be, that can neither be divided, nor enjoyed in common. Then, The Law of Nature, which prescribeth Equity, requireth *That the Entire Right; or else, (making the use alternate,) the First Possession, be determined by Lot.* For equall distribution, is of the Law of Nature; and other means of equall distribution cannot be imagined. *Of Lots,* there be two sorts. *Arbitrary,* and *Naturall.* Arbitrary, is that which is agreed on by the Competitors: Naturall, is either *Primogeniture* or *First Seisure.*[2]

> I come from a dizzy land where the lottery is the basis of reality.[3]

The place is ancient Babylon. The writer is Borges. His sinister, allusive story recounts how life in Babylon came to be totally ruled by the drawings of a mysterious lottery run by the equally mysterious, possibly apocryphal, "Company." At first, the lottery was merely an ordinary, mercenary game run by merchants, open only to those rich enough to gamble. In the course of time it became predictable and therefore boring and unpopular — until the organizers started to interpolate a few unfavourable tickets among the winning tickets: these decreed fines to be paid by those who drew them. As a result, the game's popularity was much enhanced: losers with penalty tickets cheated the lottery by refusing to pay and some were jailed for this refusal. Soon, the unfavourable tickets simply stipulated jail sentences, not fines. The organizers were by now known as "the Company."

At this point the plebeians of Babylon, deprived of the seductive uncertainties of the game, in which they could not afford to take part, revolted, demanding to be allowed to participate. This "caused the Company to accept total power" — at the people's request. The lottery became "secret, free and general" and "every free man automatically participated in the

1 Originally published on pp. 190-202 of *Political Studies* 32 (1984). Copyright © 1984 *Political Studies*. Reproduced with permission from Blackwell Publishing Ltd.
2 T. Hobbes, *Leviathan* ed. C.B. MacPherson (Harmondsworth, Penguin, 1968), 212-213.
3 J. L. Borges, "The Lottery in Babylon," in *Labyrinths* (Harmondsworth, Penguin, 1970), 55. All other quotations from Borges are from this story.

sacred drawings every sixty nights which determined his destiny until the next drawing." Both social roles and individual actions and other, "impersonal" events, were now determined by lot. In other words, the entire life of Babylon was regulated by the lottery. "At times, one single fact—the vulgar murder of C., the mysterious apotheosis of B.—was the happy solution of thirty or forty drawings." Further modifications were introduced to intensify chance: the result of one draw could be amended or negated by further draws. "No decision is final, all branch into others." That is the story—but finally the narrator, alias Borges, discusses the nature of chance itself, which dictates that spurious accidents and errors should be interpolated into events seemingly determined by the lottery; errors have been introduced even into the narrative. The role of the omnipotent Company, about which there are as many theories as there are about the nature of God, is also discussed—inconclusively, of course, for chance offers no conclusions.

Borges's very short story calls into question all our metaphysical certainties about causality, self-identity and divinity. It satirizes the reality which we like to think of as ordered by showing the infinite, ramifying network of chance events which bring about, among many others, those few events which we choose to consider significant. Consequently, it can be read as a satire on religious faith and/or on our mental structuring of the world which raises the most profound questions about free will and determination and their relation to chance. However, I want to use this equivocal allegory as a framework within which to reconsider ideas of justice and, in particular, that which prevails in our own liberal society, even though this approach can hardly avoid entanglement with questions of wider significance.

Chance and causality are often misleadingly contrasted. In Western usage, at least, chance implies chaos and unpredictability or (with respect to human action) a lack of purpose, while a caused or determined system is one of which, in principle if not in practice, we can explain the operations by reference to general rules or laws. However, this contrast is too superficial. In Babylon, despite the hegemony of chance, there *is* causality, for every chance draw determines people's actions. In a sense, then, it can be regarded as a fully determined system which, however, has a chance primary cause, that is, the lottery and no evident purpose. (It is not revealed whether the Company's "decisions" are indeed random or whether they follow some unknown blueprint and implement the Company's private purposes. But from the Babylonians' viewpoint they represent pure chance. I will also assume this, and leave aside the intriguing question of what "the Company" may signify.)

Borges portrays a system which, paradoxically, while resting on chance, is *ordered*, because chance is interpolated with delicious regularity. One result, paradoxical for us, is that the intrusion of acts of free will would be arbitrary and anarchic, and disruptive to the system. However, the Babylonians are not devoid of free will. They follow the lottery *of their own free will*; it does not determine their behaviour in the sense that the behaviour of robots is determined. In fact, their conduct is not significantly different from the rule following behaviour of people in other societies, but the rules that they follow are different. This is important in considering whether such a society could be called a just society.

First I shall contrast the institutions of Babylon with those that liberals believe to be just and then I shall discuss whether Borges's Babylon could, in a different sense, be called a just society. Finally, I will consider how the lottery principle might be incorporated in a new theory of justice.

I. Liberal Justice

It is instructive to examine the role that chance plays in a liberal, welfare-capitalist system such as our own, and how it relates to social justice. According to modern liberal doctrine, the basis of just distribution is an amalgam of the guaranteed satisfaction of minimum needs (through the welfare system) plus the allocation of rewards according to merit, in conditions of approximate equality of opportunity and competition. Liberal ideology rests on the assumption that there are natural inequalities between people, inequalities of endowment, of talent and of energy ("inequalities of desert and contribution") and that society is flexible, and structures itself to reflect and take account of these. Those with outstanding talents will, quite justly, create elevated and lucrative positions for themselves. Each individual can differentiate him/herself from others and advance beyond them, in terms of material and other goods, according to his/her achievements. It is further assumed that if the distribution of talents changes, or contributions increase, the flexible social structure and pattern of distributions will change to accommodate this fairly; productivity agreements exemplify this hope. (But we should also note, for example, the glut of unemployed graduates 20 years after the Robbins Report which led to the expansion of British universities — the system is not, after all, so accommodating). Major goods must be distributed according to merit, by due process — impartially, and treating like cases alike. Chance allocation, by contrast, is a random and arbitrary allocation of goods, according to no specifiable or justifiable criteria. The only things that liberal theory admits can properly and justly be distributed by chance are minor goods such as raffle prizes: otherwise, merit must rule.

However, the problem for liberalism is that the biggest chance distribution of all takes place when we are born and is beyond our control — the distribution of health, beauty, intelligence and other natural endowments. In societies where a strong class system operates, social status can also be regarded as a "natural" endowment. Under these circumstances, a merit-based system of social justice tends merely to reinforce natural advantages or disadvantages. The adoption of welfare measures by liberal societies in this century took place precisely and explicitly to negate these uncontrollable manifestations of chance occurring at birth which, if allowed to operate unmitigated, would make a system based solely on competition and merit unjust. Thus, in theory at least, policies for producing equality of opportunity make everyone equally capable of benefiting via the system of reward. The assumption underlying all this is that social positions and distributions are essentially not given or fixed, but man-made.

Borges's story, by contrast, presumes that society consists of certain fixed or given roles into which individuals—mere ciphers, subjects of chance—are slotted. There will always be a condemned man—no need that whoever draws this lot should have qualified for the role by responsibility and guilt. Likewise, in Babylon, there will always be the slave—no need that he should have deserved his status, as long as someone fills the position. Absurd? I think not. I would argue that Babylon is structured like all other societies. In every society certain functions must be performed, primarily to maintain the social system, functions such as leadership and arbitration. From this perspective individuals are of secondary importance, even if the social system is justified as being, ultimately, for the good of the individuals. The allegory demonstrates that in Babylon, certain functional roles exist—the priest, the merchant, the criminal—and that it matters little who fills them. No special credentials are needed, the social machine runs on. This challenges the liberal conviction, or delusion, that social roles and institutions are determined by the operations of free will, talent and ingenuity, and that society is flexible, and mobility possible. Borges's assumption to the contrary may offend our beliefs on this score, but his account is not unrealistic. Individuals born into any society are indeed confronted by structures and roles which seem preordained, into which they must fit themselves, to which they must adapt.

In the allegory, then, the idea of a society flexibly structured according to individual merits and achievements, is rejected; Borges offers instead a model of a seemingly traditional society of just the kind which liberal ideology was developed to undermine, that is, a feudal, hierarchical, theocratic society. But there is a crucial difference, namely, the regular interpolation of chance in the allocation of roles so that nobody is condemned or enfranchised to inhabit one level of the hierarchy indefinitely. In fact, the allegory contains a fatalistic insight about the persisting necessity for certain elements in *any* social structure, which undermines key elements of liberal theory concerning the nature of society and justice. Equally, it threatens the egalitarian axioms of socialism. This is not an

insight which I particularly like; however, it has an important consequence for any conception of justice. This can be simply stated: if the structure of society is partly or wholly determined in certain respects and
necessarily entails inequalities (i.e. different roles with different intrinsic
values and/or different rewards attached to them), and if people are *more*
equal than are the roles (i.e. roles and rewards are highly differentiated,
people less so) injustice will result from any once-for-all distribution. In
such a case, justice lies in a repeated chance allocation and re-allocation of
individuals to the various roles with their concomitant rewards. This
injunction takes into account people's desires and talents which, as
Hobbes argued, might be considered approximately equal (especially
desires) and dictates that chance should be employed both to randomize
and in the long term to (approximately) equalize the allocation of roles and
rewards. But in Babylon, people's talents and desires, apart from their
desire for risk are of secondary importance; there we see at work a radical
egalitarianism not based on human respect, but rather on the needs of the
system.

Yet perhaps Babylon is not so distant from our kind of society. We could
read the story as a satirical critique of capitalism and of the liberal theory
of justice, one which shows them to be based on a mere illusion of equality
of opportunity and freedom. At a fundamental level, contrary to appearances, the Babylon which Borges depicts is in essence like our own society,
with its established roles and institutions, rewards and penalties. And
what we like to see as orderly, willed, rational and just is portrayed by him
as being determined by chance (that is, the distribution of roles and
goods). The moral is that, though we have the illusion that we choose our
roles, they are really chosen for us. The nature of society is in principle
already determined, our lots are cast once, at birth, and these determine to
a large extent our actions and successes and failures for a whole lifetime,
given the relatively inflexible social structure. But the role which this pur-
est of chances plays in our society is concealed and diminished at the conceptual level by the doctrines of equality of opportunity and human rights
and at the concrete level by formal and substantial equalization processes
(such as civil rights, education and health care) which mediate natural
inequalities, although very imperfectly. So the system is erroneously perceived as one not based on chance but ordered on just and rational principles. The illusory doctrine of free will gives us the impression that we
control our own lives, and even control social events. But we might as well
abandon this delusion, the allegory implies, and acknowledge the role
which the chance of birth and subsequent accidents of fate play.[4]

---

4   An alternative preferred by some is to call chance "the will of God," which, at least, maintains
    the comforting assurance that *someone* is in control of the whole process and administers it in
    the interests of justice, if somewhat mysteriously.

If social mobility and equality of opportunity really functioned in our society, it might be just. But we have all the traditional structures which Borges caricatures with no corrective element of choice (except in relatively trivial personal matters) and no further corrective element of chance (except on the same superficial scale) after the great lottery of birth. The story, then, presents us with the unauthorized version of our own system, intensified in its affective power by grotesque and exotic details. Our social system is based on fixed positions (with concomitant rewards) and unequal chances, because equality of opportunity does not, and indeed cannot, exist in the way that we envisage it. Life is an unjust lottery. Borges exposes the shortcomings of such a system by heightening the role of chance to the point of ridicule.

II. Babylonian Justice

But is the role of chance in Babylon actually as arbitrary and unfair as it is in our own society? While chance (qua accidental inequality) in our society militates against social justice (whether that is seen as resting on need, equality or merit) and undermines a supposedly fair and ordered system because its role is unacknowledged or camouflaged by myths of desert and merit, in Babylon it has a corrective and redistributive effect. The saving grace there is that the Babylonians have a sporting chance to change their positions every 60 days, whereas, by and large, we are stuck with our roles for life.

The Babylonian system departs from our own in two crucial respects. First the role of chance is fully recognized and accommodated. Since chance necessarily plays a role in the distribution of goods and positions in society no matter what system of justice is in operation, its potentially invidious effects (i.e. the distribution of goods to some, evils to others) are counteracted by ensuring that chance is interpolated on a regular or systematic basis so that nobody suffers from drawing a losing ticket for more than 60 days. Consequently, the Babylonian distributive system satisfies what I would consider to be the two basic conditions for justice: *impartiality*, through its random operation, and a *reduction of inequality* by its approximate equalization of outcomes for individuals in the longer term, through a selection of winning and losing tickets. A second difference is that the Babylonians in the story freely chose their system, which we did not, *pace* the social contract theorists. I shall now elaborate these two differences, in reverse order, to tease out the theory of justice implicit in Borges's story.

I would argue that the inauguration of the total lottery parallels the social contract as envisaged ideally, because the Babylonians chose it freely. This means considering briefly the free/determined opposition in relation to the Babylonian system. I said earlier that the lottery does not destroy the free will of the Babylonians, but harnesses it; men freely follow chance, just as we would say that we obeyed democratically elected governments of our own free will. (This partial resignation of freedom of choice is not thought to impair free will, as Elster argues.[5]) But free will and liberty are not synonymous: liberty connotes opportunities for the exercise of the power of choice which we call free will. How much liberty do the Babylonians have? Clearly, once the total lottery was established, they ceased to have liberty as liberals conceive of it (for example, the opportunity to change jobs, etc.), being committed to follow the destinies allotted to them. But, although their liberty in the fullest sense is restricted, they have not become automata: they still choose to follow their destinies. The significant feature is, however, that originally they begged the Company, alias chance, to take over and to make their choices: this is a parallel case to the social contract, defined as voluntary submission to the authority of another or others. The people of Babylon freely forwent their freedom of action, to be dictated to by chance, but chance cannot be called a tyrant, for it is an absence of purpose.

According to some theorists, a voluntary and total sacrifice of freedom like this is self-invalidating; Locke denies that we can freely choose to become slaves, as this is to choose to forgo choice, to negate our human essence. This puzzles me, for it is not illogical or dehumanizing to choose to sacrifice part, or even all, of my freedom. People make such partial sacrifices all the time — they take jobs, sign agreements, vote for representatives. Every promise or contract is a partial sacrifice of freedom, usually undertaken in the hope of benefits prized more highly than the freedom which is surrendered. Some religions invite us to make just such a choice, to sacrifice our freedom wholly and to place ourselves in God's hands; this is the burden of the famous speech put into the mouth of the Grand Inquisitor by Dostoevsky.[6] "Choose certainty" is his message. The Babylonians, by contrast, choose chance as their taskmaster, but the choice is equally free. It cannot be said, except by paternalists (who subvert their own case by denying the validity of others' choices) that the choice to forgo choice or freedom of action is self-invalidating. It is certainly not self-contradictory. Nor can it be said that its outcome is necessarily unjust, if it is freely undertaken, although we may think such a choice imprudent or suicidal.

In fact, if we accept that the Company in Babylon represents pure chance (and is not Borges's metaphor for God or a totalitarian regime), various liberal and conservative philosophers, because of the views they hold about freedom, would be committed to arguing that free submission to chance should be condoned. Hayek, for example, holds that submission to accidental forces, the forces of the market, impinges less on our freedom

5   Jon Elster, *Ulysses and the Sirens* (Cambridge, Cambridge University Press, 1979), ch. II.
6   Fyodor Dostoevsky, *The Brothers Karamazov*, vol. 1 (Harmondsworth, Penguin, 1958), 292-305.

than submission to the control of other human beings such as planners. He, no doubt, would prefer the lottery to any human power since he justifies the market on similar grounds, although his faith in the market might lead him to prefer it to the lottery. Whether submission to the lottery is detrimental to freedom, therefore, depends on what view is taken of liberty and of whether it can properly be used to make rational, liberty-limiting choices in order to obtain other benefits. I think it can. Choosing a lottery system is not in itself more detrimental to freedom than electing a new government.

There are parallels between Borges's model and Hobbes's social contract which further demonstrate that the Babylonian form of society is voluntary and based on consent. The early Babylonians gave themselves up voluntarily to an absolute sovereign, chance. The rule of chance signifies *risk, surprise* and *variety*. These original Babylonians were motivated above all by an inveterate love of gambling, Borges suggests, but we might surmise that they were also moved by the desire for opportunity and variety within a rigid and hierarchical system, that is, by a desire for more equal chances. Like the original social contract, the total lottery was not harmful to the freedom of the generation that chose to submit. But is there a problem with later generations, who are simply dictated to by the lottery? It might appear to them as a coercive authority not of their choosing. However, it is reasonable to assume that succeeding generations would be equally titillated by the uncertainty and variety which lottery created and would continue to obey its dictates for that reason, just as, for Hobbes, later generations, sharing the innate timidity of their forefathers, would obey the sovereign to avoid regression to a state of anarchy, even though they were not party to the contract.

Hobbes's social contract theory relies, of course, on a contrary reading of human nature to that of Borges, on people's desire for certainty, order and security; the original contractors' descendants continue to obey the sovereign out of prudence, to gain these ends. Formally the models of Hobbes and Borges are similar, despite these opposed assumptions. An original population, inhabiting a "dangerous" environment, gives up its freedom of action to attain certain benefits. In both cases later generations continue to obey voluntarily because of the benefits which obedience brings, although they did not actively choose to forgo their freedom as did the first generation.

As this parallel suggests, there is a skeleton of a social contract to be found in Borges's story, which justifies the sovereignty of the lottery. It can also be used to explain why the Babylonian system, contrary to appearances, represents a possible form of social justice. To illustrate this further, I shall examine the similarities between the Babylonian social contract and that hypothesized by Rawls in *A Theory of Justice.* The Babylonians contract in to chance and ignorance of their futures in the face of a certain, structured reality; the men of Rawls's Original Position contract in to certainty (qua the two principles of justice), given the uncertain, unstructured nature of their future reality, which is hidden behind the "veil of ignorance." Both these manoeuvres give rise to a procedural, not a substantive, theory of justice, i.e. one which specifies processes, not outcomes. One of Rawls's major assumptions is that men are not risk-takers, a crucial assumption that leads to the choice of the maximin operational rule and the more substantive difference principle. This assumption has provoked controversy about Rawls's account of human nature. If it were modified slightly the maximin rule would disappear. Or if it were modified for just some of the people in the Original Position (for example, by deciding that 50 per cent of them are risk-takers, while 50 per cent want security) they would never reach agreement on the rules of justice.

Barber argues against Rawls that some people *would* risk becoming slaves if there were even a significantly smaller chance of becoming slave owners.[7] Thus, a modification of the non-risk-taking assumption to make it more psychologically realistic would mean that all the forms of society which Rawls wants to rule out *ab initio* as being intrinsically unjust would have to be readmitted for consideration. Barber's example is not preposterous: the most dedicated gamblers do risk, and often lose, their whole fortunes. And Borges's Babylonians are gamblers to a man: the thrill of submitting to chance outweighs the costs. This assumption, the contrary to Rawls's, is not per se less likely. For the Babylonians, as was said, the attraction of chance is that it satisfies appetites for variety, risk and surprise which a stable, predictable system of justice could not. Risk, surprise and variety are, in Rawlsian language, primary goods for the Babylonians which take precedence over the primary goods which Rawls commends such as wealth, rights and freedom. Of course, those goods also exist in Babylon, but are unevenly distributed and continually redistributed. The Babylonian social contract, then, is one made by men with different proclivities and priorities from those imagined by Rawls.

But a vital element of Borges's story, that which gives it its power and horror, is that the system into which the Babylonians contract is not a vacuum but a society rife with inequality, cruelty and grotesque and barbaric customs and punishments. There is seemingly no maximin rule in operation here, since anyone might draw the lot of the condemned man or of the victim of an assassination. But, in fact, the minimum is located elsewhere, in the guaranteed excitement of the draw which compensates even for a possible future loss of life or limb. (In any case, why should inveterate risk-takers invoke the maximin principle?)

7   Benjamin Barber, "Justifying Justice: Problems of Psychology, Politics and Measurement in Rawls," in *Reading Rawls*, ed. Norman Daniels (Oxford: Basil Blackwell, 1975), 297-298.

But what would someone who took rights seriously, a respecter of persons, say about the system of rough justice in Babylon? Or, to pose the question differently, does the fact of free and voluntary entry into a system that would be adjudged unjust by other criteria make it just? In Rawls's case this question does not arise as he so contrives his theory that free and rational choice leads to a society that would be judged just by other generally accepted liberal criteria. This is precisely what makes his argument open to the charge of circularity. In Borges's story we have something resembling a just and universal contract which nevertheless leads to outcomes which would be judged unjust by egalitarians *and* human rights *and* "entitlement" theorists. Yet I would argue that the outcome can still be regarded as just if we accept that the original Babylonians could not change the system and therefore lit upon a procedure to make it as just as possible. Consider the first generation of Babylonians, those who clamoured for inclusion in the lottery and for its extension to all aspects of daily life. This generation was confronted by a hierarchical, Byzantine and inhumane socio-political system which must have seemed highly unjust to those born into the lower echelons with no hope of escape; instead of overthrowing the system (a substantive reform presumably beyond their powers) they chose procedural reform and, by choosing the lottery, inserted into the system a form of justice through the randomized distribution of wealth, status and privilege: justice based on impartiality (through randomness) and an equalizing tendency (through repetition of draws). Chance distribution is certainly a feasible method of just allocation for positional goods, and every role in the Babylonian hierarchy is, literally, a positional good. In the case of "goods" which are actually evils (for example, being a slave) it is equally just that they should be frequently redistributed by chance. Given that the social and political system of Babylon could not be changed, the lottery served to make this unequal and inhumane society more just through a procedure guaranteeing impartiality and, in the longer term, equal life chances.

If the Babylonians agree to submit to the lottery, then, they cannot reasonably complain about any particular allocation, for justice lies in the procedure and in the repeated recasting of lots. To object would be like agreeing to play the card game "Cheat" and then complaining that everyone else was cheating. In Babylon, the intrinsic injustice (from an egalitarian or a liberal viewpoint) of the social system, is counteracted by the corrective justice of the lottery. Any incorrigible injustices which might occur in one draw for some individuals (e.g., drawing the lot of the condemned man) are justified because the procedural justice of the lottery has already been quasi-contractually agreed by the participants in exchange for its positive benefits, surprise and variety.

We might also note that the lottery in Babylon and the difference principle in Rawls's theory have similar functions. The difference principle is
chosen because further roles are hidden behind the veil of ignorance, in
the hope that it will regulate inequalities and lead to greater equalization
in the longer term—although many critics argue that it does not go far
enough towards this. The lottery is chosen because future roles are known,
and some are dreadful; but it also functions to equalize people's chances of
receiving good and bad allocations in the long term. One of the original
uses of the lottery in Greece was to distribute goods of unequal value to
people of equal merit such as plots of land, some more fertile than others,
to ex-soldiers. The Babylonian lottery, like other lotteries, regards individuals as equal—equal ciphers—to whom a range of intrinsically unequal
goods must somehow be distributed. It is thus in a sense based on radically egalitarian premises although, as was stated, this egalitarianism does
not arise from a respect for persons.

In summary, then, the Babylonian lottery can be seen as a just distributive procedure firstly because of the elements of contractualism, due process and impartiality in its constitution. Some people might argue that
these elements alone guaranteed its justice. Secondly, from the perspective
of someone who believes that a key component of justice is equality, I
would argue that the equalizing effect which arises from the random,
repeated casting of lots, also makes it a just system, given the immutable
nature of the Babylonian social structure. The lottery serves to make an
intolerable system more just and therefore more bearable by the circulation of inequalities. I would not, of course, argue that *any* chance distribution is just (for this would imply that any system whatever could be
regarded as just): it is the complete impartiality of the Babylonian lottery
and the repetition, which are in themselves fair, which bring about an
egalitarian form of justice.

III. Justice through Lottery and Rotation

By now I have embroidered and dissected Borges's fable out of all recognition although not, I hope, too perversely. I have suggested that there is a
moral tale for liberals in it, and also the outline of a radically different conception of justice. But, in circumstances other than those of Babylon, could
the justice of the lottery really be superior to "arranged" justice?

The premise of the lottery is that perfect equality of welfare, functions
and resources is unattainable. Chance negates the need for equality at a
primary level (i.e. equality of material goods, etc.) and substitutes it at a
secondary level, much like Rawls's two principles. It can therefore be
regarded as a procedural conception of justice, but one which, like that of
Rawls, rests on substantive assumptions and has substantive implications.
Let us assume that it is beyond our power to change the stratified nature of

society in most respects, although we may alter the forms that stratification takes, and institute social minima. This assumption implies that the ideally flexible anarchist society and the ideally equal socialist society are both impossible. Even so, we may still wish to achieve a form of justice based on an equalization of average outcomes over a lifetime for individuals. Then, surely, the interpolation of chance in the form of a lottery is an appropriate device for producing just average outcomes, provided that the draws are frequent and regular — a provision to give everyone a "fair chance" which modifies, but does not abolish, the idea of chance allocation. The lottery as a procedural device does not specify final outcomes, for it ensures that outcomes shift continually. Since people are primarily concerned with justice in their own lifetime, one throw of the dice per lifetime, as usually happens, does not constitute justice,[8] whereas a lottery does.

However, I am inclined to agree to some extent with Rawls about people's desire for certainty and a maximin principle, so I would concede that a pure lottery (where some might draw a run of losing or winning tickets) is too extreme and far too similar to our present system. A lottery does not guarantee an equitable distribution, but randomizes the unfairness of any non-equal distribution: in the very long term, randomization would probably equalize the distribution of good and bad chances per person, but social processes work in the short term. There is also the problem of one-off draws (drawing the condemned man's lot, etc.). I think that this need not concern us here, since I want to consider how a lottery might operate in a humane society, rather than in Babylon. (But we might note that drawing lots is a time-honoured way of deciding who shall undertake dangerous missions: the worst, one-off risks are probably most fairly allocated by a lottery system when they occur in a society which is otherwise relatively risk-free).

I am not contemplating the institution of a radical, act-determining lottery such as Borges describes, where responsibility for actions is eliminated and personal identity almost annihilated. I am considering how the lottery might operate as a device for achieving distributive justice with respect to roles and resources, to improve a society which contains necessary inequalities but which already guarantees human rights and a social minimum, for humanitarian reasons. Evidently, the lottery has two major disadvantages — uncertainty, and the possibility of a run of losing tickets for some individuals. Uncertainty (which can also be a source of pleasure) is to some extent inherent in the lottery although it could be modified by the regularity of draws and the guarantee that no draw would reduce indi-

---

8   Not even if this were said to even out over generations, as in the romantic novel where the slave's child becomes the master; this still does not satisfy existing individuals, on whose desires justice in their own time must primarily be based (although, of course, their desires may include an improved quality of life for their children).

viduals below the social minimum. The problem of a run of winning or losing tickets could be solved by devising a system which guaranteed that nobody would draw a "losing" ticket more than twice, say, in a row. (This assumes that people could more or less agree on what counted as goods and evils, or as winning and losing tickets). It would also be possible to allow for the voluntary surrender of "good" tickets which people did not value; for example, a non-musical person who drew a ticket for a year at the Paris Conservatoire could surrender it and draw another. A lottery modified in these respects could be an instrument of social justice in our own society, if more radical reforms are considered unfeasible.

Alternatively, a *regular rotation* of goods and evils, including necessarily differentiated roles or positions, would be a fair way of distributing and circulating ineradicable inequalities and would achieve many of the benefits of the lottery. The argument for rotation of functions (as opposed to resources) depends, as does that for the lottery, on the assumption that people are roughly interchangeable and that no unique talents are needed for the occupation of particular positions. Neither system would work well in a highly specialized economy like our own—though I would argue that all such economies and the social systems based on them are doomed to some degree of injustice. But other forms of society, in which lottery or rotation would be suitable, are conceivable. Many Utopians have advocated role rotation in the small communities which they envisaged. Fourier, for example, in his theory of "attractive labour," suggested that individuals should work at as many as eight jobs in turn, each day. And Marx, in the famous passage (usually considered ironic—but who knows?) about being a hunter, shepherd, fisherman and critic in turn, touches on the same idea.

If the interchangeability of roles which lottery or rotation presuppose is considered unfeasible for a society such as ours, on the grounds of differentiated functions and skills, another possibility is to separate people's productive roles from their rewards. Then, indivisible and positional rewards could be distributed by lot or by rotation, first taking account of basic and special needs. It might be argued at this point that rewards should be distributed equally, once they are separated from functions, but this presupposes a completely different, far more homogeneous, economic system. Most industrialized societies are materially structured in a way which necessitates differential rewards unless the whole system is to be destroyed—large incomes for the upkeep of large houses, and so on. I would argue that, in order to maintain an industrial economy (and for other reasons, such as for the sake of variety and richness of life) it would be preferable to retain these differentials and to give everyone the chance of experiencing different levels of wealth and different styles of living, rather than to abolish all differentials and revert to an inevitably more simple, more uniform economic system.

If the course of action suggested above were taken, the term "reward" would lose its meaning. But such an arrangement would ensure that people did jobs for which their talents suited them. Even then, all the jobs for which no special skills were needed—for example, the jobs of politicians—could be distributed regularly by lot or rotation. In fact, there have been numerous proposals for the distribution of political power by lot, although such suggestions remain at the periphery of political theorizing, perhaps because of the vested interests which militate against such non-elitist dispersal of power. Lottery was occasionally used in the political arrangements of ancient Greece, and Aristotle thought that the election of leaders meant that power would go to the rich or to those who wanted it, whereas the choice of leaders by lot would avert this danger. Proposals for government by rotation have also been made, usually by those trying to eradicate entrenched privilege. Almost the only example of rotation in the public sphere in Britain, the jury system, is, of course, based on the principle that some functions can be carried out by *anyone,* and require no special skills, a supposition that also underlies some early, radical theories of democracy.

There are, I think, good reasons for believing that a degree of rotation, or even the use of a modified lottery principle, in the allocation of public office would have an ameliorating effect on our institutions. It would prevent the formation of elites—or, rather, undermine existing elites—and produce a wider dispersal of political knowledge, which would surely be desirable. Representative democracy, after all, has hardly had the effect of politically educating the people and increasing their power and responsibility. The allocation of office by rotation would go some way towards achieving these ends and would still be democratic in the proper sense of the word. Rotation is not the same as pure chance: it pays some attention to people's desire for a guaranteed supply of certain things. By contrast, the lottery is based on the idea that surprise and risk are themselves a major part of what people desire. But there is room in society for both principles, and they could operate in harmony unlike, say, rotation and the principle of entitlement. If we could ensure that people's basic needs are securely satisfied and that highly specialized jobs (which carry their own rewards in terms of work satisfaction) were appropriately filled, there would be sound reasons for distributing non-specialized jobs and scarce goods above a guaranteed minimum via a modified lottery system or by rotation, especially in the case of scarce luxuries. This would add to the spice of life. Such a system would mitigate the two major kinds of social injustice which the ineradicable inequalities in the structure of our own society (plus the inelasticity of supply of some goods) produce:

1.   The injustice of the fact that not everyone can live, say, in Chelsea simultaneously. Such inequalities are externally determined.

2.   The further injustice of the fact that some people with lesser talents or resources cannot, under any merit-based or entitlement system of distribution, ever hope to live in Chelsea. This inequality is intrinsic to our liberal system.

The solution to these problems is not to raze Chelsea to the ground, or Chelsea-ize the rest of Great Britain, but to ensure that everyone has a sporting chance of living there for a time, or a guaranteed turn of living there.

I have tried to show that chance, under certain conditions, could play an important part in mitigating injustices and structured inequalities, and that a modified lottery system, perhaps in conjunction with planned rotation, would be a feasible mechanism for achieving social justice in the distribution of some goods and positions, although not all. The adoption of such methods would not necessarily negate other concepts which we associate with social justice, such as merit (i.e. there could still be praise or honour for a job well done), but would subordinate them in the interests of greater equalization of people's life chances, the ultimate aim being that everyone should have a fair chance of enjoying every sort of position and good for part of their lives and should also take a fair share of the less pleasant duties which society imposes. Furthermore, if everyone understood and agreed to such procedures, the likelihood of resentment at inequalities would be considerably reduced — as in a democratic system where losers console themselves that it may be their turn next time. At least, people would not feel that allocations were being made by those with vested interests, or according to inappropriate criteria. The lottery/rotation system would also mitigate natural inequalities to some extent by preventing people from capitalizing on their natural advantages or from having extra social stigma added to their natural disabilities. Of course, there are irreducible differences between people: in our society, being a woman, being black, being handicapped are examples of such natural differences which often attract additional artificial (i.e. social) disadvantages. While a rotation or a lottery system could not eradicate these differences, it would at least divorce them from the allocation of goods or positions.

"The Lottery in Babylon" challenges the commonplace that chance, or a lottery, is the negation of a just ordering of society. The moral of the tale, as I have read it, is that the lottery can function as a corrective for the injustices inherent in any society founded upon stratification and inequality — that is, any conceivable society. In developing arguments in support of the lottery, I am, of course, making the fundamentally egalitarian assumption that people do not have different intrinsic "worths" which should be differently rewarded. Doubtless, for this and other reasons, my arguments will be anathema to those who argue for desert- or merit-based theories of justice, but the shortcomings of merit as a criterion both in theory and in practice are well known. The injustice of capitalist society is that those who have much get more: the use of the lottery and rotation could alleviate, or even eliminate, this injustice.

Richard G. Mulgan[1]

Lot as a Democratic Device of Selection

I

When democrats need to select an official, form a committee or appoint a representative, they naturally turn to election as the most appropriate method of selection. Other methods, such as hereditary succession, auctioning of offices or cooption by incumbent officeholders, seem unfair and unjust by comparison, because they do not allow the whole group to share equally in the process of appointment and because they deprive equally qualified people of an equal chance of being selected. Only election seems to imply equal opportunity for all. There is, however, an alternative, equally democratic method of selection which is usually not considered — the lot or "sortition." Historians of democracy recognize that the lot was a key institution of ancient Greek democracy but today it appears as an oddity, perhaps appropriate for the quite different conditions of the ancient Athenians, but not worth considering as a procedure which would possibly be used in a modern democracy.[2] The last major political theorist to have taken the lot seriously was Rousseau. Like Montesquieu, whom he quotes,[3] he regarded lot as the method of selection most suitable for democracy, though democracy itself, where all citizens shared equally in all functions of government, executive as well as legislative, was an impossible ideal.[4] In the eighteenth century, classical Athens still remained the prime instance of democracy and its institutions were naturally taken as

---

1   Originally published on pp. 539-560 of *Review of Politics* 46 (1984). Copyright © 1984 Cambridge University Press. Reproduced with permission of Cambridge University Press.

2   It is not referred to by, for example, Robert A. Dahl, *A Preface to Democratic Theory* (Chicago and London: University of Chicago Press, 1956); Giovanni Sartori, *Democratic Theory* (Detroit: Wayne State University Press, 1962); Jack Lively, *Democracy* (Oxford: Basil Blackwell, 1975); Carole Pateman, *Participation and Democratic Theory* (Cambridge: Cambridge University Press, 1970); J. R. Pennock, *Democratic Political Theory* (Princeton: Princeton University Press, 1979).

3   Montesquieu, *De L'Esprit des lois* 2:2.

4   Rousseau, *Contract Social* 4:3; cf. 3:4.

typically democratic. But Rousseau marks the end of the city-state as a subject of other than purely historical interest in political thought. As the city-state was eclipsed by the nation-state, representative government, rather than government by citizen assembly, became established as the most appropriate form of popular government and was identified with "democracy." It was therefore natural for election, the key device of representative government, to be seen as the essentially democratic mechanism for selecting leaders and for the lot to be discarded as no longer useful or interesting. This neglect of the lot by modern democrats is unfortunate. Not that elections should be abolished and all representatives chosen by lot—even in ancient Athens, election was always used alongside the lot and, as we shall see, election can involve substantial advantages from a democratic point of view. Nonetheless, the Athenian experience of lot is worth reviewing because it shows that the lot was based on principles still recognized as fundamental to democracy. Moreover, there are still some situations in a modern community where lot may be considered a more democratically appropriate method of selection than election.

II

We may begin with a brief survey of the positions filled by lot in democratic Athens. By "democratic Athens" we understand Athens after the reforms associated with Ephialtes and Pericles in the mid-fifth century until the fall of the city to the Macedonians toward the end of the fourth century. In the first place, lot was used to fill two major institutions, the Council and the courts, which assisted the assembly in its conduct of public business. The Council prepared the business for the assembly and supervised the implementing of the assembly's decisions. This Council, more recent in origin than the old aristocratic council of elders, the *Areopagus*, consisted of five hundred members, fifty from each of the ten *tribes*, chosen for a year by lot.[5] (The *tribes* were military and administrative units each made up of citizens from a number of varied localities, urban and rural.) The ten sections of fifty members each took turns to serve as a committee (*prytany*), virtually in permanent session. The order in which these sections served was determined by lot, as was the identity of the Council member who was to preside each day over both the *prytany* and Council and also over the assembly if it met on that day. The popular courts consisted of "juries" of several hundreds, occasionally thousands, of citizens who decided most private legal suits and also some more specifically political questions, such as the legality of the conduct of former officials. (The distinction between legal and political questions, however, was not at all sharp or clear. Great latitude was allowed in what sort of evi-

---

5   Aristotle, *Constitution of Athens* 43.2.

dence was allowed and many apparently private disputes were political in character.) The courts were seen as acting on behalf of the citizen body as a whole and were chosen by lot from a panel of six thousand citizens.[6] (The size of the Athenian citizen body is not known exactly and clearly fluctuated during the classical period. It is usually estimated at between thirty and forty thousand.)[7]

Lot was also the most common method of selecting public officials. The main exceptions were the various military leaders, including the overall commanders, the generals or *strategoi*, as well as minor officers, such as the *taxiarchs* (infantry commanders) and *hipparchs* (cavalry commanders), who were elected.[8] Certain officials, concerned with financial administration were also elected. But all the rest were chosen by lot. The most prestigious officials chosen by lot were the ten *archons* who had important legal and religious duties, such as collecting legal evidence, presiding over courts and organizing religious ceremonies.[9] After their year of office they joined the *Areopagus*. Earlier, the *archons* had been the major magistrates in Athens, with considerable judicial and executive powers. They had been appointed by popular election, from members of the wealthiest families. Later, and by degrees, lot had replaced election as the method of selection. First, the *archons* were chosen by lot from a preelected panel of five hundred consisting of fifty from each of the ten tribes.[10] Later, the preliminary selection was itself made by lot. Apart from the *archons*, there were many other administrative officials chosen by lot. The Athenian practice was to divide administrative duties among a large number of different boards or committees, each charged with a specific, well-defined area of responsibility.[11] In his *Constitution of Athens*, Aristotle refers to the ten *poletai*, who let out public contracts,[12] the ten *apodectai* or collectors of public revenues,[13] the ten *astynomoi* or city commissioners who supervised the streets, the ten *agoranomoi* or market inspectors,[14] and so on. The normal term of office was one year with, in almost all cases, a ban on reappointment—the important democratic principle of alternation or "ruling and being ruled in turns" as Aristotle describes it.[15]

6   Aristotle, *Constitution of Athens* 24.3, 63-69.
7   Cf. A. W. Gomme and R. J. Hopper, "Population (Greek)," in *Oxford Classical Dictionary*, 2nd ed. (Oxford: Oxford University Press, 1970), 861-863.
8   Aristotle, *Constitution of Athens* 43.1, 61.
9   Aristotle, *Constitution of Athens* 56-59.
10 Aristotle, *Constitution of Athens* 22.5.
11 A.H.M. Jones, *Athenian Democracy* (Oxford: Basil Blackwell, 1969), 104.
12 Aristotle, *Constitution of Athens* 47.1.
13 Aristotle, *Constitution of Athens* 48.1.
14 Aristotle, *Constitution of Athens* 51.1.
15 *Politics* 1317 61-2.

Participation in the lot was for the most part voluntary, as was attendance at the assembly. Candidates for office had to submit to a preliminary investigation, the *dokimasia*, which was concerned simply with questions of technical eligibility, such as whether the candidate was genuinely a citizen or had held the office before; it did not extend to the wider question of administrative ability or fitness for the job in question.[16] Whether the number of names put forward regularly exceeded the number of positions to be filled is not definitely known. If it did not, the effect of the lot would have been considerably reduced; selection would, in practice, have occurred at the earlier stage where it was decided whose names should go forward to the lot. For the Council, which required five hundred fresh members each year and on which a citizen could serve twice in his life but no more, it may have been necessary to drum up candidates, an obligation which would fall on the leaders of the local *demes* or villages. (The *demes* were themselves organized democratically, with their own assemblies and mayors, *demarchs*, who were democratically appointed, though whether by lot or election is not clear.)[17] Serving on the Council, after all, was one of the few public duties undertaken by Socrates, which suggests that it was a duty required of most citizens, even those who were not particularly active in public life.[18] For jury service it seems that most who wished to serve were able to,[19] though the use of the lot prevented them or anyone else from knowing which court they would belong to or which cases they would hear. For the various boards of magistrates, there were normally more candidates than positions, though occasionally no selection was necessary and the accusation could be made that potential competitors had been bought off by a candidate wishing to secure automatic selection.[20]

What was the rationale behind the Greek use of the lot? Though associated particularly with the radical democracy of the fifth and fourth centuries, lot was a device of ancient origin. It occurs several times in Homer, the earliest extant Greek literature, as a means of deciding who should take precedence when there was no obvious reason for preferring one person to another. Thus, in the funeral games at the end of the *Iliad*, the order in which the contestants line up for the chariot race is determined by lot.[21] Similarly, in the *Odyssey*, when Odysseus decides to send half his men to examine Circe's house, the choice of which half should go and which half

---

16   Aristotle, *Constitution of Athens* 55.3-4; Charles Hignett, *A History of the Athenian Constitution* (Oxford: Clarendon Press, 1952), 232.

17   Hignett, *Athenian Constitution*, p. 136, n 5.

18   Plato, *Apology* 32b.

19   Jones, *Athenian Democracy*, p. 37.

20   E.S. Staveley, *Greek and Roman Voting and Elections* (London: Thames and Hudson, 1972), 51, 110-111, n. 80.

21   *Iliad* 23:350-56.

should stay is made by lot.[22] Sometimes the process of drawing or casting lots is accompanied by a prayer asking the gods to choose the best person. For instance, at one point in the *Iliad*, the Achaeans must choose a champion to fight against Hector in single combat. Nine warriors volunteer and put their tokens into Agamemnon's helmet. Meanwhile,

> the people, holding up their hands to the gods, prayed to them. Then would murmur any man gazing into the wide sky: "Father Zeus, let Aias win the lot, or else Diomedes Tydeus' son, or the King himself of golden Mykenae." So they spoke, and Nestor the Gerenian horseman shook the lots and a lot leapt from the helmet, that one they all had wished for, the lot of Aias.[23]

This and similar passages[24] have suggested that the rationale of the lot for the Greeks was religious or supernatural.[25] On this view, a choice by lot was not so much a random choice as a decision referred to the gods who knew the right answer when men did not.[26] The supposed religious basis of the lot is supported by the fact that it was used in religious contexts, such as deciding the order in which suppliants should approach a priest or oracle.[27] Moreover, in his *Laws*, Plato, no great supporter of the lot for choosing political leaders, stipulates "the divine chance of the lot" as the proper method for selecting priests, thus entrusting the choice "to the god himself to ensure his own good pleasure."

Support for a religious interpretation of the lot might be found in similar practices and attitudes in biblical society. Lot was used by the Jews for dividing up land,[28] and for deciding who should go into battle.[29] In the book of Proverbs, Solomon recommends lot as a means of settling quarrels which will determine God's will.

> The lots may be cast into the lap, but the issue depends on the Lord.[30]

In the Acts of the Apostles, when a replacement is to be found for Judas as twelfth disciple, two names are put forward and the final decision between them is made by lot. On this occasion the drawing of lots is accompanied by a prayer.

> Then they prayed and said, "Thou, Lord, who knowest the hearts of all men, declare which of these two thou hast chosen to receive this office

---

22 *Odyssey* 10:206.
23 *Iliad* 7:177-182 (translated by Richmond Lattimore).
24 Cf. *Iliad* 3:316.
25 See N.D. Fustel de Coulanges, *The Ancient City* (Garden City, NY: Doubleday, 1956), 182; cf. J.W. Headlam-Morley, *Election by Lot at Athens* (Cambridge: Cambridge University Press, 1933), 7, n. 2.
26 Aeschylus, *Eumenides* 32; Euripides, *Ion* 416.
27 *Laws* 579c.
28 Numbers 26:52-56. Thanks are due to Douglas Campbell for providing biblical references.
29 Judges 20:8-10.
30 Proverbs 16:13; cf. 18:18.

of ministry and apostleship which Judas abandoned to go where he belonged." They drew lots and the lot fell on Mathias, who was then assigned a place among the twelve apostles.[31]

Are we to conclude, then, that the Athenians of the classical period, when choosing *archons* or councillors by lot, were not so much leaving the decision to chance as handing it over to the gods? This religious interpretation of the lot has been vigorously contested.[32] If the lot had been an indication of the gods' will, it has been argued, officials chosen by lot would have used the fact of divine preference in their defense when their political careers came under attack in the courts. But this does not happen. There is no clear evidence of anyone attributing his selection to the direct intervention of a god. Instead, people chosen by lot commonly referred to themselves simply as having been appointed "by chance."[33]

Moreover, opposition to the use of the lot was not seen as blasphemous. For instance, if the decisions of the lot were really thought to have been divine decisions, the well-known criticisms of the lot made by Socrates and others would have been considered breaches of religious piety. However, there is no suggestion in the many different accounts of Socrates that these criticisms were ever considered as contributing to the charges of impiety. Indeed, it is Xenophon, the chronicler of Socrates most concerned to demonstrate his religious orthodoxy, who gives the fullest account of Socrates' objections to the lot.[34]

At the same time, a completely rational and secular interpretation of the lot is probably mistaken. Its continued use in religious ceremony and for selecting religious officials suggests that the lot retained an aura of divine authority, at least for some people on some occasions. There was a close connection between religious and other areas of social life, including politics. It is unlikely that a procedure which was appropriate in specifically religious contexts would *never* carry similar connotations when used for selecting political officials. Furthermore, attributing a choice to chance is not in itself evidence of an entirely rational view of the lot. Though Chance (Tyche) was distinguished from the more personal and approachable gods, such as the Olympian gods or local deities, it could still be seen as a divine force.[35] It is described by the poet Pindar, as the daughter of Zeus

31   Acts 1: 24-36 (*New English Bible*).

32   Headlam-Morley, *Election by Lot*, 4-12.

33   Headlam-Morley, *Election by Lot*, 10-11. In the *Republic*, Plato recommends that the rulers' selection of marriage partners be concealed behind an ingenious system of lots so that those who come off badly may blame "chance and not the rulers" (460a).

34   *Memorabilia* 1.2.9.

35   See E.R. Dodds, *The Greeks and the Irrational* (Berkeley: University of California Press, 1951), 42; cf. Kenneth. Dover, *Greek Popular Morality* (Oxford: Basil Blackwell, 1974), 138-141.

and a character in Sophocles refers to it as "divine."[36] Significantly, Plato, when talking of the lot in the *Laws*, couples both "the god" and chance as directing its operations:

> It is necessary to make use also of the equality of the lot...and in doing so to pray, calling on the god and Good Tyche to guide for them the lot right towards the highest justice.[37]

These passages suggest that some Greeks of the classical period may have considered the selection of public officials by lot to be guided by a mysterious supernatural force, just like other unpredictable and apparently random phenomena, such as changes in weather or personal accidents. As such it was appropriately accompanied by a prayer asking for a fortunate outcome.[38]

However, though Tyche might guide the fall of the lot and might be worth soliciting with a prayer, this would not in itself provide a conclusive reason for using the lot rather than some other method of selection, such as election or hereditary succession. All traditional practices had religious underpinnings and were associated in some way with the gods. A preference for the lot rather than, say, election, should not be seen as straightforward preference for the decision of a god over the decision of men but more as a preference for one type of divinely sanctioned method rather than another. The difference lay in the fact that lot did not operate through human judgment or control whereas other methods did. The decision to use the lot was thus a decision to opt out of a conscious determination of an issue or selection. This choice itself could not be referred to the gods, but would have to depend on human judgment, on accumulated wisdom and on the calculation of advantage. Thus, even if we accept that the Greeks looked on the lot as divinely determined, if we wish to discover the reasons which led them to use it, we may place the religious aspect on one side and may concentrate on the empirical world of practical experience.

Why, then, did Athenian democracy make such extensive use of the lot? One important reason was that it expressed the democratic commitment to political equality. As Aristotle recognized, political conflicts between the proponents of different types of constitution, such as aristocrats, oligarchs and democrats, were not simply, or even primarily, struggles between different self-interested groups seeking power and property for themselves. They were also ideological contests between different conceptions of justice, that is between different principles or criteria for distributing the

---

36   Pindar, *Olympian Odes* 12.1; and Sophocles fragment, cited Hugh Lloyd-Jones, *The Justice of Zeus* (Berkeley: University of California Press, 1971), 162, n. 6.

37   *Laws* 757e; cf. 690c.

38   Aristotle's account of chance in Physics II 4-6, it will be remembered, assumes that chance events, though exceptional, are causally determined not random events.

goods of society.[39] The conception of justice peculiar to democracy was that social goods should be divided equally among all free citizens.[40] Equality of distribution was implicit in the original slogan of the democrats, *isonomia*, "the fairest word of all" according to Herodotus,[41] which incorporated the notions of equality (*ison*) and law/rights (*nomos*). Among the goods to be distributed equally in a democracy was political office. The values of Greek society had always emphasized success and achievement, recognized and authenticated by the community at large.[42] Positions of leadership and public authority were naturally associated with virtue and prestige. To hold office was to lay claim to the respect of one's city as someone deserving of distinction. Indeed, a common Greek word for "office" is *time*, meaning generally "honor" or "reward." Political office was thus a good in itself, a social value, like wealth or military prowess, which individuals would admire and be willing to compete for. In a democracy, therefore, political office, like any other "honor" or good, should be distributed equally among the citizens.

Political equality was sought through a number of different institutional mechanisms. All major issues were decided in the sovereign body, the assembly, in which all citizens had an equal voice. Other decisions, as we have seen, were shared widely among the citizens by dividing administrative functions among a large number of different boards or committees and by restricting the length of tenure, usually to one year. Lot was also an essential part of this equalization of authority.[43] Because lot was the traditional method of choosing between people who were thought equally deserving, selecting administrative officials by lot, particularly officials who occupied positions of prestige, such as the *archons* or the president of the Council and assembly, was a public expression of democracy's commitment to the equality of all citizens.

Athenian democracy always recognized that some positions, particularly military command, required special skills and would need to be exempt from the lot. Lot, in Aristotle's words, was used by democracies "for all offices or *all but those which require experience and skill*."[44] When special skills were required the normal democratic method of selection was

---

39 Cf. *Politics* 3. 9.
40 Aristotle, *Politics* 1280a 24-5, 1317b 2-7.
41 *History* 3.80.
42 Cf. A.W.H. Adkins, *Merit and Responsibility* (Oxford: Clarendon Press, 1960), ch. 3,8,10.
43 Staveley, *Greek and Roman Voting*, 54-57, argues that alternation (or rotation) was fundamental and lot merely subsidiary, the most convenient method of selection once it has been decided that offices will be held in turn. Certainly, alternation was an important democratic principle (cf. Euripides, *Suppliant Women* 405-8; Aristotle, *Politics* 1317b 20-22) and lot was frequently coupled with alternation as the normal method of ordering those who are to take turns. Nonetheless, lot would have been independently significant as an expression of distributive equality.
44 *Politics* 1317b 22.

election which did not presuppose the same degree of equality as the lot. Even if the positions in question were open to all citizens and even if all citizens had a right to vote in the elections, elections were still a means of choosing the best or most deserving candidates, not a means of choosing between equally deserving candidates. Indeed, in this respect, election could be seen as an aristocratic, we might say "meritocratic," rather than a democratic device, because it was aimed at finding the best candidates.[45] Election might imply that all citizens were equally good judges of merit, but not that they were equally meritorious. Democratic elections thus encouraged equality of political opportunity rather than strict political equality. It was this aspect of democracy, the career open to talents, which was emphasized by the Thucydidean Pericles in his famous praise of Athenian democracy:

> Advancement in public life falls to reputation for capacity, class considerations not being allowed to interfere with merit; nor again does poverty bar the way. If a man is able to serve the state he is not hindered by the obscurity of his position.[46]

Significantly, lot does not figure at all in the funeral speech, though other writers, such as Herodotus,[47] Plato[48] and Aristotle,[49] mention it as a prominent characteristic of democracy — one reason, perhaps, why the funeral speech has been particularly appealing to modern democrats.[50]

The assumption of the lot, that there were many public offices for which experience and skill were not required, shocked opponents of democracy, like Socrates and Plato. Socrates, for example, complains in Xenophon's *Memorabilia*, that nobody would choose a pilot or carpenter or musician by lot, though if these positions were badly filled they would cause far less harm than bad political appointments.[51] But use of the lot, it should be noted, did not imply that superior ability and experience were not *discernible*, only that they were not *required* for the job in question. It is most unlikely that the Athenians were unaware of differences in capacity among those who filled the various positions appointed by lot. The president of the assembly, for example, was selected by lot but there must have been some incumbents who did a much better job than others. Similarly, in the various boards or committees there must have been some whose con-

---

45 Aristotle, *Politics* 1273b 40-41.

46 Thucydides, *The History of the Peloponnesian War* 2.37 (translated Crawley).

47 *History* 3.80.

48 *Republic* 561a-b; 557.

49 *Politics* 1317b 20-21.

50 Cf. Frank M. Turner, *The Greek Heritage in Victorian Britain* (New Haven and London: Yale University Press, 1981), 187; George Grote, *History of Greece* (London: John Murray, 1862), iv, 267-275; John Stuart Mill, *Essays on Philosophy and the Classics*, ed. J.M. Robson (Toronto: University of Toronto Press, 1978), 333-334.

51 See above, n. 34.

tribution was outstandingly good and others who had to be carried by their colleagues. Other characteristics of Athenian government, such as alternation and the use of boards rather than individual magistrates, would have helped to prevent the damage done by incompetent individuals; indeed, this may have been part of their rationale. Incompetence was seen to occur but could be safely ignored in all but the most vital executive functions, such as military command. Participating in the various public offices was an honor which should be shared as equally as possible among all the citizens, even at the price of a certain degree of inefficiency, and lot was vital as a means of selecting citizens at random, regardless of their personal qualities.

Equality of desert was thus the main ethical assumption underlying use of the lot. But there were other political effects of the lot which will have formed part of its overall rationale. For example, one consequence of selection by lot was a reduction in competition for political office and in the opportunities for factionalism. Aristotle mentions election contests as a possible cause of revolution and refers to the experience of the city of Heraea where election was replaced by lot in order to avoid election intrigues and competition for office.[52] Similarly, the pseudo-Aristotelian *Rhetoric to Alexander* refers to lot as a means of reducing *stasis* or political disorder,[53] and we may assume this point to have been a commonplace of Greek political thinking. Not that the use of the lot at Athens removed all factionalism or political competition. Within the assembly itself, or before the courts, political opponents would regularly clash in argument and would seek to destroy each other's reputations. Vigorous competition surrounded positions, such as the generalship, which were chosen by election. Nonetheless, considering the great number of offices to be filled each year, choosing so many by lot would have helped to reduce the level of conflict and to confine it to the more significant issues.

More important, from the democratic point of view, were the ways in which lot helped to sustain the main constitutional principle of Athenian democracy, namely the dominance of the assembly. The democratic constitution was the creation of leaders like Cleisthenes, Ephialtes and Pericles, aristocrats who owed their ascendance to popular support in the assembly and feared their more oligarchical opponents' influence elsewhere. The other branches of government, such as the Council, the courts and the various magistrates, were organized, not to check or balance the power of the assembly, as a modern democrat might expect, but to maintain it. Use of the lot had a number of advantages from this point of view. For instance, because the outcome of a lot could be neither controlled nor

52   *Politics* 1305a 28; 1303a 14-16. Cf. William Lambert Newman, *The Politics of Aristotle*, volume 4 (Oxford: Oxford University Press, 1887-1902), 306-307; Plato, *Laws* 757e.

53   1424a 12-20.

predicted, there was less chance that individual officials or bodies would be suborned by hostile interests. No one going to a meeting of the assembly could predict who was going to preside. This was a consequence not just of appointing officials by lot in the first place but of assigning them their particular duties by lot as near as possible to the time when the duties were to be performed. More generally, the lot contributed to the general weakening of executive power on which the supremacy of the assembly depended. Psychologically, selection by lot would tend to counter any feeling of superiority on the part of those selected. As we have seen, selection by lot was attributed to chance. Though some may have seen chance as a mysterious and supernatural force, being chosen by lot was not considered to be evidence of any particular competence or skill. By contrast, someone who had been appointed by popular election would naturally have thought that he had some special capacity, at least in the opinion of his fellow citizens. The person chosen by lot would have felt less confident in the value of his opinions in relation to those of his fellow citizens. For this reason he would have been more likely to follow the wishes, whether actual or anticipated, of the assembly as a whole.[54] This would again lessen the tendency of public officials and administrative boards to usurp the authority of the assembly.

Where important decisions could not be taken by the assembly itself, they needed to be referred, where possible, to bodies which could be relied on to act as the assembly would have done. This applied particularly to the Council and the courts which had substantial political and legal responsibilities and could have seriously weakened the authority of the assembly if they had developed as independent sources of power. In both cases, lot helped to protect the assembly by selecting a reasonably representative sample of citizens. The popular courts, it may be remembered, had been created as a direct extension of the assembly. In earlier times, the assembly had acted merely as a court of appeal and then as a court of first instance for some major political charges, such as treason. Cases were sufficiently few for the assembly as a whole to hear them all.[55] But when the reforms of Ephialtes gave jurisdiction in almost all matters to the people, the volume of business required the "people" to meet much more frequently than the full assembly was able to. Hence, the creation of the large juries to act on the assembly's behalf. Being a cross section of the citizen body, they could be expected to act in the same way as the assembly would have if it had been able to hear all cases. Similarly, the democratic Council was created in order to protect the assembly's interests against opposition from the older, originally more aristocratic, council, the *Areopagus*. In the case of the Council, alternation, the complete change of membership every year, was

54 Hignett, *Athenian Constitution*, 231.
55 For the history of the courts, see Hignett, *Athenian Constitution*, 96-97, 200.

vital in preventing it from acquiring authority as a body of accumulated political experience like the Spartan Gerousia or the senate in republican Rome. But, as with the courts, the random sample provided by the lot helped to secure representative membership.[56]

If bodies selected by lot were to provide a representative cross section of the assembly, two conditions needed to be met. First, all citizens would have to be eligible for selection. The importance of eligibility seems obvious but has sometimes been overlooked, particularly in discussions of the historical development of the archonship.[57] When everyone is eligible the lot is democratic; but if only a few are eligible, the lot, as Aristotle remarked,[58] is oligarchic in effect, and less democratic than an election where all citizens have a vote even though only the wealthy may be eligible for office. Secondly, the number to be appointed to any body had to be sufficiently large. The courts and the Council were likely to mirror the wishes of the assembly not just because their members were appointed by lot from all citizens but also because of their sheer size, the fact that they

56   These bodies were not always precisely accurate cross sections of the citizen body. Juries in the fifth century may have contained a preponderance of older citizens of the poorer class who were attracted by the small *per diem* allowance; in the fourth century, both the courts and the Council seem to have had slightly less than their fair share of poorer citizens. It is also true that only a minority of eligible citizens regularly attended the assembly. Thus a cross section of the citizen body was not necessarily a cross section of the assembly and vice versa. Nonetheless, we do not hear of any permanent or deep-seated clash of interests between the assembly on the one hand and the courts or Council on the other; this confirms the assumption that a panel of jurors or the members of the Council in any year, being appointed by lot, would be near enough to a cross section of the assembly as a whole (Jones, *Athenian Democracy*, 106, 123-124).

57   Three stages may be identified in this development: (1) election by all citizens of candidates drawn from the wealthiest class; (2) election by all citizens of a panel drawn from the wealthy from which final selection was made by lot; (3) selection by lot from among all citizens (Staveley, *Greek and Roman Voting*, 33-40). This development might appear to be progression towards greater democracy (Hignett, *Athenian Constitution*, 173-192; W.G. Forrest, *The Emergence of Greek Democracy* (London: Weidenfeld and Nicolson, 1966), 204-212). However, the change from the first to the second stage, from direct election to the combined method of lot from a large preselected group, diminished rather than increased the ordinary citizen's control over the archonship. While the *archons* were elected, the people could guarantee that these magistrates, who still made important legal decisions and who had a significant influence on public policy in general, would be generally sympathetic to a majority of citizens, even if they were all drawn from the wealthy classes. Introduction of the lot, while the archonship remained restricted to the wealthy, would have reduced the likelihood of popular leaders; it would be more likely to have produced a cross section of the wealthy, supporting the interests of the wealthy rather than the poor. This first change, therefore, from election to lot, sometimes seen as part of the inexorable development of the power of the Athenian *demos*, could have been reactionary in intent, aimed at diminishing the populism associated with the office of *archon*. If so, the intention was ultimately unsuccessful because the result of introducing lot for the archonship was to reduce the status and importance of the office itself and to transfer popularity and political influence to the elected generals. Indeed, it could be argued that this was the real purpose of the change, to diminish the importance of the *archons* by altering the method of their selection, from election which confers status and authority, to lot which does not. Whatever the real motives behind this particular reform (and there is no firm historical evidence beyond the bald description of the change in the *Constitution of Athens* 22.5), we can see that lot is not a democratic method unless all citizens are eligible to be selected.

58   *Politics* 1300 b 2.

were made up of hundreds of citizens. The larger the body, the more chance that it would be a cross section of the citizen body, and the less chance that it would be subverted by personal or sectional interests. Both the courts and the Council were deliberative rather than executive bodies. They could hear arguments, make decisions and exercise a general supervision over those who implemented the decisions. But there were many administrative and executive duties which they were too large to carry out and which needed to be entrusted to smaller groups or to individuals. Here it was harder to prevent the accidental selection of people who might turn to be unrepresentative or improperly partial. This argument was neatly turned against the democrats by Isocrates, a fourth-century critic of the fully developed democracy, and a nostalgic admirer of an idealized, moderate form of democracy supposedly instituted by Solon. He disapproved of the way in which the lot ignored differences in merit and he advocated election as a means of securing good leaders. He also argued that election was more democratic than lot,

> since, under the lot, chance would decide the issue and the partisans of oligarchy would often get the offices; whereas under the plan of selecting the worthiest men, the people would have in their hands the power to choose those who were most attached to the existing constitution.[59]

In practice, as we have seen, potential damage from officials chosen by lot was reduced by dividing administration into a large number of clearly defined functions, thus severely circumscribing the area of individual initiative and discretion allowed to the officials. But this was not always possible. In cases where considerable discretion was entrusted to a few individuals, Isocrates' point had more force: use of the lot might actually threaten the interests of the assembly.

However, it was precisely for this type of office, such as the generalship, that the Athenians dispensed with the lot and relied instead on election. As we have seen, one reason for electing generals and other military commanders was that these positions called for superior skills and experience. But another reason has now emerged, the fact that election helped to make these officers accountable. By electing generals individually, the citizens could be assured that they were choosing people generally sympathetic to the democratic constitution; they could also choose people who supported a particular strategy or policy. Moreover, this accountability was enhanced by the possibility of repeated tenure of office. Athenian generals, hoping for reelection, would be anxious to keep faith with the assembly. Lot, combined with alternation, certainly diminished status and made officials diffident about getting out of step with their fellow citizens. But election and reelection created formal, personal links between the person chosen and the people who had chosen him and on whose behalf he acted.

59 *Areopagiticus* 23.

It thus made the selection of the occasional maverick less likely and, though it elevated the status and authority of those chosen, it also made them personally more responsible to their electors. This contrast between lot and election can be described in terms of two types of representation. Lot, particularly when combined with large numbers, was a method of selecting "typical" or "descriptive" representatives, that is, people who were literally representative or typical of the citizen body as a whole, in the sense that they shared the same characteristics. Election, on the other hand, was the appropriate method to choose representatives in the sense of agents, those who would act for the people and pursue the people's interests without necessarily being typical members of the people.[60]

We may summarize our conclusions about the Greek use of the lot as follows. First, it was generally seen as an appropriate and divinely sanctioned method of just distribution when deciding how to allocate a recognized good (or evil) among a group of people considered equally deserving. Indeed, its use might signify a conscious determination to treat people as equals in the face of claims that they were unequal. Politically, the lot was an expression of the democrats' belief that all citizens deserved an equal share in public honor and the rewards of office. It also had certain political consequences. (1) It was a means of reducing the extent of factionalism and competition surrounding the appointment of officials. (2) It helped to prevent interests hostile to the assembly from suborning or unduly influencing particular bodies or officials. (3) Together with alternation and the division of duties, it helped to reduce the authority of officials delegated to act on behalf of the assembly. (4) Provided that all citizens were eligible and a large number could be chosen, it could produce bodies which were typically representative of the citizen body as a whole and could be trusted to act on the assembly's behalf. On the other hand, in comparison with the lot, election was the appropriate democratic device when skill and experience were required, and when it was necessary to delegate to individuals, either singly or in small groups, power to act on behalf of the assembly in ways which could seriously harm or benefit the assembly's interests. In such cases, the interests of the people would more likely be served by electing persons of known competence and loyalty than by risking the randomness of lot.

III

What is the role of the lot in modern democratic societies? In everyday social life, lot is still firmly established as a method of just distribution. When some benefit or disadvantage is to be distributed among members of a group, when no members of the group are more deserving than any

60   Cf. A.H. Birch, *Representation* (London: MacMillan, 1971), 15; Hanna F. Pitkin, *The Concept of Representation* (Berkeley: University of California Press, 1967), chs. 4,6.

others and when the benefits or disadvantages cannot be divided, then the most appropriate method is still to leave the decision to chance.[61] There are many different procedures used — tossing a coin, cutting cards, drawing straws — but they are as deeply embedded in our daily patterns of behavior as they were in Homer's or Aristotle's.

Many of these occasions for the lot are humdrum or trivial — who should take first turn on the swing, who should have the last piece of pie, which team should bat first. Or lot may represent a method of last resort if other decision procedures have produced a tie or deadlock. For instance, in advertising competitions, it is standard practice to have a rule that, if there are more correct entries than prizes, lots will be drawn between them. But some cases are far from trivial and lot is often by no means the method of last resort. One general area where lot is common is in the distribution of new opportunities for economic gain. The normal commercial method of distributing scarce resources is to allow a market to allocate them to those willing to pay the most. But this approach is not always considered appropriate or fair. Balloting remains acceptable as an alternative means of distributing new shares or newly divided allotments of land. Balloting for land has ancient classical and biblical authority and has been regularly used, especially in colonial or newly developing societies, where governments or settlement companies have opened up new land. In New Zealand, for instance, one of the original colonizing companies, the New Zealand Company, distributed its sections or urban and rural land by ballot,[62] and ballot remains the normal method of distributing new farms among aspiring young farmers or new mortgages to building society members.

Lot is also used to decide the supreme question of life and death. Some form of ballot is common for determining who should undertake military service. Certain categories of person may be excluded as physically unfit or as vitally needed on the home front, but a choice between the rest is considered invidious as involving a judgment that some people's lives are inherently more valuable than others, a judgment that democratic societies and their governments may be reluctant to make. Lot figures similarly in those tragic dilemmas of life and death where some lives must be lost while others are saved and where the value of one person's life must be consciously weighed against another's. In the famous nineteenth-century

---

61   Cf. Brian Barry, *Political Argument* (London and New York: Routledge and Kegan Paul, 1965), 88-89; John Rawls, *A Theory of Justice* (Oxford: Oxford University Press, 1971), 374; Bruce A. Ackerman, *Social Justice in the Liberal State* (New Haven and London: Yale University Press, 1980), 285-289.

62   William H. Oliver with Bridget R. Williams, eds., *The Oxford History of New Zealand* (Oxford and Wellington: Oxford University Press, 1981), 60.

American case of Holmes,[63] people who had been shipwrecked and found themselves in an overloaded lifeboat had thrown some others overboard in order to save their own lives. The court found them guilty of murder but held, interestingly, that their action would have been defensible if the issue of who was to be jettisoned had been decided by a ballot. More recently, lot has been seriously considered as a possible means of distributing access to scarce and expensive medical treatments, such as kidney machines. In this instance, however, both the medical authorities and the public at large have been reluctant publicly to embrace the concept of complete equality of desert implied by the lot. By implying that there are equally deserving people whose lives cannot be saved, lot has the disagreeable consequence of highlighting scarcities which society could overcome if it wanted to. Other methods, on the other hand, such as delegating the decision to a panel of medical experts and/or laymen, are less stark. They allow for degrees of desert and provide at least the appearance of allocating to the most deserving. Unlike the lot they do not require the deliberate sacrifice of anybody who is equally as deserving as the lucky ones who are saved.[64]

Lot is thus still well established as a method of deciding between equally deserving cases. What of its use for selecting public officers? In at least one such area, the choice of jurors for jury trials, lot is the normal method. The rationale for choosing jurors by lot closely follows that we identified among the Greeks. Trial by jury is trial not by experts but by "good men and true," average citizens, or at least average citizens who have not disqualified themselves by some fault or crime. Athenian juries may have been much larger and may have had much wider discretion and jurisdiction; nonetheless, modern and ancient trial by jury shares the same ideal of trial by a random cross section of citizens on behalf of the citizen body as a whole. In addition the fact that selection by lot is uncontrollable and unpredictable is obviously one of the main advantages of using it for appointing juries. Courts are expected to be nonpartisan and to present an impartial verdict on the individuals that come before them. Lot lessens the chances that juries may be corrupted by rich and powerful interests.

Elsewhere, however, modern democracy relies almost entirely on election as the democratic method of selection. Given our conclusions about the democratic benefits of elections, this is hardly surprising. As we have seen, elections are particularly important where special skills are required and where individual officials are given a considerable degree of initiative and discretion. Both of these conditions apply to modern representative

---

63 *United States v. Holmes*, 26 Fed. Cas. 360, cited in Guido Calabresi and Philip Bobbitt, *Tragic Choices* (New York: Norton, 1978), n. 114.

64 Calabresi and Bobbitt, *Tragic Choices*, 41-44. See also Douglas Rae, *Equalities* (Cambridge, MA: Harvard University Press, 1981), 172-173, n. 9.

government. With the growth of large specialized bureaucracies, government itself has become a complex and specialized profession. The distance between legislatures and ordinary citizens makes the personal accountability which election provides particularly necessary and valuable. No one, therefore, would dispute that election is the key device of modern democracies or seriously claim that popular control over governments would be increased by appointing a legislature by lot from among the citizens.

But central government is not the only area in which democratic procedures may or may not be used. As de Tocqueville and Mill realized and recent democratic theory has rediscovered,[65] a democratic society is one where there are opportunities for equal participation in decision-making in all the various groups and organizations, central and local, political and nonpolitical, which are included within the nation-state. In terms of size and cohesion of interest, many of these groups closely approach the type of society in which Greek democratic procedures flourished. In many institutions, such as trade unions, schools, churches, sports clubs and other community associations, such general business as is necessary is often carried out by occasional full meetings open to all members, with the day-to-day or week-to-week business conducted by a few officers or a committee. These officers are typically selected by election at an annual general meeting. In such cases, the democratic objections to the lot are much less pressing. Most of the tasks carried out by a PTA Committee, a parish vestry or a union executive could be done by any small group of members selected at random. Indeed from the point of view of democratic theory there would be a number of advantages in using lot rather than election. The control of the group as a whole over its own business and what is done in its name would be considerably increased by the tendency of lot-appointed officers to defer to the wishes of the membership as a whole. Moreover, the divisiveness associated with competitive elections could be avoided without any loss of political equality. A recent, perceptive study of small-group democracy has pointed out that small communities place a high value on harmony and cohesion;[66] consequently individuals are unwilling to risk causing conflict by such actions as contesting elections. However, where elections are regularly uncontested, the power to appoint passes to those who nominate, usually those who already hold office. Certain people, particularly of the articulate, professional middle class, tend to monopolize leadership and to dominate those less confident of their abilities and less willing to put themselves forward. This systematic inequality had been the major source of disillusion among those democrats who put their faith in grassroots participation or

---

65   See, e.g., Pateman, *Participation and Democratic Theory*.
66   Jane J. Mansbridge, *Beyond Adversary Democracy* (New York: Basic Books, 1980), 59-71.

small-scale democracy. Lot, along with the attendant devices of alternation and division of duties, would be admirably suited to solving the problem of involving everyone without causing friction. It would prevent the emergency of oligarchical cliques and would spread the opportunity to participate much more widely among the community.

Admittedly, selection by lot does not automatically make the less confident more willing to come forward, particularly if participation in the lot is itself voluntary. Nonetheless, the complete break between selection and a person's individual qualities, which the lot provides, would be more likely to encourage participation from those who doubt their own individual worthiness. Many democratic theorists profess a belief in human equality and the educational effects of political participation. It is therefore surprising that lot has not been taken seriously as a selection mechanism. It is not as if balloting were not well established as a distributive device in many other aspects of our social life. Yet, in selecting officers, election, not lot, is automatically thought of as the democratic device. The present writer, for instance, regularly suggests to his students, who pride themselves on their commitment to democracy, that they appoint their class representative by lot. But they either remain politely amused by his apparent eccentricity or become scandalized when they realize he is being serious.

The reasons for our unwillingness to use the lot to select officials must be deep-seated and for the present a few brief and speculative suggestions may suffice. First, modern democrats appear to be deeply committed to a belief not only in inequalities of ability but also in their relevance to the allocation of administrative and political responsibility. We may have confidence in the judgment of the group as a whole, when meeting in plenary session, but less in the capacity of individual members. Thus, we may believe that everyone is equally capable of judging merit — hence the widespread support among democrats for popular election or the referendum. Beyond this, however, the prevailing principle is equality of opportunity or the career open to talents, rather than strict equality of participation through alternation and random selection. For almost any position, it is true, some people may make a better job than others but we do not seem prepared, as the Greeks were, to overlook these undoubted differences for the sake of achieving greater equality. Secondly, we are also committed to the voluntary principle that the administrative chores associated with any organization should be done by those who want to do them. So long as there are enough volunteers coming forward or those in office wish to carry on, the others will feel content to let them and will not perceive a duty to participate. Indeed, while the number of volunteers remains sufficient, social pressure, the fear of appearing pushy or ambitious for office, may actually discourage people from coming forward. This, in turn, helps to preserve the position of the self-perpetuating oligarchies which run most organizations. Perhaps, also, we are less inclined than the Greeks to see office as an honor, an intrinsic goal to be distributed equally among all the membership. We take a more instrumental view of politics and political office, judging them by their capacity to deliver other, nonpolitical goods and not as activities to be engaged in for their own sake. We place more emphasis on democratic *rights*, the opportunity to exert influence when we wish to achieve some particular purpose, and less on the inherent value of holding office. In this respect, Greek democracy was helped by the immediacy of its aristocratic ancestry. The pride and pleasure in assuming positions previously monopolized by the nobility, and still so monopolized in neighboring cities, was fresh and potent. Nonetheless, even if our collective memory of aristocratic privilege has dimmed and political office has lost the glamor of exclusiveness, it remains true that any position of responsibility, however humdrum, implies some degree of collective respect and authority. Any community which places a high value on social and political equality will want to share these positions among its members as equally as possible. To this end, lot, with its random disregard for personal characteristics and individual differences, deserves to be included as at least one of the weapons in the democrat's armory.

Lewis A. Kornhauser and Lawrence G. Sager[1,2]

Just Lotteries

Social institutions employ different sorts of procedures for allocating benefits and burdens. In western, industrial societies these procedures fall into three somewhat crudely drawn categories. Two of these are common and carry with them familiar justifications from political philosophy. Adjudicatory mechanisms measure claims for benefits or for relief from burdens against standards of social value or entitlement. The justification of an adjudicatory mechanism flows more or less straightforwardly from the pedigree and substantive soundness of its allocational metric. Markets permit persons to trade towards benefits or away from burdens. The justification of a market mechanism is typically found in its ability to reveal and respect individual preferences and hence social value, and the extent to which it facilitates the autonomous choices of its participant traders.

The third category of allocative device is neither common nor easy to locate on the map of political philosophy. Lotteries are distinguished most prominently by the fact that they eschew rather than embrace identifiable elements of personal desert or social value; lotteries are driven by chance, not reason. Attempts to justify the apparent caprice of allocations by lot are further confounded by the fact that the rare occasions upon which social entities have been moved to employ lotteries typically have involved grave rather than trivial stakes. Lotteries thus appear in just the sort of cases — the allocation of (scarce) kidney dialysis machines and military conscription — where merit, utility and autonomy seem to figure with

[1] Originally published on pp. 483-516 of *Social Science Information* 27 (1988). Copyright © 1988 Sage Publications. Reproduced with permission of Sage Publications.
[2] Seminars at the New York University and Boston University Schools of Law greatly aided us in clarifying our thoughts, as have extended conversations with Ronald Dworkin. For discussions on moral theory generally we owe him and Frances Kamm a larger debt. The Filomen D'Agostino and Max E. Greenberg Research Fund of the New York University School of Law provided financial assistance which we gratefully acknowledge. Responsibility for the views expressed of course remains ours alone.

special force, making the blind choice of allocation by lot especially prob-lematic.[3]

In this essay we try to make some sense out of lotteries. Our concern is with social allocations that do not involve express agreements of the com-peting claimants to the pertinent social good. We will refer to instances of such social imposition of allocations by lot as "social lotteries." There are two questions that any satisfactory account of these rather mysterious allocative devices must answer: first, when is it morally appropriate to allocate social benefits (including the benefit of being exempt from a social burden) by lot? And second, assuming that in a given instance an alloca-tion by lot is morally appropriate, what are the essential procedural quali-ties of a lottery that enable it to fulfill its morally appointed role? We can provide a shorthand for these inquiries, asking in the first instance what makes a lottery *just,* and in the second, what makes a lottery *fair.*

Naturally, these two inquiries are interactive rather than hermetic. One cannot inquire into the justness of lotteries without knowing in some detail what counts as a fair lottery, and conversely, one cannot know the details of what counts as a fair lottery without knowing the requirements of the moral theory pursuant to which some form of allocation by lot is appropriate. As

---

3   Our tripartite classification of allocation mechanisms is neither mutually exhaustive nor mutually exclusive. Most obviously, we have ignored voting (or legislative) mechanisms as allocation devices. As we make clearer in Section I, we consider allocations of "scarce" goods among equally entitled individuals. These allocation problems might best be regarded as the second stage in a two-stage decision process. In the first stage society decides how many resources to devote to those who prove to be equally entitled; in the second stage it decides how to allocate the goods among those entitled. In many instances we invoke legislative mechanisms at this first stage. We also often use legislative mechanisms at the second stage to select among adjudicatory, market, and chance mechanisms to govern the second-stage allocation. Consequently voting mechanisms enter into the analysis in a different and often prior stage.

To understand why this classification scheme is not mutually exclusive, we must elaborate a bit on the nature of the different mechanisms. In an adjudicatory mechanism, the arbiter makes two judgements. The first determines the relevant choice criteria; the second identifies the candidate who, on these criteria, ranks highest. This second step is a factual or evidential one. Litigation, the paradigmatic example of an adjudicatory mechanism, deploys the evidence before a neutral arbiter who then makes a decision. Other evidential mechanisms, however, exist. We might consider a competition or a tournament as a device for identifying the person who best meets the criteria implicit in the tournament: those qualities necessary for success. If we believe that a benefit should be awarded to the swiftest runner, organizing a 100 meter dash may be a reasonable way to identify the most deserving individual. Similarly, if we believe a given prize should go to the person who most desires it, then an auction market may be a reasonable way to determine who desires the good most. Thus, on this account, a market is one "sub"-mechanism for determining who best meets some predetermined choice criteria.

After the identification of the appropriate choice criteria, but before the inquiry into the relative ranking of the candidates, the distribution of the prize among the candidates is uncertain. In this sense every adjudicatory mechanism looks, in part, like a lottery. We explore this point below in our discussion of impersonality and "opaque" lotteries.

Finally, on this account, we may interpret legislative mechanisms as adjudicative. When the adjudicatory criterion identifies some other attribute or value as relevant, voting may serve to aggregate judgements as to who possesses the identified value. On these issues, see Lewis A. Kornhauser and Lawrence G. Sager, "Unpacking the Court," *Yale Law Journal* 96 (1986).

with all such problems, however, one is obliged to start somewhere. We have chosen to begin with the comparatively narrow, procedural question of what makes a lottery fair, and to build from there to the question of when it is just to use a lottery mechanism at all. Thus, some aspects of our fairness discussion will necessarily be contingent on issues that will not be aired until we take up the question of what makes a lottery just.

We set these inquiries against the backdrop of a class of moral theories which roughly can be call rights-based. We put utilitarianism to one side, if only because the analysis of lotteries is unremarkable for the utilitarian. Normally a utilitarian will prefer allocative procedures that are positively linked to utility, like markets, or appropriately tuned adjudicatory mechanisms. Allocation by lot will commend itself to the utilitarian if and only if the costs of allocation by a more conventional mechanism exceed its utility-seeking advantages, resulting in a lower social utility net of allocation costs than the expected yield of a lottery. This is likely to be the case only when definitive utility information for substantive allocative criteria is costly or impossible to obtain.[4] Rights-based theories, in contrast, postulate the existence of rights or other robust forms of entitlement in many important allocative contexts. Such entitlements offer analytically more interesting prospects for the use of lotteries than does the imperative to maximize utility.

I. What Makes a Lottery Fair?

A lottery allocates a benefit (sometimes called a "prize") among a designated group of potential beneficiaries ("candidates" who comprise a "pool") according to a stipulated procedure (the "payoff condition"). The payoff condition is stipulated by some person or persons with the authority to effectuate the allocation (the "allocating agency").

When we think of allocating a benefit "by lot," we have in mind payoff conditions on the order of those that turn on the toss of a fair coin, the roll of a fair die, or the drawing of a lot from a thoroughly mixed set. In the very idea of a "fair" coin or die there inheres the element that drives our naive view of what makes a lottery itself fair, *equiprobability:* when and

---

4   A utilitarian might adopt a lottery to break ties among possible allocations with equal utility outcomes, or to avoid allocative disutilities like envy, disappointment or the perception of injustice.

A committed and energetic rule utilitarian, of course, could rebuild a "rights-based" theory of political morality by moving it to a foundation of utilitarianism. To be sure, this would restore interest to question of the justness of lotteries. But such a utilitarian should be quite content with the analysis that follows, which assumes some more or less familiar form of "rights-based" theory, and thus attempts to consider the justness of lotteries in a moral environment that is quite congenial to the mediating rules/rights to which she is committed.

Typically, rights-based theories will leave a substantial domain for social decision making that is unconstrained by sharp limitations of rights. Within this domain, concerns of social utility will prevail, and within this domain social decision-makers following a rights-based protocol might employ social lotteries for utilitarian reasons.

only when a lottery's payoff condition gives each member of the pool an objectively equal chance to receive the benefit do we think of the lottery as fair. But this preanalytic sense of what makes a lottery fair requires closer scrutiny on two levels. First, a close account of what kinds of payoff conditions are objectively equiprobable yields some startling results: under many common circumstances, for example, loaded dice, weighted coins and other mechanically "biased" mechanisms can provide a lottery with objective equiprobability. Second, despite our initial sense that equiprobability is both a necessary and sufficient condition of a fair lottery, there are substantial arguments for the less restrictive requirement of *impersonality* in its stead. Impersonality for these purposes is a negative quality; it denotes a refusal to prefer or disprefer members of the lottery pool because of their attributes or circumstances.

We address these questions in turn.

The mechanics of equiprobability

Consider first a simple and pure example of a satisfactory payoff condition: each candidate draws, after a thorough random mixing, one of six lots, each of which is inscribed with a number from 1 to 6; a fair six-sided die is then rolled and the prize is awarded to the candidate whose lot corresponds to the number on the upturned face of the die. There is no doubt that this payoff condition is equiprobable, and no doubt that this is a fair lottery, entirely appropriate to any circumstance where our moral theory permits or insists upon a distribution by lot among the six candidates.

Suppose, however, we change the lottery, and we use a "loaded" die which always favors one or more of its faces. The lottery remains fair, and moreover, its fairness can still be explained by observing that the possible outcomes are equiprobable. When a payoff condition employs more than one device that we traditionally think of as "random," we do not require that every included device be equiprobable, but only that the payoff condition as a whole function equiprobably, and thus that each candidate have an equal chance of success overall. This is the principle of *convolution,* and it functions in our loaded dice variation on the pure lottery as follows: however badly biased the die may be, the equiprobability of the initial fair draw of the numerically inscribed lots produces equiprobability overall in the candidates' chances of getting the prize.[5] To understand why this is so, suppose the worst version of our loaded die case, with a fair draw of lots followed by the roll of a die that always comes up the same, say with its

---

5   Suppose the die rolls a 2 with probability 1/2 and a 5 with probability 1/2. Candidate i has a 1/6 chance of drawing number 2 and a 1/2 chance of winning if she does draw number 2; she has the same chances with regard to drawing number 5 and winning with it. Her overall chance of success is therefore

$$(1/6) \times [1/2 + 1/2] = 1/6.$$

A similar calculation applies for any distribution P_i as in note 8.

"6" face upturned. Now suppose a second lottery in which we announce that the winning candidate will be the person who draws the lot marked "6," then have a fair draw. In principle these are the same lottery, with the roll of the loaded die in the first instance functioning merely as a rather ornate and delayed way of saying that the winner is the person who draws the lot marked "6."

There is nothing conceptually remarkable about the principle of convolution, but it explains why many lotteries with quirky or unknown elements subsumed within their payoff conditions are fair. In our loaded die case the payoff condition can be thought of in two stages: first, the linkage stage, in which an individual is associated with a particular outcome, and second, the bounty stage, in which the winning outcome is chosen. If either of these stages is subject to an objectively equiprobable choice mechanism, the resulting lottery will be equiprobable, no matter how odd, complex, or biased the other stage may be. Thus, if we go back to our original draw-lots-then-roll-die example, and stipulate that the lots are drawn from a hat under circumstances where we are unsure that the draw from the hat is equiprobable but where we know the die to be fair, the lottery remains equiprobable.[6]

The equiprobability requirement is more generous than it may appear in another respect as well. Let us distinguish three temporal points in the lottery process: (1) the *invocation moment,* when the allocating agency commits itself to an allocation among the candidates on the basis of a stipulated payoff condition; (2) the *vesting moment,* after which no intervening circumstance can change the outcome of the lottery; and (3) the *equiprobability moment,* which is the moment at which the payoff condition satisfies the requirement of equiprobability. The question is what if any temporal relationships among these three points are necessary. One such relationship is required by the very nature of the lottery process. The vesting moment must come after the equiprobability moment; if all the candidates have an equal chance of winning the lottery at time t, it must be the case that at t the payoff condition has not yet vested. Our cases so far have embodied a second temporal relationship as well, which may seem to be required by equiprobability but in fact is not; namely, that the equiprobability moment come after the invocation moment.

This second relationship suggests itself because it seems wrong at first blush for an allocating agency which is required to use an equiprobable payoff condition to choose a contingency that has already vested, with the

6 Let P_i denote the probability that candidate A will draw the lot numbered i. Then A's chances of success in the lottery are given by summing over i the probability of his drawing i times the probability of i being the winning outcome, or

$$1/6[P_1 + P_2 + P_3 + P_4 + P_5 + P_6] = 1/6$$

since the sum of the P_i must equal 1, regardless of the distribution.

winners already chosen. Certainly, if the allocating agency knows the identity of the winners at the time it designates the payoff condition and invokes the lottery, the lottery can be neither equiprobable nor fair. But suppose that a payoff condition is objectively equiprobable at time t, that it vests at $t+1$, and that at $t+2$, without any knowledge of the outcome of the payoff condition, the allocating agency institutes a lottery which depends upon the payoff condition. Does anything prevent such a lottery from being treated as equiprobable and fair?

Consider two lotteries. In Lottery Alpha, faced with an allocation of one benefit among six candidates, we realize that remarkably enough we have a friend in a distant city who has a fair die on each face of which is inscribed a letter, and that the letters fortuitously correspond with the first letter in the first names of each of our candidates. So we call our friend, who is scrupulously honest, and ask her to roll the die and tell us what the winning letter is. Clearly this is an equiprobable lottery, and clearly it is fair. In Lottery Beta we call our friend on a whim and ask her to roll the die, write down the result (without saying anything about it), place the paper in an envelope, seal it with her special seal, and mail it to us. Later our need to make a one-in-six allocation arises, and we announce our intention to base the allocation on the winning letter in the envelope which is already making its way to us. There is simply no plausible reason to regard Beta with any less favor them Alpha. Ignorance of the outcome of the Beta roll permits us to treat the earlier moment of equiprobability as if it persisted up to the moment that we open the envelope and read what is written on our friend's terse missive. We can call this constructive persistence of equiprobability the principle of sustained fairness.

In combination, the principles of convolution and sustained fairness qualify many oddly constructed lotteries as equiprobable. Indeed, they are so potentially generous in their scope as to make it a matter of some challenge to avoid equiprobability. The improbable circumstance of a six-sided die with just the right letters on it on our Alpha and Beta lotteries, for example, was important to our story because an ordinary die would have required a linkage between the six candidates and the faces of the die, and many of the processes that would suggest themselves at the linkage would be equiprobable, and hence — per convolution — would enable the lottery as a whole to satisfy the equiprobability requirement.

Impersonality as a competitor to equiprobability

Equiprobability has very powerful sanitary characteristics. By suppressing all reasons for making an allocative choice, an equiprobable payoff condition necessarily suppresses bad reasons. Imagine that we yet again confront a choice among six candidates, and realize that there happen to be six potential delegates of our allocative authority of whose proclivities we are quite certain, as follows:

1. Misogynous Max, who will choose candidate A because A is the only male candidate.

2. Monstrous Max, who will choose B because of her race.

3. Mercantile Max, who will choose C because she is professionally successful and hence "productive."

4. Medical Max, who will choose D because she is the youngest and healthiest of the pool.

5. Manipulable Max, who will choose E because he is sweet on her.

6. Matriarchal Max, who will choose F because she is his mother.

If we choose among the Maxes by the roll of a fair die or by some other equiprobable mechanism, the choice among the six candidates will be equiprobable, and the various "bad"[7] reasons of the Maxes will be offset and neutralized. In effect, equiprobability absorbs[8] bad (and good) allocative impulses, by reducing them to proxies for the candidates themselves. If the payoff condition is equiprobable overall, the outcome is in this sense sanitary.

But if this sanitary quality is all that is needed to make a lottery fair, then equiprobability is a sufficient but not a necessary condition of fairness. A less demanding condition, *impersonality,* can match the sanitary virtues of equiprobability. An impersonal choice is one that (a) ignores the attributes or circumstances of the candidates *as reasons for choosing among them,* and (b) does not depend upon attributes or circumstances of the candidates that plausibly could be expected to figure as reasons for choosing among them.[9]

---

7   Mercantile and Medical Max may not look all that bad under some moral theories and for some allocations. But what appeal they have is in the direction of permissible adjudicatory standards. These Maxes would be acting on criteria that would not be morally appropriate in the equal entitlement cases which we posit as permitting or demanding allocation by lot. See pp. 185-197.

8   Equiprobability leaves a trace of a bad reason for allocative choice behind, in that the members of society will know that in some sense that bad reason was part of the allocations machinery. Some bad reasons, like race, may come freighted with unacceptable symbolism under these circumstances. See our discussion of informal fairness on pp. 146–152.

9   Our definition of impersonality may not itself be necessary for the fairness of a lottery. Other weaker conditions have been suggested as necessary criteria. For example, in an interesting article, George Sher, "What Makes a Lottery Fair?" *Noûs* 14 (1980) [chapter 5 of this volume], offers a definition of a fair lottery that rests on the independence of the payoff condition from the desires (or preferences) of the candidates and the allocating agency. Our definition implies Sher's in our exclusion of the use of the candidate's attributes or circumstances as *reasons* for choice, any reason being necessarily linked to some desire of the chooser. Sher's definition, on the other hand, does not consider as relevant the qualities of the candidates used to choose. He thus offers a conception of impersonality that relies on the absence of desire of relevant persons while our conception is more extensive.

    Both Sher's conception of impersonality and ours regard certain "natural" lotteries as unfair. For example, a choice between Rose and Jasmine based on which of them is more likely to benefit humanity might be regarded as a "natural" lottery if we regard their likely benefits to

When both of these conditions are met, the sanitary virtues of equiprobability are preserved.[10]

A common class of impersonal payoff conditions consists of lotteries that are plainly based on chance, but which fail or may fail the requirements of equiprobability. Suppose, for example, that an allocating agency rolls a 365-sided die, and then allocates a prize among six candidates by awarding it to the candidate whose birthday is closest to but not later than the "date" (the nth day of the year) showing on the die's upturned face. If the allocating agency is ignorant of the birthdates of the candidates, this is an impersonal lottery. The birthdates of the candidates function as a *mechanism* for choosing, not a *reason,* since the agency is merely tagging the candidates; there is no thought that a particular candidate deserves to win because of her birthday, or that a better social outcome has been realized because a particular candidate's birthday was favored. And birthdates are "neutral" in the sense that they could not plausibly be expected to be reasons for choice. Nothing about this lottery, however, suggests that it will even approach equiprobability.[11] Suppose the birthdates of the candidates A through F are in fact spaced sequentially throughout the year, and that candidate B was born on 30 April, candidate C on 1 May, and candidate D on 1 September. Candidate B has 1 chance in 365 of winning the birthdate lottery, while candidate C has 123 chances in 365.

The birthdate lottery is suggestive of a quality that will often figure in the move from equiprobability to impersonality. Simple lotteries like our earlier dice examples are comparatively *transparent,* in the sense that it is possible to trace the workings of the payoff conditions and make reasonably accurate determinations of the probabilities that attach to various outcomes.[12] Other lotteries, of which the birthday lottery is a rather mild

humanity as somehow beyond their control or the control of the allocating agency. Sher's definition views this lottery as unfair because the choice of benefit to humanity as a criterion reflects the preference of the allocating agency; it fails our criterion because it uses an attribute or circumstance of the candidate as a reason for choice. In our later discussion, we treat mechanisms of this type as adjudicatory mechanisms. See pp. 157–158.

We share the intuitions that on occasion regard such mechanisms as fair lotteries but we would hope to explicate these intuitions in terms of our definition of impersonality and our inquiry into equiprobability. For some hints to our thinking on this matter see note 14.

10 Equiprobability, of course, satisfies these conditions, and hence is inclusive of impersonality.
11 Equiprobable chances for each of the six candidates would require that each successive birthday be spaced 60.83333 days after the previous birthday. Given a 365-sided die this is impossible. Even if we knew that each person were born in a leap year so that equal spacing were possible, such spacing is highly unlikely.
12 Throughout this discussion, our reference to "objective" probability is a reference to either (1) frequentist views resting on observed physical properties of the world; or (2) logical notions that rest on a formal theory of rational inference. In either case, the requirement of equiprobability commits one to more than a requirement of impersonality. Impersonality demands that the payoff condition be independent of the attributes and circumstances of the candidates; this requirement differs from equiprobability because it admits non-equiprobable mechanisms, in particular ones for which the probabilities are indeterminate. As we discuss in

instance, are comparatively *opaque,* in the sense that it is difficult or impossible to unravel or trace the workings of the payoff condition, and correspondingly difficult or impossible to assess the outcome probabilities. The opacity of these latter lotteries at once makes them appealing from the vantage of impersonality and unappealing from the vantage of equiprobability. If an allocating agency decides to make its award to the person whose fingerprints correspond most closely to the last suspect apprehended by the FBI, to the person with the thickest toenails, or the person with the largest pancreas—all in ignorance of any useful underlying facts—the resulting choice is impersonal but not necessarily equiprobable.[13]

The quality of impersonality is strikingly parallel to equiprobability in scope as well as sanitary effect. The principles of convolution and sustained fairness apply in full to impersonality. Thus when a lottery has both a linkage stage and a bounty stage, if either stage is determined by an impersonal mechanism the payoff condition will function impersonally overall. And by hypothesis a payoff condition that is impersonal at time t retains its fairness at $t + 1$ in the face of ignorance as to its outcome, since impersonality depends on ignorance rather than an objective state of the world like equiprobability. To understand how the principle of sustained fairness would operate in the context of impersonality, recall our earlier example of lotteries Alpha and Beta. In those lotteries the payoff condition was the roll of a fair die owned by a distant friend. In Alpha, after deciding to use her roll of the die as a payoff condition, we call her and ask her to roll it and report the result; in Beta she rolled the die and placed the unannounced result in the mail prior to our decision to use the outcome as the payoff condition. If we imagine that our friend has a loaded die, though we do not know which candidate the die favors, lottery Alpha satisfies our criterion of impersonality. Once more, however, our view of Beta should

the immediately following note, this indeterminacy cannot be resolved by reference to the principle of insufficient reason.

13 Opaque lotteries are intuitively attractive, and it is tempting to reconcile their attractiveness with notions of equal treatment by appealing to the principle of insufficient reason. The principle of insufficient reason holds that in the face of ignorance of a probability distribution, one is to assume equiprobability; more formally, when the actual or frequency probability distribution over n mutually exclusive and exhaustive outcomes is unknown, as a logical or conceptual matter one must adopt the density $1/n$ for each outcome. If we accept the principle and apply it to opaque lotteries, we will treat them as not merely impersonal but equiprobable as well. See John Maynard Keynes, *A Treatise on Probability* (London: Macmillan, 1921).

But the principle of insufficient reason is simply not a useful surrogate for objective equiprobability in any case where we believe that equiprobability matters. Suppose that we hold the birthdate lottery, and then realize that, given the actual distribution of birthdates among the candidates, the lottery was grossly inequiprobable. If we believe that equiprobability is a necessary condition of fairness, we surely could not believe that the birthday lottery was in fact fair. Opaque lotteries must find their justification in the virtues of impersonality, not equiprobability.

not change. It too satisfies impersonality because our ignorance of the outcome allows us to invoke the principle of sustained fairness.[14]

But equiprobability has a unique egalitarian virtue that impersonality can not supply. Equiprobable lotteries facilitate equal treatment ex ante.[15] Suppose we have a single good which is indivisible and two claimants of the good who each enjoy robust and equal moral entitlements to it. An equiprobable lottery has the unique capacity to divide a good probabilistically, making possible the allocation of a ½ chance of receiving the good to each candidate.

In the end, therefore, the choice between equiprobability and impersonality may come down to the question of whether the operative moral theory demands or at least places a premium on distributions by lot that include the ex ante egalitarian virtue of equiprobability. The burden of our discussion in section II is that some moral theories, under some circumstances, will make such a demand or will place such a premium. Under these analytical conditions, equiprobability is a necessary as well as a sufficient condition of a fair lottery.

Informal attributes of a fair lottery

Thus far, we have been discussing the formal requirements of a fair lottery. These requirements would attach even if the actual details of a lottery mechanism were concealed in a "black box," and the lottery was being evaluated by dispassionate, rational observers, who knew only of its abstract features — such as equiprobability or impersonality. In the real world there are secondary, pragmatic concerns that demand the attention of a fair-minded allocating agency. We can think of these as informal requirements of a fair allocation by lot.

It is obviously important that a lottery look fair, especially to the candidates. It is also important that fair lottery protocols actually be carried out by the responsible officials, rather than subverted by carelessness or corruption. Equiprobability has distinct advantages over impersonality in addressing both of these pragmatic concerns. Equiprobable payoff mecha-

---

14 We suspect that the intuition that natural lotteries that use some social or personal attribute or circumstance as a payoff condition relies in a complex way on the principle of sustained fairness. In the Rose and Jasmine hypothetical of note 9, for example, an apparent retreat behind the veil of ignorance at which time the genetic endowments and social positions of Rose and Jasmine were unknown underlies our sense of fairness of this "natural" lottery. The allocation of Rose and Jasmine to their individual characters and social standing then appears to be the result of an impersonal (in our sense) mechanism. We further suspect that this impersonality is necessary but not sufficient for the judgement of the fairness of the natural lottery. We hope to treat these and other issues in another essay devoted to natural lotteries.

15 Ex ante refers to matters as they stand before the *event;* ex post to matters as they lie after. For our purposes ex ante will usually refer to things before or at the moment that the lottery in question is instituted, while ex post will usually refer to things after the allocation dictated by the lottery's outcome has been effectuated.

nisms offer themselves up for validation and understanding,[16] while impersonal mechanisms lend themselves more readily to suspicion and subversion. A die can be tested, and if fair and followed is self-vindicating. Impersonal conditions raise problems: if transparent, they are easily manipulated on behalf of an intended outcome; if opaque, they are beyond comprehension and inspection, and can easily conceal events that violate the requirements of impersonality. Equiprobable payoff conditions have the additional advantage of being shrouded in an esthetic of equality that makes their acceptance as fair more likely.

A different sort of informal fairness-connected issue is presented by allocations which, as with the Mad Maxes lottery above, implicate rightfully deplored criteria like the race of the candidates. Although we can construct formally benign mechanisms that include the explicit use of racial identity, these mechanisms might serve to legitimate race as a criterion for other social choices where it could play a substantive role. They are also easily misunderstood or misconstrued, and very unlikely to be received dispassionately by losing candidates. We thus might well choose to preclude race and other deplorable criteria from payoff conditions, not because they inevitably make a specific lottery formally unfair, but because their use threatens both to corrupt other social institutions and to undermine confidence in the fairness of any lottery in which they appear.

II. What Makes a Lottery Just?

With a working understanding of when lotteries are fair, we now ask when lotteries are just, when it is morally appropriate to employ a fair lottery as a means of allocating some benefit (including the benefit of being exempt from a burden). We can usefully start with a claim for social lotteries that, on its surface, seems straightforward: a social allocation by lot is just when (a) the good in question is to be allocated among a claimant pool composed of persons who enjoy equal moral entitlement to the good; and (b) there is not enough of the good to go around, to effectuate an allocation to each member of the claimant pool. The logic underlying this claim is obvious; scarcity prevents a full and equal allocation of the good among the claimant pool, and a fair lottery provides a means of effecting a limited allocation while respecting the equal entitlements of the claimants.

But equal entitlement and scarcity—in this context, at least—are concepts that bristle with complications, and the apparently simple case for social lotteries that depends upon these concepts suffers in full from their difficulties. We are thus obliged to take a second and considerably closer look at each of these legs of the social lottery claim.

---

16 At least if we are considering straightforward equiprobable payoff conditions. The exotic lottery devices qualified as equiprobable by the principles of convolution and sustained fairness will not typically commend themselves on appearance of fairness grounds.

Equal entitlements

1. The meaning of moral entitlement

The moral circumstances of individuals are so extravagantly variegated that it may seem quite improbable that two or more persons would ever enjoy equal moral entitlements to a good. If this perception were correct, we would be forced to conclude either that social lotteries are of trivial, aberrant significance to a rights-based theorist, or that such a theorist would have to justify their use for allocations among unequally entitled persons.[17] But it is important to distinguish moral entitlement from moral worth and moral consequence. A person's moral worth is a measure of her general moral stature, of her rank on the scale from sinner to saint. Moral consequence inheres not in persons but in choices among states of affairs: in any given state of affairs there will be circumstances that will be valued or disvalued from the vantage of the ruling moral theory, as well as those that will be value neutral. The moral consequence of the choice of state A over state B consists of those circumstances of either positive or negative moral value that distinguish the two states.

A person's moral entitlement, in contrast, reflects the moral force of her claim to a particular good. The distribution of moral entitlement among rival claimants to a good can, under many circumstances and pursuant to plausible rights-based moral theories, be quite discrepant from the distribution of moral worth among the claimants and quite discrepant as well from the measures of moral consequence that would attach to possible allocations among the claimants. Robust moral entitlements — often called rights — typically derive their force not from a complex calculus of personal worth or a wide-ranging measure of moral consequence, but from rather stark and general features of the situations in which they arise. Hence the rights of Rose and Jasmine not to be killed by Violet can be equal, notwithstanding the fact that Rose has rather little to commend her to the world, while Jasmine has led a life of energetic virtue, has a handicapped husband who is heavily dependent on her, and is engaged in a research project of great social importance, along with colleagues who are emotionally and professionally invested in her continued work with them. Equal moral entitlements are thus less rare than the moral complexity of the world may suggest.

2. The meanings of equal entitlement

The category of equal moral entitlements, without further refinement, is too broad and undifferentiated a base upon which to found the claim for social lotteries. Equal entitlements can arise in at least four quite different entitlement configurations. First, rival claimants to a good may have no moral entitlement to it at all, and be equally entitled only in the special

---

17   Cf. John Broome, "Selecting People Randomly," *Ethics* 95 (1984).

sense that null equals null. This sort of radical non-entitlement might be true of strangers, among whom a billionaire is contemplating allocating her wealth. Second, rival claimants may have no direct entitlement to the good at all, but may be entitled to treatment as equals in the allocation process involving the good. Treatment as an equal does not demand equal treatment, but does demand that the interests of each claimant be fully and equally taken account of in the process of determining the appropriate allocation. Social allocations occur in environments that frequently may give rise to the rights of rival claimants to be treated as equals; the obligations of parents to children and of governors to the governed are classic instances of what many theorists would recognize as the obligation to treat persons as equals.[18] Third, rival claimants may not have independent entitlements to the contested good, but may be entitled to equal treatment with respect to the allocation of the good. The right to equal treatment goes beyond the right to treatment as an equal, which is its predicate: equal treatment is just that; if Rose is to be given the contested good, then for precisely that reason Jasmine is entitled to the same good.[19] The social allocation of lifesaving medical therapy may commend itself as a setting where the mortal stakes of the rival claimants give them rights to equal treatment.[20] Fourth, rival claimants to a good may have independent, but equal, entitlements to it. The equally strong rights of Rose and Jasmine not to be killed by Violet are an instance of this form of equal entitlement. Under some circumstances independent and equal entitlements may be competitive; that is, they may in effect be rights to the same good, leaving their holders equally entitled to the good. As a shorthand, we will call such independent, equal and competitive entitlements "competing entitlements" (or "competing rights"). These four senses of what it means to be equally entitled cover a broad range of entitlement force. Competing entitlements are freestanding, and in this sense absolute. Entitlements to equal treatment are conditioned on the treatment of others. Entitlements to treatment as equals are entitlements to process or rationale, not to an outcome at all. And null entitlements are reassuring only in the sense that one's rival is no more entitled than one's self.

Cases where members of the claimant pool are equally entitled to a good only in the sense of null entitlements are not particularly interesting for our purposes. Presumably they leave the allocating agency free to pursue any allocative mechanism, including a lottery, but they do not support an affirmative claim for lotteries on grounds of justness. Each of the other

---

18 See Ronald Dworkin, "Liberalism," in *Public and Private Morality*, ed. by Stuart Hampshire (Cambridge: Cambridge University Press, 1978).

19 See Kenneth W. Simons, "Equality as a Comparative Right," *Boston University Law Review* 65 (1985).

20 We return to this possibility in our discussion of the use of kidney dialysis machines, below at pp. 149–150.

forms of equal entitlement can play a role in making some form of an affirmative claim, and will figure in our discussion of such claims. We emphasize the distinctions among them here because these distinctions play out
in the analysis of justice-driven claims for social lotteries in important ways.

Equal entitlement and the justness of social lotteries

We can now begin to take up the claim that lotteries are just mechanisms
for allocations of a good to an equally entitled claimant pool when there is
not enough of the good available to satisfy the needs or desires of the
entire pool. In so doing we are getting ahead of ourselves, of course, since
we have yet to contend with the difficulties that attach themselves to the
critical notion of scarcity. But important questions arising out of the claim
for social lotteries as just connect with the notion of equal entitlement, so
we beg the reader's indulgence and set aside the problematic aspects of the
notion of scarcity for the moment.[21]

1. The exclusive claim for social lotteries

Initially, we narrow the claim for social lotteries to include only instances
of equal entitlement in the sense of rights to equal treatment or in the sense
of competing rights to the good itself, and strengthen the claim to the proposition that lotteries are the only just means of effectuating an allocation
under these circumstances. We will call this narrowed and enhanced claim
the "exclusive claim" for social lotteries, since it sees social lotteries as the
exclusively just means of allocation under the stipulated circumstances.

The exclusive claim for social lotteries depends upon the egalitarian
aspect of fair allocations by lot. The claim is in its essence simple: what a
social lottery offers is an equal division of a good that is otherwise indivisible. A lottery constitutes a probabilistic division of the good ex ante;
instead of getting one unit of the good each member of the lottery pool gets
a G/P chance at one unit of the good, where G is the number of units of the
good available and P is number of persons in the entitlement pool.[22] On
this account a social lottery is just because it permits an equal allocation of
the good consistent with the equal entitlements of the claimant pool. It is
exclusively just because the only other means of respecting those
entitlements is to make no allocation at all, an option that suffers other
justice-related liabilities.

Both of these last observations require some analysis. The proposition
that making no allocation at all is the only non-lottery means of respecting

21   We confront scarcity below at pp. 153–160.
22   The exclusive claim's stipulation that the good in question is too scarce to permit a full
     allocation to the entitlement pool presupposes that the good in some relevant sense is
     quantitatively — as opposed to probabilistically — indivisible. The concept of indivisibility is
     one of the problematic aspects of claims that depend on the scarcity of a good, since most goods
     can be divided in some quantitative way, if only by breaking them up and distributing the
     pieces. We consider indivisibility on pp. 154-155.

robust and equal moral entitlements to a scarce good requires defense against the possibility that an adjudicatory allocation is as good or better a means of doing justice among such entitled claimants. This issue is entwined with understandings of the robust forms of equal moral entitlements, and so we take it up here. Likewise, the proposition that making no allocation at all is itself infirm demands defense. The possibility of doing justice by doing nothing is more closely connected with the problems of scarcity, and so we table it until we consider scarcity below.

The equal distribution rationale which underlies the exclusive claim for social lotteries has obvious implications for our discussion, in Section I, of equiprobability and impersonality as rival understandings of the sufficient conditions of a fair lottery. Equal distribution depends on the capacity of the social lottery to provide a form of equal treatment, and hence seems better served by a conception of fairness that demands equiprobability. But even a lottery that is fair only in the sense of being impersonal may be a strong "second-best" social option under the equal entitlement conditions that characterize the exclusive claim. The more fundamental question is whether a lottery which offers the most that a lottery can offer—equiprobability—is to be preferred or dispreferred over an appropriately tuned adjudicatory mechanism in cases of robust equal entitlements.

2. The challenge on behalf of adjudication: social value as a tie-breaker

An adjudicatory allocation assumes that there is a metric of personal virtue or social value against which competing claimants are to be measured in the adjudicatory process. Since the exclusive claim for social lotteries stipulates the existence of a pool of claimants who enjoy either rights to equal treatment with respect to the distribution of some scarce good, or competing rights with respect to the good itself, it may seem that there is no relevant matter left to adjudicate with regard to these claimants. But what of the role of adjudication as a tie-breaker? On this view the equal entitlements of the claimants in effect cancel each other out, and what is left may include elements of social value that may appropriately determine the allocation among the claimants.

If the tie-breaker view is correct, then the claim for social lotteries as the only just means of allocating a good among equally entitled claimants fails. There may remain justice-based reasons to be wary of adjudicatory mechanisms in cases of this sort—indeed we will consider them when we consider the non-exclusive claim for lotteries (below, p. 152)—but they are not so definitive or pervasive as to justify the claim that the use of adjudicatory mechanisms to break entitlement ties is intrinsically unjust. In cases where the elements of tie-breaking social value loom large, and the risks of adjudicatory mechanisms are relatively small, adjudication will be a serious competitor with allocation by lot. The exclusive claim for allocations by lot thus depends on a rejection of the tie-breaker view.

This observation leads us to consider the tie-breaker argument more closely, and hence to the heart of a serious problem in moral theory. Consider the following story. Violet has lost control of her speeding car and is approaching an intersection where Rose and Jasmine stand, paralyzed with fear; her only options at this point are to hit and probably to kill either Rose or Jasmine, This is Rose of our earlier story, who has little to commend her, and Jasmine, upon whose shoulders a measurable share of the free world's well-being seems to depend. If Violet hits Jasmine, she is also likely to hit and destroy a magnificent sculpture which has been erected on the sidewalk adjacent to where Jasmine is standing.[23] Rose and Jasmine surely each have equal, independent rights not to be killed by Violet (these are good examples of what we have called competing rights). Is it nevertheless morally appropriate for Violet, who is aware of all this, to choose to hit Rose on the grounds that Jasmine's death would entail a great loss of social value?

There are two possible responses, which we will call the *dominant rights* view and, as already introduced, the *tie-breaker* view. The dominant rights view insists that it is wrong to treat competing moral claims as though they literally cancel each other out and leave the field of choice where it would be if there were no moral claims at all. In other words, it is a mistake to treat offsetting claims of robust entitlement as though they were null entitlements.

On this view neither Rose's nor Jasmine's equal right not to be killed can offer a reason for choosing one over the other, but their rights most certainly function as a reasons for *not* choosing between them on certain grounds; these moral claims of right are in competition, but they do not go away, and they entitle their holders not to be dispreferred on grounds inconsistent with their continuing rights. Rose and Jasmine each have a right not to be killed by Violet, and that right is plainly dominant over many other circumstances of social value, including any features of either's life that do not qualify her right not to be killed and including the survival of the magnificent sculpture next to which Jasmine stands. The presence of the rival claimant with an equal right does not change this basic moral fact: each continues to have a right not to be killed, on account of the statue *or any other element of social value over which her right in isolation would have enjoyed dominance.* Under non-competitive circumstances the right not to be killed is not conditioned on some threshold of moral worthiness, and the right is not conceived of as having variable weight, depending on the victim's moral worth or the moral consequence of the death of the victim. The right not to be killed is distinct from, and superior to, these

23 We were introduced to tie-breaker cases of this general sort and to the problem they embody by Frances Kamm. Her thoughts are reflected in her paper, "Choice between People: 'Common Sense' Morality and Doctors," *Bioethics* 6 (1987).

other matters. This is a fortiori true of the statue, which could never compete with the recognition of — or otherwise qualify — the right not to be killed. The dominant rights view holds that it is wrong to let these subordinated claims of social value back into the picture at this later stage of analysis and effectively permit them in turn to subordinate the rights of Rose and Jasmine not to be killed.

The argument for the tie-breaker view responds that by recognizing and acting upon attributes of social value that distinguish between Rose and Jasmine we do not subordinate the rights of Rose and Jasmine to these attributes. Suppose, for example, that it was clear that if Violet were to steer towards Rose, Rose would be killed, while Jasmine would "only" be injured if she were the target, though sufficiently seriously to place in great jeopardy her value as both spouse to her handicapped husband and colleague to her fellow-researchers.[24] Even if we were committed to the tie-breaker view of allocations to equally entitled claimants, we might well believe that Rose's right not to be killed was stronger than Jasmine's right not to be badly injured. If we did, the loss of social value that attended Jasmine's injury and the destruction of the statue next to which she is standing would make no difference; withal, we would be committed to the view that Violet was morally obliged to steer towards Jasmine. The rights of Rose and Jasmine not to be killed thus have real meaning and force in our moral analysis generally. But when we reach an impasse, and one of these rights must necessarily be violated, the tie-breaker view argues that a good reason for choosing which right is to be sacrificed is considerably better than no reason. One right has to be spent; surely a return of social value should be preferred to no return at all.

This last proposition returns us to the heart of the exclusive claim for social lotteries. The exclusive claim ultimately rests on the perception that a choice among equally entitled claimants to a scarce good based on the outcome is *not* a choice made for no reason at all. The reason for a choice by lot is that it is the only way of making some allocation while respecting the equality of rights that characterizes the entitlement pool. The lottery offers equality; it divides the scarce good into probabilistically equal units. This emphasis on doing justice to the equality demands of the situation suggests that we should further refine our analysis; thus far we have been treating as identical for these purposes the case of rights to equal treatment and that of competing independent rights. On closer consideration, the case for the dominant rights view may be considerably stronger with regard to rights to equal treatment.

Consider how we would arrive at the view that Rose and Jasmine were entitled to equal treatment with regard, say, to the allocation of kidney dialysis machines. Imagine that we were public officials charged with the

---

24   This example and the point it supports were suggested to us by Ronald Dworkin.

awful task of deciding who among a claimant pool of persons suffering from renal failure should be given access to the scarce supply of kidney dialysis machines at our disposal. Among the pool of claimants, we assume, are persons like Rose and Jasmine, who arrange themselves at opposite ends of the social value spectrum, as well as many who fall in between. Nevertheless, it seems quite plausible that we would conclude that the mortal stakes riding on the allocation of our machines made it morally wrong to distinguish among the claimants on the basis of the value to society of their continued life. To respect their personhood, to respect them as persons — we might reason — is to value their survival, and it is wrong to value the survival of one person any more or less than that of another.[25]

Having thus decided that Rose, Jasmine and the other members of the claimant pool are entitled to equal treatment, notwithstanding the consequential differences in social value signified by their lives, it would be bizarre to turn around and admit those same discrepancies in social value back into the picture as an allocative tie-breaker. We have just taken account of and discounted these matters out of moral necessity. Only by blinding ourselves to the moral reasons for concluding that Rose and Jasmine are entitled to equal treatment could we countenance a social value tie-breaker.[26]

This analysis suggests a tidy resolution of the dominant-rights issue: treat rights as dominant in the case of rights to equal treatment, and use discrepancies in social value as a tie-breaker in the case of competing independent rights. But matters do not fall out quite that simply. Given that we are operating within the confines of a moral theory that recognizes rights to equal treatment, we are likely to discover that most if not all instances of competing independent rights carry with them, or at least imply, rights to

---

25 It is important for our purposes to observe the difference between having a right to treatment as equals and having a right to equal treatment. But as this skeleton of an equal treatment argument shows, equal treatment may follow from treatment as equals under certain analytical circumstances.

26 A critic might respond that we have constructed the right to equal treatment shared by Rose and Jasmine in an implausible fashion. Such rights, it might be argued, are plausible only if fashioned on an abstract, all-other-things-considered-to-be-equal basis. On this account, once we move from behind the veil of abstraction and confront Rose and Jasmine as they are, all other things are decidedly not equal. But such a rendition of the right to equal treatment makes it a mere restatement of the right to treatment as an equal. It may be that an attractive, rights-based theory could fail to recognize rights to equal treatment, except in this redundant, per se sense of the right to treatment as an equal. If so, the exclusive case for social lotteries has to be understood as specific to that class of rights-based theories that do recognize rights to equal treatment under some circumstances.

A more modest response from the critic would be that a plausible construction of the right to equal treatment with regard to life-saving therapy would make scarcity an exception to the right. But it is hard to imagine an appealing moral theory which would find in the precious relationship of a person to her life a right to equal treatment, yet permitted that right to dissolve when exposed to scarcity. This is especially true if — as is likely to be the case in many moral schema — society is morally free to create an undersupply of goods as to which there exist rights to equal treatment. See p. 153.

equal treatment. It may be that it is appropriate as a matter of course to cede rights to equal treatment to persons who hold competing independent rights. But even failing such per se conversion of competing independent rights, we can expect that the special moral cachet underlying the independent rights in question will often be the decisive element in the analysis of a claim of right to equal treatment. Consider, for example, the competing independent rights of Rose and Jasmine not to be killed by Violet. In a moral scheme that recognized rights to equal treatment, we would expect that the impulse behind giving persons the right not to be killed would likewise inspire the conclusion that persons have rights to equal treatment with regard to not being killed by the same threat. The portability of moral reasons from the environment of independent rights to that of rights to equal treatment should be common in attractive moral theories.

In any event, decisions by social entities are likely to implicate rights to equal treatment with respect to the allocation of a good rather than competing rights to the good itself. Within the analytical domain of rights-based theories that generate rights to equal treatment of the sort we have posited with regard to the allocation of kidney dialysis machines, there will thus arise cases where equally entitled claimants pursue a good which exists in too scarce a supply to satisfy their claims, and as to the allocation of which the use of a social value tie-breaker will be morally inappropriate. Such cases demand some mechanism for treating the rival claimants equally, and lotteries commend themselves as such mechanisms.

Not all rights-based theories will recognize rights to equal treatment in the generous form we have considered, however. Absent such rights, the dominant-rights/tie-breaker issue may be more open to divergent views.[27] One's view of the issue will then be critical to one's view of the exclusive claim for social lotteries. Under the dominant-rights view, a social lottery may well be the only means of doing justice among equally entitled claimants to a good.[28] Under the tie-breaker view, a lottery may be one way of doing justice among equally entitled claimants, but to use a lot-

---

27   Even without rights to equal treatment, there remain strong claims on behalf of the dominant-rights view. The proposition that it is wrong to allow the presence of an equally entitled rights holder to be the occasion for subordinating a robust claim of right to elements of social value over which the right in question is plainly superordinate can attach to competing independent rights without regard to a right to equal treatment.

28   Other analytical consequences may also ride on the dominant-rights/tie-breaker issue. If we are committed to the dominant-rights view, the question of whether "the numbers count" (John M. Taurek, "Should the Numbers Count?" *Philosophy and Public Affairs* 6 (1977)) in life-and-death cases may become more difficult. If Violet's choice is between hitting and killing Rose or hitting and killing Jasmine *and* her husband, the idea that all three would-be victims have continuing equal and independent rights is complicated. On what grounds if any could Violet choose the death of one over the death of two? Is she required in effect to have a lottery? What would the appropriate lottery look like? Would it require the equivalent of a two-sided or a three-sided die? See Frances M. Kamm, "Equal Treatment and Equal Chances," *Philosophy and Public Affairs* 14 (1985). In contrast, the tie-breaker view simply points to the social value virtues of sparing two lives rather than one.

tery under these circumstances is to be indifferent to the social value that could be recovered by an adjudicatory mechanism, and the squandering of such social value requires some further justification.

3. The non-exclusive claim for the justness of social lotteries

The non-exclusive claim for social lotteries also assumes scarcity, but requires equal entitlements only in the more modest sense of entitlement to treatment as an equal.[29] The claim is also more modest in its payoff, arguing only that concerns of justice may commend lotteries over social-value seeking allocative devices under certain circumstances.

The non-exclusive claim rests on two propositions. First, social value-seeking mechanisms — adjudication and markets — will in some settings create or exacerbate patterns of social injustice; the risk of such distributional injustice is a good reason for social allocators to avoid the use of social value-seeking mechanisms in these settings. And second, the obligation to treat persons as equals permits unequal allocations that are justified by gains in social value but sharply limits unequal allocations that are not so justified. Given these propositions, the structure of the non-exclusive claim for social lotteries to allocate some scarce goods is obvious. On the one hand, the adjudicatory or market pursuit of social value is compromised in some circumstances by concerns that injustice will be exacerbated by such mechanisms. On the other, the obligation to treat persons as equals sharply limits social options in default of gains in social value. Social lotteries offer a means of making allocations of scarce resources that satisfies the right to be treated as an equal but does not implicate the concerns that may justifiably attach to social value-seeking mechanisms.

But neither of these founding propositions of the non-exclusive case for social lotteries is self-evident, and we want to subject each to some scrutiny. We will treat here the entitlement-connected issue of what limits the right to be treated as an equal places on social allocations in default of social value-based justifications for unequal treatment. We will postpone the discussion of the injustice potential of adjudicatory and market allocations until the related question of scarcity is addressed below.

4. The views of the right to be treated as an equal

A fair lottery is sanitary both in the sense that it does not permit factors that constitute, correlate with, or symbolically affirm extant elements of social injustice to drive allocative outcomes, and in the sense that it is indifferent and hence neutral among the members of the lottery pool. These sanitary qualities have obvious egalitarian virtues. A lottery can offer still

---

29 The arguments for the non-exclusive claim are at least as strong where there are equal entitlements in the more robust sense of entitlements to equal treatment or competing entitlements. If the exclusive claim has failed to persuade the reader, the non-exclusive claim thus gives social lotteries a second chance.

more in the service of equality; if it is equiprobable, it can effectuate probabilistically equal divisions of a good ex ante, as we have seen. The question is whether the non-exclusive claim for social lotteries, predicated as it is on the right to be treated as an equal, directs us to the more demanding condition of equiprobability or whether it is fully satisfied by impersonality. It is a question that exposes two understandings of the right to be treated as an equal.

The right to treatment as an equal promises that one's interests — one's welfare and entitlements — will signify fully and equally in the decision-making process of the relevant social entity. It is clear that this right is violated when social entities favor some persons over others for the wrong reasons. What is not clear is whether the right is violated when the social entity acts to favor one person over another for no reason at all. The right can be conceived as essentially negative, violated only when a social act is occasioned by unequal concern for the interests or entitlements of some members of the affected population. On this view, a social allocation that is genuinely arbitrary, that disfavors some persons in result but is in no sense personal to them, does no disservice to the right to treatment as an equal. The right can also be conceived in more affirmative terms, as insisting that persons be treated equally in the absence of legitimate reasons for differentiation. On this view, arbitrary and unequal allocations of social benefits are violative of the right to treatment as an equal. Equiprobability is a virtue under either view, since it can only be understood as improving the allocative picture from an egalitarian perspective. But on the first view, equiprobability merely adds a social value to the lottery process, special only in that it is a form of social value the pursuit of which does no violence to impersonality (indeed, as we have seen, on p. 142, equiprobability is a useful means of assuring honest impersonality). On the second view of the right to treatment as an equal, in contrast, equiprobability is necessary to a fair lottery.

Scarcity

1. The extent of scarcity

In most realistic problems of social allocation, such as those presented by conscription and renal failure, the scarcity of the benefit to be allocated arises not from nature or acts of God but because some social organ has decided not to produce the good in a greater quantity. Our prior discussion has thus assumed implicitly that the evaluation of these social allocations could be divided into two independent stages: (a) an evaluation of the justice of the decision determining the amount of resources to be devoted to a particular problem or group (the "production" stage); and (b) an evaluation of the mechanism used to allocate the predetermined resources among the equally entitled claimants (the "distribution" stage).

To a large extent this evaluative independence of the production and distribution stages seems justified. Obviously rights to treatment as equals or to equal treatment do not, by themselves, involve or imply entitlements to a particular level of production. Society, in these cases, has no moral obligation to satisfy completely the needs or desires of each and every claimant. Consequently, in these cases we may reasonably consider the justice of the choice determining the level of production separately from the justice of the mechanism of distribution of the scarce good.

Equal and independent rights to a good present a more complex picture. In some instances a social entity which, though able to, failed to produce and allocate sufficient goods to satisfy rights to the good itself would have acted unjustly. Such injustice arises, for example, if a wealthy society fails to produce enough food to meet the minimum nutritional needs of each of its members.[30] In other instances, however, an independent entitlement may not give rise to a full claim of social satisfaction. Our independent entitlements not to be killed, for example, do not clearly give rise to claims against society that it devote vast resources to the complete elimination of all risks and hazards or to our medical care in the event of accident.[31] Whether or not justice permits society to provide insufficient amounts of a good for distribution to satisfy independent entitlements, separate evaluation of the production and distribution decisions remains justifiable. If the scarcity is socially permissible, then evaluation of the distribution seems to stand on independent grounds. If, in contrast, the scarcity is unjust, the fact of its injustice obviously does not excuse the pertinent social entity from the obligation to allocate what is available justly. The independence of the evaluation of these two stages, however, is not complete. The reasons for devoting some definite amount of resources to those with renal failure may dictate that these resources be allocated in particular discrete bundles; these same reasons may also function to bar or at least prejudice the option of making no allocation at all. Production and distribution rest entwined in the analysis of indivisibility and of the virtue of some distribution over no distribution. Our discussions of these issues, therefore, suffer from greater incompleteness and hesitancy.

2. Indivisibility

The distribution problem does not arise from scarcity alone. If each of twenty-four equally entitled individuals lays claim to one of twelve chocolate bars, justice apparently requires that we break the bars in half and give

---

30   Such an event seems unlikely. Even in times of famine, starvation most often occurs not because production of food is insufficient but because the distribution of the produce is inadequate. See Amartya Sen, *Poverty and Famines* (Oxford: Oxford University Press, 1981).

31   The entitlement remains more than an entitlement to equal treatment or to treatment as an equal, however, in two senses. First, it only yields, in the production stage, to strong claims of social value or of other competing rights. Second, the entitlement, while it may or may not have force against society, may have force against particular individuals.

an equal piece to each claimant. Though physically and functionally possible in almost every case, we choose to frame the problem not as one of fair division but as one of just distribution of scarce goods.[32] While we might divide up kidney dialysis machines either by dismantling them and distributing their parts or by allocating each claimant a less than optimum time on the machine,[33] we see the problem, whether we choose an adjudicatory, market, or chance mechanism, as one of distributing not dialysis time but life-saving dialysis time.

In some cases the indivisibility of the goods is inherited from the production stage of the decision problem. This influence of the production stage on the distribution one seems clearest in cases where claimants only have rights to treatment as equals. In conscription cases, for example, society must choose whether to conscript anyone at all, everyone, or only some. To make the decision it weighs various social values; when it decides that concerns of efficiency dictate less-than-universal conscription, it also determines that a specific number of tours of duty of a well-defined duration and nature are required. Thus, indivisibility derives from the resolution of the production problem.

A similar influence of the production decision on the distribution problem may operate in cases of rights to equal treatment and of equal and independent rights to a good. When society chooses to allocate 100 dialysis machines (each costing $100,000) to all sufferers of renal failure, it chooses something different from the allocation to those sufferers of the ten million dollars necessary to build the 100 machines. Society also chose the form in which it wished to allocate its resources; that form requires that the allocation save lives.

At least two different reasons might explain this production-stage requirement that the distribution save lives. First, we might imagine that, prior to any individual learning whether they will suffer renal failure, everyone would prefer a substantial chance to gain therapeutically optimal access to a kidney machine to the certainty of a small piece of such a machine. As the discrepancy between the personal value of a divided

---

32 Only in the cataclysm-prone lands of moral philosophy does one confront literal, mechanical indivisibility such as when a fatal plague strikes two islands, with only one boat available and only enough time to get the serum to one island soon enough to save its inhabitants. Death is vital to these stories; it provides indivisibility by eliminating the disappointed claimants from the picture, a fact which helps to explain an otherwise remarkably morbid tendency in the storytelling exercises of modern philosophy. Death's scythe has done more for moral philosophy than Occam's Razor.

Bernard Williams has suggested in "The Idea of Equality," in *The Problems of the Self* (Cambridge: Cambridge University Press, 1973), that prestige is mechanically indivisible. But prestige frequently depends on social organization and cultural mores which are, to some extent at least, socially determined.

33 At least up to the point where the time allotted would be so short as to prevent any use of the machine at all. This minimal time would be determined by the time necessary to prepare dialysis therapy.

share of a good and the good in its undivided form grows, and as the chance of securing the good in its undivided form if it were allocated by lot grows, so too should our confidence that the good in its present form would meet this ex ante test of indivisibility.

Second, as mortal stakes cases indicate, robust rights of the equal treatment or independent variety typically arise in part because the good in question has a peculiar moral value. Certainly that is true of the view that persons enjoy a right to equal treatment with regard to the distribution of kidney dialysis machines; the capacity of these machines to prolong and enhance life is important to this claim of right. If the further division of a good would undo the claim of equal entitlement to it, that seems a powerful and independent reason for treating the good in its present state as indivisible.[34]

Scarcity and the justice of social lotteries

1. Non-allocation as a competitor to the social lottery

As in the case of indivisibility, the reasons underlying the production decision dictate that some allocation rather than none occur. We may understand this point most clearly in the conscription cases. Suppose that the production choice reduces to one among three alternatives: (1) universal national service of one year; (2) two years of service for half the population; and (3) no national service at all. In selecting among the alternatives, society will balance the constraints on liberty imposed by conscription, social assimilation benefits of universal service, defense or national service needs, and concerns of efficiency in meeting these needs. Social selection of option (2) entails preferring allocation (2) to no allocation at all.

A similar argument obtains in the case of entitlements to equal treatment or of equal and independent entitlements to a good of which society has chosen to provide an inadequate number. If society would prefer no allocation of kidney dialysis machines to one by lot (or by adjudicatory or market mechanism), it should not have allocated any resources to the production of kidney dialysis machines. Whatever reasons underlie the production decision must also explain the preference for some distribution over none.[35]

---

34 Our discussion below of commensurability is connected to both these ideals of ex ante consent and moral entitlement. When a good in its present state is incommensurable with the same good if further divided, in the sense that the capacity of a person to enjoy life is enhanced by the good in its undivided state but not otherwise, there is particularly good cause to think that, ex ante, everyone would choose to commit society to distribute the whole good. Similarly, if division of the good renders it incommensurable with full distribution there is good reason to believe that division runs contrary to the entitlement claimed.

35 Thus, the social preference of some allocation over none presents an immediate problem in the distribution phase only in the exotic cases of moral philosophy where society has a distribution problem thrust on it without having made a production decision.

Before continuing, it may be worth noting that the justification for some allocation over none is not the Pareto superiority of some distribution over none at all. Again the conscription case illustrates this clearly. If we consider only the preferences of those subject to conscription (and assume that each person would prefer no service to some service), option (3) will be Pareto preferred to both options (1) and (2). Moreover, evaluated after a lottery to determine who serves, option (2) is Pareto non-comparable to option (1) as those conscripted are worse off and those not conscripted better off. Finally, if each individual is risk-averse, option (2) considered prior to the selection of conscripts is Pareto inferior to option (1). If society selects option (2) regardless, it must do so for reasons other than its Pareto superiority.

2. *Adjudicatory mechanisms and the non-exclusive claim for lotteries*

As we have seen, even when claimants to a good are, in one sense or another, equally entitled to it, possible allocations may still differ along other dimensions of social value. In our discussion of the exclusive claim for social lotteries we argued that the dominant rights view would require the use of a lottery when entitlements to equal treatment or when competing rights were involved.[36] Here we seek to identify those qualities that recommend allocations by lot in cases of entitlement to treatment as equals or in the stronger entitlement cases when one adheres to the tie-breaker view. We shall argue that the crucial, disqualifying condition rests on the use of these criteria being injustice-exacerbating.

Recall the sanitary justification for lotteries. That justification invoked lotteries when society feared either the use of illegitimate, non-neutral criteria to allocate the good or the corruption of the agency charged with the distribution. A lottery served to insulate the allocation against the injustices inherent in these fears. The use of illegitimate criteria of selection and the corruption of officials, however, does not exhaust the ways in which adjudicatory mechanisms may prove unjust. Apparently "neutral" criteria, indeed criteria of social value, can, under some circumstances, exacerbate pre-existing injustices, or create new ones, in society.

How can an adjudicatory allocation which promotes an acknowledged social value exacerbate pre-existing injustices? The possibility appears particularly unlikely when we adopt a social value like moral worthiness. Nonetheless many of our conceptions of social value, even moral worthiness, derive from extant social conditions. The individual perceived as most socially useful may be one from a particular (higher) class family, educated at certain schools which give easier access to positions of power,

---

The opposite problem, however, may arise. Society, in the production decision, might elect to allocate no resources to a particular problem, such as renal failure. When someone suffers renal failure, however, society may find it difficult to adhere to its decision.

36   See pp.147–152.

and engaged in a profession that excludes, perhaps without the conscious effort of any member, individuals from other economic and social milieus. The award of the prize to the most efficient or most worthy may therefore reward those who have already profited most from the social structure. The conscription system used in the United States during the 1960s may provide a stylized example of the problem of injustice-exacerbation through an adjudicatory system. A motivation to adopt conscription by lot was that the system of "adjudicated" exemptions resulted in an army composed disproportionately of the poor and the black, classes who already suffered disproportionate social burdens.[37]

Moreover, systematic use of specific social values as tie-breakers in situations of equal moral entitlement may have two other adverse consequences. First, it would link the outcome of large numbers of allocations. This correlation of outcomes among various distributions[38] would further exacerbate any extant injustices. Second, the correlation among outcomes might have disincentive effects on individuals from seeking the prizes. If, beforehand, everyone knows that the winner of a prize will be the most efficient or the most worthy those without prospects of being so designated may withdraw their candidacy.[39]

3. Market mechanisms as competitors to the social lottery

Society often uses market mechanisms to solve problems of the allocation of scarce goods. As solutions to these problems, market mechanisms differ from both adjudicatory mechanisms and lotteries in at least one important respect particularly relevant here, given our decision to treat the distributive stage independently of the productive stage: markets generally solve simultaneously the production and the distribution problem.[40] Since we consider here only cases in which the number of units available for distribution is predetermined socially and unaffected by the outcome of the market process, we ignore an important feature of markets that may often argue in their favor.

To understand the circumstances under which lotteries would be preferable to markets we must understand how markets function. Market allo-

---

37 The introduction of the lottery, however, may not have altered much the social distribution of the burden, since various exemptions remained and these were still disproportionately open to the white and middle-class.

38 The outcomes may not be identical because the pool of candidates might vary slightly from allocation to allocation.
   It is possible of course that repeated use of a lottery will generate injustice because someone will prove to be lucky and win disproportionately often.

39 Conversely, of course, it gives individuals added incentive to be the most efficient or the most morally worthy.

40 We sometimes use markets only to solve distribution problems. In the United States the Environmental Protection Agency, for example, has determined levels of admissible pollution in some areas and then permitted potential sources of pollution to trade for these rights to pollute.

cations depend on two factors: (1) the distribution of preferences in the market and (2) the distribution of wealth in the market. Thus, in general, if all claimants for a good have identical preference relations, then those with most wealth will generally prevail in bidding for the scarce good. Conversely, if claimants have identical wealth, those with the most intense preferences for the scarce good will generally bid most for it. On this account we might regard market mechanisms as adjudicatory mechanisms in which the relevant criteria for allocation are identified as wealth and preference. This perspective yields three conclusions immediately.

First, for cases of entitlement to equal treatment or of competing rights, and if one adheres to the dominant rights view, markets would be unacceptable. If the dominant rights view requires the assignment of equal probabilities in this case rather than the use of tie-breakers in general, it must also prohibit the use of wealth and preference, whether determined by a market or adjudication, as a tie-breaker.[41]

Second, if use of wealth or preference as an adjudicatory criterion were injustice-exacerbating, it will remain so when it operates through a market. This argument carries particular force with regard to wealth. Wealth, after all, is often unequally (and unjustly) distributed in our society, and allocating further social benefits on the basis of wealth serves to exacerbate these inequalities and injustices.

Third, where preferences do differ among persons, and where wealth is equally distributed among claimants, markets apparently have some clear benefits over lotteries. A market insures that scarce goods go to those who value them most; a lottery assigns the goods on the basis of luck. If the goods may not be traded after the lottery, nothing assures that those who value them most will have ended up with them. Furthermore, we might, without affecting its efficiency properties, design the market mechanism so that those who lose the bidding are partially compensated for their loss out of the payments of the winners.

These conclusions suggest that lotteries will appear more desirable than markets when either claimants have shared preferences over the scarce goods (so that use of the lottery does not abandon the efficiency quality of the market) or claimants preferences are considered irrelevant to the allocation of the scarce good and when the distribution of wealth among claimants is unjust (so that use of the lottery protects against the injustice-exacerbating quality of market allocations). These two characteristics seem most plausible in cases in which the scarce good to be allocated is incommensurable with money and other material goods.

---

41 If we justify markets not on their efficiency properties but on their autonomy aspects, the analysis becomes more complex and less certain. For some competing entitlements, under the dominant-rights view, we might value autonomy sufficiently to allow that value precedence. In the face of inequalities of wealth, however, the threats of injustice exacerbating distributions might conflict with the autonomy-based justification of markets.

Suppose Iris has a debilitating disease that leaves her bedridden, in pain, unable to care for herself and unable to participate in any normal activities. Suppose further that taking a full dose of miracle drug X will restore sufferers from this disease to normal health and a p per cent dose of the drug offers a chance p of being restored to full health. In one sense, Iris's preferences for fractional doses of X seem no different from her preferences for chocolate; she prefers larger fractional doses to smaller just as she prefers more chocolate to less. Yet fractional doses of X are different because X offers the prospect of altering Iris's capacity to enjoy life. At any given level of wealth, Iris prefers to be healthy rather than debilitated; moreover, almost no payment, however large, would make her prefer being debilitated and wealthy to healthy. Thus if Iris were poor and Daisy, a second sufferer of the same disease, were rich, we would not think it appropriate to auction off the single available full dose of X. The auction, since it measures value in terms of dollars, will conclude that Daisy values X more than Iris, but we think that, because X is not commensurable with money, Iris values X as much as Daisy does. Under these circumstances a market mechanism would fail to treat Iris and Daisy equally, as well as tending to exacerbate the already existing inequalities.

Conclusion

Social lotteries, by design, are blind to all good reasons for making hard social choices. They thus pose a riddle, of the form "When is it ever reasonable to use an unreasonable mechanism for allocating scarce and valued social goods?" Most riddles are solved by changing levels of discourse, and this one is no exception. Lotteries make unreasoned allocations, but a social entity may have the best of reasons for making an unreasoned allocation, namely, the doing of justice among equally entitled claimants. Scarcity, equal entitlement, and equal treatment are crucial to the vocabulary of justification for social lotteries, and each of these ideas when pressed runs quickly to the complex and controversial. We have tried to embed our discussion of social lotteries in an analytical framework that respects the native complexity of the ethical environment. But a short form of our conclusions is possible. Lotteries are just when and because they offer the possibility of sanitary, neutral and equal allocations of social goods under circumstances where these egalitarian virtues are otherwise unavailable. The necessary condition of a fair lottery is either impersonality or equiprobability, depending on close distinctions among competing notions of equality.

Torstein Eckhoff[1]

Lotteries in Allocative Situations

Introduction

My definition of allocative situations refers to those cases where an individual or organization, which I call the distributor, allocates scarce resources, privileges, burdens or punishments among a number of potential recipients. The distributor may, for instance, be a mother or father and the recipients their children. Or the distributor and his recipients can be a teacher and his students, an employer and the employees, the staff and the inmates of an institution, a social worker and his clients, a court of law and the parties in a civil suit or the accused in a criminal trial, an administrative agency and its clients, or a state and its citizens.

A distributor who does not want to act arbitrarily has a choice of several principles of distribution: he can pay attention to the needs, fitness, achievements, merits or guilt of the recipients; or he can give each of them equal shares regardless of their personal characteristics. A third choice is to hold a lottery which distributes the chances of obtaining the values equally.[2]

In what follows, I review certain factors which may have an impact on the choice of distribution-principle. In section 1, I discuss the strategies which a rational distributor would adopt, supposing he were not bound by norms and did not have to consider recipient reactions. Such reactions and the extent to which distributors are likely to take them into account are considered in section 2. Development of social norms and enactment of laws, which in many cases regulate allocation activities, are not discussed separately. It may, however, be supposed that such norms are often products of an interplay of distributor and recipient interests.

---

1   Originally published on pp. 5-22 of *Social Science Information* 28 (1989). Copyright © 1989 Sage Publications. Reproduced with permission of Sage Publications.
2   Unequal distribution of chances is also a possibility, but I have never heard of it being practised in allocative situations. This alternative will therefore not be considered in the present paper.

In sections 3-5, different examples of the use of chance devices are discussed on the basis of the theoretical assumptions advanced in the previous sections. Since the examples are taken from different cultures, it should be borne in mind that what we regard as chance devices have often been considered a way of obtaining answers from the supernatural world. This is clearly stated in the book of Proverbs 16:33 – "The lot is cast into the lap, but the decision is wholly from the Lord." Indications of similar beliefs are found in several cultures.[3] Furthermore, if the outcome is not interpreted as a divine answer, it may more or less be considered a result of fate or luck.

The reasons for leaving decisions to a lottery can, to some extent, be the same for a distributor who believes in a supernatural interpretation of the outcome as they are for one who regards it as a pure chance device. Both can conceive of a lottery as a way of simplifying decision-making and of avoiding responsibility for the outcome. But there may be other motives for choosing the device. When discussing reasons for and against the use of lotteries in sections 1 and 2, I presuppose, when nothing is said to the contrary, that the lottery is considered a pure chance device.

I. Allocation Strategies of Distributors[4]

A rational distributor must take into account two types of reason. One type, which I call *substantive,* relates to the content of his decisions: what should the decision be in order most effectively to promote the purpose of the allocation? The other type, which I call *procedural,* refers to methods of making decisions. Some procedures are better suited than others to simplify decision-making and protect the distributor from doubt, scruples and criticism, etc. In other words, the choice of procedure is of significance for the costs involved in decision-making. It can also have other consequences. One kind of procedure may, for instance, be better suited than another for displaying distributor rationality.

Substantive considerations often make it rational to take into account recipient characteristics. For instance, if the purpose of the allocation is to improve the living conditions of the recipients, their need is certainly a relevant criterion, as perhaps also is their ability to make use of the assistance offered. If the purpose is to select people for the performance of certain tasks, their qualifications must be taken into account. And if the purpose is to punish offenders, the question of guilt is, of course, of decisive importance.

3   See Oluf H. Krabbe, "Om lodtraekning i fortid og nutid" ["On Lotteries in the Past and the Present"], *Juristen* (1944), and Vilhelm Aubert, "Chance in Social Affairs," *Inquiry* 2 (1959) [chapter 1 of this volume].

4   The questions dealt with in this and the following section are discussed in greater detail in my book *Justice: Its Determinants in Social Interaction* (Rotterdam: Rotterdam University Press, 1974): 243-323.

There are, however, situations where it is considered improper or impracticable to take recipient characteristics into account. Equal treatment according to some objective measure will, in such cases, be a natural solution. This alternative can be chosen on grounds of principle when, for instance, regard for human dignity or individual self-realization requires "everybody to count for one, nobody for more than one." Allocation of political influence through democratic elections, in which each vote counts equally, is an example. However, there are also cases where distribution according to need, fitness, merit or the like is considered proper, but where the distributor chooses objective equalization because he is unable or unwilling to find relevant differences between the recipients.

Objective equalization can be obtained in two ways: either by giving the recipients equal shares of the allocated values or by holding an even-chance lottery. The first of these alternatives has, from the distributor's point of view, the advantage that he retains control over the outcome of the allocation. Furthermore, ideals of equality are realized in a more substantial way by giving the recipients equal shares than by giving them equal chances. It is therefore quite natural that the equal-shares alternative is usually chosen if it is available.

But this is not always the case. The object of allocation can be indivisible, either because of its physical properties or because of social norms which, for instance, determine that only one person can hold a certain position. In such cases, an even-chance lottery may be accepted as a substitute for the equal distribution of shares.

Moreover, even if what is to be allocated is divisible, it may be difficult to divide it equally. The difficulty may arise because the criteria of equality are too diffuse or too complicated, or because several alternative criteria are available and none of these provides an obvious choice. In such cases, a combination of equal shares and equal-chance division is possible. As an example, we can take the division between heirs or co-owners of an estate which consists of arable land, meadow, forest and heath of varying quality. One solution to this allocation problem, which was prescribed in ancient Norse law, is to divide the estate into approximately equal units and let it be decided by lot which of the co-owners should have the different units.

I now turn to the distributor's *procedural* considerations. He must, among other things, take into account the difficulties involved in making and enforcing decisions. The activity of collecting information, weighing the evidence, deliberating the issues, making up one's mind and carrying the decision into effect can be troublesome and unpleasant. In particular, this is so when recipient characteristics, for example their needs, fitness, merit or guilt, are to be taken into account. In such cases, procedural considerations indicate that decision-making should be simplified. One way of doing this is to base the decisions on more specific and visible criteria than would seem to be ideal from a substantive point of view. An employer who holds that the best suited should be employed and who realizes that suitability for a job can depend upon many different personality traits, restricts himself, for example, to taking account of a few easily ascertainable criteria such as age, sex, education and previous experience.

Another, more radical, way of simplifying decision-making is to abandon the search for relevant recipient characteristics and to give each equal shares or, if that is not feasible, equal chances. This can be a tempting solution from a procedural point of view, but it is often unsatisfactory on substantive grounds. Whether, and under what conditions, a given solution is considered acceptable depends, among other things, on the relative value given to the two kinds of reason. The importance attached to the different conflicting reasons varies with the culture. For instance, it is unthinkable today to decide by lot whether an accused should be punished when there is doubt about his guilt. There are, however, many examples from ancient times and other cultures of this having been done — and not only in cases where the outcome is interpreted as an answer from the deity.

Recipient reactions are another factor which a rational distributor must take into account. If at least some of the recipients are greatly dissatisfied with his decisions, he may be caused inconvenience and trouble, which may make the implementation of decisions difficult. The extent to which recipients are satisfied is likely to depend partly on how just or reasonable they find the outcome of the allocation to be and partly also on their evaluation of the procedure. Among other things, it is often important to judge whether or not they consider the distributor to be impartial and whether they believe that they have had a fair trial. The factors determining recipient attitudes to allocation and the inclination of distributors to take account of these attitudes are discussed further in section 2.

It is also important for many distributors to preserve their own reputation and to present a picture of themselves — and of the organization or institution which they represent — that is apt to facilitate future decision-making. From this point of view, it can be essential to give the impression that the decisions one makes are impartial. Impartiality can be displayed in different ways,[5] but the surest way seems to be to leave the decision to a lottery. A strong desire on the part of the distributor to display indisputable impartiality is therefore a factor which can favour random selection.

Another quality which is often appreciated in a distributor is rationality, in the sense of being able to give convincing reasons for individual decisions. This can rule out the possibility of basing allocations on a chance

---

5   See Torstein Eckhoff, "Impartiality, Separation of Powers and Judicial Independence," *Scandinavian Studies in Law* 9 (1965): 12-22.

device. The fact that rationality is strongly demanded in judicial and administrative decision-making in modern Western societies is probably one of the reasons why such decisions are less frequently left to lotteries here than has been the case in former times and other cultures.

II. Recipient Attitudes to Allocation

The interests of the recipients can be related to both substantive and procedural questions. *Procedural* issues are of particular importance when the recipients make the allocation themselves. But they can also be interested in the procedure adopted when a distributor makes the allocation. It may be of concern to them, for example, to see how long it takes the distributor to come to a decision, how indiscreet and embarrassing his investigations will be, whether they will have an opportunity to argue their own interests themselves, etc.

However, when the issues are *substantive,* the recipient is likely to pay close attention to what he is himself going to receive. But he may also be concerned with questions of distribution. This is especially likely if there is a competitive relationship between himself and other recipients. The resources to be allocated may, for instance, be limited so that the more the others receive the less he will get for himself. Another source of interest in comparisons is the fact that what others receive serves as a yardstick for evaluating one's own situation. When, for instance, one talks about a high or a low income or living standard, severe or mild punishment, this has little meaning if these descriptions are not based upon comparisons. The tendency to make comparisons is probably one of the factors that help to develop conceptions of distributive justice. And when such conceptions exist, they serve as additional motives for making comparisons and evaluating distributions.

Recipients will, in many situations, prefer person-orientated principles of distribution according to need, fitness or merit, for example. On the basis of such criteria, they often demand some kind of relative equality, for instance that reward or punishment should be given in proportion to merit or guilt. There are also situations in which recipients demand equality according to an objective measurement—equal shares or equal chances. Recipients are, by and large, possibly more inclined than distributors to prefer these kinds of equalization. One reason for this is that demands for equality can be a means by which recipients defend themselves against the distributor and by which the weaker defend themselves against the stronger recipients.

The need for a defence against the distributor is particularly strong when recipients are dependent upon him, for example because he controls benefits which they need badly and which they are not able to obtain anywhere else; or because he has the power to impose burdens or punishments on them. There can be different kinds of real or imagined threat against which the dependent recipient needs to protect himself. There may ·be the danger of being refused or deprived of vital values (for example, parental affection or an employer's confidence); or perhaps the distributor will use his control over benefits and burdens as a means of manipulating the recipients. In addition, the inferior position of the recipient in relation to the distributor and his fear that competing recipients will be favoured, can in themselves be sources of insecurity. A demand for equal treatment together with other recipients can be a means of defending oneself against all these dangers. If the claim is met, so that each is given equal shares, they are relatively well insured against deprivation, manipulation and insecurity.

Random selection is well suited to meeting some of the defence needs of weak recipients, but it is poorly suited to meeting other of their needs. The recipients avoid being manipulated by the distributor, but they have neither predictability nor insurance against the deprivation of vital values.

Objective equalization can also have *procedural* advantages for both the recipients and the distributor. Both may consider it advantageous that decisions be made quickly and without detailed investigation. Furthermore, when the distributor follows a simple principle of equality, the recipients can more easily keep a check on him than when he bases himself on person-orientated criteria. It can be difficult, for instance, to verify whether or not the distributor is acting impartially when he attaches significance to such criteria as need, fitness and merit.

For this reason it can be important for the recipients to avoid person-orientated criteria. In some cases this demand is met even more satisfactorily with random selection than with the even distribution of shares. If the criteria of equality are diffuse, an attempt to give each recipient as much as the next may leave some doubt as to whether this has actually been done. Have some person-orientated considerations perhaps crept in? Such doubts are less likely to arise when a formalized random procedure is used.

The more heavily that procedural considerations weigh and the more difficult it is to find any other obvious method of equalization, the more the recipients find random selection a satisfactory solution. And the greater the importance that is attached to predictability and security and to everyone getting some of the benefits or carrying some of the burdens, the less a lottery is found suitable. The result of the interplay between these factors is that random selection seems to be most favoured when the outcome is either of very *minor* or very *great* importance to the recipients.

When the outcome is of minor importance, the fact that random selection involves a simple technique for arriving at a result will often be decisive. One can say, for instance, "The result is of no importance; we may just as well toss a coin." If more important values are involved, less stress is put upon simplifying the decision-making and more on substantive considerations which plead against leaving the result to chance. But if the value increases even further, the recipients' need for protection against partiality becomes more and more urgent. For this reason lotteries are sometimes preferred where the most vital values are at stake.

The extent to which the *distributor* is likely to take recipient preferences into account depends, among other things, on how important the outcome of the allocation is for himself. The less important it is, the easier it will be for him to yield to recipient wishes, for instance to their preference for random selection. Randomization may, in such cases, also be in the distributor's own interest since it is able to simplify his decision-making and exempt him from responsibility. That fact that he does not base the allocation on rational considerations and that he loses control over the outcome is of minor importance when he considers the result unimportant.

It follows from this that allocation by lottery is likely to be found in particular situations where the outcome is of great importance for the recipients and of minor importance for the distributor.

Let me add a few remarks about situations where the recipients themselves undertake the allocation. They may be a group of children, for example, who are to share some sweets or allot roles in a game; or they may be heirs who are to divide an inheritance, or people who are to do a job together and divide the various tasks among themselves.

If they have similar and therefore competing interests it may be difficult to reach agreement and the difficulties will tend to increase as the competing interests become stronger. Unless everyone accepts the outcome, there is a danger that no solution will be found. It is not at all certain that the minority will give way to the majority. The solution will normally be most acceptable when it constitutes a compromise, where everyone is treated equally and where it is made apparent that this is so.

A particular difficulty attached to decision-making is that none of the participants is impartial, since each has a personal interest in the outcome. For this reason, each may hesitate to take too active a part in negotiations. If one of the recipients is especially keen on producing or supporting proposals, the others may think that he is trying to butter his own bread. The rest may then become active and support other solutions with the result that the conflict becomes acute.

Since too much initiative can have harmful effects, the need arises for simple decision-making methods so that no-one has to show too much activity. This indicates that specific, highly visible and indisputable criteria of allocation should be found. If what is to be allocated is a homogeneous and divisible object, for example a sum of money or a bar of chocolate, distribution of equal shares will normally be satisfactory. This is a reasonable compromise because everyone gets the same amount and it is a simple matter of making a decision. But, if the object is heterogeneous or not measurable, it will be difficult to find sufficiently specific and indisputable criteria of equality. A way of solving the problem that is frequently used when two people are to share something between them is that one divides and the other chooses. But even though it is perhaps theoretically possible to extend the application of this method to division among more than two people, it will be too complicated in practice.

The problems of arriving at any other solution probably make lotteries a more likely choice in such cases than when an outsider acts as distributor. The great advantage of lotteries for recipients who undertake the allocation themselves is that they make the role of distributor redundant.[6] For reasons mentioned previously, the likelihood of lotteries being preferred depends, here as well as in cases where there is a distributor, on the importance of the outcome—randomization being particularly suitable when the outcome is either of very minor or very great importance to the recipients.

III. Lottery Selection of Persons for the Performance of Certain Tasks

1. Athenian democracy in the 5th and 4th centuries BC is the classical example of selection of authorities by lot.[7] The highest political authority was the *assembly,* of which all adult male citizens were members. The assembly was, in a very real sense, a sovereign body, which held forty regular meetings a year and extraordinary sessions as required. The main administrative organ was the *Council of 500,* which prepared the agenda of the assembly and supervised and co-ordinated the activities of magistrates. Candidates for the council were nominated by the population of the city districts (the *demes,* of which there were about 100). The number of candidates depended on district population and members were chosen by lot from among the nominees for a term of one year. A person might not sit on the council more than twice in his life. The majority of the 350-odd *magistrates* were chosen by lot from all qualified candidates who put in their names, so that every male citizen had a chance to take a turn in the administration. There was an age qualification of thirty for magistrates as well as for councillors. And certain offences, such as an unpaid debt to the treasury, could disqualify a person. The administration was organized into different boards on which the chosen magistrates served for a term of one

6   Unless the recipients suspect each other of cheating so that, for this reason, they need an outsider to arrange things for them.
7   My sources are A.H.M. Jones, *Athenian Democracy* (Oxford: Blackwell, 1957), and Ernest Barker, *Greek Political Theory: Plato and His Predecessors* (London: Methuen, 1960). The Athenian principles are also discussed by Aubert, "Chance in Social Affairs," 15-17 [pp. 38–39 of this volume].

year. There were no permanent civil servants, with the exception of a few hired secretaries for some of the boards.

Finally, there were the *popular law courts*. For each case, a jury was empanelled by lot from a pool of 6000 citizens chosen annually by lot. They decided both civil and criminal cases, for instance charges of peculation or malfeasance brought against magistrates and charges of treason or of "deceiving the people." They also had the power to quash any motion voted in the assembly as being contrary to the laws and to punish the author. Political trials were frequent in Athens. Popular juries were in such cases sometimes thousands strong.

The selection of administrators and juries by lot was probably considered a pure-chance device. In the surviving literature, there is no indication of supernatural explanations. The justification of the lottery seems to have been that it gave every citizen an equal chance, without regard to wealth, birth, or even popularity or eloquence. The system was criticized by Socrates, Plato and others because it made room for incompetence as readily as for competence. But it must by and large have been popular, since it was maintained for centuries.

To explain the extensive use of lotteries in allocating positions of power it is necessary to consider that other ways of selecting officials could have caused difficulties. Given the great number of councillors, magistrates and jurors and their short terms of office, popular election of all of them could have been too complicated and time-consuming. Appointments by the assembly could also have been a very complicated matter. Since all citizens were members of the assembly, their task would have been to select among themselves those who should hold the different offices. In other words, a large number of potential recipients with competing interests would undertake the allocation. As mentioned in section 2, there are special difficulties attached to this kind of decision-making which make the lottery a tempting solution.

It should also be said that most magistrates had routine tasks which many people could be sufficiently qualified to perform. In situations where outstanding qualifications were demanded from an administrative officer, e.g. in times of war or economic crisis, the magistrate was in some cases not chosen by lot, but elected by the assembly. This seems to show that considerations of expediency could determine whether the lottery system should be applied or not and it illustrates that the more important the outcome is for the distributor, the less likely it is to be left to chance.

2. In modern times, jury members are the only example of official decision-makers who are, as a rule, selected by lot. A system similar to the ancient Athenian practice, with lottery selection of both the pool of eligibles and the jury called to serve in the particular case, was introduced

in the US federal courts in 1968.[8] In other countries, a mixed system is used. In Norway, for example, a pool of prospective jurors (and lay judges) is chosen by municipal authorities. According to the law,[9] only people who, because of their uprightness, competence and independence, are particularly suitable for the task should be elected. However, it is doubtful whether this requirement is met to a great extent. Moreover, the election method does not ensure a representative cross-section of the community, as does the US system. On the other hand, in Norway, juries for particular cases are selected by lot.

This use of a chance device can be defended from two points of view: it makes for a fair distribution of burdens among prospective jurors; and it is intended to prevent jury selections from being manipulated by judicial authorities, thereby securing independent popular participation in the administration of justice. Jury selection is, in other words, a kind of allocation where, on grounds of principle, distributor control over the outcome should be avoided; and the best way of ensuring this is to leave the selection to chance.

3. With the exception of jury members, all holders of judicial, political and administrative positions in modern democracies are normally elected or appointed, not selected by lot. If we compare our systems of government with that of ancient Athens, two factors may account for the different methods of selection. The practical difficulties of arranging elections and appointments are not the same in democracies based on representation as they would have been in the kind of direct democracy practised in Athens. Furthermore, the devotion to ideas of rationality prevalent in present-day Western societies demands that important decisions should, whenever possible, be based on reason and not left to chance.

However, in cases where position-holders are elected, parity of votes raises a problem which has to be solved in one way or another. Selection by lot is a possible solution, but there seems to be a tendency to avoid this if an alternative can be found. Odd numbers of judges or committee members and tie-breaking chairmen are often used to avoiding deadlocks. Examples can also be found of a series of ballots, some of which may involve new sets of judges, being cast until a single winner is obtained.

In popular elections — of members of national or municipal assemblies for instance — it may, however, be difficult to find any solution other than a lottery when the voting results in a tie. Norwegian election law[10] provides for selection by lot when two or more political parties obtain an equal

---

8   Public Law 90-274 (USC §§ 1861-71, Supp. IV, 1969). Previously the pool of potential jurors was selected by the clerk of the court. Bias resulting from this method is discussed by Hans Zeisel in "Dr. Spock and the Case of the Vanishing Women Jurors," *Chicago Law Review* 37 (1969).

9   Court Law, 13 August, 1915, article 76.

10   Election Law, 1 March 1985, articles 51, 59, 64 and 69.

number of votes. This is extremely unlikely to happen, however, since there are several thousand voters in each constituency.

4. Outside the field of government, random selection of positions is more frequent, particularly where the potential recipients undertake the allocation themselves. Children use jingles such as "eenie, meanie, miney, mo" when distributing roles in their games. The drawing of lots is frequently used to select partners and to determine starting positions in various games and sports, e.g. who is to be white in chess, serve first in tennis or choose sides in football. Selection by lot is also often regarded as the best procedure when someone is to be chosen for an especially dangerous mission or if a life has to be sacrificed to save others.

A US criminal case from 1842 deals with a situation of the latter type, where a ship had been wrecked and one of its lifeboats was adrift in a storm. The boat was overloaded and leaked so that it was eventually on the point of sinking. On the orders of the first mate, the crew threw overboard all the male passengers apart from two married men and a small boy (a total of 14). The following day the boat was rescued. One of the crew, Holmes, was later brought to court (in the meantime, the others had disappeared) and was sentenced to six months' imprisonment. The judge instructed the jury that the passengers were entitled to be saved before the crew, apart from those crew members who were needed to navigate the boat. If none of the crew could have been dispensed with, lots should have been drawn among the passengers to designate who should be sacrificed.[11]

Typical of all these cases of random selection is that equalization is strongly indicated and is impossible to obtain by other means than an even-chance lottery. The examples I know of also seem to support the theoretical assumption, made in section 2, that randomization is considered most suitable when the outcome is either of minor or of very great importance to the recipients. In extreme cases, when lives are at stake, it is difficult to accept that any distributor should have the right to decide about the values to be sacrificed. The first mate in the lifeboat, who was otherwise in command of both the crew and the passengers, was not considered entitled to decide about their lives despite the fact that some people probably had to be sacrificed if anyone at all was to survive and despite the fact that he followed the time-honoured custom of saving the women and children. And if no-one is, or can be, designated as distributor, it becomes almost impossible for the recipients to find any solution through negotiation other than that of using random selection.

11   The case mentioned, *US v. Holmes*, is reported in 26 Fed. Cass. 360. It is discussed by Edmond Cahn, *The Moral Dimension* (Bloomington, IN: Indiana University Press, 1956).

IV. Allocation of Punishment by Lot

1. One way in which criminal justice has been distributed by lot is where the number of guilty people is so great that the authorities, for reasons of economy or mercy, do not want to punish them all. For instance, when a number of soldiers have deserted or mutinied, only every tenth or twentieth is executed while the others are released. Legal rules authorizing this method of limiting the application of punishment to a representative sample of the offenders have been in force in many countries, cf. *inter alia* Danish-Norwegian and Swedish laws from the 17th and 18th centuries.[12] The last time this law was applied in Norway was in 1814 when, after the short war that year against Sweden, a number of soldiers were brought to trial for insubordination. Four of them were sentenced to death along with every tenth man of the 114 others, who were selected by lot. All of them, however, were pardoned.

Most of the cases in which the sampling method was used were concerned with military offenders. There are, however, also examples of it being used in cases concerning civilians. In a Danish case from 1726,[13] in which all the inhabitants of a community had stolen wood from a forest, it was decided that six of them should be selected by lot and punished with six months' imprisonment.

The justification for these practices, found in judgements and legislative deliberations, was in a certain sense highly rational. It was maintained that the punishment of a small sample was sufficient to deter others from committing similar crimes and it was argued that one should not punish more people than necessary. Considerations of mercy were adduced in support of this principle and the economic consideration invoked that the execution of a great many soldiers or the imprisonment of large numbers of petty thieves would be a waste of such scarce resources as manpower and prison capacity.

The fact that the method was abandoned in the late 18th or early 19th century was probably due to the spread of Enlightenment ideas on justice. At that time there was a tendency towards more lenient punishment and a stricter equality in the administration of justice. It was no longer considered sufficient equalization to give a number of similar offenders equal chances of being punished; they should all have the same punishment.

Today the practice of selecting by lot some offenders for punishment and setting others free would certainly outrage our sense of justice. Still, this is not very different from what we are actually doing. The large num-

---

12   Birger Wedberg, *Tärningkast om liv og död* [Dicing with Life and Death] (Stockholm: Norstedt, 1935), accounts for the Swedish statutes and trials. English examples from the 17th century are mentioned by Keith Thomas, *Religion and the Decline of Magic* (London: Weidenfeld and Nicolson, 1971).

13   Mentioned in Krabbe, "Om lodtraekning i fortid og nutid."

ber of legal regulations which are frequently violated makes it impossible for the police and other law-enforcement agencies to detect and prosecute against more than a small fraction of the offences actually committed. In many cases of petty theft, for instance, no serious attempt is made to detect the offender. And the flaunting of administrative regulations is often left unpunished even if the offenders are known to the agencies of social control. Who is punished and who is not depends, to a great extent, on chance. Given the limited investigation capacity, this may be considered an advantage. If a systematic principle for the selection of cases to be investigated were applied — for example, where only the most serious offences were sanctioned — the consequences would be that groups of deviants would learn that they had little to fear. From the point of view of law enforcement, a more systematic randomization of the distribution of threats than that actually practiced would perhaps be advantageous. This would, however, be repugnant to our ideology of justice.[14]

2. Lotteries have also been used to decide questions of guilt. Several examples are found in the Bible.[15] One of them is the story of Jonah[16] who, instead of going to Nineveh to convert the gentiles, as the Lord had ordered him to do, boarded a ship bound for Tarshish. During the voyage a heavy storm threatened to wreck the ship. The crew wanted to know who on board was responsible for this disaster. By casting lots Jonah was found guilty. He was thrown overboard and swallowed by a whale and the storm blew itself out.

No doubt, the official interpretation of these lotteries in ancient Israel was that decisions were left to God. In some instances this is openly stated and the fact that the answer given by lot always came true points in the same direction. Jonah's guilt was proved by the ship being saved when he was thrown overboard. In other cases, the accused confessed his guilt when he was chosen by lot.

A somewhat similar method of resolving doubt about guilt were the ordeals used in several European countries during the Middle Ages. Here also the outcome could depend very much on chance, but it was interpreted as an answer from the deity.

This was, however, probably not the case with regard to certain Swedish and Finnish trials from the 17th and 18th centuries, in which it was decided by throwing dice which of two or more accused should be sentenced to death for murder. In these cases[17] all those accused had attacked

---

14   These suggestions are discussed more fully by Aubert, "Chance in Social Affairs," 17-20 [pp. 40–42 of this volume].

15   Joshua 7:13 ff.; Samuel 14:24 ff.; Proverbs 16:33 and 18:18; and Jonah 1.

16   Jonah 1.

17   Reported in Wedberg, *Tärningkast om liv og död*, 16-37.

the victim, but it was impossible to ascertain which of them had dealt the mortal blow.

Wedberg[18] argues convincingly that throwing dice in these cases was not (or at any rate was not primarily) believed to represent any heavenly revelation. The procedure was adopted, he contends, because *lex talionis* prescribed that a life should be given for a life, but not more than one for one. When two or more people were responsible for a murder, it was necessary and sufficient that one of them be sentenced to death. And if there were no reason to differentiate between them they should, for the sake of equality, be given the same chance of living by throwing dice.

The use of chance devices to overcome the difficulties involved in detecting offenders may, however, as suggested by Aubert,[19] have also had another function: an effective way of displaying impartiality. Furthermore, it served to remove the responsibility for a difficult choice from the shoulders of the judges.

The practice is, however, repugnant to ideas of justice and fairness prevalent in Western societies today. By leaving the decision open to chance, the officials indicate that it is of minor importance to them *who* is punished. This is a display of disrespect for individuals and one which cannot be tolerated today. We hold that each person's guilt should be considered separately and that the principle *in dubio pro reo* should be applied. This is certainly more in accordance with present ideals of fairness and human dignity than is the lottery method, but it is less apt to secure impartiality. Suspicion that evidence is manipulated by the police, or that a biased jury or judge will convict without sufficient evidence is always present.

V. Lottery Allocation of Resources and Burdens

As I mentioned in section 1, there are instances where, if prevailing norms are to be respected, material values should be divided into equal shares; but this is difficult to carry out because the criteria of equality are diffuse or complicated. It was also mentioned that one solution to this problem is to divide the values into approximately equal units and let it be decided by lot which of the recipients should have the different units.

There are many historical accounts of this method being used. When the Frankish king, Klotar, died in the year 561, his kingdom was divided by lot between his four sons. The Vikings used the same method to divide conquered land in France and Italy. Lotteries have also been used in allocating spoils of war and in distributing estates between heirs or co-owners.[20]

---

18 *Tärningkast om liv og död*, 25f.
19 "Chance in Social Affairs," 21 [p. 43 of this volume].
20 Several examples are mentioned by Krabbe, "Om lodtraekning i fortid og nutid," 170-173. See also Thomas, *Religion and the Decline of Magic*, 118-124, on allocation by lot in the 16th and 17th centuries in England.

The financial economy has reduced the need for applying lotteries in such situations. When material objects can be converted into money, it is always possible to give the recipients equal shares measured in terms of economic value. Difficulties may still arise, however, if two or more heirs desire the same object. In such cases, allocation by lot is often used when the heirs themselves are in charge of the distribution. But when a deceased person's estate is administered by a court or by an executor, other methods of allocation, e.g. auctioning, are usually prescribed. In Denmark, however, there is still a legal rule providing for solution of the problem by lottery.[21]

In situations where the object of allocation is indivisible, so that the distribution of equal shares is not possible, selection by lot has been used or proposed: for instance, the allocation of medical resources in short supply, admission to schools and universities, or public housing. However, in Western societies there seems to be a preference for person-orientated principles of distribution, e.g. distribution according to need, fitness, effort or merit. Random selection is, as a rule, found acceptable only when no relevant difference between recipients can be found. Even in cases where the time priority of applications is the only difference, the principle of "first come, first served" is often considered a more appropriate basis for distribution than random selection. This may be because time priorities can indicate differences with regard to need or effort, or because it is considered fair that the sacrifice of waiting should be rewarded.

Attitudes towards randomization also remain reserved when it comes to the official allocation of burdens. An exception to this is the allocation of compulsory military service. This is a burden which is, or has recently been, distributed by lot in many European countries, including Scandinavia,[22] and in the USA.[23]

The widespread acceptance of this practice is easy to explain: when it is found unnecessary to draft everyone who answers certain minimum requirements of fitness, a method of selection must be found; and it seems difficult to find a method more suitable than the lottery. Since the selection is of great importance for those eligible for conscription, there will be severe demands for fairness and impartiality. Hardly any person-orientated principle of distribution would be suited to meet these demands. It would be difficult to reach agreement on the criteria to be applied. Should those most fit for military service be drafted? Or should those who have the greatest need to avoid it be exempted? And how should fitness be

---

21 Administration of Estates Act, 30 November 1874, article 47.

22 This method was adopted in Norway in 1854 after Danish, German and French patterns. It has not been used in this country in the last fifty years, since all who meet the requirements of fitness are now drafted.

23 The execution of draft lotteries in the USA is discussed by Stephen E. Fienberg, "Randomization and Social Affairs: The 1970 Draft Lottery," *Science* 171 (1971).

tested or need proved? Basing the decisions on such criteria would, in any case, involve a great deal of work. There is no reason for the authorities to take on this work or to take responsibility for a large number of decisions that are likely to be criticized, since it is of little importance to them whether Peter or Paul does military service as long as both of them fulfill the minimum requirement.

In other words, we have here an illustration of the point made in section 2 that, in situations where the outcome is of great importance to the recipients and of minor importance to the distributor, random selection is more easily accepted than in other cases.

Fredrik Engelstad[1,2]

The Assignment of Political Office by Lot

Introduction

To people used to modern political processes, allocating political office by means of sortition mechanisms seems strange, and to some even incompatible with democratic procedures.[3] Yet the drawing of lots has been an enduring practice within the political institutions of societies that we consider precursors of modern democracy, notably the Athens of classical antiquity, the *communes* of early Renaissance Italy, and Switzerland of the 18th century.

It therefore seems appropriate to inquire into the more detailed mechanisms of political sortition in order to understand how and why it has been practised and with what consequences for both political efficiency and social integration.

This paper deals only with the selection of people for political office. It does not consider the use of lottery in the decision-making of office-holders, as when Caesar made up his mind to cross the Rubicon or when today the British House of Commons decides whether to treat private members' bills.[4] Furthermore, only selection for political, as opposed to academic,[5] religious or other offices, is considered. The Old and New Testaments give

1 Originally published on pp. 23-50 of *Social Science Information* 28 (1989). Copyright © 1989 Sage Publications. Reproduced with permission of Sage Publications.

2 The paper has benefited from generous comments by Jon Elster, Mogens Herman Hansen, and Maurice Pope, as well as excellent bibliographical assistance from Sven Lindblad. The author alone is responsible for possible errors or misunderstandings.

3 In April 1988 the local council of one of the Norwegian municipalities decided to allocate one liquor licence among four applicants by drawing lots. In a subsequent debate in the Norwegian parliament, the Minister for Social Affairs characterized this practice as incompatible with general principles of public administration.

4 Peter G. Richards, *Mackintosh's the Government and Politics of Britain*, 6th edition (London: Hutchinson, 1984), 162.

5 August Burckhardt, "Uber die Wahlart der Basler Professoren, besonders im 18. Jahrhundert," *Basler Zeitschrift fur Geschichte und Altertumskunde* 15 (1916).

numerous examples of selection by lot of people for priestly services. This practice was widespread too in ancient Greece.[6] However, the main point in religious lotteries is to reveal the will of God, whether it concerns selecting people, making decisions or settling questions of guilt. Here I concentrate on purely political questions, where the use of sortition may be rationally justified on the grounds of its consequences.

Finally, I distinguish between sortition and rotation of office, even if these two mechanisms are often confounded because both are practised mostly in small, unbureaucratic institutions.[7] Rotation is often used synonymously with turnover in office. This implies a relatively short term of office and usually a ban on re-election. Rotation in a stronger sense of the word occurs when there are as many as or more office terms than there are candidates. In this case, some principle must be found to determine the order of holding office. One example is the practice in Danish villages of locating farms relative to the movement of the sun in order to determine the rotation order for the office of village mayor.[8] In present-day Malaysia, a complex set of criteria is used to determine which of the rulers of the nine states in the Malaysian federation should be designated Head of State for a five-year period.[9]

A lottery, on the other hand, is a mechanism for the selection of people which may be used independently of the number of candidates or the length of office terms. Rotation in the strong sense is thus an arrangement which presupposes that *everyone* will hold office at some point in time, while sortition implies that *anyone* may be selected.

I. Key Examples of Sortition for Political Office

Sortition for political office was probably practised in several city-states in ancient Greece. But we only have systematic information about this for Athens. Within the realm of strictly political institutions in Athens, there are three types of office to consider: the archonship, the various boards of ten and the Council of 500. Although the political significance of each, as well as the relations among them, underwent great transformations during the political history of Athens, they may be treated as relatively stable elements of the shifting constitutions.

After a long period of tyrannical rule in the 6th century BC, Kleisthenes introduced several constitutional reforms from 508-7 onwards. One of them was a change in the tribal structure of Athens, something that would

6   M.H. Hansen, *Det athenske demokrati i 4. arhundre f.kr.* Vol. 5: *Embedsmaendene* (Copenhagen: Museum Tusculanum, 1979), 30.
7   See Max Weber, *Wirtschaft und Gesellschaft* (Tübingen: J.C.B. Mohr, 1922; Studienausgabe, 1972), 169ff., 796ff.
8   Joan Rockwell, "The Danish Peasant Village," *Journal of Peasant Studies* 1 (1972): 417.
9   Tan Sri Mohamed Suffian bin Hashim, *An Introduction to the Constitution of Malaysia*, 2nd ed. (Kuala Lumpur: Jabatan Chetak Kerajann, 1972), 27-34.

be of decisive importance for the formation of electoral districts. The city was divided into some 140 small municipalities — *demes* — which in turn comprised the ten tribes of Athens. Assignment for office through nomination and selection was to take place on all three levels: *demes,* tribes and city. The Council of 500 was formed by the Kleisthenean reforms as well, and was probably filled from the very beginning by the drawing of lots. In the following half century, when Athens reached a peak of political power, sortition was used to an increasing degree. From 487, the archons were chosen by lot,[10] and probably during the following two or three decades the other magistrates were selected in the same way.

In the 5th century BC Athens probably had some 700 magistrates with administrative tasks — the *archai;* so, including the Council, the number of political offices amounted to about 1200.[11] Taking into account the popular juries, several thousand tasks were assigned by lot each year. The most important offices of Athens not allocated by the drawing of lots were those of the ten *strategoi* — the military commanders — and other military offices. Some financial and religious tasks were also filled by election. All of these office-holders were elected by the Popular Assembly.

The term was usually one year for all types of office. No citizen could be a member of the Council of 500 more than twice in his lifetime. Likewise, no-one was eligible for an office he had held before, but there was no restriction on the number of different magistracies one person was allowed to fill. The consequence of the high turnover in office was that every male citizen attaining the age of thirty could expect to hold office at least once, perhaps several times, during his life.

Even if Greek philosophy decisively influenced the rest of the Western world, such was not the case with the Athenian political system. Sortition did occur in Roman politics, but mostly for allocating tasks within committees which were elected otherwise. The spirit of the Roman political system was very different from that of Athens. The city-states of northern Italy, however, had many examples of political lotteries in the period from the Middle Ages to the High Renaissance. But in this case as well there is hardly any reason to assume that inspiration from Greece was at work.

Most Italian city-states had some sort of city government comprising between six and twelve members, selected for a fairly brief period ranging down to two months. In the main, sortition was employed as a means of selecting members for this governmental board, but it might also have concerned other offices. It was in the city-state of Florence that the use of

---

10   Robert J. Buck, "The Reforms of 487 BC in the Selection of Archons," *Classical Philology* 60 (1965).

11   M.H. Hansen, "Seven Hundred *Archai* in Classical Athens," *Greek, Roman, and Byzantine Studies* 21 (1980).

political lotteries was preserved for the longest time, from 1328 up until the end of the 15th century.

Alternatively, lotteries were used to designate the board of electors given the task of appointing the leading magistrates of the city. Venice gives the most prominent example. Outside Italy this arrangement is also reported in Barcelona of the 15th century.[12] The use of lottery is also sporadically reported in 16th-century England, both for the selection of members of municipal councils and members of parliament,[13] but it did not develop into a stable institutional arrangement.

In some of the Swiss *Landsgemeinden,* sortition for the office of mayor remained in use over a period of 200 years, from 1640 to 1837.[14] In these cases, the chance mechanism was employed primarily to solve a distributional conflict. To hold political office implied the possibility of acquiring economic gain, by procuring mercenaries to foreign princes among other means. Such income fell to those holding the post of chairman in the community. The idea that everyone should have an equal chance of getting the gains of such a position quickly emerged. Consequently, the office was filled by the drawing of lots. If the lot fell to poor people with few means to exploit the office, they had the right to sell the office to the highest bidder.[15]

In the city of Basel, too, lot-drawing was employed during the 18th century to select city officials. Sortition was introduced mainly, it seems, to avoid the bribing of electors.[16]

Excepting the Lilliput state of San Marino,[17] I have found no examples of the allocation of office by lot in modern polities. However, sortition has been introduced in some cases as a part of the endeavour to democratize industrial companies. Emery cites examples where the composition of the board of directors or of planning groups within companies have been decided-by sortition.[18] Blum reports on a worker-owned company in which there is a special committee with members drawn by lot from among all the employees.[19] This committee is charged with the task of deciding whether the climate of the company is sufficiently good for the board of directors to deserve the confidence of the employees.

12 Claude Carrère, *Barcelone: centre économique à l'époque des difficultés, 1380-1462* (Paris: Mouton, 1968), 39.

13 Mark A. Kishlansky, *Parliamentary Selection: Social and Political Choice in Early Modern England* (Cambridge: Cambridge University Press, 1984).

14 Eugène Rambert, *Les Alpes Suisses: Etudes historiques et nationals* (Lausanne: Librairie F. Rouge, 1889), 226f., 276f.

15 Rambert, *Les Alpes Suisses,* 227.

16 Paul Burckhardt, *Geschichte der Stadt Basel* (Basel: Helbing and Lichtenhahn, 1942), 78.

17 Vilhelm Aubert, "Chance in Social Affairs," *Inquiry* 2 (1959) [chapter 1 of this volume].

18 Fred Emery, "Cities, Markets and Civilized Work, Anno 2000," *Human Relations* 38 (1985).

19 Fred H. Blum, *Work and Community: The Scott Bader Commonwealth and the Quest for a New Social Order* (London: Routledge and Kegan Paul, 1968). Cited after Carole Pateman, *Participation and Democratic Theory* (Cambridge: Cambridge University Press, 1970), 80.

II. Reasons for Drawing Lots for Political Office

There is no clear-cut, systematic presentation of sortition for office in the literature of political theory, no thorough discussion of what might be its strong and weak points; but sporadic references are found in the works of philosophers of Greek Antiquity, the Renaissance and the Enlightenment.[20] Later theoreticians have, for the most part, regarded it as a curiosity or ignored it altogether. Thus, a discussion of the justifications for sortition must, to a great extent, rely on arguments that are reconstructed from descriptions or casual remarks.

Justifications for the use of lottery may be of two main types. First, we may draw a distinction between normative reasons and reasons of efficiency. The normative justifications may be seen from two angles: one regarding the individual and the other considering the political system. The reasons of efficiency may also be divided into two categories: those linked to the process and those that concern the outcome of the process.

1. Distributional justifications

The strongest normative argument in favour of sortition is linked to the idea of social equality and individual welfare. In an unweighted lottery everyone has an equal chance of being selected. In a formal sense, this may also be said of elections. In modern democracies anyone may be elected president or member of parliament. But the candidates' actual chances of being elected are very unevenly distributed, due to important informal differences between them concerning social resources such as "public image," oratorical gifts, funds to spend on campaigning, the power to make threats concerning what will happen if the candidate is not elected, etc. Sortition removes the effects of these informal differences and thus prevents the formation of political elites.

On the personal level, the argument of equality may be directed towards the consideration of character formation and the sense of personal worth, or towards the distribution of extrinsic goods. Among the former, self-realization is perhaps the most important. In the Aristotelian view, participation in matters of state is the greatest of man's activities. Thus, in a democracy, the chances of attaining office should be equal for all. This idea is echoed in Montesquieu, but with a more normative twist. He does not underline equal chances of participation in decision-making as a reason for sortition, but equal chances of serving one's country (*L'esprit des lois*, 1.2.11).

Lottery may also be justified by equality of self-respect. The losers do not have to search for personal shortcomings as reasons for failing to attain office, something also mentioned by Montesquieu. On the other hand, the

---

20   See Fredrik Engelstad, "The Assignment of Political Office by Lot" (Institute for Social Research Working Paper 1/88, Oslo, 1988), for a survey.

winners will have to temper self-exaltation which may result from their
winning the election. They will know that their holding office is not due to
personal qualities different from those of most other people.[21] For similar
reasons, lots were occasionally drawn to select members of parliament in
16th-century England.[22] Candidates were usually recruited from among
the local nobility by a process of consensus formation. However, if there
emerged more serious candidates than there were seats, one might resort
to lottery in order to avoid a selection process that would be incompatible
with the existing code of honour.

The exercise of office may also be a source of material or immaterial benefits. To the extent that these benefits are linked to the position, it may be
argued that the position should be equally accessible to everyone. Such
benefits may not necessarily take the form of money or goods. In given situations, social relationships may be just as important. Holding office for a
period brings a better chance of educating oneself politically as well as of
developing contacts with other powerful people, all of which may be
regarded as investments that may return profit after the term of office has
ended. However, holding office may also be a disadvantage in terms of
either goods or time or both. The fact that office requires time and effort
was stated by Rousseau as a principal reason for sortition (Du contrat social
4.111).

2. Representation

The most common conception of democratic representation embodies the
idea of someone acting on behalf of someone else. Representatives
embody the general will, the interests and the preferences of the electorate,
commonly mediated by the party system. Against this idea may be set a
notion of descriptive representation. This implies that the representatives
are conceived as "standing for," rather than "acting for," those they represent. Or in the words of John Adams, the legislature "should be an exact
portrait, in miniature, of the people at large."[23]

This idea is intimately linked to the persuasion that citizens should be
autonomous and equal, as discussed above. But it also has a separate
meaning connected with the representative body. If it is true that elections
tend to restrict candidates to the wealthy and well-educated part of the
population, a certain misrepresentation of the interests and the preferences of the electorate will inevitably follow. Even if representatives have
as their conscious goal to embody the popular will, they will hardly be

---

21 Richard G. Mulgan, "Lot as a Democratic Device of Selection," *Review of Politics* 46 (1984): 549
    [p. 123 of this volume].
22 Kishlansky, *Parliamentary Selection*, 15, 67ff.
23 Hanna F. Pitkin, *the Concept of Representation* (Berkeley, CA: University of California Press,
    1967), 60.

able to do so without also taking into account their personal interests as a ruling group.

Thus, selecting representatives by lottery may be the best way of bringing the interests of the majority into the representative body. Undoubtedly, the assembly has to be fairly big to give an accurate picture of the population at large. But in an assembly of between 400 and 700 members, the deviations from a suitable interpretation of "popular will" furthered by elections will probably be much more important than those created by the chance mechanism.

3. Efficiency as related to the process

Compared with many other methods of selection, sortition may usually be performed with low expenditure of time and other resources. This is especially true when there is a single decision to be made. Instead of long debates, the matter may be settled instantly by tossing a coin. This argument of economy has been used in favour of drawing lots, for instance in deciding parents' custody rights in cases of divorce in order to avoid law suits that are both time-consuming and emotionally painful for the parents as well as the child.[24]

Furthermore, sortition may be performed easily when there is a very high number of candidates and a corresponding difficulty in establishing an exact list of all who are eligible. Candidates may be grouped, as happened for instance in ancient Israel in the selection of a scapegoat. First, one tribe was drawn from among the twelve, then one clan in the tribe, one family in the clan and one individual in the family. A somewhat similar procedure was used for the draft lotteries in the USA in the late 1960s. Instead of drawing individuals directly, birthdays were used as the unit of selection.[25]

Another type of argument for procedural efficiency points to the already-mentioned fact that informal resources of the candidates are made irrelevant by drawing lots. This implies that social resources that would be wasted on campaigns and similar activities may be utilized more productively to achieve societal goals.

Likewise, sortition may be employed to avoid illegitimate coalitions or the bribing of electors with the aim of "fixing" the result of the elections. As an example, the widespread use of such "Praktiken" was the principal reason for the introduction of a lottery for the selection of city-council

---

24   Jon Elster, "Solomonic Judgments," *University of Chicago Law Review* 54 (1987); and "Custody by the Toss of a Coin?" *Social Science Information* 27 (1988).
25   Stephen E. Fienberg, "Randomization and Social Affairs: The 1970 Draft Lottery," *Science* 171 (1971).

members in 18th-century Basel.[26] A similar case is mentioned by Aristotle (*Politics* 1303a 15).

Drawing lots may also prevent important social conflicts. Electoral campaigns easily lead to unnecessary polarization between candidates, unfounded election promises and hostility between groups. Such social costs disappear when the choice is made by a neutral mechanism that is not susceptible to influence (Aristotle, *Politics* 1305a 28).

4. *Efficiency as related to the outcome*

The fact that it is impossible to know who will be selected for a political office may contribute to diminishing social damage or waste. A striking example is the group of magistrates in Athens who were in charge of inspecting the building and maintenance of warships in Piraeus. They were selected by lottery for one year. This made it very difficult for ship-builders to bribe the control committee.[27]

A similar point may be made for conspiracies against the state. If nobody knows who will be a member of the city council in a month or a year, an attempt on the life of a leading official becomes more difficult. Likewise, the mechanism of sortition may subdue the motivation for conspiracy. Many potential conspirators will perhaps be among those drawn next time. Such arguments were voiced particularly in the context of political life in Florence.[28]

A related mode of thought was found in Athens. Combined with a short term of office and a ban on the re-election of officials, sortition prevented the development of a privileged group of officeholders which, in the long run, might have evolved into a new ruling class. Under given conditions, this meant that a maximum of power rested with the Popular Assembly. However, it should be mentioned that this was not a necessary consequence, even if it was intended by Athenian democrats. The power of the Assembly was not contingent upon the turnover of the magistrates alone, but on stability in the other political offices as well. This is discussed further in section V.1.

III. Arguments Against Political Sortition

The arguments against the use of sortition in the political process may also be classified into normative reasons and reasons of efficiency. The normative reasons fall into two categories: those regarding ex ante normative considerations and those concerning the outcome.

26 Burckhardt, "Uber die Wahlart der Basler Professoren," 31.
27 J.W. Headlam, *Election by Lot at Athens*, 2nd ed. (Cambridge: Cambridge University Press, 1933), 162.
28 John M. Najemy, *Corporatism and Consensus in Florentine Electoral Politics, 1280-1400* (Chapel Hill, NC: University of North Carolina Press, 1982), 302f.

1. Ex ante normative arguments against lotteries

The most general argument against sortition takes as its point of departure the ideal of rationality. Society as it actually exists is far from rational, but it is the vocation of mankind to make it more rational. Accordingly, to introduce a chance mechanism into the political process is to take a step in the wrong direction.[29]

Closely related to this thought is the idea of human responsibility. People charged with making social decisions, such as judges or politicians, bear the responsibility of making the best possible decision, taking all relevant arguments into account. In the feasible set of decisions, there is always one that is the best, and it is the responsibility of the decision-makers to select this one. This point was made by William Godwin (*Enquiry Concerning Political Justice*, 1793, chap. II.6.X).

There is also a weaker and more pragmatic version of this idea. Admittedly, in some cases it may be impossible to single out the best decision. One might just as well throw dice to decide the case. However, if this were allowed, it would easily function as an invitation to avoid a series of other disagreeable choices, where rational and responsible decisions would be required, by introducing lotteries there as well.

2. Normative reasons concerning the outcome

Selection by lot may indirectly weaken the moral obligations of those who are selected. As they are picked by chance, they may not feel responsible towards society in the same way as those who know that they are elected by their fellow citizens. Thus, even if sortition reduces the chances of corrupt actions, it may have the undesired effect of enhancing the moral corruption of those holding office.

On the societal level, political lottery may lead to a reduction in the chances of implementing popular will, as pointed out by Isocrates (*Areopagiticus* 23). Candidates for office vary in their dedication to the social goals and values of the majority. They also vary in their ability to interpret and implement popular will. Thus, even though elections may entail the development of social elites, they also give enhanced opportunities for controlling who is going to hold office.

3. Efficiency

The most widely used argument against political sortition is that it does not permit the selection of the most talented people to fill the office (e.g. Socrates in Xenophon's *Memorabilia* 1.2.9). In many situations, the drawing of lots may lead to a considerable loss of social efficiency; in extreme cases,

---

29 See Peter C. Fishburn, "Acceptable Social Choice Lotteries," in *Decision Theory and Social Ethics: Issues in Social Choice*, eds. Hans-Werner Grottinger and Werner Leinfellner (Dordrecht: D. Reidel, 1978), 137.

the results will be socially disastrous. However, the net loss of social efficiency may be less spectacular because of the motivational gains caused by a system where everyone is eligible.

The argument of efficiency carries proportionally less weight as criteria of preselection (see section 4.2) are strengthened. In an aristocratic society — understood as "the rule of the best" — such preselection is supposed to take place prior to the selection of officeholders, either by birth or by property. The strictest example of preselection is found outside the political realm, in the appointment of professors at the University of Basel in the 18th century. For the final selection, lots were drawn between three candidates who were all judged competent by a professional committee.[30] However, in most of the interesting cases of political sortition, preselection on the basis of talent has not held a prominent place. This is the case even in an oligarchic society like 14th-century Florence. Thus, the argument of talent cannot be dismissed as irrelevant on empirical grounds.

It is hard to conceive of a society where sortition is the only mechanism used for selecting officials. In practice, formal elections to some positions and informal selection processes mediated by kinship or other ties have played an important role. A crucial question, therefore, is whether and to what extent the drawing of lots may be combined with other selection processes. The Athenians found a balance between the civil magistracies filled by lot, the military and financial magistracies filled by elections, and the Popular Assembly with access for all male citizens. The problem of talent may also be counteracted by the design of the structure of positions. The positions allocated by lot are mostly the membership of committees, and not singular offices. In Athens, the board of ten was the most common form, with one member from each *deme*. In this way, the probability of drawing some talented members was fairly high.

An assumption that is often made implicitly is that the use of sortition is restricted to small groups or small-scale societies.[31] However, this argument should be seen as deriving from the argument of talent. In smaller groups, existing differences of talent may become less visible due to group dynamics. It is hard to see why the size of the collectivity should in itself make lotteries less efficient than elections or other selection procedures (see also section 2.3). Thus, the question of size should not be treated as a separate argument.

IV. The Place of Lottery in the Selection Process

The main point of the lottery is of course that it is a mechanism for making random decisions. But the decision to use and, if desired, how to use this

---

30 August Burckhardt, "Uber die Wahlart der Basler Professoren."
31 For an explicit argument see Mulgan, "Lot as a Democratic Device," 555 [pp. 129–130 of this volume].

mechanism may not be taken randomly. Indeed, it is possible to conceive metalotteries designed to decide randomly when the random mechanism should be used and possibly to allocate different weights to the alternatives. But use of the lottery very easily becomes meaningless if the decision-making body deprives itself of the possibility of anticipating possible outcomes.[32]

In the following sections, I make an attempt to "lay out" the political decision-making process by the selection of people for offices, and discuss how the lottery may enter the process at various stages and affect the outcome differently. To do so, it is convenient to distinguish between those selection processes where the point is to select candidates in the last instance by lottery and those where the lottery serves as an auxiliary mechanism in the election of candidates. This distinction is not clear-cut as the two cases may be combined. But at any rate it may be useful to give a separate account of the cases where the final selection of candidates is *not* performed by drawing lots.

1. The lottery as an auxiliary mechanism

In this section I describe how the lottery may be used (i) as a part of the procedure for verifying the result of the election; (ii) as a part of the election procedure; (iii) as a mechanism to select electors; and (iv) as a way of determining the order of filling the office from among several candidates selected simultaneously.

From Sparta we have an example of the use of lottery to ascertain the actual result of the election. As sign of voting, the cries of the voters were used. Gilbert (after Heinberg) describes the election of the Spartan *gerontes*, where the

> people assembled in the Apella and the candidates for office went through the assembly in an order previously determined by lot. He at whose passing the people raised the loudest cry was held to be elected. The loudness of the cry was judged by men shut up in a house near the Apella, from which they could hear the cry, but not see the assembly.[33]

In ancient Rome, lotteries were rarely used in politics, but there is an important example concerning the voting procedure itself. Voting in political assemblies was performed according to group, with voting groups consisting of tribes, voting one after the other. The voting order was determined by lot. After the first tribe had voted, the result was made public. One reason for determining the order of voting by lot could be that the

---

32 The intricacies of metalotteries are vividly described in an entertaining novel, *The Dice Man* (New York: W. Morrow, 1971) by Luke Rhinehart.

33 Gustav Gilbert, *Constitutional Antiquities of Sparta and Athens* (London: Swan Sonnenschein & Co, 1895). Cited after John Gilbert Heinberg, "History of the Majority Principle," *American Political Science Review* 20 (1926): 54f.

vote of the first groups might influence the vote of subsequent groups.[34] An alternative interpretation by Pope[35] is based on the rules for deciding the result of the election. A candidate would be considered elected as soon as he had gained one half of the votes. The rest of the votes would then not be taken. In the case of an election with two candidates, where both had equal support among the electorate, it would be to their decisive advantage that their supporters vote early.

Furthermore, lotteries may be employed to determine the boundaries of the electorate. Another example can be given from Rome: Latins, who did not belong to the Roman tribes, had voting rights in the city, but were not allowed to take part as a separate group. Consequently, lots were drawn to determine to which of the tribes the Latins should be allocated, something that might have a decisive influence on the voting of that tribe.

More significant examples of the determination of the electorate by sortition are found in several of the Italian city-states of the Renaissance. Most prominent of these is Venice, where the election of the doge was accomplished through a very complex process. The election lasted five days and went through ten stages, two each day. The process started in the Great Council of the city, from which thirty members were selected by sortition. By a new draw, this group was reduced to nine members, who then selected a new group of forty, all of whom had to be elected by at least seven votes. The process continued this way, through nine stages with five sortitions and four elections, until the fifth day, when a group of forty-one people was designated. These in turn elected the doge.[36] Even if the process were more elaborate in Venice than in most other city-states, there are similar examples from other Italian cities, among them Bologna, Parma, Brescia, Vincenza.[37] The same procedure is also recorded in 16th-century England for the selection of both borough officers and members of parliament.[38]

In the city of Basel, a mixed system was practised during the 18th century. The body of electors was given in advance. However, the electors were divided by lot into three or six subgroups, each of which nominated one candidate for the office. Lots were then drawn among the nominees.[39]

Finally, sortition may be used to determine the order of succession of candidates who are already appointed by some other procedure. The term of office of the Athenian Council of 500 was divided into ten segments,

34   E.S. Staveley, *Greek and Roman Voting and Elections* (London: Thames and Hudson, 1972), 155.
35   Personal communication. See also Maurice Pope, "Athenian Festival Judges—Seven, Five, or However Many," *Classical Quarterly* 36 (1986).
36   Robert Finlay, *Politics in Renaissance Venice* (London: Ernest Benn, 1980), 141f.
37   Arthur M. Wolfson, "The Ballot and Other Forms of Voting in the Italian Commune," *American Historical Review* 5 (1899): 11f., 19f.
38   Kishlansky, *Parliamentary Selection*, 36.
39   Burckhardt, "Uber die Wahlart der Basler Professoren," 35.

with the fifty representatives of each tribe acting as a presiding committee for one period. The order of the tribes was determined by lot. An analogous procedure is known from Siena of the 13th and 14th centuries. On some occasions, the city council in fact acted as an electorate, by pointing out candidates worthy of filling the positions in the same council in later periods. According to a complicated set of rules, the candidates were divided into groups of nine, each of which would then constitute the city council in one of the subsequent periods. Slips of paper, on each of which was written the name of a group, were closed in waxen balls and deposited in a chest. The order of succession was determined by drawing a new ball each time a new council entered office.[40] The effects of this arrangement were in many ways similar to those in Florence described in the following section.

2. Selection of candidates

When candidates are to be selected by sortition, the process must go through at least two stages. It has first to be determined who is eligible, and then the draw among candidates can take place.[41] The first stage is the more interesting of the two. Once the list of candidates is drawn up, the process continues more or less automatically, even if it happens that the selection of candidates influences the final selection procedure, or vice versa. I return to this case below.

First comes the establishment of a formal rule designating those entitled to take part in the political process. In Athens, this differed according to the office to be filled. In the Solonian constitution, only members of the two upper tax classes were eligible for the office of archon. Later the hoplites, the third of the four classes, were included. The lowest class was also excluded from the various boards of magistrates, and from the Council of 500, but only de jure.[42] Likewise, those inhabitants who were not Athenian citizens, i.e. born of Athenian parents, were excluded from office.

In addition to such formal delineations, there will often be a substantial delimitation excluding candidates considered incapable or unworthy of holding office, for political institutions will usually feel a need to protect themselves against madmen or potential traitors. In Florence this responsibility was handled by a committee of trusted men, who were summoned from time to time to scrutinize all citizens with regard to their eligibility for political office. The official aim of the committee was to prevent the selection of men who did not have the confidence of the majority. But secondarily, the committee also aimed to exclude candidates of low social

---

40   William M. Bowsky, *A Medieval Italian Commune: Siena under the Nine, 1287-1355* (Berkeley: University of California Press, 1980), 60.
41   See also Aristotle, *Politics* 1300b 2.
42   See also A.H.M. Jones, *Athenian Democracy* (Oxford: Basil Blackwell, 1978), 105.

rank, even if this was not stated officially. Renaissance Florence was governed by an unstable coalition of nobility, finance magnates and merchants. These groups constituted the most important recruitment base for political office. At the same time, Florentine politics was dominated by a continuous conflict between the oligarchy and the middling and small artisans. A major concern was the criteria for eligibility for the city council, the Council of Twelve. After a revolt by the lower classes in 1378, the list of candidates was broadened substantially to include middle-class artisans and merchants.

Naturally, the right to sit on such a scrutinizing committee will also be the object of political conflict. The use of sortition is meaningful if it fulfils the important task of anticipating and, to some extent, preventing such conflicts. In Florence there was consequently also a complex process, in several stages, for the selection of the scrutinizing committee. This process went through several rounds of sortition, in a way somewhat similar to the appointment of electors for the choice of doge in Venice.[43]

Eligibility, however, is not only a question of formal citizenship or political confidence. In Florence, where the term in office of members of the Council of Twelve was two months, there were other limitations as well. One lay in the rule that a member could not be re-elected within a period of two years; another in the fact that possible candidates might be travelling abroad and thus unable to serve on the council. Others were not eligible as long as they were sentenced to debt prisons. In Florence, the selection of council members was performed by drawing names from special bags, as already mentioned. Those candidates who were temporarily ineligible had their names deposited into another, smaller bag, the *borsalino*. Originally, the *borsalino* was designated only as a place to keep the slips containing the names of temporarily ineligible candidates. However, over a long period, a very complex set of rules gradually developed, implying drawing from both the small and the large bags. This arrangement favoured those who had already served on the council, i.e. the oligarchy, and was implemented as a response to the extension of the pool of eligible candidates during the second half of the 14th century. When rules of eligibility are put under political pressure, the selection of candidates may undergo a slow displacement if the process of lottery allows small changes that are insignificant when regarded separately; but which over time may add up to a substantial result.

In Athens, the system for controlling candidates was far less elaborate than that in Renaissance Italy. No committee was formed to judge the suitability of each candidate before the draw. On the other hand, those selected for office were exposed to a comprehensive and fairly tough control. Before taking office, they had to speak before a popular court. Here all

43   See Najemy, *Corporatism and Consensus*, 122.

the selected candidates had to answer questions regarding their family and past conduct. New hearings might take place both in the middle of the term or at the end, when they concerned the way that each magistrate fulfilled his office.

Establishing a list of suitable candidates may also be complicated by a widespread unwillingness to serve a term in office. The Athenians often had difficulties in filling the list with volunteers. Thus the conscription of candidates for sortition was often necessary. The unwillingness to serve in office may have had at least two causes. To hold some of the offices could be fairly costly to the candidates, both in terms of time and money.[44] In addition, many citizens, especially those in the lower classes, may have feared the scrutinizing hearings, and not least the possibility of being exposed to disdain and insult from members of the higher classes.

Both in Athens and in Florence, it was an important principle that the selection of candidates should be representative of the smaller geographical units of the city-state. In Florence, two persons from each of the six vicinities were drawn for the Council of Twelve. In Athens the ten tribes were represented by an equal number of people for the seats in the Council of 500, but in such a way that the representation was roughly proportional to the *demes*, which were of unequal size.[45] For the majority of the magistracies, as well as the different internal functions of the council, candidates were selected by tribe.

3. Varieties of two-stage sortition

Two-stage sortition was also in practice for long periods in Athens. However, this arrangement concerned only the selection of archons,[46] not members of councils or other officials. Each tribe selected by lottery ten candidates for the archonship, in the second stage one of whom was drawn from each tribe. At first sight, this practice appears meaningless. Why not select one candidate at once?

The two-stage lottery probably succeeded a two-stage selection of archons by vote, with the tribes nominating candidates and the Council of Areopagus performing the final selection.[47] But the historical antecedents do not explain why the practice persisted for more than 150 years. Thus, some of the underlying properties of two-stage selection should also be explored.

Staveley forwards the hypothesis that preselection by lot may have served as a mechanism to secure a sufficient number of candidates for the

44   Hansen, *Det athenske demokrati*, 38.

45   Headlam, *Election by Lot at Athens*, 56.

46   In fact, a triple sortition may have taken place. In addition to two stages in the selection of candidates, the different offices of the archontate may also have been allocated to tribes by lot. See Mabel Lang, "Allotment by Tokens," *Historia* 8 (1959): 88.

47   Buck, "The Reforms of 487 BC."

final selection of archons. If the number of candidates became too small, the officials could have the option of raising the number by conscription, and then drawing lots to choose among the conscripted men.[48] The unintended consequence of such a system would very easily be that less willing people were selected at the cost of those striving for the office of archon.

This hypothesis may also be elaborated in a somewhat different direction. If archons were chosen in one step among those who volunteered for the office, the most ambitious candidates would most easily be chosen. This would enhance the possibility of increasing the political power of the archonship. However, one of the important functions of sortition was to lessen the importance of the archonship and other elite offices. By the process of two-stage selection, one is assured of a high number of candidates, and thus the chances of average citizens to be elected become substantially greater.

Other forms of two-stage lottery also deserve mention. The allocation of tasks by sortition within groups whose members have already been drawn by lot may be regarded ex post as a two-stage sortition process. The internal division of labour in the Council of 500 is the most conspicuous example of this type. Another form of ex ante two-stage procedure was practised for a fairly long period in 5th-century Athens, when a large number of the magistracies were filled on the *deme* level. As the *demes* varied in size, the number of magistracies were allocated to the *demes* according to population. In a central lottery in the Theseus temple, each year several hundred offices were redistributed among the *demes* and then filled by sortition within each *deme*. This procedure was abandoned, however, because some of the *demes* started selling offices.[49]

V. Consequences of Filling Office by Sortition

There are two reasons why the effects of political sortition should be viewed separately from the justifications for their introduction: (i) the intended consequences may not be attained due to distorting mechanisms; and (ii) important unintended by-products may emerge. Among the intended consequences, attention should be focused on questions of distribution, as this is where we may come across important differences between ideals and reality.

1. Distributional consequences

That an unweighted lottery creates equal chances for all candidates, as long as fraud is avoided, is trivial. But the use of the chance mechanism presupposes some institutional arrangement. The important question, then, is whether sortition within a given institutional context creates

48   Staveley, *Greek and Roman Voting and Elections*, 37f.
49   Hansen, *Det athenske demokrati*, 32.

greater equality than an alternative mode of selection applied to the same set of candidates. We may compare a sortition situation with one of direct elections, and ask if the distribution of the probabilities of being selected is more weighted in one case than in the other. If we take the cases of Athens and Florence, the answer is probably that in both cases sortition is the more egalitarian mechanism.

For Athens, we must compare the informal differentiation due to the fact that rich candidates have better opportunities of conducting campaigns than had poor candidates, with the effect that the control mechanism favours the well educated who have good training in rhetoric and are used to standing up in large assemblies. The poor candidate must compete with the rich, either with respect to money or competence and rhetorical ability. In the second case, he may be in a weak position; in the first case, the task is virtually hopeless. There is thus reason to believe that over time, a system of direct elections will serve the interests of the rich better than one of sortition. But what about the facts? Questions have been raised about the extent to which the Council of 500 was filled by well-to-do people.[50] Demographic evidence, however, suggests that almost every citizen must have served on the council.[51]

In the case of Florence, the important difference among candidates did not lie in wealth, but in social influence. The system was generally fairly closed, but has been described as being such that, when a person was nominated, his chance of eventually being drawn was very great. For long periods at least, the sortition process was more clearly directed towards the order of succession of candidates rather than deciding whether a candidate would hold office or not.[52] Accepting the narrow base of candidates, it can hardly be doubted that the system worked in a more egalitarian way than direct elections would have done. If successive elections with the same people standing as candidates had been held, it is almost unthinkable that all the candidates would have been elected, but simply in a different order.

Another problem of distributional consequences is encountered if some, but not all, offices are allocated by lot. This was an important feature of the Athenian political system, where the military offices were filled by election in the Popular Assembly. There was no limit on the number of times a person might be re-elected commander. An obvious consequence of this system is that the power of the *strategoi* was enhanced, compared with that of the civilian magistrates. So, even if sortition equalizes power within one sphere of the political system, it may weaken this given sphere in comparison with others.

50   Jones, *Athenian Democracy*, 106.
51   Hansen, *Det athenske demokrati*, 36.
52   Najemy, *Corporatism and Consensus*, 115.

This line of reasoning should be modified by two considerations, however. The first concerns the amount of power held by the people. If magistrates had been elected, or even were employed on a more permanent basis, the possibility of their serving as a counterforce vis-à-vis the military commanders would no doubt be increased. The power of the military offices would be reduced; however this would hardly be to the benefit of popular participation, but rather to the profit of the magistrates as a group. To some extent, popular participation would be sacrificed in order to counter the concentration of power among the *strategoi*. Secondly, the question of legitimacy should be considered. Even if institutions experience a loss of effectiveness because of the sortition mechanism, this may be compensated to the extent that the drawing of lots strengthens the legitimacy of political participation. These two arguments indicate that, even if it is true that "a combination of lots and elections leads to a concentration of power among those elected,"[53] it does not necessarily follow that alternative modes of selection would lead to a more equal distribution of power.

2. Effects on social integration

The distributional effects of sortition may also influence social integration. I have already mentioned that the drawing of lots may prevent conspiracies. This argument may be generalized, inasmuch as the citizen's support for the political institutions will be strengthened by his knowing that he himself may be drawn. His chances of being drawn are naturally small, but they are not nil, and they are no greater for anyone else (with the reservations already mentioned). Conversely, he who wants to be selected but does not gain office cannot put the blame on others.

In addition to the integrative effects linked to equality of chances, there are also effects on social integration due to the ritual aspects of sortition. The act of drawing lots will itself often be both solemn and exciting.[54] These ritual aspects had a very different form in Antiquity and in the Renaissance. In Athens the drawing took place in public. Little is known about the exact procedures; some of the drawings may have been located in each *deme*,[55] but some were also held in the centre of the city, where thousands of people were gathered, as was the case with the selection of jurors.[56] At any rate, these events must have been a source of important public ritual.

---

53   Hansen, *Det athenske demokrati*, 36.

54   In her short story "The Lottery," Shirley Jackson conveys vividly the excitement of the act of drawing lots. See "The Lottery," in *The Lottery* (New York: Avon Books, 1965).

55   Jones, *Athenian Democracy*, 105.

56   Sterling Dow, "Aristotle, the Kleroteria, and the Courts," *Harvard Studies in Classical Philology* 50 (1939).

Each year several thousand offices and tasks were allocated by lottery. A substantially higher number of candidates had to be nominated. Thus the integration of the political system was not only due to the equality of chances, but must also have been furthered by the fact that each citizen had to be a candidate several times over. And those who were not candidates must often have watched the exciting game. Even if it stems from a totally different epoch, an account from the Swiss *Landsgemeinden* retains some of the flavour of the event. Rambert describes how the elders look back on the time when fate decided the choice:

> Mais les vieillards et même les hommes d'âge mûr se souviennent d'avoir vu plus d'une fois fonctionner les huit boules enveloppées de noir, et tous sont d'accord pour dire que les élections actuelles sont pâles en comparaison; c'était un spectacle que celui de tout le peuple dans l'attente et de la brusque et libre exposition de sa joie, de sa surprise et de sa mauvaise humeur, selon les caprices du hasard.[57]

The Renaissance cities of northern Italy present a different picture. Here, except for the solemn prelude, the drawings were not surrounded by festivity and excitement. On the contrary, they were to a great extent characterized by secrecy, especially in the case of candidate nominations. In Siena, they took place in secret meetings where only a few magistrates and priests were present as witnesses.[58] The name of the person who was actually nominated was kept secret in Florence also. None of the citizens, except the scrutiny committee, could know if they were nominated or not. But they could keep hoping.[59] One good reason for keeping the nominations covert was that, if those who had been rejected found out, their hostility towards the city would be greater. One may ask if the uncertainty due to secrecy weighed more heavily than the enhanced integration due to the chances of being drawn, such that the net result would be negative. Against this assumption, one may argue that secret decisions, even if they concerned central parts of personal life, seem to have been both widespread and accepted in an Italy on the borderline between the Middle Ages and the Renaissance.[60] Many guild rituals point in the same direction.

Without posing the question of causal direction, one may regard the differences between Athens and Florence concerning secrecy and publicity in the light of certain religious conceptions of the times. The Athenians pictured the gods as capricious, but fully understandable. On the contrary, however, 14th-century man experienced God's ways as inscrutable, his

---

57 Rambert, *Les Alpes Suisses*, 276f.
58 Bowsky, *A Medieval Italian Commune*, 60.
59 Najemy, *Corporatism and Consensus*, 302.
60 Daniel Waley, *The Italian City-Republics* (London: Weidenfeld and Nicolson, 1969).

wisdom as transcending human understanding and his modes of being as filled with grace.

VI. Some Possible Explanations of the Use of Political Lotteries

It would be fruitless to aim for a general theory explaining the use of sortition for filling offices. Each historical situation is unique and must be explained by the bundle of causal factors present in the given situation. To understand why sortition had been used in any one society, it is necessary to describe the interplay between the intentions and plans of the social actors and the structural conditions within which they had to act. Detailed explanation of the use of sortition, in the cases described above, is a historical task clearly beyond the scope of this article. However, I have sketched some factors of a more general character.

1. Intentional factors

There are a host of different reasons for introducing sortition into politics, as already discussed in section 3. Many of them have no doubt been implicitly or explicitly present in the cases recorded. The justifications may have been the wish to prevent the bribing of electors, avoid social conflict, allocate offices that imply extra benefits or burdens, or to broaden the base of political participation.

Viewed separately, such justifications may explain why the lottery has been introduced at a given point in time, but they are not sufficient to explain why this arrangement develops into a social institution that is maintained over decades or even centuries.

One possible reason for the maintenance of sortition lies in the normative structure. Political sortition may gain normative support from its historical roots in religious customs. Other normative justifications may stem from secular ideology, such as the wish for political equality. However, political institutions may only exceptionally be explained by normative factors alone. A society without well-established routines for rational consideration of means and ends will hardly be viable in a world dominated by civil and military power struggles. Consequently, religious roots or political ideals may explain the introduction of lotteries, but not their maintenance over time.

If sortition is to be more than a short-lived curiosity in social life, the social actors must be able to cope with the problems linked to social efficiency. They are not bound to understand them fully. But they must at least find some sort of modus vivendi by constructing a social edifice containing niches where talent does not play an important role, or combining the individual offices into committees or other types of structures that will ensure the presence of a minimum of personal ability.

In principle, this construction of social institutions may develop by trial and error, or by other processes where random decisions are at play. But it must be said that many circumstances have to coincide for this to happen. In. societies in which political lotteries have played a prominent role, this has hardly been the case. These are societies with a high degree of rationality, where important philosophical and artistic breakthroughs have taken place. This is obvious for Athens and Florence, but 17th-century Basel also had an academic culture of very high standing. The political actors had an intellectual grasp of the functioning of lotteries and were able to evaluate several of the consequences springing from them.

The question may be raised as to how elaborate this rationality actually was. A common argument, cited earlier, implies that the use of lotteries means the abdication of reason. It follows from this view that rationality in these societies was rather undeveloped. They represent an immature, even juvenile, position in the history of human rationality. Against this, it may be argued that, on the contrary, they represent an exceptionally high degree of rationality, captured in Pascal's conception of "L'esprit de finesse:" the deepest rationality is the one which understands the limits of rationality and thus understands when it is rational to abstain from rationality.[61]

It is perhaps impossible to decide unequivocally whether a given society employing political sortition belongs to the grey zone between traditional and rational societies, or whether, on the contrary, it represents a deeper form of rationality. But perhaps it does not really matter. For our purposes, it is sufficient to point out that political sortition will develop more easily in two types of society: those that are half-way to being rational and stand on the threshold of developing a stronger rationality in social life, and those that are "post-rationalist" in the sense that social arrangements are allowed to reflect the insight that, in some settings, it may be rational to abstain from rationality.

2. Social structural factors

In principle, political lotteries may develop on the basis of any type of social condition. However, it may be interesting to focus on some factors common to the social situation in Athens and Florence, even if this cannot in itself explain the acceptance or rejection of political lotteries.

In both cases, we are confronted with city-states which had a strong sense of civic spirit. This feeling of a common cause had as its condition among other things a long period of economic growth, leading to changes in the class structure of society. New compromises between classes and

---

61   Otto Neurath, "The Lost Wanderer of Descartes and the Auxiliary Motive," in *Philosophical Papers 1913-1946* (Dordrecht: D. Reidel, 1983).

factions in the city-state were built upon a broadening of the power base and a strengthening of the political participation of the lower classes.

These structural features were common to larger geographical areas in both Greece and in northern Italy. The formation of a great number of city-states in a period of rapid social change made these areas into a sort of natural laboratory for experimentation with political constitutions. Thus, on the macro level sortition may be regarded as one of several possible procedures brought forward by trial and error, and then tested in practice.

But such arrangements are not introduced and maintained by themselves. There must be one or more groups supporting them and seeing it to be in their own interest to protect them. This was without doubt the case in Athens. For the lower classes, sortition was the choice, from among a number of feasible arrangements, that focused in the clearest way on the possibility of participation for all citizens. At the same time, it had the favourable effect, from the citizens' point of view, of securing maximum influence for the Popular Assembly, to which every citizen had access. Political sortition was adopted not least because the lower classes regarded it as a vehicle for breaking the consensus of the elite.

In Florence, the picture was somewhat different. The political system had a more oligarchic character than in Athens. Sortition was introduced partly to restrain factionalism among kinship groups in the upper strata. In this respect, sortition had the opposite consequence of what was found in Athens, as it led to enhanced elite consensus. At the same time, the arrangement was also partly in the interest of the lower classes for reasons similar to those in Athens. Sortition made it possible to raise the question, in a pertinent way, of who was really eligible for office. Among other occasions, this happened in a dramatic way in the rebellion of 1378. At the same time, however, the drawing of lots contributed to the preservation of elite power, as long as the elite could decide in secret who were to be considered as candidates.

The success of a social institution is not only dependent on which interests it is designed to serve; it is also a function of the consequences that follow. Three types of consequence may be distinguished, and three corresponding questions may be raised. The first concerns intended consequences. Are they in fact attained? Secondly, unintended consequences, both positive and negative. What are the net effects of the unintended consequences as perceived by the actors? Thirdly, the question may be raised of whether sortition is compatible with other social institutions and practices. This last point is discussed in connection with factors that may lead to the abolition of lotteries.

The foregoing discussion suggests that intended consequences concerning equality were attained to a certain degree in both Athens and Florence. Likewise, expectations of reducing bribery or corruption were largely met.

It had also been pointed out that political sortition probably had favourable effects on social cohesion. The experience of being a candidate, the rites surrounding the drawings and the excitement connected to the outcomes contribute to strengthening the legitimacy of the political system, and give the citizens a more intense feeling of taking part in social life. At the same time, these are effects that may hardly be evoked in favour of the introduction of sortition. Thus they may explain why lotteries are maintained rather than why they are introduced.

3. Reasons for the abolition of sortition

There may be several explanations for the fact that sortition is not maintained as a procedure of selection for office. The nearest at hand concerns military conquest. Both in Greece and in northern Italy the arrangement was abolished because city-states practising sortition were conquered by states unwilling to tolerate it. However, the argument is weak, as lotteries obviously may be diffused in the same way, something that happened not least in Greece, where the Athenians implemented their own political arrangement in the cities they conquered. Consequently, military reasons do not sufficiently explain the lack of political lotteries in modern societies.

Internal strain may be created if sortition becomes incompatible with other institutions and practices. A Weberian conception of rationalization as the motor of history might regard sortition as a prerational mode of selection which is not compatible with social institutions changing in the direction of rationally justified arrangements. However, we have pointed out that the abdication of rationality cannot necessarily be considered as irrational. On the contrary, in given circumstances it may involve a deeper understanding of the implications of rational action. A general explanation of this type consequently rests on several implications, such as: (i) societies like Athens and Florence had not attained this deeper form of rationality, but were rather prerational in their nature; (ii) the growth of social rationality necessarily goes through a phase with enhanced rationality, but lacking this insight; and (iii) only at a later stage may it be expected that the deeper type of rationality be established. Without going into substantive discussion of these assumptions, it may at least be said that they are very strong.

As a short conclusion, I sketch a mode of thought that incorporates the points made above, but ties them together in a somewhat more complex way. Political change in Western societies has most of all been characterized by the concentration of power in big national unities and among a small group of actors. Political government has been built on a demand for maximal predictability. The concomitant growth in democracy and ideals of political participation has taken place on the basis of this development. What we know as modern democracy is not a further development of types of government known from small city-states or rural communities. It is rather a further development and tempering of the monolithic power structure of the national state. This type of centralized power has been strongly opposed to the unpredictability that is at the heart of sortition processes. When lotteries have once been employed in smaller societies but are now not practised in greater unities, this is not necessarily an effect of size. It is more probably the case that the power structure that has allowed the growth in power and size of societies has been incompatible with sortition as a selection mechanism. The growing centralization has, in its turn, led to greater social complexity and enhanced claims for political participation. Perhaps this will stimulate renewed considerations of lottery procedures within politics as well as other social spheres.

Willem K.B. Hofstee[1]

Allocation by Lot:
A Conceptual and Empirical Analysis

In 1989 the Soccer Club of Peize, represented by six youths and a trainer, won a national TV quiz. The prize consisted of 50 tickets for the Holland-West Germany soccer match, which were scarce and highly valued because of an atavistic rivalry between the two countries in this respect. The Club Committee decided to have lots drawn for the tickets and to ask the winners to contribute DFL30 to the club funds for the purpose of buying a TV set for the club canteen. The six boys who had won the quiz, and who had already received personal presents, were not given priority in the distribution of the tickets; this decision was later reversed under heavy pressure amounting to, among other things, anonymous telephone threats to the club chairman.

Many more illustrations could be given for the strong feelings of aversion that are often evoked by using lottery as an allocative mechanism. On the other hand, rational arguments in favour of lottery have been put forward. Elster[2] discusses three types of indeterminacy that might justify random choice between options. One is strict equioptimality, as in choosing between cans of Campbell's tomato soup. A second is equioptimality within the limit of what it pays to find out, that is, the case in which the cost of gathering more information would exceed the marginal utility of the superior option. The third is the incommensurability of options; one might say that, in this case, any investments into the choice procedure are fruitless a priori.

The present analysis takes the contrast between aversion and argument as its point of departure. Its scope is allocative problems and particularly those situations in which some public *authority* distributes scarce indivisible goods among *people*, rather than problems of choice between *goods*

1   Originally published on pp. 745-763 of *Social Science Information* 29 (1990). Copyright © 1990 Sage Publications. Reproduced with permission of Sage Publications.
2   Jon Elster, *Solomonic Judgments* (Cambridge: Cambridge University Press, 1989).

from a private point of view, whether individual or institutional. In the context of allocation, the question about the feasibility of lottery may be analysed as follows: from a rational point of view, the *efficiency* of distributive mechanisms is at stake, as it is in other problems of rational choice. However, the interplay between the allocative authority, the target subject, and the general public or common interest introduces two further aspects of feasibility. One is *justness*, that is, the extent to which the mechanism is compatible with written and unwritten rights. The other is *acceptability* in an empirical rather than a normative sense, and especially acceptability to the subjects of allocation. Undoubtedly there are all sorts of interactions — conceptual, historical, empirical — between these three criteria. However, the reduction of these economic, juridical and social points of view to each other appears to be unsatisfactory.

Efficiency

A first question is whether allocation by lottery can be rational from an economic point of view. In reply to Elster's statement summarized above, I argue that it cannot. My approach takes two steps, the first of which consists of making his three variants collapse, and the second of showing that lottery is generally not rational.

The first variant, strict equioptimality, is a limiting case with a zero probability of occurrence. Few experienced shoppers, for example, would agree to the appropriateness of even the extreme example of choosing between cans of Campbell's tomato soup. In practice, one would take the closest one and inspect its ultimate consumption date, rather than carry out a mental lottery. Advanced players of bridge can point to a case where a defender plays his best when trying to execute such a mental lottery, namely, when that defender has the queen and jack doubleton; similar situations may arise in other games where it pays to be unpredictable. For practical purposes, however, strict equioptimality is non-existent.

Incommensurability is to be disregarded for a quite different reason. Once the possibility of incommensurable options is entertained, the idea becomes infinitely contagious. No two applicants for a job or school, requests for a research grant, or cans of soup can evermore be argued to be commensurable. The admission of possible uniqueness of options instantly kills rational choice altogether. Conversely, the perspective of rational choice presupposes commensurability — see, for example, the classical statement by Coombs.[3] In that perspective, even multi-attribute utility degenerates into comparability. Indeed, options may have different scores on a number of attributes; the very idea of rational choice, however,

---

3   Clyde H. Coombs, *A Theory of Data* (New York: Wiley, 1964), 284-291.

brings about the possibility of aggregating these scores into a composite score.

What remains is the general case of indeterminacy. Barring trivial cases, any two options will differ in many respects, and it is usually difficult to aggregate their merits and demerits in a cogent and systematic manner. The argument, then, is that the cost of a systematic procedure of comparison may outweigh the marginal utility of the superior option.

Granting the validity of this conclusion, the second step of my argument consists in pointing to a third procedure that is, under the circumstances, generally superior to both lottery and laborious decision-making. This is the alternative of sloppy choice. It may take the form of intuitive decision-making, or turning a screening device — which is used to ensure that applicants, grant requests, parents claiming child custody, and the like, meet minimal standards — into a fully fledged selection procedure providing a complete ranking, or other sloppy procedures. Their marginal cost is essentially zero. Their validity tends to be low but positive. From an efficiency point of view, even the laziest stereotyping is usually superior to random choice.

There are limits to this argument. One follows from the fact that the efficiency perspective is limited as such — unless one would wish to stretch it to an extent that would make it tautological. Other limitations may be encountered within the rational perspective. Selection of students for closed studies is an example. Considering the isolated problem of selecting applicants for medical studies, there can be no doubt about the efficiency of using grade point averages in high school. However, from the national or institutional point of view that is relevant here the appropriate model is not selection but placement, by which individuals are distributed over studies, closed and open, in such a way that the overall utility is maximized. The complications that arise under the placement perspective are exemplified by the fact that in The Netherlands the academic discipline with the highest number of applicants per slot is veterinarian studies.[4] The admission system is highly selective in terms of grade point average. It is hard to maintain that the national interest is better served by the superior treatment of pets that is the probable main result of this policy, than by a system that would relegate some of these bright youngsters to other intellectual endeavours. Thus the efficiency principle may encounter its own limits and become perverted.

Incentive effects constitute another complication. Elster[5] discusses self-mutilation by young men in systems where disability leads to auto-

4   Cf. W.K.B. Hofstee, "The Case for Compromise Models in Educational Selection and Grading," in *On Educational Testing*, eds. Scarvia B. Anderson and John S. Helmick (San Francisco, CA: Jossey-Bass, 1983).

5   *Solomonic Judgments.*

matic exemption from military service. The asymmetry between exemption and admission is considered in the last section of this article. In admission to closed studies, selection on the basis of grade point average may demotivate the large majority of mediocre students (it they correctly perceive achievement to be mainly a function of talent) and therefore lower the average achievement. Admission by lottery would avoid creating the disincentive. However, an important question is whether incentive effects are administratively legitimate in the sense that authorities can account for their decisions in terms of such effects: the paradoxical and disrespectful nature of the account may well undermine authority in the long run.

Finally, incentive effects may pertain to the authority itself. By using lottery for admission to closed studies, for example, the authority may create more dissatisfaction with the scarcity of slots than by using selection (as the rejection of candidates has a person-blaming rather than a system-blaming implication), and thereby keep itself committed to solving the scarcity problem. However, such creative detours also hardly satisfy the criterion of public accountability.

These complications, subtleties, or even perversions are not to obscure the primary argument about the inefficiency of lottery. The general conclusion from this section is that random assignment is not justifiable on rational grounds. If there is an argument for lottery, it is to be sought beyond rationality.

Justness

The second question to be discussed is whether lottery is just, as distinct from efficient. In order to illustrate the distinction, I emphasize the contrast between admission and selection problems, for example, admission to higher education versus personnel selection. The contrast is meant to be ideal-typic; some of the blurrings that are favoured in real life are discussed later.

Selection entails comparative judgement of individuals, whereas admission is absolute. Selection typically consists of filling one or more slots with the best applicant(s) in terms of expected net productivity, whereas admission is typically not so restricted, and hinges upon qualifications that are assessed without reference to other candidates. (Philosophically, there may be no such thing as an absolute judgement; what is meant here is that in the executive phase, comparisons among individuals are not in order, only comparisons between a person and a preset standard). In terms of scaling, selection presupposes an ordinal scale, without a natural threshold point; for admission purposes, the full emphasis is upon the threshold, and individual differences above or below the threshold are irrelevant. In terms of decision-making, selection errors are measured in loss of utility, whereas for admission errors the appropriate unit of measurement is regret.

In everyday reality, there are all sorts of blurrings of the distinction between admission and selection. For a particular high-level job, all available applicants may be found wanting, which implies that absolute thresholds have emerged. An applicant may complain about not getting a particular job for which he or she was qualified, thereby implicitly treating the situation as an admission problem. The complaint may even receive wider acknowledgement where social considerations are part of the hiring policy, as in the case of affirmative action, which can be viewed as a partial transformation of selection into admission. On the other hand, private schools may favour highly selective "admission" policies; in *numerus clausus* situations even in public education, many local decision-makers automatically favour an approach of personnel selection in choosing future students. All this is not to say that the distinction between selection and admission is useless or even vague; on the contrary, it may help to clarify misunderstandings that frequently arise between interested parties.

The distinction between admission and selection paves the way for an allocative principle that differs from efficiency — namely, rights. Rights (or qualifications, or entitlement), rather than expected future productivity, are associated with admission as distinct from selection. With respect to allocative issues in areas like education, health and welfare, entitlements are documented in the Declaration of Human Rights, the Strasbourg Treaty, etc.

From an economistic point of view, one may be tempted to reduce rights to efficiency. The fact that admission to universities, for example, is conditional upon prior qualifications, may be interpreted in terms of the predictive validity of such qualifications for future success. There are at least two objections against this interpretation. One is practical: economic and juridical principles may conflict with each other in concrete cases. A public school, for example, cannot admit a highly intelligent student without a proper diploma at the expense of a mediocre student possessing the diploma. So irrespective of their origin, rights lead their own life and may become counterproductive. The other, more fundamental objection is that rights may not be based on prospective efficiency considerations at all. In many cases they refer to a retrospective principle like merit or credit, in other words, a personal or generic balance sheet. Rights are acquired individually, through past effort, or bestowed upon a group of persons generically on the basis of sex, race, nobility, etc. In the latter case, they inherit assumed credit left by their ancestors. Positive discrimination, for example, compensates a present generation for lack of recognition of the merits of earlier ones. (I concur with the ethical individualism position taken by

Elster[6] according to which vicarious credit is unacceptable. However, the principle does appear to play a role in defending positive discrimination, so it is retained here for analytic purposes.) There is no logical connection between a person's credit and his or her expected future productivity, so the two should be kept apart in analysing the feasibility of allocative mechanisms.

Having argued that lottery is generally not efficient, I propose that it is just under certain conditions. Whereas the probability of two persons being equally fit is zero from the rational point of view, equality is the very point of departure in the context of human rights. If rights are conditional, as in admission and in many other allocation situations, the presumption is that at the very least those who are qualified are to be treated as equals; in other words, the condition is to be interpreted *a contrario* in the sense that the posing of additional requirements is not justifiable. Thus if scarcity arises, lottery is the only just procedure (barring the options that are mentioned by Elster[7] under the heading of "Absolute Equality," namely, the dividing of goods or their denial to everyone, neither of which is appropriate in the present context); all other procedures, including queues or waiting lists which require additional differential effort, introduce improper demands on the applicant.

Against this reasoning, some would argue that equal distribution of indivisible goods cannot exist at all. Equality in lotteries means that everyone has an equal chance of receiving the good, for example, admission. The objection is that individual probabilities are devoid of meaning, and that all that is registered by the individual is the fact that some are admitted and some are not, thereby violating equality. The argument is a sophism[8] because it implies that people cannot distinguish between, for example, two treatments that would offer them a chance of survival of 10 per cent and 90 per cent (as each offering would be devoid of meaning, so that their comparison would *a fortiori* make no sense), and that is an absurd implication.

A far more serious objection pertains to the rules of justness that lead to the conclusion that lottery may be suitable in a sense. Rights, especially written law and rules, are best conceived as fallible operationalizations of very abstract underlying principles, in this case, credit, equality, and perhaps fitness or need; moreover, these principles do not at all coincide. Basing one's actions on such fallible rules, even if justifiable, may not meet the criterion of wisdom, to be circumscribed as keeping an eye on the future of

6   Jon Elster, *An Introduction to Karl Marx* (Cambridge, MA: Cambridge University Press, 1986).

7   Jon Elster, "Local Justice," *European Economic Review* 35 (1991).

8   See W.K.B. Hofstee, "'Jan heeft een kans van .70': Drogredenen met betrekking tot individuele kansuitspraken" ["'John has a chance of .70': sophisms with respect to individual probability statements"], *Kennis en Methode* 3 (1979).

humankind. In the practice of civil law, for example, wisdom consists of taking the needs and interests of the parties into account, in addition to their legal positions.[9] Conversely, personnel selection as a rational enterprise faces boundary conditions of a social and individual nature. Because of this higher-level uncertainty, the mixed system of weighted lottery in admitting Dutch youngsters to *numerus clausus* studies,[10] apart from being a political compromise, may be taken as testimony to the wisdom of the Dutch authorities.

It should be emphasized that the notion of wisdom was used here without reference to political categories such as acceptability and consent; thus far, the analysis is meant to be axiological, not empirical.

Principles and Mechanisms

Rationality and justness are principles that underly allocative mechanisms; they may be invoked to account for the use of such mechanisms. Acceptability is another matter; it is an empirical criterion not a normative principle. Before turning to empirical issues, an attempt is made here to answer two remaining conceptual questions, namely, whether other principles have to be considered, and what the relation is between principles and allocative mechanisms.

Principles of allocation

Taking the question about the feasibility of lottery as the pivotal issue, two major principles of allocation have been discussed: efficiency and justness. The justness principle branches into the principles of credit and equality: some people deserve to be allocated certain goods; in the absence of such considerations, equality prevails. The credit principle may be viewed as a special case of equality, that is, as conditional equality; for systematic purposes, however, I reverse the emphasis and take equality as a special case of credit, namely, as the absence of legitimate considerations of differential credit. Finally, it has been noted that credit can be individual or generic, as in the case of affirmative action or other cases of privilege.

In addition to this list, the principle of need is often mentioned. In the context of allocation of scarce indivisible goods by an authority, there is not much room for the need principle, as it is difficult to formulate any rules about differential need, even though the concept may have a general appeal. In many cases, therefore, need is no more than a redundant label for considerations of equality or credit. Probably the most fruitful conception of need in this context is discretionary. It covers cases where the

9   Jan ten Kate and Peter J. van Koppen, *Determinanten van privaat rechtelijke beslissingen* [*Determinants of decisions in private law*] (Arnhem: Gouda Quint, 1984).
10 See, e.g., W.K.B. Hofstee, "Test und Interviews zur Voraussage des Studienerfolgs" ["Tests and interviews for predicting academic success"] in *Hochschulzugang in Europa* [*Higher Education in Europe*], ed. Wolfgang Mitter (Weinheim: Beltz, 1979).

authority feels exceptionally sorry for some particular person, but does not wish to turn the exception into a rule. Need is thus a non-principle, or a limiting case of a principle. This is again not to deny that the idea of need may underlie allocation in general, only to state that its differential application is a marginal affair.

Assuming that no other basic principles can be found, the following structure may be formulated: we have three principles, namely, efficiency, credit and the discretionary principle of need. Subjects of an allocation procedure may or may not differ among themselves in their standing with respect to these principles; if they do, differences may be either strictly individual or vicarious, as in the case of generic credit. Table 1 contains the structure. Not all combinations will appear to make sense at first, without the following explanation.

TABLE 1
Structure of allocative principles

	Rational: "fitness"	Justice: "credit"	Discretionary: "need"
Individual	selection	honouring	exception
Generic		priority	
No difference		equality	

The application of the rationality principle to individual differences in fitness is usually called selection, for example, personnel selection. An interesting case arises when efficiency is combined with generic differences based on, for example, race, sex, nationality, etc. Such cases of discrimination represent a frontal clash between rationality and justness. On the one hand, there is no doubt that discrimination pays off: empirically, the predictive value of these characteristics is generally positive. On the other hand, discrimination is always inadmissible because the set of so-called bona fide requirements is empty; there is no prior reason, for example, why a soprano should be female and a bass male. In this clash, justness is the clear winner. The instructive implication is that efficiency as such is a second-rate principle in allocative contexts. Personnel selection, where that principle is generally accepted, hardly counts as an allocative problem because the involvement of public authorities is at best marginal.

The cell representing absence of differential fitness is empty because of the argument presented earlier: under the viewpoint of efficiency, equioptimality is a zero-probability case.

In the central column of Table 1, the top line represents the honouring of individual efforts to qualify. Positive discrimination, here labelled priority, is another example where justness beats efficiency. An interesting disparity should be noted at the empirical level between the wide acceptance of affirmative action, which is counterproductive, and the lack of acceptance of equality as operationalized in the lottery mechanism, which is merely nonproductive.

Finally, if the conception of need as a discretionary principle is accepted, only individual exceptions come under that heading, and generic need is a contradiction in terms. Absence of differential need, like differential fitness, also makes no sense. Once the possibility of interindividual utility comparison is granted, the probability of finding two persons with equal need becomes zero.

Allocation mechanisms

Selection, honouring, priority, equality and exception take an intermediate position between abstract principles and concrete allocation mechanisms. A list of such mechanisms is provided by Elster.[11] Table 2 summarizes the associations between mechanisms and principles. Roughly, a mechanism may be positively or negatively associated with a principle, or be neutral towards it. Mechanisms can be applied in a positive or a negative manner. Ability is applied negatively in exemption from military service; new applicants may be preferred to those of last year in school admission, amounting to a negative waiting list; sex, race, age and seniority may be applied negatively as well as positively. In compensatory education, there is a risk of rewarding lack of achievement and incurring the consequent incentive effects. Lottery is the only mechanism that cannot be reversed. In the following, only positive applications are considered.

TABLE 2

Associations between allocative mechanisms and principles

	Fitness	Credit		
		Individual	Priority	Equality
Lottery	0	0	0	+
Ability Testing	+	0	0	0
Queues	±	+	0	+
Sex, Race	+	0	+	0
Achievement	+	+	0	0
Age	+	0	+	+
Seniority	±	+	0	0

---

11   "Local Justice."

With the exceptions of lottery and ability testing, mechanisms embody more than one principle. Queues and waiting lists are applied irrespective of personal characteristics, and they cater to equality in that respect. An element of honouring individual credit, however, enters especially into queues. It is argued, moreover, that perseverance testifies to motivation and, therefore, to fitness, although that argument is sometimes reversed to the extent that waiting lists are said to constitute a negative selection criterion. The primary principle in positive discrimination on the basis of race, sex etc. is priority because of generic credit. Although counterproductive in the short run, affirmative action tends to be argued also in economic terms, and the argument may be valid in the long run. Achievement as an allocation mechanism primarily honours individual effort, but is also predictive of productivity. Age, as a criterion for receiving privileges such as the right to vote and to drive, represents generic credit and fitness, but it also represents equality because the coming of age befalls every individual. Seniority primarily honours individual credit, but also relates to productivity, albeit in an ambivalent manner; the experience or human capital argument is counteracted by considerations of high salaries and loss of flexibility.

The list is not complete; nationality and geography, for example, are missing. However, it may serve to illustrate the idea of oversaturation of mechanisms by principles. Preference for impurity is further illustrated by the frequent use of strategies consisting of serial (conjunctive) connections of mechanisms, as in the case of weighted lottery, or parallel (compensatory) connections, as in point systems.

Acceptability

Turning to the empirical issue of the acceptability of mechanisms, two recent studies are briefly reported. The first of these relates to the theme of mixed principles that has come up repeatedly in the earlier analysis. The second study is an experimental investigation of the relation between allocative problems and principles. It focuses specifically on the hypothesis formulated by Elster,[12] among others, that lottery is more suitable for exemption than for admission problems.

Study 1: Admission to advanced medical training

Until recently, the procedure for admission to advanced education for general medical practitionership in The Netherlands was as follows. Among the many applicants (about 1600 for 260 vacancies in 1989) a lottery was conducted; the lucky applicants were entered into local selection procedures consisting of an interview by a panel of three doctors. A diffi-

---

12 *Solomonic Judgments.*

culty arose when one of the local panels decided that the interview provided insufficient grounds for selection and subsequently installed a second lottery; the rejected candidates sued the school and won, to the effect that they had to be admitted. This incident, and general dissatisfaction with the procedure, led to a phase of reconsideration. The present study was carried out in that context. In the present reporting, however, the focus is upon the theoretical question of whether subjects of allocation procedures prefer mixtures of principles over pure solutions.

Methods and results

A questionnaire was sent to 540 people registered as candidates for the schools for general medical practitionership. The response rate was 55 per cent. Respondents were asked to give their answers in terms of general desirability rather than personal interest. The questions, together with the response percentages, are given in Table 3.

TABLE 3
Questions about admission to advanced medical training,
and answer percentages

1. Given a limited number of slots, the procedure should be:	
(a) Waiting list	16
(b) Lottery	1
(c) Selection	27
(d) A mixture (see below)	57
2. Assuming that a mixture would be chosen, what should it be?	
(a) Lottery and waiting list	6
(b) Waiting list and selection	79
(c) Selection and lottery	8
(d) All three	7
3. Assuming a selection procedure, what should it consist of?	
(a) Interview	17
(b) Internship	1
(c) Achievement tests	1
(d) GPA basic medical education	1
(e) Psychological tests	0
(f) Other	2
(g) A combination of (a) to (f)	79
4. What kind of procedure, in your judgement, is preferable?	
(a) Procedures with definitive rejection of candidates	15
(b) Procedures by which rejection is not definitive	85

Discussion

The respondents were opposed to one-track mechanisms (item 1) and instruments (item 3). Among the single instruments, the interview, which is a mixture in itself, is the only one that gathers more than a handful of votes; most respondents, however, prefer a buffering. Lottery, the only single-principled mechanism in this context (because selection may refer to achievement and/or ability testing) appears to be the least acceptable (items 1 and 2). Preference for fuzziness and indeterminacy is also illustrated in item 4. Together, the results provide consistent support for the proposition that solutions to allocative problems are less acceptable the purer they are.

Study 2: Allocative problems and principles

The second study to be reported here was designed to investigate the differential acceptability of allocative solutions depending on the kind of problem. Particularly, the solution profiles for selection and admission problems were expected to differ. Furthermore, a hypothesis formulated by Elster[13] was tested, namely, that lottery is more acceptable in problems of exemption than in positive allocation.

Between exemption and allocation there is a formal correspondence: exemption is allocating exempt status to a person. The substantive difference, however, may be expressed as follows. In exemption problems, a choice has to be made between individuals such that some will remain in their present state (e.g., in a lifeboat) whereas others will incur something undesirable (e.g., being thrown overboard); in positive allocation, the alternative to the present state is desirable (e.g. receiving an organ for transplantation).

Method

The problems presented were taken from Elster's[14] list (E1 to E4 concern exemption; A1 to A4 positive allocation).

E1 *Life Boat*: The boat is overloaded and a storm is impending.

A1 *Transplantation*: The number of donor organs is insufficient.

E2 *Tax Audit*: The comptroller can audit only a fraction of the tax forms.

A2 *Restitution*: Not all requests for restitution of tax payments can receive timely treatment.

E3 *Lay-offs*: Because of shrinkage of the labour organization, forced lay-offs are inevitable.

A3 *Promotion*: Only some of those who are eligible can be promoted.

E4 *Conscription*: Only some of those who are fit need to be called upon.

---

13 *Solomonic Judgments.*
14 "Local Justice."

A4   *Quota*: More people apply for immigration than the number a country wishes to admit.

The digits refer to pairings; in all four cases, an attempt was made to have an exemption problem mirrored by a positive allocation problem. Two questionnaires were constructed, one containing the problems E1 to E4, and the other A1 to A4. To both questionnaires, a fifth problem was added, namely, *Closed Studies*. In the E-questionnaire, the phrasing was: "some of the applications for a particular study cannot be honoured." In the A-questionnaire, the phrasing was: "For a particular study, admission is restricted." In the present definition, *Closed Studies* is an A-problem. The context and the corresponding phrasing, however, might make a difference.

The following solutions were presented to the respondents:

I.   *Lottery*, decision by chance.

II.   *Priority*, based on sex, race, age, etc.

III.   *Honouring*, of personal merit from the past.

IV.   *Selection*, on the basis of the expected future value of the person.

The solutions are meant to represent equality, generic credit, personal credit and fitness, respectively.

One hundred second-year students of psychology at the University of Groningen received the questionnaires by mail. The E and A versions were distributed randomly. The number of responses was 66, divided evenly between E and A versions.

The respondents judged each problem for each solution, using a three-point scale running from "acceptable" to "not acceptable." They were invited to comment.

Results and discussion

The mean acceptability ratings of the solutions for the problem are given in Table 4. Clearly, problems have their own profiles; in particular, the selection problem A3 differs from the admission problem A5 in the expected direction. The fact that lottery has the highest overall acceptability, in sharp contrast to Study 1, can be explained by a difference of subjects (psychology students versus medical doctors) or procedure (fictitious versus real-life problems), or both. Priority is judged to be marginally acceptable for A1, *Transplantation*, and E3, *Lay-offs*; these exceptions to its overall lack of acceptability are probably artefactual: a number of subjects commented that sex and race were out of the question, and that only age might provide an acceptable basis for decision-making. Age, however, in this context represents efficiency (as in the *Transplantation* problem) or personal credit (as in *Lay-offs*) rather than generic credit. Therefore, the acceptability of privileges may be concluded to be quite low with the present respondents.

TABLE 4

Means of acceptability ratings or exemption (E)
and positive allocation (A) problems,
on a scale ranging from +100 (acceptable) to -100 (not acceptable)

		Lottery	Priority	Honouring	Selection
E1:	Lifeboat	64	-36	-82	-52
A1:	Transplantation	36	06	-88	-36
E2:	Tax audit	94	-67	-55	-76
A2:	Restitution	70	-63	-88	-94
E3:	Lay-offs	-03	00	42	55
A3:	Promotions	-15	-45	73	76
E4:	Conscription	79	-42	-64	-06
A4:	Quota	48	-39	-27	-39
E5:	Closed studies	76	-79	-48	15
A5:	Closed studies	76	-85	-24	06

The specific hypothesis that, in addition to general descriptive purposes, motivated the present study was that lottery is more acceptable in problems of exemption than in problems of positive allocation. The design of the study contained two approaches to test this hypothesis. First, a matching was attempted between the problems E1 and A1, E2 and A2, and so on; secondly, one and the same problem, *Closed Studies*, was presented as the last problem in both lists, therefore in different framings. The latter operation was unsuccessful. The acceptability ratings of lottery for both framings were identical (Table 1, bottom row). In fact, all four solutions received quite comparable ratings for the two framings of the *Closed Studies* problem (with the possible exception of *Honouring*, which is difficult to interpret, however, as this solution is not consistently less popular in exemption problems), thus testifying to the comparability of the two respondent samples. The most likely interpretation of this failure to achieve a framing effect is that the problem is well-known to Dutch students and therefore resists framing.

The matching operation in itself was quite successful. The rank order correlations between the solution profiles of paired problems, omitting the *Closed Studies* pair, averaged .75, whereas the average correlation between all other pairs was -.19. In terms of their pairings, the exemption problems all show greater acceptability of lottery than do their positive allocation counterparts. This result is all the more striking as no other solution shows such a systematic pattern. In sum, the indications are that lottery is associated with exemption rather than with positive allocation problems. This finding supports the otherwise subtle distinction between the two classes of situations.

Acceptability of Mechanisms: General Discussion

Several aspects of the empirical findings in the two studies invite further reflection. To begin with, preference for compromise solutions has appeared in an earlier study[15] where Dutch youngsters opted for weighted lottery in admission to *numerus clausus* studies rather than straight lottery or selection. That study differed from the present Study 1 in many respects: the data were gathered in the late 1970s, the respondents were high-school students, and the problem was different. These differences are expressed in the findings; in particular, straight lottery was not massively rejected as it was in the present study. The preference for compromise, therefore, seems to be all the more robust.

An appealing parallelism may be noted between these inclinations on the part of the subjects and the political process. Allocation principles are to some extent associated with political mainstreams. Efficiency appeals primarily to liberal-democrats, equality and priority to social-democrats, and personal credit and need to the christian-democratic tradition. A plausible prediction is that parties will attempt to implement these values when an allocative problem is placed on the political agenda. Only the necessity for bargaining in multi-party democracies can explain the resulting compromises. So if there is wisdom in impurity, as I have argued, the wisdom is in the democratic system rather than in the politicians or parties.

The intriguing suggestion that comes out of the empirical studies on acceptability is that the consent of the subjects is with compromise as such; in other words, preference for compromise is an individual rather than just an aggregate phenomenon. To say that the subject prefers compromise is not an instance of holistic bad taste.

To the extent that this finding is generalizable, it frontally opposes ideas ventilated by many commentators who deplore the fuzziness of politics and depict it as a threat to democracy. In a direct test of the hypothesis that citizens opt for compromise, one should confront voters with a thought experiment in which they are made individually responsible for the composition of their parliament. I expect that only supporters of small parties

15   Hofstee, "The Case for Compromise Models."

would go so far as to take all the seats, or even an absolute majority; that uncompromising attitude would be precisely the reason why these parties are so small.

A possible objection to the present reasoning is that the observed tendency to compromise is an artifact of the prior conceptual separation of underlying principles. However, the behaviour as well as the arguments of local decision-makers (as opposed to subjects) are probably well captured by the conceptual distinctions proposed here. For example, an inventory of the admission procedures to professional colleges in The Netherlands[16] revealed many instances of straight lottery and other one-track strategies designed by autonomous local authorities. (If the argument is accepted that wisdom resides in fuzziness, then the logical consequence is to remove allocative decisions from local control, with the possible exception of hardship cases.)

Compromise does not mean that an even mixing of principles is indicated for each allocative problem. First, the principles entertain their own pecking order. In authoritative allocation (as distinct from private selection), justness seems to dominate efficiency; within the domain of justness, generic privileges have a tenuous status. Secondly, the finding that problems have differential solution profiles is probably generalizable. Among these differences, the association between lottery and exemption versus admission especially merits further discussion.

At least part of the explanation for the disparity may be that lottery functions as a default option because of the inapplicability of other mechanisms to problems of exemption. Ability tests, for example, are used to reject military enlistees but can hardly be used purposely for exemption. To exempt the highest scorers would be illogical from the institutional point of view (certain stereotypes about the institution notwithstanding), and conversely, exempting low scorers would amount to using a test for unintelligence, which is a contradiction in terms. Another example of an inapplicable mechanism is the waiting list, which is the closest competitor to lottery because it is also impersonal. In admission problems, the waiting time tends to become stationary in due course because the number of people who drop out approaches the number of new applicants. With respect to exemption problems, however, the number of those who volunteer to be drafted (corresponding to the applicants for admission who waive their rights) might never approach the number of new "candidates," with the result that the age of new recruits would quickly mount to eighty and over. Other principles and mechanisms like priority (in particular, sex and vicarious credit for one's brother's service) and personal credit, which are applicable without paradox, do play a role in exemption situations as they do in admission. The remaining gap, as it were, is filled by lottery.

16   Hofstee, "Test und Interviews."

The reason why the pure-principled solution of lottery is politically acceptable for exemption from military service may be sought in the fact that the problem is low on the political agenda. Whereas admission restrictions infringe upon human rights to be vindicated by authorities, few people would care about a scarcity of military slots.

Conclusion

The present conceptual and empirical analysis of principles and mechanisms in allocation took off from a contrast between aversive reactions to lottery and arguments in its favour. I have attempted to show that the aversions are not irrational, because lottery itself cannot be arrived at from a rational point of departure. Under certain circumstances, lottery can be justified by the principle of unconditional or conditional equality. In this perspective, aversions against lottery need not be interpreted as contempt for justice, but may be viewed as objections to single-principled solutions in general. Preference for compromise was demonstrated empirically at the individual subject level. Speaking normatively, I presented the case for such buffered solutions in terms of wisdom.

By its character, this laborious attempt to unravel things, only to fuse them into fuzziness, is comparable to the case of a neurotic person who engages in a seven-year psychoanalysis and comes out as neurotic as before, but more at ease with the neurosis. Allocative problems, like humans, may defy more definitive solutions.

John Broome[1]

Fairness

This paper presents a theory about fairness, as it applies to the distribution of goods between people. I shall concentrate particularly on random lotteries. Sometimes a lottery is the fairest way of distributing a good, and my theory explains, better than any other theory I know, why this is so. That is the main evidence I offer for it. But the theory is not limited to lotteries; it is intended to apply whenever goods are distributed between people. I shall use the fairness of lotteries as a guide to fairness in general.[2]

I

It often happens that there are several candidates to receive a good, but the good cannot be divided up to go round them all. The good may be very important; it may even amount to the saving of the candidate's life. For instance, not enough kidneys are available for everyone who needs one. As a result, some people are denied treatment for their kidney failure, and consequently die.

   For each candidate, there will be reasons why she should have the good, or some of it. (I mean prima facie reasons, which may be defeated by other reasons.) Amongst them will be the benefits, to the candidate herself and to other people, that will result from this candidate's receiving the good. When the good is the saving of life, these benefits will depend on how much the candidate enjoys her life, what responsibilities she has to other people, and so on. Then there may also be other reasons. One may be desert: some of the candidates may deserve the good, perhaps because of services they have performed in the past. For the moment, suppose all these reasons can be weighed against each other. (I shall question this later.) Then for some candidates, the reasons why they should have the

1   Originally published on pp. 87-101 of *Proceedings of the Aristotelian Society* n.s. 91 (1990-1991). Copyright © 1991 the Aristotelian Society. Reproduced with permission of Blackwell Publishing Ltd.
2   Elsewhere, I have applied the theory to the distribution of divisible goods such as income. See my "What's the Good of Equality?" in *Current Issues in Microeconomics*, ed. John Hey (New York: MacMillan, 1989), and my *Weighing Goods* (Oxford: Blackwell, 1991), ch. 9.

good will be stronger, on balance, than for others. Let us call one person a "better" candidate than another if she has stronger reasons in her favour.

How should it be decided which of the candidates should get the good? Several procedures might be used. One is to have some authority judge the merits of the candidates, and select the best. But this procedure has its costs. The job of assembling and assessing the necessary information may be expensive and time consuming. The responsibility of deciding who is to live and who to die (if that is in question) may be an intolerable emotional burden. Furthermore, the authority may not actually succeed in picking the best candidates. It may choose the candidates who best meet corrupt or prejudiced criteria, rather than the ones who are actually the best.

One procedure that avoids the costs and dangers of deliberate selection by an authority is to apply some fixed rule. (There is a risk of corruption or prejudice in setting up the rule, but not once it is set up.) And it may be possible to devise a rule that goes some way towards selecting the best candidates. For life saving, the rule of picking the youngest will do this. Age will certainly be one of the factors that helps determine which candidates are the best. Other things being equal, it is better to save a younger person than an older, because it does more good to the person who is saved: it gives her, on average, more years of life. So there is some correlation between a person's youth and how good a candidate she is.

A lottery is another procedure that avoids the costs and dangers of deliberate selection. Unlike a well-chosen fixed rule, though, it is no more likely to pick the best candidates than any others. So what advantage can it possibly have over a fixed rule? Plainly, only that it is sometimes fairer. But how can this be so? How can a lottery be fairer than a rule such as picking the youngest, which has a tendency to select the better candidates? Answering this question is the main test that has to be passed by any account of the fairness of lotteries. To answer it properly demands a particular theory of fairness in general; only this theory, which I shall describe in Sections III and IV, is able to explain adequately the fairness of a lottery.

II

Before coming to the theory, I shall first set out what I think it needs to account for: the facts about the fairness of lotteries that need to be explained.

First: a lottery is by no means always fair. It would not, for instance, be a fair way of choosing whom to award the prize in a violin competition. So in explaining the fairness of lotteries we shall need a criterion for distinguishing when lotteries are fair from when they are not.

Second: our account of the fairness of lotteries cannot simply be that lotteries are good tie breakers, appropriate only when the reasons in favour of different candidates are exactly balanced. The two examples below show that it is sometimes right to hold a lottery even when reasons are not exactly balanced. In any case, if a lottery were appropriate only for breaking a tie, its value would be insignificant. It will hardly ever happen in practice that reasons balance exactly. And if ever they do, the slightest change in one of them would mean they were no longer balanced. Then, if it was right to hold a lottery only for breaking a tie, it would no longer be right to hold one. So the value of a lottery would be lexicographically dominated by other values. (Section VI, however, qualifies this point.)

Furthermore, to say that lotteries are good tie breakers fails to explain their fairness. When there is a tie, it does not matter which candidate is chosen. What is required is simply a means of getting the decision made. A lottery is a handy means, even when no issue of fairness arises. When I cannot decide between two restaurants for dinner, I may toss a coin. This is not in order to be fair to the restaurants, but simply to avoid the fate of Buridan's Ass. When it comes to a choice, not between restaurants, but between candidates for some good, a lottery is sometimes more than just a handy means of getting the decision made when there is a tie. It is sometimes a better means than others because it is fairer. We, therefore, need a separate explanation of why it is fairer.

Thirdly: the fairness of a lottery does not consist solely in the fact that it overcomes the costs and dangers of deliberate selection by an authority. I have already explained that selection by a fixed rule is likely to be a better way of doing that. And even when it is possible to choose the best candidates deliberately, without cost and without corruption or prejudice, there is still sometimes a case for a lottery. The following two examples make this point, and also the second point mentioned above.

The first example is about games. Most games begin by holding a lottery to settle which player starts in the most favourable position (playing white, say). Fairness requires this. But normally some players will be better candidates for the favourable position than others, as I defined 'better candidate' in Section I. For instance, usually more joy will be caused in total by the victory of one player rather than another, so a greater expectation of benefit would result from giving that player a favourable start. Let us suppose there is a referee who, without prejudice or corruption, is easily able to pick out the best candidate. It would still be wrong to leave the decision to the referee rather than a lottery.

The second example is a dangerous mission. Someone has to be sent on a mission that is so dangerous she will probably be killed. The people available are similar in all respects, except that one has special talents that make her more likely than others to carry out the mission well (but no more likely to survive). This fact is recognized by her and everyone else. Who should be sent? Who should receive the good of being left behind? It could plausibly be thought that the right thing is simply to send the talented person. But it is also very plausible that doing so would be unfair to her, and that fairness requires a lottery to be held amongst all the candidates. These two views are not incompatible. It may be that fairness requires a lottery, so that it would be unfair not to hold one, but that in this case fairness is outweighed by expediency, so that on balance it is right to send the talented candidate without a lottery. This depends on the circumstances. If it is vital that there should be no slip in the execution of the mission, the unfairness will be tolerable. But if a less than perfect performance is acceptable, more importance can be given to fairness. In some circumstances, fairness will win, and a lottery should be held.

III

Those, then, are the facts. How can they be explained? In this section and the next, I shall present my theory of fairness. I mean it to apply to the distribution of any sort of good, whether indivisible or not. In Section V, I shall come back to indivisible goods and lotteries.

When a good is to be distributed, for each candidate there are reasons why she should have some of it. These reasons together determine what ought to be done: how the good should be distributed. But how, exactly, do the reasons combine together to determine what ought to be done? As I shall put it: how do reasons work? There are various views about this.

One is *teleology*. Teleology claims that the good ought to be distributed in whatever way maximizes overall benefit.[3] So the only sort of reasons it recognizes for a particular candidate to get the good is a benefit that would result. Imagine the good being distributed one unit at a time. Each unit should go to the candidate whose receiving it would produce the most benefit; this will normally ensure that overall benefit is maximized when all the units are eventually distributed. At each stage, the reason for giving a particular unit to one candidate is the benefit that would result; the reason for giving it to the next candidate is the benefit that would result from that; and so on. All these reasons should be weighed against each other, and the unit allocated to the candidate for whom the reason is strongest. So we can say that reasons are combined together by *weighing up*. This is how reasons work in teleology. Weighing up goes along with maximizing.

Other views disagree with teleology. One, for instance, claims that some reasons are *side constraints*. A side constraint determines directly what ought to be done; it is not subject to being weighed against other reasons. Rights are often thought to be side constraints. Suppose that, amongst the candidates for a good, one has a right to some part of it. Suppose it is her income, for instance, which she has earned. Then side-constraint theory

---

3   There are non-maximizing versions of teleology; see Michael Slote, "Satisficing Consequentialism," *Proceedings of the Aristotelian Society* 58 (1984). But for simplicity I shall ignore them here.

says simply that she should have it; no question of weighing arises. The theory may acknowledge the existence of teleological reasons too, which work by weighing up. It may allow that weighing up is appropriate amongst other candidates, but not for a candidate who has a right.

I am going to describe a third type of reason, which works in a third way. To introduce it, I shall first draw a distinction of a different sort amongst the reasons why a candidate should get the good: some of these reasons are duties *owed to the candidate herself*, and others are not. I shall call the former *claims* that the candidate has to the good.

The distinction between claims and other reasons is easy to grasp intuitively. Take the dangerous mission, for example. One candidate is more talented than the others. This is a reason for allotting to the others the good of staying behind. But the other candidates' lack of talent gives them no *claim* to this good. It may be right to leave them behind, but it is not owed *them* to do so. Whatever claim they have to this good, the talented candidate has it also.

The distinction can appear even within teleology — indeed within utilitarianism. All utilitarians think that if a person would benefit from having some particular good, that is a reason why she should have it. But some utilitarians think this reason is a duty owed to the person — a claim — and others think it is not. William Godwin, for one, thought it was a claim. "Every man," he said, "has a right to that, the exclusive possession of which being awarded to him, a greater sum of benefit or pleasure will result than could have arisen from its being otherwise appropriated."[4]

The difference is nicely brought out by the attitude of utilitarians to changes in the world's population. Henry Sidgwick[5] believed an action was right if it maximized the total of good enjoyed by people in the world. So he believed one should promote growth in population if the extra people brought into existence will have good lives, and no harm will be done to people already living. But this is clearly not a duty owed to the people who will be brought into existence. One cannot owe anyone a duty to bring her into existence, because failing in such a duty would not be failing anyone. Sidgwick, then, evidently thought that the duty to benefit people is not owed to those people themselves. On the other hand, a utilitarian view promulgated by Jan Narveson[6] is that one should promote the good of existing people or people who will exist, but there is no reason to increase the total of good in the world simply for its own sake. So the fact that the extra people will enjoy good lives is no reason to increase the world's population. Narveson is evidently motivated by the thought that, whatever duty there is to promote a person's good, it must be owed to the person

4   *Enquiry concerning Political Justice* (Baltimore: Penguin, 1976), 703.
5   *The Methods of Ethics* (New York: Macmillan, 1907), 414-416.
6   "Utilitarianism and New Generations," *Mind* 76 (1967).

herself. Consequently, there can be no duty to bring a person into existence.

It is clear, then, that there is a distinction between claims and other reasons. It is not so clear which particular reasons are claims and which are not. Even utilitarians, I have been saying, disagree about this. And if we recognize nonutilitarian reasons, there is further scope for disagreement. If we accept *desert* as a reason why a person should have a good, it is perhaps an uncontroversial further step to take it as a claim. But *need* is more controversial. If a person could benefit from a good, that is no doubt a reason why she should have it, but, despite Godwin, we may be reluctant to accept it is a claim. If, however, the person needs the good, perhaps we should accept that. Perhaps, for instance, a person who needs a kidney has a claim on it. But this is controversial.

In this paper, I am not going to engage in controversy over which reasons are claims and which are not. I shall take it for granted that some are: that some reasons why a person should have a good are duties owed to the person. And I shall concentrate on asking how these reasons, whichever they are, *work*. How do claims combine with each other and with other reasons, in determining what should be done?

IV

Some teleologists, as I say, recognize the existence of claims. But they suppose claims work by weighing up, just like other reasons. They think that the right thing to do, and the right way to distribute a good, is determined by the balance of reasons, whether claims or not. They throw claims and other reasons all together on to the same scales, in the same maximizing calculation.

But the fact that conflicting claims are duties owed to different people gives rise to an alternative intuition. Simply weighing claims against each other may not seem enough. Weighing up is the treatment we would naturally give to conflicting duties owed to a single person. Applying it between different people may not seem to be giving proper recognition to the people's separateness.[7]

In particular, weighing up claims does not seem to give proper attention to *fairness*. Take the example of the dangerous mission again. All reasons are evenly balanced, apart from the special reason for sending the talented candidate: she will perform the mission better. So weighing up reasons must conclude in favour of sending this candidate. But that seems unfair to her. It might be the right thing to do under pressure of expediency, but nevertheless it seems unfair. The talented candidate has a claim to the good of being left behind, and her claim is as strong as anyone else's. Yet when it is weighed against other people's claims, and the further reason

---

7   The *locus classicus* for this view is John Rawls, *A Theory of Justice* (Oxford: Oxford University Press, 1972), 22-27.

that she will perform the mission better, her claim is overridden. Weighing up seems to override claims, rather than respect them.

It is fairness that matters here because the particular business of fairness is to mediate between the conflicting claims of different people. But I need to qualify this remark slightly. Certainly, fairness is *only* concerned with claims, and not with other reasons. Suppose there is some reason why a person should have a good, but she has no claim to it. Then if she does not get the good, that may be wrong, but she suffers no unfairness. It cannot be unfair to deny her a good she had no claim to in the first place. On the other hand, it is possible that some claims are outside the domain of fairness, and work in different ways from the one I shall be describing. I shall say more about this possibility later, and for the time being I shall ignore it. I shall assume that all claims are mediated by fairness.

Weighing up claims is not enough, then, because it does not give proper attention to fairness. It would not even be enough to give claims extra heavy weight in the course of weighing up. The example of the dangerous mission shows this too. However much weight is given to claims, each person's claim to the good of staying behind is still the same. So the claims will all balance, and the talented person will still be sent, because of the extra reason. But this is unfair to her.

What, then, *does* fairness require? It requires, I suggest, that *claims should be satisfied in proportion to their strength*. I do not mean "proportion" to be taken too precisely. But I do mean that equal claims require equal satisfaction, that stronger claims require more satisfaction than weaker ones, and also — very importantly — that weaker claims require some satisfaction. Weaker claims must not simply be overridden by stronger ones.

This suggestion merely extends and tightens up a principle that is often taken for granted: that people identically situated should be treated identically. Economists call this the principle of "horizontal equity."[8] It is, like my generalization of it, inconsistent with teleological maximizing. To see why, imagine two people have equal claims to some good, but that, if the good is divided between them, less benefit will be produced in total than if it is all given to one. Then maximizing implies it should all go to one, but horizontal equity says it should be divided.

The heart of my suggestion is that fairness is concerned only with how well each person's claim is satisfied *compared with* how well other people's are satisfied. It is concerned only with relative satisfaction, not absolute satisfaction. Take a case where all the candidates for a good have claims of equal strength. Then fairness requires equality in satisfaction. So if all the candidates get the same quantity of the good, then fairness has been perfectly achieved, even if they get very little, or indeed none at all.

8   See, for instance, Anthony B. Atkinson and Joseph E. Stiglitz, *Lectures on Public Economics* (New York: McGraw-Hill, 1980, 353-355.

To be sure, all is not well if they get none at all. For each claimant there is at least one reason why she should have some of the good: the reason that constitutes her claim. Claims should be satisfied, therefore. But it is not *unfair* if they are not, provided everyone is treated proportionally.

Everyone's claim to a good should, prima facie, be satisfied. Indeed, if there is any reason, whether a claim or not, for a person to have some of a good, she should have some. Call this the "satisfaction requirement." Normally, this requirement cannot be fully met for everyone. What does it require then? I suggest it requires maximizing of satisfaction. This implies that, to meet this requirement, claims will have to be weighed against each other and against other reasons; I think weighing up and maximizing are appropriate for the satisfaction requirement. But then also fairness requires that claims should be satisfied in proportion to their strength. Claims, therefore, give rise to two separate requirements: they should be satisfied, and they should be satisfied proportionally.

It will normally be impossible to fulfill both requirements completely. Consequently, the two will themselves have to be combined together in some way, to determine what should be done, all things considered. Here again, I suggest that weighing up is appropriate: the demands of fairness should be weighed against the demands of overall satisfaction. In some circumstances, no doubt, it will be very important to be fair, and in others fairness may be outweighed by expediency.

In summary, claims work like this. Together with other reasons, they go to determine the satisfaction requirement by weighing up. And claims together determine the fairness requirement by the proportionality rule. Then the fairness requirement is itself weighed against the satisfaction requirement.

Evidently, claims in my theory do not work as side constraints; they do not necessarily prevail. This may be a limitation of the theory. I defined claims as duties owed to people, and it may be that within this class there are some claims that are genuinely side constraints. If some claims are side constraints, they are not covered by my theory. My theory is limited to the subclass of claims that work in the way I have described. Call these "fairness-claims." It might be a convenient piece of terminology to say that fairness is a subdivision of *justice*, and that justice is concerned with all claims, but fairness only with fairness-claims.

Consequently, I cannot pretend to have defined claims independently of the notion of fairness, and then shown how fairness applies to them. The subclass of claims I am talking about is partly identified by the way they work, and this is itself determined by the theory of fairness. Nevertheless, I believe the subclass of fairness-claims picked out this way is an important one. It may even include all claims. And for brevity I shall continue to use the term "claim" for fairness-claims only.

The merit of the theory is that it shows a way claims can work, without simply being weighed up in the manner of teleology, and also without being treated as side constraints. Robert Nozick argues for side-constraint theory largely on the grounds that teleology is mistaken. He concedes that these grounds are inadequate if there is a third alternative.[9] My theory of fairness offers one.

It shows how a claim can stop short of a *right*, considered as a side constraint. This fills a significant gap. It seems implausible that anyone has a right to a research grant from, say, the Ford Foundation. But if the Ford Foundation decides to distribute research grants, it should surely deal fairly with the applicants. Someone who was rejected on inadequate grounds would have a just complaint. But how can this be, if she had no right to a grant in the first place? My theory explains how. If her application is good enough, she has a fairness-claim. Consequently, *if* other people are receiving a grant, she should receive one too. In "Claims of Need,"[10] David Wiggins considers just what sort of a claim is generated by need. Again, it seems implausible that a person has a right to whatever she needs. So what can her claim be? I suggest it might be a fairness-claim, which implies that *if* needed resources are being distributed, the person should have a share.

V

Now let us concentrate once more on cases where the good to be distributed is indivisible, and there is not enough to go round.

Take a case, first, where all candidates have equal claims. It would be possible to satisfy their claims equally, as fairness requires, by denying the good to all of them. There may be occasions when it is so important to be fair that this is the right thing to do. But it would totally fail to meet the satisfaction requirement, and normally the demands of fairness will not be enough to outweigh this requirement completely. It will be better to use as much of the good as is available.

In that case, the candidates' claims cannot all be equally satisfied, because some candidates will get the good and others will not. So some unfairness is inevitable. But a sort of partial equality in satisfaction can be achieved. Each person can be given a sort of surrogate satisfaction. By holding a lottery, each can be given an equal *chance* of getting the good. This is not a perfect fairness, but it meets the requirement of fairness to some extent.

It does so, of course, only if giving a person a chance of getting the good counts as a surrogate satisfaction of her claim. This seems plausible to me. After all, if you have a chance of getting the good you may actually get it. It

9   *Anarchy, State and Utopia* (New York: Basic Books, 1974), 29n.
10 In *Morality and Objectivity*, ed. Ted Honderich (London: Routledge and Kegan Paul, 1984).

is quite different from merely giving the claim its proper weight against other reasons; that does not satisfy it in any way. Suppose, in the example of the dangerous mission, that the talented candidate was sent because of her talents. She could make the following complaint. She has as strong a claim to staying behind as anybody else. Her claim was weighed against other reasons. But this overrode her claim rather than satisfied it. It was never on the cards that she might actually get the good she has a claim to. But if she was sent because a lottery is held and she lost, she could make no such complaint.

Next, take a case where several people have claims to a good that are roughly, but not exactly, equal. Perhaps, for instance, they all need the good, but not exactly equally. And suppose again that there is not enough to go round them all. Fairness requires satisfaction in proportion to their claims. So if the good goes to the people with the strongest claims, the others will not have been fairly treated; their claims will have been overridden. And if it goes to other people, the unfairness will be worse. So unfairness is once again inevitable. But once again it can, if the circumstances are right, be mitigated by giving everyone a chance of getting the good. Ideally, each person's chance should be in proportion to the strength of her claim: the lottery should be unequally weighted. (At first, it is particularly puzzling how a weighted lottery could be fair.[11] If it is fair for some people to have a greater chance than others, that means they more ought to have the good. So why not let them have it without a lottery? My theory explains why not.) But even a lottery at equal odds may be fairer than giving the good directly to the candidates with the strongest claims. This depends on a complicated judgement. The result of a lottery will generally be that the good goes to candidates who do not have the strongest claims. This is less fair than the result of giving it directly to those who do. The likelihood of this less fair result will have to be weighed against the contribution to fairness of the lottery itself. But it is clear that, if claims are close to equality, holding a lottery will be fairer than not.

A subsidiary point. We have agreed that fairness requires everyone to have an equal chance when their claims are exactly equal. Then it is implausible it should require some people to have no chance at all when their claims fall only a little below equality.

When claims are equal or roughly equal, then, a lottery is *fair*. Whether it is *right* to hold one is then a matter of weighing the fairness it achieves against the likelihood that it will not meet the satisfaction requirement, which in this case requires the best candidates to be selected. The conclusion will depend on how important fairness is in the circumstances. But

11   In "Taming Chance," in *The Tanner Lectures*, Volume 9, ed. Sterling M. McMurrin (Salt Lake City: Utah University Press, 1988), Jon Elster mentions two examples where weighted lotteries have been used in practice.

there will certainly be some circumstances where it is better to hold a lottery than to choose the best candidates deliberately.

A lottery should be held when, first, it is important to be fair and, second, the candidates' claims are equal or roughly equal. These conditions may occur quite often. They do not require an exact balance of all considerations; claims may be equal or roughly equal even when other considerations are not balanced at all. Consider, for instance, life-saving medical treatment such as kidney replacement. It seems plausible that, in these matters of life and death, fairness is particularly important. And it seems plausible that everyone has a claim to life, even if on other grounds some are much better candidates than others. Maybe older candidates have weaker claims than younger, since they have already received a greater share of life. But even so, the candidates' claims may be nearly enough equal to make a lottery appropriate.[12] This explains why a lottery may be better than the rule of picking the youngest. If an older person has a claim to the treatment, even if it is a weaker claim than a younger person's, it demands proportional satisfaction. A lottery provides at least a surrogate satisfaction: a chance. But the rule of picking the youngest gives no sort of satisfaction at all. It simply overrides the claims of older people. So it is less fair.

That is how my theory of fairness explains the value of lotteries. It satisfactorily accounts for the facts set out in Section II.

VI

I know no alternative theory that explains the value of lotteries as successfully as mine. I cannot review all the alternatives here, but I do need to deal with one that may seem promising at first.[13]

In Section I, I spoke of the "best" candidates for a good, as though the notion was clear cut. But when the judgement between candidates depends on comparing reasons of different sorts, it often seems impossible to weigh the reasons against each other in a precise way. How, for instance, when comparing candidates for life-saving treatment, should one's *joie de vivre* be weighed against another's family responsibilities? The impossibility might be in the nature of things: some reasons might simply be incommensurable with each other. Or it might be practical: we might have no practical way of making the comparison accurately, even though in principle the reasons might be commensurable.

---

12 The arguments of Lewis Kornhauser and Lawrence Sager in "Just Lotteries," *Social Science Information* 27 (1988) [chapter 8 of this volume], are closely parallel to mine in many ways. The main difference is that their arguments permit these authors to recommend a lottery only when claims are exactly equal.

13 An argument like this is used by Jonathan Glover in *Causing Death and Saving Lives* (Baltimore: Penguin, 1977), 203-227, and by Nicholas Rescher in "The Allocation of Exotic Life Saving Therapy," *Ethics* 79 (1969).

This indeterminacy suggests the following defence of lotteries. A group of candidates might not be exactly tied — all equally as good as the others — but even so none might be definitely a better candidate than the others. Or it may be that some members of the group are actually better candidates than others, but we cannot in practice know which. Suppose there is only enough of the good for some of this group. Then, just as a lottery has a natural role as a tie breaker when there is an exact tie, it may be appropriate here for the same reason. Here we have a tie within the limits of comparability. And whereas I said in Section II that an exact tie will be very rare, a tie within the limits of comparability may be common. For life-saving medical treatment, for instance, once the medically unsuitable candidates, and perhaps the very old, have been eliminated, it may be that all the remaining candidates are tied within the limits of comparability. We may not be competent to judge between them.

However, I do not think this argument accounts adequately for the value of lotteries. For one thing, it does not explain their *fairness*. As I said in Section II, the role of a tie breaker is simply as a device for getting the decision made. No question of fairness need arise. The new argument merely extends this role to a wider domain: a device is needed to get the decision made when the weighing up of reasons has gone as far as it can.

Furthermore, if there is no separate reason why a lottery is fair, it is doubtful that it is even going to be the best way of breaking the tie. A fixed rule may well do better, for the reason I gave in Section I: it has some tendency to pick better candidates. Picking the youngest may well do better in the case of life-saving treatment. To be sure, this reason is more questionable in our present context. I said in Section I that, in an arbitrary group of candidates for life saving, the younger ones are more likely to be better candidates than the older. Now, though, we are not dealing with an arbitrary group, but with a group that is tied within the limits of comparability. A candidate's youth is one of the considerations that should already have been taken into account in admitting her to this group. Within the group, therefore, the younger people should generally have fewer other considerations in their favour than the older ones; on balance they should be more likely to be good candidates. However, I doubt that in practice, when a lottery is defended on grounds of incomparability, it will often be for a group of people chosen in this finely balanced way. For instance, the group may consist of all the candidates except the medically unsuitable and the very old. For such a group, picking the youngest would be a better tie breaker than a lottery. In any case, this argument from incomparability provides no reason why a fixed rule should be *worse* than a lottery. It fails the test I mentioned at the end of Section I.

David Wasserman[1,2]

Let Them Eat Chances: Probability and Distributive Justice

Introduction

Jon Elster reports that in 1940, and again in 1970, the U.S. draft lottery was challenged for falling short of the legally mandated "random selection."[3] On both occasions, the physical mixing of the lots appeared to be incomplete, since the birth dates were clustered in a way that would have been extremely unlikely if the lots were fully mixed. There appears to have been no suspicion on either occasion that the deficiency in the mixing was intended, known, or believed to favor or disfavor any identifiable group. If the selection was non-random in the way charged, Elster asks, was it unfair?

Elster's question suggests the more general issues I will address in this paper: what moral functions do lotteries serve and what features must they have to serve them? I will focus on one kind of setting in which lotteries are used: to allocate an indivisible good among equally-entitled claimants.[4] I will consider how a lottery can respect those equal entitlements by exploiting uncertainty or chance.

1   Originally published on pp. 29–49 of *Economics and Philosophy* 12 (1996). Copyright © 1996 Cambridge University Press. Reproduced with permission of Cambridge University Press.

2   A version of this paper was presented to the University of Maryland Philosophy Colloquium. I am grateful to Alan Strudler, the editors of *Economics and Philosophy*, and an anonymous referee for their comments on earlier drafts.

3   Jon Elster, "Taming Chance: Randomization in Individual and Social Decisions," in *Solomonic Judgments* (Cambridge, MA: Cambridge University Press, 1989), 45-46.

4   Although the concepts of "equal entitlement" and "indivisibility" are critical to the scope of this paper, I have very little to say about them by way of preliminary analysis. I will be less concerned than some authors in this area about the ways in which the claimants to a good can be said to be equally entitled — by having equal and independent rights to the good, rights to equal treatment with respect to its allocation, or merely the right to be treated as equals (this trichotomy is derived from Lewis A. Kornhauser and Lawrence G. Sager, "Just Lotteries," *Social Science Information* 27 (1988), 494-495 [pp. 144–145 of this volume]). I think that the last form of entitlement is too vague to impose clear constraints on the allocation process, while I

The draft lotteries that Elster describes place two general conceptions of probability in opposition. On the one hand, the lotteries were not known or believed to favor any specific registrants — before they were conducted, each registrant had the same expectation of being drafted. On the other hand, some registrants actually had better statistical odds than others of being drafted. Ian Hacking calls these two conceptions of probability "epistemological" and "statistical" (1975, pp. 12-13).[5] While there is a long-standing disagreement about whether fair lotteries require statistically equal odds, the rationale for that requirement has never been clearly articulated.

If there are two distinct conceptions of probability involved in the appraisal of lotteries, there are also two distinct views of how a lottery exploits probability to achieve fair treatment. These views can be characterized as distributive and procedural.

The distributive view holds that lotteries treat equally-entitled claimants fairly by giving each claimant some intangible good in equal measure, when an equal division of the good to which they have a claim is not possible or can only be achieved with a significant loss of value. The good equally distributed by a lottery is a chance or expectation of (receiving) the scarce good. Thus, Kornhauser and Sager claim that:

> [W]hat a social lottery offers is an equal division of a good that is otherwise indivisible. A lottery constitutes a probabilistic division of the good ex ante; instead of getting one unit of each good each member of the lottery pool gets a G/P chance at one unit of the good, where G is the number of units of the good available and P is the number of persons in the entitlement pool. *On this account a social lottery is just because it permits an equal allocation of the good consistent with the equal entitlements of the claimant pool.*[6]

The procedural view can, at least initially, be defined by contrast. It holds that the fairness of lotteries does not consist, or consist entirely, in the distri-

---

think the first two impose the same ones: any lottery that satisfies one will satisfy the other. I am also not concerned, except by way of contrast, with voluntary gamblers, who have entitlements to a specific allocation process, not an independent claim to its prize.

I will call a good "indivisible" if it cannot literally be divided without a nearly complete loss of whatever it is valued for, where "literal division" may include such arrangements as time sharing. (I will also be interested in partially-divisible goods, whose net value is reduced but not eliminated by equal division.) Clearly, a good can be indivisible for some purposes or people but not others, e.g., an iron-lung or respirator may be indivisible for stroke victims but not scrap metal dealers, but I will not worry about such complications.

5   Ian Hacking, "Duality," in *The Emergence of Probability: A Philosophical Study of Early Ideas about Probability, Induction, and Statistical Inference* (Cambridge, MA: Cambridge University Press, 1975), 12-13. Hacking argues that most contemporary accounts of probability fit under one conception or the other: frequency and propensity accounts are statistical, while personal (subjective) and evidential- or logical-relation accounts are epistemological. Elster ("Taming Chance," 43-46), makes a roughly parallel distinction between objective and subjective probability; I prefer Hacking's terms, because I think that some epistemic accounts. e.g., those involving the logical relation between a hypothesis and a body of evidence, are clearly objective.

6   Kornhauser and Sager, "Just Lotteries," 496 [p. 146 of this volume], emphasis supplied.

bution of something in equal measure to all of the claimants, but rather, or also, in the use of an allocative procedure that respects the claimants' equal entitlements. A procedural account of lottery fairness must explain how an allocative procedure can respect the claimants' entitlements except by giving the claimants something in equal measure. One view is that it does so simply by preventing bias or partiality in the allocation of the indivisible good. I will call this view "prophylactic." While there may be some disagreement about what constitutes bias and partiality, and what is required to prevent them, those who accept a prophylactic view agree in regarding the procedural virtues of a lottery as entirely negative: as preventing the indivisible good from being allocated for bad reasons.

Neither of these accounts of lottery fairness appears committed to a statistical or an epistemic conception of probability. The distributive account requires odds determinate and intersubjective enough to effect a "probabilistic division" of the good. But such odds can be secured by mechanisms with equal frequencies or equal propensities, by equally balanced evidence for each claimant's satisfying the payoff condition, or by the convergence of the probability-assignments made by the lottery participants. The prophylactic version of the procedural account does not appear to require equal probability at all. The procedure must prevent bias and partiality in the allocation of the good, but that arguably does not require the lottery to provide any form of equal odds at any stage of the allocation process.

In this paper, I will offer an account of lottery fairness which is procedural but not exclusively prophylactic. I will argue that lotteries also serve an expressive function, which does require a minimal sort of epistemic equiprobability. I will argue that in order to express an equal commitment to each claimant's receiving the scarce good, those who control the allocation process must have no reason to believe that any claimant is more likely than any other to satisfy the payoff condition. In Part I, I will illustrate this epistemic requirement with two examples borrowed from Kornhauser and Sager, discuss the sense in which it can be said to provide equal odds, and describe the expressive function it serves. In Part II, I will defend this requirement against arguments that respect for the claimants' equal entitlements demands less—the mere absence or prevention of improper control over the scarce good—and against claims that it demands more—statistical equiprobability.

In Part III of the paper, I will point out several difficulties in understanding the fairness of lotteries in distributive terms, as the "probabilistic division" of the good and the allocation of equal chances of receiving it. I will conclude that the rejection of the distributive view may have practical significance: if we do not regard lotteries as providing any kind of outcome equality, we should be less tempted to see them as reducing the need for the greater production or more equal division of scarce resources.

I

Consider two lotteries described by Kornhauser and Sager:[7] in the pancreas lottery, the good is awarded to the claimant with the largest pancreas; in the fingerprint lottery, to the claimant whose prints are most like those of the last suspect arrested by the F.B.I.[8] Neither lottery yields statistically equal odds. In both, the statistical probabilities are either 0 or 1, since one claimant already satisfies the payoff condition. The pancreas and fingerprint lotteries offer the same kind of equiprobability found in Elster's draft lotteries: although the claimants' statistical odds are not equal, no one involved in, or observing, the allocation process has any reason to believe that it favors an identifiable claimant or group of claimants.[9] If there is no evidence available to the allocator or the claimants suggesting that any specific claimant has a larger pancreas than any other, or has fingerprints more like those of an unknown suspect, then either lottery will be as fair as the toss of an unbiased die as a means of allocating a scarce good among equally-entitled claimants.

Some people may not share the intuition that the pancreas and fingerprint lotteries are as fair as the toss of an unbiased die. Although I cannot deny the possibility of irreconcilable differences in intuition, I suspect that any tendency to regard these lotteries as less fair arises from the strong but unexamined conviction that a lottery cannot be completely fair unless each claimant actually has a chance of getting the good. In Part II, I will challenge this conviction, arguing that fairness requires nothing more than the uncertainty which the liver and pancreas lotteries provide.

It is debatable whether that uncertainty gives the claimants equal odds in an epistemic sense. On a subjective theory of probability, it would only do so if the claimants happened to assign equal odds to their chances of satisfying the payoff condition, or if minimal coherence compelled them to do so. On an evidential-relation account, it would depend on whether there could be said to be equal evidence for each claimant's satisfying the payoff condition, rather than no evidence.[10] Whether or not the most

---

7   "Just Lotteries," 490 [p. 141 of this volume].

8   Sher suggested the largest liver as a payoff condition. See George Sher, "What Makes a Lottery Fair?" *Noûs* 14 (1980): 205 [p. 87 of this volume; Sher has "smallest liver"].

9   Elster calls this condition "epistemic randomness" ("Taming Chance," 44). It might seem that if the pancreas and fingerprint lotteries were fair, the draft lotteries should be even fairer, since they also gave each claimant an actual chance of winning the good, albeit not an equal one. In Part II, I will argue that this additional feature of the draft lotteries may really be a moral liability.

10   In the pancreas and fingerprint lotteries, there will be evidence for each claimant only if we count as evidence the fact that all claimants have pancreases or fingerprints, and perhaps the fact that none of the claimants has symptoms (e.g. of diabetes or disfigurement) that would make him more or less likely to satisfy the payoff condition. If we cannot treat the former as evidence, and eliminate the latter by stipulation, the claim of equiprobability would have to rest on the controversial principle of indifference, which assigns equal odd to each outcome in a mutually exclusive, jointly exhaustive set.

epistemic accounts of probability would regard the claimants' odds as equal in the pancreas and fingerprint lotteries, I think that ordinary usage would (or would at least recognize a sense in which they were equal), and in the remainder of this paper I will describe those lotteries as epistemically equiprobable.

The pancreas and fingerprint lotteries clearly satisfy the prophylactic function of lotteries. Because it is "difficult or impossible to unravel or trace the workings of the payoff condition," these lotteries are, and appear to be, protected from bias and partiality.[11] But the procedural function of these lotteries is not merely prophylactic. It is also expressive. In adopting payoff conditions which no participant or observer has reason to believe are more likely to be satisfied by some claimants than by others, these lotteries display an equal commitment to each claimant's receiving the good.

Perhaps the most familiar and convenient means of expressing an equal commitment to each claimant's receiving the good is the use of a randomizing device, like a die, roulette wheel, or hopper. These devices owe their expressive success, or so I will argue, not to any actual contingency in their outcomes, but to the fact that they are broadly recognized as establishing payoff conditions that no participant or observer has any reason to regard as favoring any claimant. An equally clear, if less familiar and convenient means, of expressing an equal commitment to each claimant's receiving the good would be to exploit impending discovery rather than apparent contingency. If physicists are about to weigh a new subatomic particle, or astronomers are about to count the stars in a distant cluster, and the current state of their knowledge is equally consistent with any weight or number within a given range, the assignment of claimants (whether random or not) to equally-spaced weights or numbers within that range would express an equal commitment, as clearly and firmly as a die toss, to each claimant's receiving the good. As with a die toss, expressive success would not depend on the claimants' suspense or satisfaction: either type of lottery could be fairly held during the claimants' nap-time, or over their (unreasonable) protests.[12]

One obvious issue for an expressive account is *whose* knowledge and belief counts in determining whether there is any reason to believe that some claimants are more likely than others to satisfy the payoff condition. I have thus far avoided this issue by assuming the same knowledge on the

11   Kornhauser and Sager, "Just Lotteries," 490 [p. 141 of this volume].

12   Some readers may be unhappy with the characterization of this procedural function as expressive, particularly if they are not comfortable with expressive accounts of other social functions, like punishment. Why not simply claim that the allocator makes an equal commitment to each claimant by choosing a payoff condition that he has no reason to believe favors any of them? I think it is useful to treat the lottery as expressing that commitment, because it lets us frame many questions concerning the fairness of lotteries in terms of the clarity with which their payoff conditions display a moral posture towards the claimants.

part of all parties. But the information available to the allocator, claimants, and observers will often differ, and intuitions about the fairness of the lottery may differ as well. Would the pancreas lottery, for example, be less fair if each claimant had previously received the confidential results of an MRI, revealing the comparative size of his pancreas? If some but not all of the claimants had received those results? If one or more doctors knew the results for one or more claimants?

These are reasonable questions, but they do not require definitive answer it the claimants or observers have reason to believe that some specific claimants are more likely than others to satisfy the payoff condition, then even if they recognize that the allocator lacks their knowledge, they may find it hard to regard his use of that payoff condition as expressing an equal commitment to each claimant's receiving the good. The conditions for the adequate expression of those commitments may vary with culture and social context. For example, the greater the public interest in the allocation, the broader the ignorance about who is favored by the payoff condition may have to be. What I contend is that, at a minimum, the allocator cannot employ a payoff condition that he believes favors a specific claimant, because his use of such a condition could not express an equal commitment to each claimant.

II

It might be thought that the expressive function I have attributed to fair lotteries required either more or less than the epistemic equiprobability provided by the pancreas and fingerprint lotteries. On the one hand, it might be argued that a lottery expressed an equal commitment to each claimant's getting the good simply by avoiding or preventing bias or partiality in the allocation of the good. On the other hand, it might be argued that a lottery could only express an equal commitment to each claimant's getting the good by ensuring, through statistically equal odds, that each actually had an equal chance of getting the good. I will consider these challenges in order.

A.

George Sher argues that the fairness of a lottery lies solely in assuring that the allocation of a contested good among equally-entitled claimants is not influenced by the preferences of the allocator for a specific candidate or allocative criterion. The allocator must respect each claimant's "strongest equal claim" to the good[13] — equal to every other claimant's and stronger than anyone else's. By distributing the good to satisfy his own preference for a specific claimant or type of claimant, the allocator would violate

13 Sher, "What Makes a Lottery Fair?" 213-214 [pp. 93-95 of this volume].

those claims. A fair lottery avoids such a violation by ensuring that the good is not awarded on the basis of the allocator's preferences.

On Sher's view, an allocator would be guilty of an inappropriate exercise of dominion even if he adopted a fixed rule, like always choosing the youngest candidate for dialysis, that avoided the risks of personal favoritism or advantage-seeking. By imposing a criterion for allocating the good that favored one type of claimant and was (presumably) not accepted by all of the claimants, such a rule would violate their strongest equal claims to the good. Fairness in the allocation of a scarce indivisible good thus requires more than the absence of personal favoritism or corruption.

Sher's analysis has one strikingly permissive implication, however: using a payoff condition which accords with the allocator's desire that the good go to a particular claimant does not make the lottery unfair if that was not the allocator's reason for choosing the condition. A lottery would be fair even if the allocator knew the choice of a given payoff condition would give the good to his preferred claimant, so long as he chose that payoff condition "on some basis which is totally distinct from his preference...".[14] Such a lottery, however, would strike most people as manifestly unfair, even if the allocator could somehow provide credible assurance that he had an independent basis for his choice. It is instructive to see where Sher's account goes wrong.

On Sher's analysis, a lottery will be unfair only if the allocator indulges a preference for a claimant or type of claimant that is not shared by all the claimants.[15] Sher holds, for example, that an anti-semitic allocator could fairly assign the good to the claimant who had the fewest Jewish ancestors, as long as all the claimants shared his preference.[16] This seems far too relaxed a view of what is required to respect the claimants' equal entitlements, for two reasons. First, it suggests that the only way the allocator can fail to respect those entitlements is to assert a superior title. But this is surely mistaken. An allocator who simply handed the good to the nearest claimant, to rid himself of the unpleasant responsibility of allocating it, would hardly assert a superior title. But his "allocation" would clearly fail to respect the claimants' equal entitlements or express an equal commitment to each claimant's receiving the good.

---

14   Sher, "What Makes a Lottery Fair?" 208 [p. 90 of this volume].
15   Sher ultimately adopts the following necessary and sufficient conditions for lottery fairness:
      A lottery L is fair if and only if there is no person q such that (a) q desires that L's contested good be awarded to a particular claimant or type of claimant, and (b) q's desire is not shared by all the claimants to L's contested good, and (c) q knows that his performing an action of type A will increase the probability of his desires being satisfied, and (d) q performs an action on the basis of that desire.
      Condition (d) excludes payoff conditions only if they are selected to satisfy the allocator's desires. Condition (b) permits even those payoff conditions, as long as the allocator's desire is shared by all the claimants ("What Makes a Lottery Fair?" 212) [pp. 92–93 of this volume].
16   "What Makes a Lottery Fair?" 209 [p. 90 of this volume].

Second, in permitting the allocator to indulge his own preference if it is shared by all the claimants, Sher treats their claims in inappropriately proprietary terms. Although he insists that "it is no part of our concept of the strongest claims to goods that a person with such a claim is entitled to delegate the relevant good as he prefers,"[17] the conditions for a fair lottery that he ultimately adopts allow for a kind of delegation that is not consistent with respect for the claimants' equal entitlements.

Thus, consider the allocation of a single liver within a claimant pool consisting of former New York Yankees star Mickey Mantle and several avid Yankees fans. Sher would permit the allocator, also an avid Yankees fan, to give the good to the claimant with the highest lifetime major-league batting average, as long as all of the claimants accepted that payoff condition.[18] I think that most people (even avid Yankee fans) would find that payoff condition manifestly unfair. While it might be fair for Mantle to get the liver by default—if every other claimant opted out of the lottery in deference to him—it would not be fair to give Mantle the liver on the basis of a payoff condition which transparently favored him. The adoption of such a payoff condition could not express an equal commitment to each claimant's receiving the good, even if every claimant endorsed it.

It might be argued, however, that the problem is simply that Sher's conditions are not prophylactic enough. To respect the claimants' equal entitlements, it is not enough for the allocator to *refrain* from exercising improper control over the scarce good; the lottery must be structured in a way that *prevents* him from exercising such control even if he is inclined to. This stricter standard would prohibit, per Kornhauser and Sager,[19] all payoff conditions that "plausibly could be expected to figure as reasons for choosing among" the claimants. And, given the possibility that the allocator *might* use any payoff condition known to favor some candidate as a means of favoring him, adequate prevention might even require a payoff condition not known to favor any claimant.[20]

I think this stronger prophylactic account is also mistaken, however, even if it could be construed to require the same epistemic equiprobability as an expressive account. The fairness of a lottery need not vary with the stringency of the safeguards against bias and corruption. If we knew that the allocator in the pancreas lottery had access to MRI scans of the claim-

17   "What Makes a Lottery Fair?" 213 [p. 94 of this volume].

18   This payoff condition, unlike Sher's "fewest Jewish ancestors," would not involve a preference that was inherently objectionable, which is a confounding factor.

19   "Just Lotteries," 489 [p. 139 of this volume].

20   Alternatively, it could be argued that a lottery was fair whenever the allocator refrained from exercising improper control, but that he would exercise such control whenever he acted to satisfy his own preferences regardless of whether the claimants shared them. But this view would still permit the allocator to choose a payoff condition that he knew, but did not intend, to favor one claimant, since he would not be controlling the allocation to satisfy his own preferences. Yet the knowing use of such a payoff condition still seems manifestly unfair.

ants' internal organs, we might worry that he had some knowledge of their comparative pancreas sizes. But if we later ascertained that he never saw the scans, we would regard the allocation of the scarce good by pancreas size as fair. While we might seek to impose safeguards in the future, their absence would not affect our appraisal of the fairness of the present allocation.

We might, finally, understand the prophylactic function quite differently than Sher, as eliminating inegalitarian reasons for allocating the good rather than improper control over it. To respect the claimants' equal entitlements is just to ensure that the one who gets the good does not get it for a reason inconsistent with the others' equal entitlements. But this rationale would still allow the allocator to use a payoff condition known to favor some claimants over others, as long as it could not plausibly be regarded as a reason for choosing among them. And that is too permissive. If an allocator, indifferent among the claimants, has a choice between such a payoff condition and one which he has no reason to believe favors any claimant, fairness compels him to choose the latter.

B.

Other commentators, notably Kornhauser and Sager,[21] have questioned whether the epistemic equiprobability provided by the pancreas and fingerprint lotteries is adequate to respect the claimants' equal entitlements. They suggest that a lottery in which the odds are equal only in this epistemic sense is not as fair as one where the odds are statistically equal. In this section, I will examine some of the reasons for thinking that statistically equiprobable lotteries enjoy this moral advantage. While I have been focusing on the expressive function of lotteries, the preference for statistical equiprobability may have a different source.

1.

One reason for demanding statistical equiprobability, which does not fit neatly under any of the moral functions I have outlined, reflects the conviction that a lottery can only be fair if its outcome results from an irreducibly random or probabilistic process. The argument can be spelled out as follows: 1) an equally-entitled claimant to a scarce good has only been treated fairly if he has, at some time after the lottery is invoked, an equal chance of getting the good; 2) to have an equal chance, it must be the case at that time that he *could* get the good; 3) for it to be the case at that time that he could get the good, it must not be causally determined which claimant will satisfy the payoff condition; 4) lotteries equiprobable only in an epistemic sense rely on payoff conditions whose satisfaction is causally determined, and thus do not provide equal chances. But there are counterfactual interpretations of the "could" in 2) that do not require the

21   "Just Lotteries."

indeterminism demanded by 3) — interpretations under which 2) might be satisfied by a lottery equiprobable only in an epistemic sense; for example, if some relevant fact had been different, a claimant with a very small pancreas would have had the largest one. If the defender of statistical equiprobability insists on an interpretation of "could" that requires indeterminism, he is committed to holding that even a statistically equiprobable lottery, for example, employing a fair die, would be unfair in a deterministic universe, and that seems absurd.

A number of other arguments could be made for the greater fairness of statistically equiprobable lotteries, corresponding to the different moral functions that lotteries are thought to serve. It could be argued that statistical equiprobability is necessary for the distributive function of lotteries: for the "probabilistic division" of the scarce good and the resulting allocation of equal chances. The argument would have two steps: 1) only statistically equal odds are determinate enough to effect a probabilistic division (or, at least, the minimal epistemic equiprobability found in the pancreas and fingerprint lotteries is not determinate enough); 2) one moral function of a lottery is to effect a probabilistic division of the good. I am uncertain about 1), since the odds yielded by equally balanced evidence, or even by the absence of relevant evidence, are arguably as determinate as those yielded by a randomizing device. But if my argument in Part III is correct, we need not resolve 1), because 2) is false: it does not make sense to view the fairness of lotteries in distributive terms.

It might also be argued that statistical equiprobability is required for the procedural functions of a lottery: the elimination of bias and the expression of an equal commitment to each claimant's receiving the good. Concerning the first, prophylactic function, the advantage of statistical equiprobability would be at most a matter of degree: if the allocator used a die we knew to be fair (and knew that the allocator believed to be fair), we could be confident that the allocation of the good was insulated from bias and corruption. But we might be as unsure about the fairness of the die, or the allocator's belief in its fairness, as we would be in other cases about the absence or balance of evidence required for epistemic equiprobability.

Turning finally to the expressive function, it might be argued that, given our social understandings and conventions, statistical equiprobability more clearly expresses an equal commitment to each claimant's receiving the good than (mere) epistemic equiprobability. But this need not be the case. While I have argued that there are constraints on the way we can express equal commitments, for example, that the choice of a payoff condition known to favor some claimants would belie our commitment to the others, I think we have considerable freedom of expression in this domain.

Because standard randomizing devices are convenient and familiar, they offer an easy and economical way of displaying equal commitments, with all the advantages of a cliché. In expressing those commitments in a more novel or idiosyncratic way, as in the pancreas and fingerprint lotteries, we may risk confusion or misunderstanding (e.g., because of uncertainty about whether ignorance about the payoff condition is universal), but we may also achieve greater expressive vigor. A payoff condition that exploited an impending scientific discovery, like the weighing of a subatomic particle or a census of stars in a distant galaxy, to secure epistemic equiprobability, might well express an equal commitment to each claimant even more emphatically than the use of a standard randomizing device. Moreover, the historical associations of such devices may obscure the expression of that commitment: to the extent that they have been used to invoke God's judgment about the best claimant, they have assumed that the claimants were not equally entitled. An idiosyncratic but epistemically equiprobable payoff condition like pancreas size may be less likely to carry such historical baggage.

2.

Defenders of statistical probability would still insist that there are cases in which the discovery that the odds were not statistically equiprobable would lead us to reject a lottery as unfair. Some epistemically but not statistically equiprobable lotteries do seem unfair on first impression, for example, where the prize is to be awarded by a die that turns out to be biased toward the "6." But if neither the allocator nor the claimants had reason to suspect the bias, the odds would have been epistemically equal, in the sense I have been using that term. Any feeling of unfairness seems to arise from disappointed expectations, from confusing the requirements of fair lotteries and fair gambles, or from a concern about long-run distributional effects.

A losing claimant might feel cheated in discovering that he actually had below-average odds, *if* he was led to expect that his odds were statistically equal. The mechanics of some lotteries may engender those expectations: the random drawing of a birth date or name and the toss of a biased die both involve (apparent) contingency, and they both resemble procedures that confer statistically equal odds. The claimants may feel disappointed or suspicious when they realize that they do not.

In contrast, the pancreas and fingerprint lotteries do not even appear to involve present contingency. Less may be more: because the participants have no expectation of statistically equal odds, they have no reason to feel disappointed or cheated upon finding the odds unequal. And there is no moment before the lottery vests when the claimants can perceive themselves as having unequal odds.

Some of the perceived unfairness in the biased-die case may also come from mistakenly assimilating it to a voluntary gamble. A gambler may well have a strong claim of unfairness if the die turns out to be biased, even if she only threw it once, since she has not gotten what she paid for—a die that had statistically equal odds of landing on any of its six faces, and a gamble that was attractive to her because of risk-preference or superstition. The claimants to an indivisible good have no such interest in a specific chance device, and they would have no complaint on discovering that the die was innocently biased, at least if it was to be used only on this one occasion. If we are not misled into believing that a lottery's odds are equal in a frequentist sense, and we do not regard the claimants as gamblers contractually entitled to such equality, we should find nothing unfair in an epistemically but not statistically equiprobable lottery.

Kornhauser and Sager might offer an alternative explanation for our acceptance of lotteries that offer only epistemic equiprobability: that our ignorance of who is favored by a statistically biased procedure may result from the prior operation of a statistically equiprobable mechanism. If claimants were initially assigned die-faces by lot, for example, and the lot-drawing were statistically equiprobable, the lottery would also be. Even if the die only landed on "6," each claimant would have had a statistically equal chance of being assigned that face. This is what Kornhauser and Sager call the principle of convolution: a lottery which is equiprobable at any one stage will be equiprobable overall.[22]

Few innocently-inequiprobable lotteries, however, will have such a statistically equiprobable prior stage. Typically, faces are assigned on some arbitrary but inequiprobable basis, for example, first-come, first served, claimants' preference, or allocator's whim. Despite the lack of a statistically equiprobable prior stage, however, a lottery that assigned faces in any of these ways would not be compromised by the discovery of an unsuspected bias.

Perhaps the firmest intuitions about the need for statistical equiprobability arise in settings where there is concern about the long-term distributive effects of the lottery. Consider the controversy over the draft with which this paper began. The challenge to the lotteries was based on a claim that the numbers in the hopper (corresponding to birth dates) had not been adequately mixed, so that the odds of any particular number being drawn were not equal. If only one name were being drawn for a special assignment, the accidental failure to adequately mix the names would not make the draw-

22   "Just Lotteries," 486 [pp. 136–137 of this volume]. Kornhauser and Sager (486-487 [pp. 137–138 of this volume]) also argue that a lottery can be rendered effectively equiprobable by a random assignment process occurring before it is invoked. Their principle of "sustained fairness" holds that this statistical equiprobability, or the fairness it secures, may be sustained by ignorance of the results of this process, although by the time the lottery has been invoked there is no possibility of any claimant but one satisfying the payoff condition. Although I cannot develop the argument here, I believe that the notion of sustained fairness rests on a confusion, about what the claimants have equal chances at, or what fairness required them to have equal chances at: the good itself, as opposed to equal chances of satisfying the criterion eventually chosen to be the payoff condition.

ing unfair, since neither the allocator nor the potential conscripts would have any idea of who was (dis)favored, and there could be no distributional objection to the choice of one individual rather than another. But repeated drawings may have a disproportionate impact on identifiable groups.

Thus, if the lottery had drawn names rather than birth dates, there might have been a legitimate concern about the long-run distributional effects of a departure from randomness. If the names were entered geographically, non-randomness would mean that certain regions were likely to be disproportionately conscripted; if the names were entered alphabetically, that certain "regions" of the alphabet, and consequently, certain ethnic groups and families, were likely to be disproportionately conscripted.

Yet any disproportion actually yielded by the biased hopper *could* have been yielded by a fully stirred one. This suggests that the disproportion itself cannot be the basis of the objection; that the distribution is unfair only because it was produced by a procedure that had an objective tendency to produce such disproportions. But if this is the objection, why would it not apply as well to the selection of a single individual, who also was discovered ex post to have been more likely than others to be selected?

Our concern for disfavored groups may, however, have an explanation that does not assume the need for statistical equiprobability in choosing among individuals. We regard it as undesirable as a matter of distributive justice that a disproportionate number of people from the same geographical region or ethnic group get conscripted. But we cannot guarantee that this will not happen even with a statistically equiprobable lottery. Moreover, the attempt to "correct" such a lottery to avoid disproportion is a cure worse than the disease: we would have to hold corrective lotteries to eliminate some members of the over-conscripted group and replace them with people from other groups, an adjustment that would carry the stigma of quotas and the burden of deciding which groups deserve proportionate representation. Instead, we simply insist on the procedure least likely to yield any such disproportion — a statistically equiprobable lottery. We will not tolerate an incompletely-mixed hopper, despite its *epistemic* equiprobability, because it is too likely to yield such disproportions. Even retrospectively, we find its use improper, whether or not it can be said to have violated the right of the disfavored group to equal treatment. In contrast, the selection of any particular individual is no less desirable in distributive terms than the selection of any other, so we are not concerned if the procedure is found, ex post, to have been more likely to pick one rather than another; we do not care if the unknown statistical odds of selecting particular individuals are grossly unequal.

3.

There is, however, another kind of mistake that challenges the necessity of epistemic equiprobability for lottery fairness: where the claimants or the allocator believe that the odds are statistically *unequal*, but they are in fact equal, for example, where the die everyone thinks is biased (e.g., because of a random run of sixes) turns out to be fair. It might be argued that if the resulting allocation seems fair even when the good is awarded to the apparently favored party, it must be because the lottery offered what fairness requires — statistically equal odds. But a weaker conclusion can explain the apparent fairness of this lottery: statistical equiprobability may purge bias in the absence of epistemic equiprobability.

If we conclude that either epistemic or statistical equiprobability suffices for lottery fairness, however, we face the problem of finding a rationale that encompasses both. It can hardly be said that the allocator expresses an equal commitment to each claimant's receiving the good when he uses an apparently biased die for the purpose of favoring some claimant. It might be argued that a common rationale can be found in the prevention of improper control by the allocator: the fairness of the die, like the belief in equal odds, prevents the allocator from exercising improper control.[23] But a lottery which permits the allocator to use a die he reasonably believes to be biased can hardly be said to protect against improper control, since his failure to exercise control is due solely to his mistaken belief, and not to any safeguards in the lottery procedure.[24]

In light of the difficulty in finding a common rationale for epistemic and statistical equiprobability, it might be better to concede that there are two different ways a lottery can respect the claimants' equal entitlements, and two corresponding senses of lottery fairness: the first depends on the participants' knowledge and beliefs, the second on the physical properties of the allocative device. A lottery unfair in the first sense — designed to serve the allocator's preferences or reasonably believed to favor an identified claimant — can be purged of its taint by the inadvertent use of a statistically equiprobable allocative device.

III

It is tempting to find the fairness of lotteries in the distribution of something of equal value to each claimant, because it seems plausible to regard lotteries in general as giving something of value to each participant. If we can assign a value to the good itself, then we can assign a value to the expectation of receiving it: its actual value discounted by the odds of receiving it. We can certainly find a market for this kind of good: people

---

23   I owe this suggestion to an anonymous reviewer.

24   At the very least, a proponent of the "prevention" rationale would have to explain how that rationale was satisfied in these circumstances. If the prophylactic function is satisfied merely by the absence of improper control, then the discovery that the die was unbiased would reveal the lottery to have been fair in the same way as the discovery that the allocator did not prefer the claimant apparently favored by that die, or did not use that die in order to favor him. But as I argued in Part IIA, this absence-of-control standard is far too permissive.

buy millions of lottery tickets each year, usually at a price well above the odds-discounted value of the prize.

The distributive view of lotteries does not require that the scarce good have a monetary value. We can talk, as Kornhauser and Sager do, of a lottery "divid[ing] a scarce good into probabilistically equal units" or of "allocating a chance of receiving the good"[25] without placing a price on the good or any probabilistic share of the good. We can say that probabilistic shares are valuable, and that larger shares are more valuable than smaller shares, without committing ourselves to more than an ordinal ranking.

A.

But even if it makes sense to regard expectations as intangible goods, and thus to regard the claimants as receiving something of equal value by participating in the lottery, it may not make sense to regard the fairness of the lottery as consisting in the distribution of an intangible good to each claimant. Clearly, a lottery is not fair merely because it distributes something of equal value to each equally-entitled claimant. An allocation procedure that did not confer equal expectations would not be fair if it gave each claimant something else in equal measure (besides the scarce good, of course), even something of great value.

What is it about expectations that makes them uniquely appropriate as (partial) moral substitutes for the actual good? Kornhauser and Sager hold that expectations can be regarded as probabilistic "units" of the indivisible good, so that the lottery can be regarded as effecting a symbolic or figurative division of that good. This suggests an analogy to other forms of shared ownership in indivisible goods, like shares in a corporation or time shares in a condominium. But the analogy founders on the simple fact that a lottery does two things: it gives each claimant an equal expectation of the good, but it also gives one claimant the good. Unlike the rights conferred by stock shares, or the access conferred by time shares, the value conferred by the probabilistic shares in a lottery is shared only briefly before passing to a single claimant. It is this awkward asymmetry which makes the distributive view problematic.

If the distribution of probabilistic shares plays a critical role in making the lottery fair, it can only be in offsetting or mitigating the unavoidable inequality in the distribution of the scarce good, in a way that the equal distribution of any other substitute good would not. But the claim that equality in expectations offsets or mitigates inequality in the distribution of the scarce good seems to require a comparison of the probabilistic share of the good that each claimant gets ex ante with the actual good that one of them gets ex post. And that comparison raises a number of vexing questions.

25   "Just Lotteries," 499, 491 [pp. 149, 142 of this volume; Wasserman slightly misquotes Broome].

For example if a claimant gets a probabilistic share of the good, and then gets the good, should he be regarded, in assessing the fairness of the disposition, as getting something besides the good, or does his probabilistic share "merge" with the good? Is a lottery with more claimants less fair, because it gives each claimant a smaller probabilistic share, and thereby does less to mitigate the inequality between the winners and the losers? Is a lottery less fair, for the same reason, if it has "no distribution" as one possible outcome, thereby reducing each claimant's expectation?

Consider one specific problem in detail: if it makes sense to treat an expectation as a good, it also makes sense to ask whether the value of that good increases the longer it is held by the recipient. Both positive and negative answers, however, have perverse implications for the fairness of the lottery: if the expectation gains value the longer it is held, it will be fairer, all things being equal (e.g., if the value of the good does not decline), to wait as long as possible for the lottery to vest, so as to mitigate the inequality between winner and losers by giving each claimant greater value. But we normally seek to resolve disputes over goods as soon as possible, or whenever it is convenient: we find no independent value in delay.

Alternatively, if the value of the expectation does not depend on how long it lasts, it might seem fairer to have as many semi-final stages as possible, since those stages would confer additional, valuable odds on some claimants, further offsetting the inequality between the winners and some of the losers without taking anything of value away from the other losers. Thus, a lottery with only one draw would give all n claimants odds of $1/n$; a lottery with a first draw that eliminated half the claimants and a second draw that awarded the prize would also give all the claimants initial $1/n$ odds of winning, but would, in addition, give the survivors of the first draw additional odds of $2/n$. A three-draw lottery would have the same advantages over a two-draw lottery, and so on. Since each further draw would confer greater odds on some claimants, fairness might seem to require that we have as many draws as the number of claimants permits.[26]

Each additional draw, however, would also create an inequality in expectations between some ultimate losers — the (semi-) finalists — and others. Would this inequality be outweighed by the offset to the inequality between the winner and the (semi-) finalists? Such questions do not arise

---

26 John Broome, "Uncertainty and Fairness," *Economic Journal* 94 (1984): 627-629, makes a similar argument against the claim that we have independent reasons for promoting equality in expected utility, apart from promoting equality in actual utility. When, in the case of scarce and indivisible goods, actual equality is impossible, equalizing expected utility may not be desirable. Broome denies that it is reasonable to wait as long as possible to hold an equiprobable lottery, or that it is fair to hold a second lottery after the first selects a winner, in order to prolong the expectation of equal utility. But Broome's stated objection to a second lottery is too narrow — that it constitutes "tampering with the results of a fair random process" (p. 628). If the lottery was intended from the outset to have two rounds, there would be no tampering in holding the second.

on a procedural view, on which there would be no reason to regard the number of stages in the lottery as affecting its fairness. While extra stages might be desirable in gaming lotteries, since they would extend the entertainment and suspense, they would serve no moral function in the allocation of a scarce good among equally-entitled claimants.

B.

There is, however, an argument that we must live with the conceptual difficulties in treating the fairness of lotteries in distributive terms, since almost any metric of distributive justice besides welfare or utility can be regarded as involving chances at welfare or utility. Indeed, "opportunity for welfare" is one leading candidate for the appropriate metric of equality.[27] But even metrics that are not explicitly probabilistic often have a probabilistic element. Thus, equality of resources does not guarantee equality of welfare, since the same bundle of resources may yield very disparate levels of welfare or utility, and that disparity is, in part, a matter of luck. One argument against using resources as the metric of well-being is just that those chances are, and are known to be, unequal: some people—those with certain impairments and diseases—are (known to be) likely to get far less welfare or utility from the same resources than others. But when the welfare derived from resources depends on the vagaries of taste and the market, equal resources will confer roughly equal odds of welfare. Similar claims are made about punishment as a de facto lottery— that a given sentence will have a widely varying impact on those who receive it, so that the best that we can be seen as doing is conferring equal expected punishment.

But the fact that there is a probabilistic component to standard metrics of well-being and punishment does not make chance itself an appropriate metric. As the special provisions we make for impairment and disease suggest, we try to some extent to equalize the actual impact of allocations and sanctions and to take into account some of the claimants' circumstances in determining what counts as an equal allotment or sanction. If we do not take account of certain circumstances that affect the welfare "payoff," like a person's tastes or temperaments, it is either because of the practical difficulty of doing so, or because we think it inappropriate to take them into account, either because the person is responsible for them, or because they are too integral to her identity to be regarded as part of the outcome she receives.

In contrast, the difference in the actual impact of chances for a prize on those who do and do not receive it obviously has nothing to do with their choice or identity—it is due to the brute operation of the lottery. Thus, in

---

27   Richard Arneson, "Equality and Equal Opportunity for Welfare," *Philosophical Studies* 54 (1988).

any situation where a group of claimants are found to be equally entitled to a specific good or service, we have no reason save economy to equalize their expected rather than their actual outcomes.[28]

C.

A middle ground between the procedural and distributive views has been mapped out by John Broome, who argues that the procedural role of lotteries cannot account for their fairness, while the distributive role is misconceived. Fairness for Broome requires that "claims should be satisfied in proportion to their strength."[29] Using a lottery "simply as a means of getting the decision made" is not a matter of fairness, because it serves that function "even when no issue of fairness arises," for example, in choosing between two restaurants for dinner.[30]

While Broome insists that the moral virtue of lotteries cannot be merely procedural, he also rejects, for reasons somewhat similar to those I have presented here, the claim that lotteries achieve a distributive fairness by conferring equal expected outcomes. Broome sees no virtue in equalizing expected outcomes as opposed to actual outcomes, except to the extent that the former is achieved by a fair lottery. What makes a lottery fair, however, is not that it distributes equal or proportionate odds, but that it provides partial equality of satisfaction[31] or surrogate satisfaction.[32]

One question raised by Broome's analysis is how the partial equality of satisfaction differs from the equality of expected satisfaction claimed by Kornhauser and Sager. Kornhauser and Sager do not suppose hungry claimants can actually eat chances, and it is not clear how the consideration claimants receive by getting a chance is less misleadingly described as a partial equality of satisfaction claims than as an equality of expected satisfaction.

The distributive character of Broome's approach is suggested by his reasons for endorsing proportional lotteries for some unequal claims. Claims to indivisible goods sometimes vary substantially in strength, and when they do, it raises the question of whether justice is best served by an equiprobable lottery, a direct award, to the individual with the strongest claim, or a proportional lottery. Broome believes that competing claims will often vary too much to treat as roughly equal, but not enough to directly award the good to the stronger claim.[33] In such cases, "each per-

---

28   Moreover, the degree of welfare or utility that a person derives from his bundle of resources is, aside from envy and vicarious pleasure, independent of the welfare or utility that another person derives from her bundle. This is clearly not true of lottery odds, since the success of one claimant precludes the success of others.

29   "Fairness," *Proceedings of the Aristotelian Society* 91 (1990-1991): 95 [p. 225 of this volume].

30   Broome, "Fairness," 89 [p. 221 of this volume].

31   Broome, "Fairness," 97 [p. 227 of this volume].

32   Broome, "Fairness," 100 [p. 229 of this volume].

33   Sher and Kornhauser and Sager confine their discussions to lotteries among claimants with some sort of equal entitlement—Kornhauser and Sager ("Just Lotteries") believe that equality

son's chance should be in proportion to the strength of her claim: the lottery should be unequally weighted." Yet Broome believes that the outcome of such lotteries will sometimes be less fair than a direct award to the strongest claimants, since the good will often go to someone with a weaker claim. The decision to use a proportional lottery rests on the balance of unfairness: "the likelihood of this unfair result must be weighed against the contribution to fairness of the lottery itself."[34]

A distributive view of lottery fairness seems more congenial to such a weighing, since it treats lotteries as giving something of value to the claimants even if they do not receive the scarce good. On a procedural view, that treats the lottery merely as respecting the entitlements of the claimants, it is not clear that we would disrespect weaker claims by directly awarding the good to the strongest claim. That would depend on the nature of the competing claims.[35] If respect for the weaker claims did compel us to give them some chance of satisfaction, it is not clear that there would be *any* injustice in letting the good go to a weaker claimant.

Moreover, if there were injustice in letting the good go to a weaker claimant, it is hard to see how a procedural view could weigh the likelihood of such injustice against the disrespect to the weaker claims in a direct award to the strongest claim. Since a procedural view would not treat the distribution of expected value as offsetting inequality in the distribution of actual goods, it would not treat the lottery as making a "contribution to fairness" that could be weighed against the (risk of substantive injustice in the actual allocation of the good. Thus, Broome's qualified endorsement of proportional lotteries seems to assume that unfairness in the allocation of actual goods can be offset by the distribution of expected value. And that seems to require the distributive view of lottery fairness that Broom rejects.[36]

---

of one sort or another in claims to life-saving resources is quite common, and quite robust against differences in merit and social value. Broome ("Fairness") employs a more finely-grained conception of equality in claim-strength, but thinks equiprobable lotteries should extend to claims that are only roughly equal.

34   "Fairness," 99 [p. 228 of this volume; Wasserman slightly misquotes Broome].

35   As a threshold matter, it seems that a proportional lottery can only be appropriate if the claim is such that a proportional division would have been appropriate for a divisible good: it is hard to imagine claims that could be satisfied with proportional odds but not shares. The acceptability of proportional shares or odds will depend upon the character of the competing claims. The right to some prizes, like an Olympic Gold Medal, arises solely from doing the best, so that any difference in performance eliminates any claim to the prize. On the other extreme, bankruptcy claims are based on free-standing rights that scarcity brings into conflict, and a proportional division is required when it is possible.

36   Proportional lotteries might be defended as expressing the greater but not overriding strength of the stronger claim, but this would be a rationale quite different from Broome's. The few examples of the actual use of proportional lotteries suggest yet a third rationale: a concern for the long-run distribution of actual goods. In the land and medical school lotteries described by Elster ("Taming Chance," 47), the proportional odds ensured the desired overrepresentation of

IV

In conclusion, even if it makes sense to regard lotteries as giving something of value to each participant, the fairness of a lottery among equally-entitled claimants to a scarce good cannot be understood in terms of such a distribution. Lotteries are fair if they respect the claimants' equal entitlements to the scarce good; they do so simply by distributing the scarce good in a way that cannot reasonably be seen by the allocator or the claimants as favoring any claimant.

The distinction between distributive and procedural lottery functions might have little or no practical or moral significance in a world of fixed resources that were either wholly divisible or wholly indivisible; a world where the supply of goods was fixed and where those goods either could be divided with no loss of net value, or would lose all value in being divided. Divisible goods would be allocated equally among equally-entitled claimants, while indivisible goods would be assigned by lottery, unless we preferred the more astringent fairness of giving them to no one.

But we live in a world where we can divide resources with only partial loss of value, and we can increase the production of goods to reduce or eliminate their scarcity. Both options have significant costs: there will be a loss of net value in dividing a good whenever the sum of the parts has less value than the undivided whole; there will be greater scarcity elsewhere if we increase the production of this good.

If we see a lottery as distributing something of value besides the good itself, or as partially satisfying the demand for that good, we may be more inclined to reject the costs of increased division or production. We may be more inclined to give the undivided good to one claimant and let the rest eat chances, or to maintain the existing scarcity of that good rather than to divert productive resources from other goods. If, on the other hand, we see lotteries as having only the procedural virtue of respecting equal entitlements by allocating disputed goods in a manner not known or reasonably believed to favor any claimant, they will offer a less attractive alternative to the more equal distribution of resources. We may be more willing to incur the costs of fuller division or increased production.

particular groups, like veterans and widows, without the need for an explicit quota. Such lotteries can be seen, over the long run, as allocations of proportional shares to groups.

Sigmund Knag[1,2]

Let's Toss for It: A Surprising Curb on Political Greed

> But anyone who deliberately tries to get himself elected to a public
> office [in Utopia] is permanently disqualified from holding one.
>
> Thomas More, *Utopia*

Nowadays elections are almost universally regarded as the keystone of
political affairs. Besides paying taxes and perhaps serving in the military,
average citizens participate in political life mainly by voting. Although
people disagree about election procedures and often feel disgust with election outcomes, hardly anyone today doubts that elections provide the only
way to establish, legitimize, and control a government. Historically, however, general elections have been the exception rather than the rule for
selecting and guiding governments. Alternatives include various auto-
cratic or despotic systems and processes and, in more democratic systems,
methods that supplement or substitute for elections. Among the latter is
lot-drawing, also known as sortition (from the Latin root *sort*, meaning

---

1   Originally published on pp. 199-209 of *The Independent Review: A Journal of Political Economy* 3
    (1998). Copyright © 1998, The Independent Institute, 100 Swan Way, Oakland, CA 94621-1428
    USA; info@independent.org; http://www.independent.org. Reprinted with permission from
    the publisher.
2   The author requested inclusion of the following note with his reprinted paper:
    After the present article appeared in print in 1998, the editor of the *Independent Review* alerted
    me to a commendable article in *Public Choice* that same year by an American and an Italian
    scholar, Jay S. Coggins and C. Federico Perali, on the theme of lot-drawing in ducal Venice.*
    The authors provide historical background; they describe and summarise the process of
    electing a new Doge; they discuss — against a background of decision theory from Condorcet to
    Andrew Caplin and Barry Nalebuff and beyond — the pertinence of the actual majority
    requirements laid down by the framers of the election rule; and they print a translation from
    the Italian of the election rule, which dates from 1268. They think the procedure served through
    the centuries to contain factionalism, corruption and instability. — Sigmund Knag, October 10,
    2010.
    *Jay S. Coggins and C. Federico Perali, "Sixty-Four Percent Majority Rule in Ducal Venice:
    Voting for the Doge," *Public Choice* 97 (1998).

"lot"). This procedure has intriguing characteristics and effects as well as potential for present-day utility. In this article I discuss its history and nature and consider some possible applications in the American political system.

Instances of Lot-Drawing

In the fifth century B.C., the Athenians filled their civic offices in two ways, either by the random operation of the lot (*kleros*) or by election. Most office-holders were selected by lot. Aristotle, among others, viewed lot-drawing as the more democratic procedure and election as the more aristocratic.[3] Scholars are not sure about the exact procedure used: Was the selection made from all those eligible or, at least in some instances, from those eligible and willing to serve? Lacking enough willing citizens, was compulsion used? Did the Athenians sometimes select from a short list of citizens eligible, willing, and qualified to serve? Although the evidence is inconclusive, it seems likely that "sortition from among volunteers" was the rule, at least in a number of cases.[4] Holders of the most important offices, the archonships, were selected from a short list, direct election having been abolished in 487-86 B.C. and replaced by sortition from (probably one hundred) preselected candidates of the two highest classes of citizens. After about 460 B.C., all four classes of citizens were eligible for archonship. Later the appointment process became one of straightforward double sortition—two rounds of lot-drawing.[5] Before taking office, the selected candidate underwent a scrutiny (*dokimasia*) in which citizens could object to his character or record.[6] Athens had many civic offices, most with only modest power and many requiring only part-time service. Except for membership in the Great Council (the *boulê*), offices typically could be held only once in a citizen's lifetime. This system fostered *participation, rotation*, and *amateurism*: Many citizens participated in wielding power; rotation in office prevailed; and the outlook of the ordinary citizen pervaded the civil service and the judiciary. Including the *boulê*, "about one thousand posts had to be filled year in and year out from among citizens aged at least thirty" in a citizenry of "between thirty or forty thousand or so above the age of eighteen." In addition, some six thousand served as dicasts (jurors) in the courts.[7]

In the heyday of their republic, the Venetians selected their lifetime leader, the Doge, by a complex system involving lot-drawing. The system had developed through the Middle Ages, becoming ever more complex to

---

3   David Stockton, *The Classical Athenian Democracy* (Oxford: Oxford University Press, 1991).

4   Stockton, *Classical Athenian Democracy*, 115-116.

5   Stockton, *Classical Athenian Democracy*, 108-109.

6   Stockton, *Classical Athenian Democracy*, 110-111.

7   Stockton, *Classical Athenian Democracy*, 112.

avoid manipulation, before being codified in 1268. The procedure consisted of a series of ten ballots that alternated between sortition and election. All participants had to belong to the Great Council, which included several hundred members of the most prominent families. The steps were as follows:[8]

1. The *ballottino*, a boy chosen at random, draws thirty names by plucking balls out of an urn, thus setting the process in motion with a blind draw.

2. Those thirty are reduced to nine by a blind draw.

3. Those nine put forward forty names, each of which needs at least seven of the nine possible votes.

4. Those forty are reduced to twelve by a blind draw.

5. Those twelve put forward twenty-five names.

6. Those twenty-five are reduced to nine by a blind draw.

7. Those nine choose forty-five new names, each of which needs at least seven of the nine possible votes.

8. Those forty-five are reduced to eleven by a blind draw.

9. Those eleven choose forty-one, who must not have been included in any of the reduced groups that named candidates in earlier steps.

10. Those forty-one then choose the Doge.

The Venetian system seems devised to make it impossible for any individual, family, or coterie to plant candidates or exercise undue influence. However convoluted the procedure, it supported a republican government that lasted a thousand years, until 1797.

Selection of a new Dalai Lama in Tibet involves a baroque procedure. By traditional esoteric divination, a committee of priests identifies a boy destined by the gods to become the lifetime head of government and the high priest of the country's major Buddhist sect. The boy is treated as a prince and educated for his office, which he eventually assumes. This procedure differs from lot-drawing because it gives considerable influence to the priests. But it includes an element of chance because no one can predict what sort of man the boy will become. It also precludes self-promotion and power-seeking by candidates: no candidates, no campaigning.

Historically many positions of leadership have been filled by hereditary succession. This involves randomness because heredity itself is an arbitrary yet objective criterion, and no one can know what sort of person the

Birger Dahl, *Venezia, et kulturhistorisk eventyr* (Oslo: Tell Forlang, 1994), 14-16.

new monarch or prince will be. In this case the randomness does not entail participation, rotation, or amateurism. The king represents a dynastic interest and a political class. Still, an old-fashioned monarch is not beholden to any particular interest, which allows him to take a broad and long view if he cares to do so. Needless to say, the monarchical principle of legitimacy has long since fallen out of favor among opinion leaders.

In countries with a jury system, the jury is formed by lot-drawing. Names typically come from local census or voting rolls and are subject to elimination on grounds of insanity, criminal record, or other bona fide reasons. Counsels may also have the right to exclude some jurors, though they may not put forward any person for inclusion in the jury.

Amateurism and Representativeness

A system of universal lot-drawing for public office would create proportionality in the sense of giving public officials roughly the same composition as the general citizenry without giving disproportionate weight to people with any narrow set of characteristics. Thus, if x percent of the citizens are one-legged, red-haired, nearsighted, nonsmoking Methodist cabinetmakers, one would expect to find that about x percent of the officeholders fit that description. Such proportionality differs from that usually discussed by electoral reformers. Conventional proportionality aims at the proportional representation of political parties or, more broadly, groups defined along occupational or geographic lines. By implication, every economic interest should have a correctly weighted influence in dividing the benefits dispensed by the government. Accordingly, determination of the type of characteristic to be represented tends to be highly selective — race and sex are currently fashionable. Universal lot-drawing leads to amateurism and individualism, whereas proportional representation leads to professionalism and corporatism.

A large political entity, such as a nation-state, cannot fill every public office by random selection, nor has any national legislature been composed in this way. On a local or regional level, however, it would be possible to form a legislative council by drawing the name of, say, one out of every hundred eligible citizens, thereby creating not an elected assembly but a "stand-in folkmoot" — a diminished version of the real thing.[9] As a universal system, sortition belongs to the small-scale participatory democracy of the parish, the municipality, and the historic city-state, not to the

---

9 James Fishkin, a professor of government at the University of Texas, has carried out experiments with "deliberative polling," using a representative group of citizens similar to what I call a "stand-in folkmoot." His tentative conclusion, reported in the *Economist* of May 16, 1998, is that such a group of laymen is capable of dealing rationally with complex political issues, given some counselling by outside experts and debate within the group.

large republic. But the modern world does present some interesting examples of amateur officeholding and broad participation.

The Amish people in North America furnish one such example.[10] They belong to a German-Swiss Protestant religious brotherhood, conspicuous by its members' old-fashioned dress and manners. The Amish communities are agrarian, largely autonomous, and self-sufficient. The group's main offices — bishops, preachers, and ministers of the poor — are held by unpaid amateurs (men only) selected by the leaders of the congregation according to traditional rules and by general consent. The humility ideal of the religious doctrine prohibits putting oneself forward as a candidate or campaigning for others. Some appointees find their selection to office troubling, but they cope with it. Many Amish women volunteer to train briefly as teachers or nurses and then serve without pay in those capacities.

As already mentioned, jury systems exemplify random selection as well as broad participation and rotation.

Many rural communities, though less now than previously, practice rotation of communal duties, usually unpaid, among local citizens.

Many associations also expect members to volunteer to serve as officers or functionaries or to accept such duties when asked to do so.

Even modern governments retain unpaid honorary officials, such as justices of the peace in Britain and the United States, honorary consuls, and holders of various local offices of a legal nature. In these cases we find amateurism though not randomness or broad participation.

In a large polity such as a state or federal union, the use of random selection more often applies to particular officials or to cases that cannot be dealt with otherwise.

In a representative system, the most obvious means of achieving amateurism is not sortition but term limits or part-time officeholding by people who retain their ordinary jobs. The Swiss, who use the latter even in their federal parliament, call it the "militia system" of politics.[11]

The Nature of Lot-Drawing

Allowing decisions to hinge on chance has a long and fascinating background. Historically, especially when information has been scarce or both sides of an issue have had considerable merit, people have often trusted in chance — perhaps in combination with a bit of human interpretation or intuition — employing such means as augury (divination from omens), haruspicy (inspection of the entrails of sacrificial animals), Delphic oracles, Chinese fortune bones, the throwing of dice, and the tossing of sticks.

10 John A. Hostetler, *Amish Society*, 4th ed. (Baltimore; Johns Hopkins University Press), 105-111.
11 Martin Fenner and Beat Junker, *Bürger, Stat und Politik in der Schweiz*, 5th ed. (Basel: Lehrmittelverlag des Kantons Basel-Stadt, 1989), 75, 78-79.

Because random selection by its very nature seems irrational, some may reject it out of hand, but the unfathomability of sortition also makes it a tool for creating legitimacy and efficiency. Accepting the principle of random selection and knowing that chance has given rise to a public decision, one has little to complain about if one dislikes the outcome. On the other hand, because of the claim that electoral democracy epitomizes perfect rationality, an election may engender vociferous complaints by those disappointed in its outcome. Many people may also find the long debate before an election exhausting and frustrating. If postelection disappointment were frequent and acute, the very legitimacy of the electoral system would be endangered. Popular wisdom understands the utility of the luck of the draw. When a quarrel has continued for a long time without anyone's changing his mind, someone may suggest "tossing for it." The result of the toss settles the matter, the loser swallows his dismay, and life goes on. As Guglielmo Ferrero remarks, no principle of legitimacy is entirely rational, but that deficiency does not prevent a given principle from working well in practice if it is adhered to consistently and faithfully.[12]

Powerful as they are, reason and analysis generate reliable answers only where the relevant facts, well defined and accepted, are at hand; where the objectives are clear and agreed upon; and where the alternatives are few. But such conditions rarely exist. When reason has done what it can, something else must complete the job: intuition, faith, or chance. Of these, only chance is objective and has no bias.

With random selection of officeholders from the citizenry at large, there are no candidates and no campaigning. This is a quiet procedure. Only when lot-drawing is combined with election or appointment do self-promotion and campaigning appear.

By its objectivity, sortition avoids the engagement of passions and interests. Discussion can continue forever, but once Fate has spoken, one must be silent. One may doubt human counsel but not the finger of God. The quietness of the process gives it dignity; the absence of manipulation confers legitimacy on it. Thus, sortition is especially apposite for selecting one among equals for the distinctly unequal position of holding the right to command others. (To exclude unfit persons before the final draw, other procedures may be necessary.)

Politicization: The U.S. Presidential Race

The U.S. presidential election system illustrates a maximally politicized election process. By politicized, I mean simply that considerations of merit and utility as understood by the typical citizen take second place to the desires of political insiders and organized special interests. We cannot, of

---

12 Guglielmo Ferrero, *Principles of Power* (New York: Putnam, 1942).

course, "take the politics out of politics." Politics will be partisan, and politics will never be snow-white. Still, if a democracy is not to be a sham, it must strive to serve the general rather than any particular interest.

In the present perspective, the main elements of the American presidential election process are the following. First, the various subgroups in each party put forward candidates regarded both as friendly to the subgroup and as having a reasonable chance of winning; of course, the candidates must be fairly well known and willing to run. Then, in each party, the various subgroups compete to get the party to accept their candidates as the party's candidate; again, the successful candidate must make himself known and acceptable to all and make a case that he can win. Then, in the final campaign, each party spends a vast amount of money and effort to make sure that its candidate is well known, well liked, and a possible winner. Throughout the process, launchers, candidates, and supporters eagerly search for sponsors outside the political system—individuals, groups, and organizations willing to supply voters or funds. The ultimate winner gets monarchic powers for four years, during which he must work in various ways to repay his launchers and sponsors, especially if he hopes to secure reelection.

Clearly, the system turns on self-promotion by candidates, eager maneuvering by initiative groups inside the political system, deal-making with outside special-interest groups, and calculations of candidates' salability. Moreover, the campaigning to publicize the name and policy positions of candidates requires much money, partly because the United States is an immense country. So money is the major consideration. Traits of the American character, such as brashness and the worship of financial success, compound the insidious predominance of money in campaigning. A president's great capacity to affect the material conditions of individuals, groups, and firms by wielding his statutory and discretionary powers colors the entire process.

Because so much of the selection procedure occurs before the choice is at last put before the public, the system as such does not ensure that the man elected is the one regarded as best qualified by the public.[13] One recalls Gaetano Mosca's acid dictum that a representative is someone whose friends have arranged for him to be elected. Further, the system practically ensures that the two (or more) final contenders will be men reared by the political establishment, beholden to it, and constituting no threat to it—in short, men such as Bill Clinton and Bob Dole. The system also ensures a great deal of sound and fury as the contenders attempt to convince voters that the choice is one between night and day. The earnest voter might be pardoned for feeling, during the throes of a presidential campaign, that

---

13   M.J.C. Vile, *Politics in the USA*, 3rd ed. (London: Hutchinson, 1984), 86.

the best outcome would be for the two candidates to stop their electioneering, engage in a manly duel, and shoot each other dead.

The all-importance of money in American presidential campaigning means that if a party or a party subgroup has confidence in the winning potential of its candidate, the rest is regarded as a matter of money. Even an independent candidate may perceive a fighting chance if he has money or celebrity status. Personal wealth and a gambler's self-confidence can buy the aspirant a place in the public eye, at least for a (perhaps considerable) time, as illustrated by the recent campaigns of Ross Perot and Steve Forbes. Whoever seeks the candidacy must promote and publicize himself; in this endeavor, modesty is not a virtue but a liability. Nor does anyone view the president as "above politics." The indignities of the campaign make it hard for the bruised survivor to establish his authority.

One may view a presidential campaign, not unreasonably, as a gamble with rather favorable odds and astounding gains — provided one has, or is, a candidate with good communication skills, an entrenched position in a political party, and access to ample funds, which in turn implies good connections to special-interest groups for whom one's victory has high value. From an insider's perspective, one sees campaign spending, not unrealistically, as having the power to better one's odds considerably or even decisively. For the outside interest group, campaign contributions are simply business investments with a calculated chance of paying off. So, from all sides come cries of Take me! No, me! No, me! and the suggestive crackling of dollar bills. Surely one must wonder whether the sort of person likely to engage in this huckstering and enjoy it — the endlessly flexible, ever smiling, eagerly self-advertising type — is likely to be the person best suited to lead the country.

Disciplining U.S. Presidential Elections

The Founding Fathers had a plan, though unfortunately not a very good one, for imposing discipline on the presidential election process (see paragraphs 1-4 of article 2, section 1, of the U.S. Constitution, partially superseded in 1804 by the Twelfth Amendment). They prescribed a two-step procedure, whereby the people in the several states would elect the members of an Electoral College, who in their greater wisdom would then vote on the presidential candidates. The president of the U.S. Senate would announce and confirm the winner or, in the extraordinary case that no candidate achieved an absolute majority, leave it to the House of Representatives to choose a winner from among the three top vote-getters. The Founders feared voter immaturity and mob politics, and paternalistically they trusted in the principle of leaving the actual selection to elected representatives. Whatever the wisdom of such a principle, history has rendered it hollow: The pressures of party politics have ensured that, although the formal mechanism remains the same, today's electors are bound by their party mandate to vote for the party's candidates; hence, the outcome of the election turns entirely on the party composition of the Electoral College. In other words, indirect election works as if it were direct. The safeguard, such as it was, has collapsed. Only the pointless complexity of the procedure remains.

Later reforms added further complications but failed to dispel the curse of oligarchy. The system of presidential primary elections, adopted by many states early in the twentieth century to ensure direct popular control of the nomination of party candidates, has not lived up to its promise. Nor are the party conventions for selecting a presidential candidate all they seem. "Conventions could be managed by party leaders so that they became a façade for oligarchic control by professional politicians."[14] A good recent example was the Republican national convention in San Diego in August 1996: the party's presidential candidate, Bob Dole, had already been selected before the convention began.

Including an element of lot-drawing in the selection of a given official would make the investment of money and effort by an individual or his campaign backers unnervingly risky. If, for example, the final selection were by blind draw and the final pool contained nine or twelve names instead of the usual two, the odds of any particular candidate's winning would be far different from the fifty-fifty of a conventional, closely contested election. The salient point is that no additional spending of money or effort or compromises could ensure victory or appreciably improve one's chance of winning. Inscrutable, immovable, unbuyable chance would be decisive, and the vicious cycle of individual self-promotion, cynical compromise, and blatant investment of money by pressure groups would be stopped. The dynamics of selection for office would be altogether different. Insurers talk about "uninsurable risks," which are incalculable and therefore beyond the bounds of actuarial science. Something similar (an "unfinanceable bet") would obtain in a presidential race in which chance removed crucial choices from human influence. By including elements of random selection in the choosing of a president, such a system would drastically reduce the importance of money.

A reformed system of presidential election could employ sortition in several ways: (1) to compose an electoral college from a larger body; (2) to eliminate names from an elected body of candidates; (3) to pick the final winner from a pool of candidates. It is not necessary that a blind draw make the final selection; alternatively, one could require a strong majority in an election, with random selection as a disciplining fallback option. The objective to bear in mind is that the procedure somehow blight the natural inclination of political insiders or special-interest outsiders to further their own interests by manipulating the workings of the selection process. Fundamentally that objective can be achieved only by reducing their expectation of a profit from manipulation. Including an element of chance at one or more suitable points in the procedure is the only expedient sure to have that effect. Recall the system devised by the Venetians; they knew what they were up against.

Curbing Particularism, Centralization, and Partiality

Selecting a president in a federation such as the United States combines two kinds of problem. First is the general problem of ensuring competence or impartiality in an elected leader, which we have just considered. Second is a federalist requirement: maintaining the legitimacy of the union despite its size and diversity. This raises the perennial issue of centralization versus states' rights. The federalist problem pertains to every sort of higher federal institution. Concerns about federalism often become entangled with concerns about impartiality.

A process involving lot-drawing could diminish conflicts grounded in particularism or regionalism in a federal system. To select a federal official, one might proceed by drawing from a pool of names put forward by the constituent states. Thus, the states would propose, but luck would dispose; no state could impose its candidate, and no state could complain that the result was unfair. By removing bones of contention, random selection would cement the union, bolster its legitimacy, and conserve political energy. By offering an alternative to appointment by the central government, such a process would check centralization.

Processes involving lot-drawing can also help to ensure both the competence and the impartiality of officeholders. For an office requiring specific professional skill or political experience, a two-step procedure could be adopted: first, a conventional selection of a pool of qualified candidates, to ensure competence; then a final selection at random, to thwart politicking. Selection of judges, for example, might proceed according to this procedure. It might also be used to select police officers, election officials, and members of various local boards.

Appointing Supreme Court Justices

Concerns about competence and federalism surely arise with regard to the selection of justices of the U.S. Supreme Court. One would hope that the professional soundness and political impartiality of the justices would not be twisted by political partisanship or expediency. To stand above politics is part of the Supreme Court's very raison d'être. Alas, the present system of presidential appointment of justices subject to the approval of the Senate fails badly, producing a maximum of politicization in both the selection process and the composition of the Court. Federalism suffers, too. The union is not supposed to be a unitary state. According to the Tenth Amendment, "The powers not delegated to the United States by the Constitution, nor prohibited by it to the States, are reserved to the States respectively, or to the people." Federalism touches the Supreme Court directly because one of its functions is to adjudicate disputes arising between the federal government and the states. Appointment by the federal government predisposes the justices to side with the federal government. This bias generates a dangerous drift toward a unitary system because a subservient Supreme Court is unlikely to check centralizing actions by the federal government. To counteract such drift as well as the politicking that endangers political impartiality and professional soundness, reform of the judicial appointment process deserves consideration.

I suggest a two-step system.[15] First, create a pool of qualified candidates by having each state nominate candidates from among its own judges. Second, fill the actual Supreme Court vacancy by a blind draw from that pool.

Such a procedure would bring about many changes. (1) It would eliminate the rewards of justice-selection politicking at the federal level; (2) the justices, no longer the creatures of the federal government, would have less inclination to expand the power of the central government; (3) political vetting of judicial candidates would occur only in the states, where genuine support for federalism would carry more weight than it does in national politics; (4) the rewards of justice-selection politicking in the states would have small expected value, because no state's candidate in the federal pool would be assured of actual appointment; (5) reaching the Supreme Court via state selection, the justices would give greater support to states' rights, but their possible particularisms would tend to balance each other out and, in any event, to matter less than they do now. The likelihood that the Court would consistently favor a particular state would be small, whereas under the present system the likelihood that the Court will favor the federal government over the states is great.

Cutting Gordian Knots

Sortition could serve in some cases as a fallback measure: If a political body were unable to agree on a decision by deliberation and voting, it could resolve the matter by casting lots. Agree or else. Such a threat would have a disciplinary effect, helping to end unreasonable or dishonest holdouts. Thus the mere threat of decision making by sortition could become the sword that cuts Gordian knots.

Consider a case in which a parliamentary body agrees in principle but disagrees on details, and as a result the relatively trivial disagreement produces "gridlock," preventing the implementation of the principle. For

---

15   John F. Knutsen of Oslo suggested this constitutional idea to me.

example, in a budget debate a majority of the legislature favors reducing the budget, but each party has pet projects it will not give up, thereby blocking overall reduction of spending. Such a deadlock could be resolved by dividing the problem into two parts and applying lot-drawing as a goad to agreement. First, the legislature decides on the budget total; then it considers which elements to cut, under the threat that if agreement is not reached, the overall excess of spending will be eliminated by random deletion of individual projects. Under this constraint, the members must choose between chosen cuts and randomly selected cuts, and the relative undesirability of the latter may spur them to reach agreement quicker.

Another possibility is to use random selection in the appointment of an official from a limited list of candidates by an electoral college subject to two constraints: first, the winner must gain unanimous approval or, perhaps, a strong majority such as three-fourths; second, if the college does not make a selection in step one, the winner will be selected by blind draw from the list of candidates. The potential for proceeding to step two would greatly diminish the expected profit of any elector from holding out against a good candidate for manipulative motives, such as extracting concessions from other electors. In this system of selection, either the winner would have a strong majority of votes, which would make him more than the representative of one party, or he would be simply the lucky candidate, which would attest that he does not owe his office to manipulation by any particular interest. Either way the winner would have secured legitimacy lacking under present methods of selection.

Conclusion

However difficult it might be to adopt the use of sortition in political decision making, the device deserves serious consideration by constitutional reformers. Our present methods of decision making are not so fine that they cannot be improved, and including an element of sortition is not nearly so daft as it may sound when first proposed.